D1174049

MAINSTREAM of AMERICA

Mainstream of America Series ★

EDITED BY LEWIS GANNETT

THE AGE OF
THE MOGULS

Books by STEWART H. HOLBROOK

THE AGE OF THE MOGULS

IRON BREW
A Century of American Ore and Steel

THE YANKEE EXODUS
An Account of Migration from New England

ETHAN ALLEN
A Biography

THE STORY OF AMERICAN RAILROADS

HOLY OLD MACKINAW
A Natural History of the American Lumberjack

LOST MEN OF AMERICAN HISTORY

BURNING AN EMPIRE
America's Great Forest Fires

LITTLE ANNIE OAKLEY & OTHER RUGGED PEOPLE

FAR CORNER
A Personal View of the Pacific Northwest

THE AGE

OF

THE MOGULS

STEWART H. HOLBROOK

DOUBLEDAY & COMPANY, INC., *Garden City, N.Y., 1954*

For Sibyl

Contents

FOREWORD

THE men in this book have been described variously during a century as giants and Titans, and more often as rogues, robbers, and rascals. But never as feeble. The least of them had a splendid audacity and a vital energy that erupted in astonishing ways.

They had certain traits in common. They have usually been treated as a class. Yet all were men of devout and adamantine individualism, hence differed from one another in greater degree than was the case with the mass of their fellow Americans. Each had an overpowering sense of acquisitiveness. None subscribed to the dogmas of the philosophers which deal with what ought to be, but held stoutly to the proposition that what is and shall be is determined by the *forces at work*. That they understood the forces at work must be clear from their accomplishments.

A few were foreign-born. The first Astor was a German, the first Guggenheim a Jew from Switzerland, the first Du Pont a Frenchman. Carnegie was a native Scot, James J. Hill virtually a Scot though born in Canada. Marcus Daly came from Ireland, Insull from England. The others were native Americans, mostly of the so-called Puritan or New England stock. Exceptions include the Vanderbilts, who were of Dutch; Frick, Schwab, and Heinze of German; and Cyrus McCormick and Thomas Lawson of Scotch-Irish ancestries. Jay Gould was descended from Nathan Gold, an English Jew who settled in Connecticut in early colonial days and married a Yankee girl.

The group may be arbitrarily divided into the three categories of promoters, bankers, and industrialists, with merchants in the latter group. Cooke, Morgan, and Stillman were primarily bankers.

Among the promoters were Fisk, Gould, Gates, Lawson, Rogers, Flagler, and Insull; among the industrialists Carnegie, Rockefeller, McCormick, Armour, Frick, Ford, and the Du Ponts. The Guggenheims were both promoters and industrialists. Mellon covered the entire field. Hill, Harriman, Villard, and the first two Vanderbilts belong, as great railroadmen, in a special niche. The Astors were the most successful real estate operators.

When we come to individuals, the group immediately defies further classification and takes on striking contrasts, as between Daniel Drew and Jim Fisk. Both were country lads and there any similarity ends. All his long life Drew dressed and played the part of an illiterate yokel in the big city, a sort of rustic fallen among thieves, who spent his evenings, often quietly drunk, in a cheap hotel room reading the Bible and chewing tobacco. The diamond-lit Fisk was ostentatiously a libertine, fit to carouse with the playboys of Gaius Petronius.

Carnegie was the greatest self press agent of his class. Rockefeller, until he was very old, worked heroically if unsuccessfully to keep his name out of the papers. And until the second-richest American was made Secretary of the Treasury, Andrew Mellon's name was wholly unknown outside Pittsburgh.

Henry Clay Frick was "the hardest man to see." Philip D. Armour perhaps the most approachable. In arrogance, no one could best Pullman, the sleeping-car king. Hill was probably the most irascible; he once fired an unoffensive employee simply because his name was Spittles. Jay Cooke enjoyed an unsullied reputation for honest dealing and was a genial, kindly, and considerate man. Morgan the elder, when bogged down in Manhattan traffic, directed his chauffeur to charge ahead by way of the sidewalk.

The grossest legends appear to have attached to the Big Four of California, namely, Stanford, Huntington, Crocker, and Hopkins. Either they earned their reputations, or they were victims of a consistently bad press. Nor have apologists been able to do much to improve the standing of Jay Gould, or anything at all for Drew and Fisk.

The present book is not overly concerned with the comparative business ethics of these men of money. The best of them made "deals," purchased immunity, and did other things which in 1860, or 1880, or even 1900, were considered no more than "smart" by their fellow Americans, but which today would give pause to the most conscientiously dishonest promoter. The rules have a way of changing every decade or so. In 1934 a jury found Insull guilty of nothing. Twenty years later his methods would land him behind bars. Indeed, under present-day rules, almost every man in this book would face a good hundred years in prison.

My account will not attempt to pass judgments on matters that have baffled moralists, economists, and historians. I happen to believe that no matter how these men accumulated their fortunes, their total activities were of the greatest influence in bringing the United States to its present incomparable position in the world of business and industry. But I shall use neither gilt nor whitewash. Nor tar.

These were tough-minded fellows, who fought their way encased in rhinoceros hides and filled the air with their mad bellowings and the cries of the wounded; while their determined womenfolk badgered them into erecting monstrous houses that were much like the ennobled bathrooms of ancient emperors. The men were as magnificent in their piratical wars as they were pathetic in their dude clothes, trying to eat with a *fork,* wondering how best to approach a chaise longue. They were a motley crew, yet taken together they fashioned a savage and gaudy age as distinctively purple as that of imperial Rome, and infinitely more entertaining.

STEWART H. HOLBROOK

Portland, Oregon,
March 1953

PART ONE

THE ERA
OF
BRASS
KNUCKLES

Chapter 1 **NOON**

CORNELIUS VANDERBILT, commonly called the Commodore, was last seen taking the air in April 1876. He was then eighty-two years old. Yet confining him to his mansion at 10 Washington Place in New York City required the stoutest efforts of a regiment of physicians and the pleadings of his young and second wife, Frank, of whom he was most fond.

It is improbable that the astonishingly vital old man would have paid them any heed had he not read, in the *Tribune* of April 11, of the death of A. T. Stewart, the department store magnate, and reflected, too, that William B. Astor was already five months in the grave. Things of that sort, happening to contemporaries, tend to leave a man open to reason.

The Commodore was richer than Astor, richer than Stewart. He was the richest man in the United States. In New York he was much admired, not for his charities, which were few, but for his bluff manner, his dash and energy, and his public comments, which were forceful, often humorous, and wondrously illiterate.

The Commodore's hulking figure, likened by some to that of Silenus, was familiar to all New York. It was encased, no matter the weather or the occasion, in a fur-lined overcoat and a plug hat. Many thought he looked like an English archbishop, with his bright blue eyes and pink countenance fringed with whiskers from his ears down to the parochial snow-white choker, perhaps the last high stock in the city, which he retained when flightier men gave way and changed to the vulgarly stylish product of Troy and the new four-in-hand cravats.

Though conservative and almost antique in his dress, there was nothing shy about Commodore Vanderbilt. His handsome features appeared on every bond certificate of the New York Central and the Lake Shore & Michigan Southern railroads; and on both sides of the great head lamp of the *Commodore Vanderbilt,* fastest locomotive engine of the New York Central. The whole massive figure, fur-lined coat and all, stood in bronze before the St. Johns Park freight terminal. Esthetes might sneer. Sneers did not affect the Vanderbilt lines, which continued to pay investors eight per cent, often more.

For many years New Yorkers had been made familiar with the Commodore's habits. He was an early riser. It was his custom to glance at the morning papers, then to break his fast with the yolks of three eggs, a lamb chop, toast, and a cup of tea into which he invariably put twelve lumps of sugar. He then drove in a topless buggy to his office in Bowling Green. There in an hour or so, aided by one clerk, he transacted business, gave a few hints to his son William, then drove home for a good solid midday dinner. When he drank, which was not often, he liked a tumbler full of straight gin.

Afternoon usually found him driving in Central Park or racing horses along the Harlem Lane speedway with Robert Bonner, the New York *Ledger* publisher. Friends seldom went driving twice with the Commodore, for he was a fiend on the road. Occasionally he was seen in Wall Street, and often at the Manhattan Club, where he liked to play whist. Evenings of late years, however, he was at home, and here to please his youthful wife he had been trying hard to forego the pungent waterfront language he had picked up in his ferryboat days. It was a difficult thing to do. The Rev. Charles F. Deems found him one day in tears and was so astonished at the spectacle he barely managed to ask what was the matter. "Oh, goddamnit!" the old man replied. "I've been a-swearing again, and I'm sorry."

Now, in early May of 1876, clever mongers of stocks, hearing that the Commodore was confined to his home with some ailment or other, confided to Wall Street reporters that the old gentleman was actually dying and that his agents were unloading his stocks.

The young men of the press hastened to 10 Washington Place. Young Mrs. Vanderbilt admitted them to the parlor and explained that her husband's disorder had almost entirely disappeared, that the rumors of mortal illness had no truth. Just then the whole mansion seemed to vibrate as a roaring avalanche of profanity came rolling down the stair well. It was the old man himself. He had crept from his couch to listen, and now he spoke. "I am *not* dying," he bellowed. The reporters then heard him say something to the effect that even if he were dying, he would arise from his death's bed to knock all hell out of them wretches who start rumors and provide a big job for the undertakers. The boys went back to their papers to write that the Commodore still lived.

But he was declining, and when another report of his passing came out of Wall Street, the New York papers set up a deathwatch at 10 Washington Place. The Commodore was furious when he heard reporters discussing his health in front of his own home. His wife protested to them. The reporters then chipped in to engage a room almost across the street from the Vanderbilt home. There they played cards and had beer and sandwiches brought in, detailing one of their number to watch comings and goings at No. 10.

But the Commodore was not to be hurried in his going. Spring turned to summer. Autumn arrived. Christmas found the reporters still in their vidette. Meanwhile, two of the Commodore's physicians died, and the Rev. Henry Ward Beecher remarked unkindly in public that the press noted the rises and falls of Mr. Vanderbilt's temperature as though they were a part of the daily weather report.

The family, the retainers, and the physicians were having their hands full. When one of the surviving doctors recommended champagne to the patient, the old man seemed to figure a moment, then replied: "I guess sody water will do." One did not become wealthy drinking champagne.

Yet, when he overheard his wife remark, in reply to one of the doctors who suggested more woolen blankets on the patient's bed, that they were "very expensive," the Commodore exploded. "Goddamn the expense!" he said. "Buy a bale of 'em."

He was constantly demanding "more of them cookies" which, for some reason or other, were given him in short ration. Once, when he had asked for more cookies and was instead given a bowl of soup, he took one mouthful, then heaved soup, spoon, bowl and all clear across the room. "Who in damnation salted that soup?" he cried.

On occasion, and without notice to his conventional physicians in attendance, he would call in "Dr." William Bennett, who said he was an electric healer. One time Bennett found the Commodore howling like a wild beast, wondering aloud "why God was persecuting him so," but he "responded immediately" to magnetization and the electric healer "left him sleeping placidly."

Meantime, and despite family protests, the Commodore enjoyed what he said was Art, and sat for hours gazing at a shocking painting, Aurora, the gift of his pretty if somewhat scandalous friend Tennessee Claflin, who was herself a sort of magnetic healer and spiritualist. The Commodore had set her and her sister Victoria Woodhull up as stockbrokers and helped them to found a weekly paper that discussed everything, even sex. It seems unlikely that the hardheaded old man was ever a thorough convert to spiritualism, but he played at it, possibly on the theory that one can never be certain about such matters. He also had saltcellars placed under the legs of his bed as "health conductors."

But his health did not improve, and his devoutly Christian wife, knowing the lateness of the hour and horrified at the Commodore's pagan superstitions, labored hard to make him see the true light. She had a small organ moved to his bedroom, and there she played while the sons and daughters, together with their children, gathered to sing old hymns. These and the soothing Dr. Deems, Baptist pastor added to the ménage by Mrs. Vanderbilt, gradually weaned the old man from the deplorable errors of his thinking.

Early on the morning of January 4—it was now 1877—the old gentleman suddenly sat bolt upright in bed. "Frank!" he called to his wife. "Frank! Sing me my hymns!" Frank broke out with "Come All Ye Sinners, Poor and Needy," while Dr. Deems intoned the Lord's Prayer. At 10:51 A.M. the Commodore died.

By noon, says the biographer of the Vanderbilts, the flags of the Manhattan and the Union clubs were at half-mast. The engravers at *Harper's Weekly* were busy making a cover portrait of the late great man. The closing hours of Wall Street trading showed the Commodore's stocks to have made slight gains. This would have pleased him most of all. Death, nothing, could shake the value of the Vanderbilt lines. It was, as an observer remarked, evidence of the Commodore's genius. Even though "$50,000 of absolute water" had been poured for each mile of his railroad system, this so-called watered stock took account of "the boundless values which adhered to his property through its completion as a supreme monopoly over common highways of trade." That was the great thing. Vanderbilt had "discovered and taken the then new way of imperialism and monopoly."

In clubs and in Wall Street offices, old New Yorkers related stories of the late Commodore's humor; and Henry Clews, the stock market chatterbox, recalled that when one of Vanderbilt's numerous sons-in-law needed $50,000 to enter a tanning venture and went to the Commodore to borrow it, the old gentleman asked how much he expected to make from the investment. "About five thousand dollars a year," replied the young man. "Boy," said the Commodore, "I can do better than that with $50,000. Tell you what I'll do. I will pay you $5,000 a year hereafter, and you may consider yourself in my employ at that salary." Others recalled the Commodore's great virility and spoke of the difficulty of getting pretty housemaids, or even just housemaids, to remain long in the Vanderbilt ménage.

Now that the first great mogul of American capital and industry was dead, he must be laid away. After a brief service at his home, followed by a sermon at the Church of the Strangers, the body was taken to Staten Island, home of Van Derbilts since early in the eighteenth century. Here the horses "toiled with difficulty through the falling snow," and the Commodore was at last interred in the Moravian cemetery at New Dorp. By the graveside stood a score of the family and many old friends, and even a few business enemies, including Peter Cooper, Thurlow Weed, Frank Leslie, Samuel Ward, and old Daniel Drew, a scarecrow knee-deep in snow, threadbare as usual, leaning on the umbrella he used for a cane.

It was a giant they buried. Said the New York *Herald:* "The impression made upon the community by both Stewart and Astor was a faint one compared to the deep mark of Vanderbilt." From the cover of *Harper's Weekly* peered the old man, and inside one read that he was ". . . unfalteringly faithful to his engagements . . . and though not much of a churchman was never skeptical." Then it came to something of genuine importance. The deceased, said *Harper's Weekly,* was "the owner of 28 steamboats, no one of which was lost by fire, explosion or wreck while in his employ." In that era of steamboat disasters, a more arresting statement could hardly have been made, unless it was one in the *Herald* saying of Vanderbilt that "the rights and welfare of the smallest stockholder [in his railroads] were as well guarded as his own."

That his own welfare had been well guarded was soon apparent when it became known that the Commodore's estate ran to $105,-000,000 before taxes, and almost as much after taxes, for in that day government was a ghoul of modest wants.

What nobody remarked, simply because nobody could know,

was that Commodore Vanderbilt had died at high bright noon— noon, that is, for his own class of men, the aggressive and spectacularly successful leaders of commerce and industry, the great moguls of capital. Never again, after 1877, were the moguls to be wholly free, as they had been before, to work their financial wonders without protest from labor, criticism from the public, and harassment by government.

Great fortunes, larger than Vanderbilt's, were to be made after 1877, but not with impunity. A new era had set in. The giants and near giants who followed the Commodore, including his own able son, were never to know a moment when they were not under fire.

Out of the last six months of the year of the Commodore's death came the first effective labor unions the country had seen. Along with the unions came the first serious efforts of government to make it increasingly more difficult for one man to accumulate and leave an estate of $105,000,000.

Accompanying these harassments, and perhaps their actual source, was a radical change in public temper and a new viewpoint: Through the smoke of the tremendous violence of 1877 the capitalist was seen clearly to be an ogre, the natural enemy of man, of the Republic, and of God.

Chapter 2   PRIMITIVES

THE astonishing fortune left by Commodore Vanderbilt was in large part the result of his activities during and right after the Civil War. In this span of less than two decades his wealth had increased one hundred times over. It could not have happened in the United States until then. The period of Vanderbilt's vast accumulations was the first rich growing season for American multimillionaires.

In 1855 Vanderbilt had been listed as merely one of nineteen New Yorkers whose wealth was estimated at more than one million dollars. Nor was he high on the list, which was topped by the twenty millions of William B. Astor, second of the line, whose father had done well enough in the fur trade.

The bulk of the Astor fortune had come chiefly from increased values of New York City and adjacent real estate. John Jacob Astor, the poor immigrant from Germany, got his liking for land from a crafty deal he began working on as early as 1809, when a browsing lawyer told him that 51,012 acres of Putnam County, New York, did not legally belong to the more than seven hundred families who had bought these farms from the state of New York and had been living upon them since just after the end of the Revolutionary War.

This very land, the lawyer told Astor, had been originally the estate of Roger Morris, a Tory, and had been confiscated by New York. New York had no legal right to do so, for Morris held the land on a life lease only; and, said the lawyer, no state could confiscate a life lease. Either the state's officers had not known this basic law, or they had disregarded it as pettifoggery.

John Jacob Astor acted promptly. After satisfying himself on the point, namely that one third of Putnam County legally belonged to the heirs of Roger Morris, all of whom lived in England, he set out to buy off the heirs. This he accomplished for approximately a hundred thousand dollars. Then he notified the seven hundred farmers they were trespassers. The poor, dumbfounded farmers appealed to the state. The state at first refused to recognize Astor's title. Astor refused to recognize the state's. After a long battle in the courts, the state compromised in 1827 and granted Astor $500,000.

Astor did not mind the abuse heaped upon him by the public. He continued his real estate ventures. His favorites were heavily mortgaged farms on Manhattan Island, such as the Eden farm, a portion of which is now Times Square. Astor got it for less than a song. During the panic of 1837, he foreclosed on some sixty farms or parcels of land on Manhattan. Though he was by then the richest man in America, he did not become a spender. He liked beer, tobacco, and draughts; and his biggest outlay was perhaps the pensioning of an old friend, whose duties were to converse in German and, as Hone the diarist remarked, "to be Astor's train bearer and prime minister." This surely was modest enough compared to one of his descendants who bought his way into the British peerage and died Viscount Astor of Hever Castle.

In summing up the career of the first John Jacob Astor, the New York *Herald* said that at least half of his fortune should have been left to the people of New York City because the value of his property had been "augmented by their aggregate intelligence, enterprise and commerce." As for Astor himself, he had exhibited at best only "the ingenious powers of a self-invented money-making machine."

Perhaps the same could have been said of several other large fortunes of the fifties and the forties. Stephen Whitney, large landowner, ranked next to Astor in wealth in 1855. After him come James Lenox, a man of property, then assorted Rhinelanders, Schermerhorns, and Goelets. The Goelets started as ironmongers, the Schermerhorns as ship chandlers, the Rhinelanders as bakers. But their new affluence had come from real estate. The Goelets, for instance, had for sale or rent a great deal of the land along Fifth Avenue from Union Square to Forty-seventh Street.

Shipping had brought four million dollars to William Aspinwall by 1855. The Belfast emigrant, Alexander T. Stewart, whose death had given pause to old Commodore Vanderbilt, had made his pile as New York City's first merchant prince, mostly in retail and wholesale dry goods. Just below the nineteen millionaires of 1855 stood no less a public character than Phineas T. Barnum. From the exhibition of midgets, mermaids, two-headed calves and such, he had accumulated $800,000, and was probably better known than any of the nineteen top money-making machines.

More typical of the new captains of industry like Vanderbilt was Peter Cooper, who had made his million from the manufacture of glue and isinglass; and George Law, son of an Irish immigrant, whose million had come from New York City's first horsecar lines.

In Philadelphia, probably the first fortune in 1855 was that of the Drexels, father and sons, and its founder was the most unusual of the new millionaires. He was Francis Martin Drexel, born in the Austrian Tyrol, who had come to the United States in 1817 as a portrait painter. For the next decade he followed his profession, and got as far afield as South America. Here he also trafficked in currency. Returning to Philadelphia, he opened a note-shaving business that was successful from the first. During the early years of the California gold rush the Drexels made a great deal of money as bankers.

New England's early fortunes had come from the sea, neither as fish nor yet as sperm oil, but from trade with foreign parts. By 1855, however, the brothers Brown of Rhode Island had long since proved that Americans, as well as the English, might become wealthy by manufacturing cotton. By then, too, members of the remarkable Lawrence family of Massachusetts were promoting railroads from the profits of their own textile mills.

Possibly the first New England millionaire had made his stake as early as 1830. He was Israel Thorndike, and typical of the change from seaborne to industrial fortunes. Thorndike began to make money as captain of a privateer in the Salem-Beverly fleet during the Revolution. He took many rich prizes. After the war he engaged in trade with the Orient, but soon moved to Boston, where he invested in the still new and risky manufacturing ventures of Massachusetts and New Hampshire. When he died in 1832, his estate was valued at one and a half million dollars, probably the largest fortune in New England.

The really great American fortunes of business and industry, however, had to await the urgent demands of the Civil War and the coincident and monstrous corruptions that have accompanied all American wars from the one starting in 1775 to that ending 170 years later.

Because he was a precocious youth who got under way early in life, Cornelius Vanderbilt had the benefit of not one but two wars. Perhaps he should be considered the first of the American mogul class. He was also one of the greatest. He early appreciated the values of monopoly. Although he thought the public should pay aplenty for the benefits of monopoly, he believed those benefits should be real. Both Rockefeller and Carnegie, and other successful industrialists, possibly profited by his pioneering example. He knew how to buy, or at least sway, the acts of judges, of public officials of all sorts, and of legislatures. He knew how to get extra-curricular help from the federal government, including regiments of marines when wanted. Old Vanderbilt even set the pattern of elegance and display followed, though greatly expanded, by so many of his class who came later.

Born on Staten Island in 1794, Vanderbilt was only seventeen when he prevailed on his mother to lend him a hundred dollars with which to buy a two-masted barge called a periauger. He hoped to "earn a living" from it by ferrying people and goods in New York Harbor. A year later, Great Britain and the United States went to war. A British fleet soon menaced New York, and the American commissary general called for bids to transport supplies to military posts around the harbor.

Young Vanderbilt's bid was accepted. He quickly gained a reputation for reliability and daring. No voyage stumped him. He'd deliver supplies anywhere, at any time, no matter where the British ships lay. Late in 1813, when the enemy was repulsed at Port Richmond, the commander of that post wanted to inform authorities in New York immediately. A high sea had every ferry beached. Vanderbilt went to the commander. "I'll carry you across," he said, "but I'll carry you under water halfway." He did, too, and the party reached the Battery thoroughly drenched and bailing furiously.

Young Vanderbilt was tall, strong, and energetic. He was also as tough as anything to be found on the waterfront. He added two other small boats to his fleet and kept them busy to the end of hostilities. He had done very well, having repaid his mother and put aside a thousand dollars. With this he purchased a condemned schooner from the government, and in her raced the New York oyster fleet to the beds off Virginia. The oystermen of that day were a hard lot, many of them no better than pirates. They fought ferociously for favored positions at the beds. What later was called highjackery was common. Vanderbilt enjoyed the business thoroughly. He fought or bullied his way to the best positions, loaded his condemned schooner till her deck was awash, then struck out for New York to beat all hands to the market. In his old age, Vanderbilt recalled that he sold his first cargo of oysters at a profit sufficient to pay for his ship.

He married. He built two larger schooners and entered the coastwise trade. At twenty-three he possessed almost ten thousand dollars of capital. He had earned, because of his ability and possibly also because of his outstanding profanity, the nickname of Commodore, by which he was ever after known.

The alert young roughneck had watched the progress of the new steamboats. They seemed to be coming in fast. But, so far as the waters around New York were concerned, they were a monopoly of the Fulton-Livingston combination. This politically powerful group had prevailed on the legislature to grant it exclusive right of steam navigation in New York waters. Either you paid Fulton-Livingston for a license, or you did not operate there with steam. Vanderbilt thought this an interesting condition. In 1818 he sold his profitable sailing schooners and hired out at sixty dollars a month to operate the steamer *Bellona,* which belonged to Thomas Gibbons of New Jersey. Gibbons kept his boats out of

New York waters. He wanted neither to pay the license, nor to challenge the Fulton-Livingston combination.

Young Commodore Vanderbilt never dreamed of applying for a license, or of keeping out of New York Harbor. He started immediately to operate the unlicensed *Bellona* from New Brunswick, New Jersey, to Manhattan. Aaron Ogden was the first to protest. He was a New Jersey operator who had paid the license to run *his* boats to New York City. He obtained an injunction against the *Bellona*. Vanderbilt not only paid it no heed, but went ahead deliberately to provoke incidents. Among other things, he designed and flew a special flag from the *Bellona's* mast. On the flag was a challenge. *New Jersey Must be Free,* said the legend. This created something of a sensation. So did the truculence with which Vanderbilt ran his craft. He docked her at wharves belonging to opposition steamers. If any resistance were offered, or even intimated, Vanderbilt and his crew of shoulder-hitters were ready for battle. The *Bellona,* by now one of the best-known boats in American waters, continued to ply such routes as her commander thought best for business.

After six years of futile attempts at force and at law, during which the *Bellona* never missed a voyage, the Ogden line at last managed to have the case heard before the United States Supreme Court. To defend the Gibbons line, Vanderbilt engaged Daniel Webster. The Court's mind, doubtless helped somewhat in its thinking by Webster, found for Gibbons and his *Bellona.* The state act creating the Fulton-Livingston monopoly was declared unconstitutional. The outcome was no more pleasing to Vanderbilt than apparently it was to most of New York and New Jersey, and the Commodore was hailed as a deliverer. "We owe to him," said a prominent citizen, "the freedom of the seas as applied to us locally."

The liberator of the local seas was now ready to start his own line of steamers. Within a few months he had two boats operating on Long Island Sound and the Hudson. His reputation must already have been formidable, for Robert Livingston Stevens, who had been successfully running boats on the Hudson, immediately withdrew, saying he feared what the Commodore would do at rate slashing. The new line did just that, and the North River Association, a combination of operators, were so alarmed that they bribed Vanderbilt to remove his vessels and to agree not to compete for ten years. The bribe amounted to a nice monthly income.

There appeared meantime, however, a gaunt, rustic figure, Daniel

Drew, who was to give battle to Vanderbilt for thirty years. Noting the Commodore's early success on the Hudson, Drew put on a boat, the *Water Witch,* and cut rates below Vanderbilt. In her first season Drew's vessel dropped some ten thousand dollars. Vanderbilt jeered. Drew said nothing, that is, to Vanderbilt; but to the citizens along the river he said that Vanderbilt was robbing them blind with excessive rates. Drew cut his own rates again, then sat back waiting for the Commodore to buy his nuisance line. The Commodore did, too, and paid handsomely to get Drew off the river, just as the North River crowd paid Vanderbilt to cease and desist.

Vanderbilt kept building boats. He started a run to Boston, another to Providence. Each vessel he built was better than the one before. The Vanderbilt ships had much to do with the trend that inspired the term "floating palaces." The *Commodore Vanderbilt* when launched in 1846 was the finest vessel New Yorkers had ever seen.

The Commodore was doing well. He had a comfortable though not grandiose house built on Washington Place in New York into which he moved his increasing family though not his wife. She did not want to leave Staten Island. She was promptly committed to a private sanitarium and given several months in which to reflect. In the spring of 1847 she was released and "went obediently to her new home in the city."

The gold rush to California opened new vistas to the imagination of the Commodore. He got all available maps. He talked with all manner of people who had made the voyage to the west coast by the various routes, then he settled on Nicaragua as the crossing place. He procured from the weak government of that country a charter for the Accessory Transit Company, then sent men to build docks on the east and west coasts. He also had crews improving the channel of the San Juan River and laying several miles of fine macadam road. Meanwhile he began construction of a fleet of seagoing steamships. When all was ready, the Commodore advertised that his route to the gold fields was two days shorter than that by Panama. He set his passenger fare below that of all other lines. Almost at once he garnered a large part of the traffic.

For forty years the Commodore had applied his great energies to business, and his business had prospered. It was now time for his first vacation, which was to occupy much of 1853. His was to be a holiday fit for an American king of commerce; not just a voyage to Europe and the grand tour of the Continent, such as so many rich Americans had been content with. And because it set the pattern which many of his countrymen were to follow, once they had made their piles, the Commodore's vacation deserves attention.

While getting his Accessory Transit Company under way, Vanderbilt was also having a nice little steam yacht built, the *North Star,* 270 feet overall, with a beam of thirty-eight feet. Her like had not been seen afloat. Naples granite went into her. So did marble, rosewood, satin, and plush—by the ton, foot, and yard. Though her décor was said "to evoke the Age of Louis XV," the ceiling and walls held medallion paintings of essential Americans, Washington, Franklin, Clay, Calhoun, and Webster—but no Jackson or Jefferson. "Fastidious silk lambrequins and lace curtains" adorned all the berths. Gilt touched everything that would take and hold gilt.

Loading his wife, ten of his twelve children, together with sons- and daughters-in-law, and a few grandchildren, into the *North Star,* the Commodore thoughtfully added to the ship's list his personal physician and wife, and the Rev. Dr. John Overton Choules and wife. Not that the Commodore himself felt need for the holy man, but rather the conventions of great wealth seemed to call for an ecclesiastical retainer. The Rev. Dr. Choules fancied himself something of a literary character, and his copious notes resulted in an unconsciously humorous history of *The Cruise of the Steam Yacht North Star.*

This first great yacht of an American citizen left New York on the night of May 20, 1853, her decks fairly blazing with rockets and roman candles as she passed Staten Island in salute to the Commodore's aged mother, who lived there in senility. Before the vessel had fairly left American waters, the Commodore was bustling about anxiously to learn how the *North Star* was performing, badgering her officers. Throughout the long voyage, which took the Vanderbilt party to England, Russia, Germany, France, and Italy, the Commodore apparently showed more interest in the performance of his yacht than in anything met or seen. He constantly visited the engine room. He watched coal consumption carefully. Now and then he called for short bursts of speed. He wanted to know what the vessel would do with a little urging.

The *North Star* virtually stunned England, both press and

people, even though most of the "exalted personalities" declined
invitations to meet the Vanderbilt party. The London *Daily News,*
after describing the incredible elegancies of the yacht, went on to
speak of Mr. Vanderbilt, calling him a legitimate product of his
own country, one of "the tamers of the great forces of nature."
These were the new kind of men who were to dominate the world.
All decent Tories must have shuddered to contemplate the *Daily
News's* vision of things to come. The old rulers, such as the Percys
and the Howards, said that paper, have become merely "faded
distinctions that formed the glory of the ruling classes centuries
back." The *News* thought it time "that *parvenu* should be looked
upon as a word of honor."

Though titled England and the gentry ignored, as well as they
could, this American parvenu and his seagoing yacht, the Vanderbilt party nevertheless made a tremendous impression on a people
who were later to grant peerages to American parvenus and hail
as their greatest statesman the son of an American woman reared
in Brooklyn.

Russia was more hospitable, and the party was made welcome
by the Grand Duke Constantine, who placed a carriage of the
Emperor at their disposal, from which the Commodore viewed
the palace of Peterhof. In Paris the Commodore saw a military
review at Versailles and had some boots made by M. Forr. In
Italy both Mr. and Mrs. Vanderbilt sat for the American sculptors
Joel Hart and Hiram Powers.

But what Commodore Vanderbilt thought of Europe and its
people is regrettably not known. All the opinions expressed in the
fatuous Rev. Dr. Choule's *History* are his own, and of little or no
interest.

One thing is certain. The Commodore returned from his long
voyage with his abilities unimpaired. On reaching his office in New
York he learned that in his absence certain of his associates in the
Accessory Transit Company had made notable progress in using
the powers of attorney granted them when he left: they had sold
his interests down the river. Letting go a string of gorgeous oaths,
he quieted sufficiently to dictate a classic letter to the Messrs.
Charles Morgan and C. K. Garrison of Accessory Transit. It was
brief. "Gentlemen," ran the letter. "You have undertaken to cheat
me. I won't sue you, for the law is too slow. I'll ruin you. [Signed]
C. Vanderbilt."

Although the Commodore failed to ruin Morgan and Garrison,

he crippled and humbled them, and he also regained control of Accessory Transit. To achieve these ends, he converted the *North Star* into an elegant passenger steamer for the Panama run. He added two other ships. He organized the Opposition line to California and cut fares to new lows, including a steerage rate of only thirty-five dollars.

The three established lines, including Accessory Transit, asked for quarter. Vanderbilt was happy to sell the *North Star* to the United States Mail line, and his other vessels to the Pacific Mail. The Messrs. Morgan and Garrison were also obliged to satisfy his claims against them, which were far from modest; and the company they had "stolen" from Vanderbilt failed to pay any dividends. The Commodore bought heavily and was soon elected president of Accessory Transit.

While these things were going forward, that strange character William Walker, a native of Nashville, Tennessee, turned up in Nicaragua with a small band of Nicaraguan exiles and malcontents. After a little shooting they unseated the tiny country's President and installed their own man, who proceeded to revoke the Transit Company's charter. This action was inspired by cash advanced to the ursurpers by Morgan and Garrison. When Nicaragua's new President died, shortly after taking office, Walker himself became head of the republic.

That President Walker had erred when he favored Morgan and Garrison, instead of Vanderbilt, soon became evident. Without leaving New York, the Commodore persuaded the governments of four neighboring republics to organize "a defensive alliance" against Nicaragua. He directed a couple of his freebooting associates to organize and lead an invading force, for even in those days a defensive alliance was the popular name for aggression.

The Vanderbilt generals and their gangs went tearing into poor Nicaragua. They attacked and captured Walker's main garrison, then went on to reduce all his jerry-built forts. Inside two weeks the Commodore had undone General Walker's military reputation. When Walker attempted a comeback, Vanderbilt suggested to the State Department in Washington that marines ought to be sent to Nicaragua to "protect American interests." The marines landed, and deported Walker.

Now that its route was open again the Accessory Transit could resume operations. Commodore Vanderbilt was again in command. He announced as much. But Transit did not resume its run. The established lines wanted no more Vanderbilt competition, and their officials agreed to pay him $56,000 a month simply to forget his great desire to carry gold seekers cheaply to Eldorado.

The Nicaragua affair was possibly in the mind of a writer on the New York *Mail* who, years later in commenting on the Commodore, wrote that "his adamantine good sense in all business matters was known to all who tested it, especially if they ventured on the assumption of its decay."

While Vanderbilt's war in Nicaragua was progressing to its predestined victory, the Commodore found time to survey transatlantic mail and passenger service. The only competition to the great Cunard line was that offered by the American ships of E. K. Collins of New York. With a subsidy from Congress, the Collins line seemed to be making money. Vanderbilt proposed that he too enter the business with alternate runs. Collins replied that he could not make the ships pay even without competition from Vanderbilt. "Then," said the Commodore, "you've got into a business you don't understand."

Without subsidy, Vanderbilt put two vessels on the New York-Southampton-Le Havre run. He built a new ship, SS *Vanderbilt,* which in her first season made the fastest time to Europe and took the Blue Ribbon previously held by the Cunarder *Persia.* Vanderbilt asked Congress for subsidies, which were refused. He then announced to all the papers that his ships would gladly carry the mails to England free of charge. This offer, though not accepted, plus the fast runs of Vanderbilt ships, had a blighting effect on the Collins line. Its vessels departed and arrived with not more than half of the passenger space occupied. In 1858 the line went into receivership.

Though he had ruined the Collins line, Vanderbilt must not have found transatlantic business profitable enough to suit him. It seems probable, too, that he had at last come to think there might be something he could do in the new steam railroad business. In any case, he sold his transatlantic line, retaining only the SS *Vanderbilt,* which he turned over to the government in 1861, shortly after the outbreak of war.

The Civil War also took one of the Commodore's sons, George, who had been trained at West Point and served on the frontier. Young Vanderbilt was in the Shiloh campaign, and died later of what was said to have been exposure in the famous rivers-of-blood engagement.

Though the Commodore himself was sixty-eight years old, in

1862 the government asked him to become its wartime shipping agent in New York. The tough old man threw himself into furious activity, and although war's end found him charged with having bought worthless tubs at high prices for the government—naturally exacting a commission for himself—his name was finally expunged from the Senate resolution of censure. Instead, Commodore Vanderbilt was among those citizens to whom a grateful Congress presented a medal for loyal and meritorious service. By the end of the war, too, he was the only citizen of his country worth more than twenty millions of dollars.

Chapter 3 BOLD NEW TALENTS

THE Civil War did more for and to the United States than to abolish chattel slavery. It changed our transportation system, acting as a kind of hothouse forcing process on railroads. The necessity of carrying hundreds of thousands of troops and their supplies called for swift expansion of rails in the North. This was done so well and quickly that many historians of the four-year struggle have credited railroads with playing a major part in settling the issue.

The demands of war did other things, such as hastening transformation of the North from a country of farmers and small manufacturers to a highly organized industrial region. The voracious waste of war showed its infinite power to stimulate all the productive forces of the people. A great boot and shoe industry grew up in New England during the last two years of fighting, specifically to supply the needs of soldiers. The necessity of feeding the same men created the new packing plants in Chicago. McCormick's reaper, patented long before war began, had to await that tragedy before it and other agricultural machinery made much headway. The making of guns in frantic haste caused expansion of what had been a doddering iron and steel industry. It was much the same with nearly all manufacture. And even before the war ended, a great migration had started as both natives and foreigners set out to see what lay beyond the Mississippi.

With the war, too, came what moral philosophers have said was moral decay in wholesale volume, an apparently illimitable increase in man's natural cupidity. Scandals uncorked during and right after the fighting showed that soldiers had been given clothing and blankets made of shoddy, technically a material of reclaimed wool, such as old rags, which gave a new term to our language. Soldiers also got boots made largely of paper; they were fed meat that had come from diseased cattle and hogs; they rode nags that had been doctored to make a sale to the cavalry. Only too often the very guns put into their hands would not shoot. One big order for such weapons, refused by ordnance officers in the East, was sold and shipped to General Frémont in the West.

Likely the moral condition of the country *was* lower than usual. Perhaps the moral philosophers should take into account the possibility that man's inherent cupidity fluctuates, like a thermometer, with the number and quality of opportunities to commit theft, legal or otherwise; that the honesty of too few men is constant. This man is incorruptible up to the figure of, say, $100,000. Many other men will gladly sell for two dollars the only piece of genuine influence they will ever possess, which is their vote. Still other men use lead slugs in pay-telephone boxes.

The ethics by which men conduct business appear to be no more constant than individual honesty. The decade after 1865 in the United States appears in retrospect to have been an extended pay-day for the vast military exploit just concluded. Somebody observed it was as if Booth's bullet had released all the chicanery and cupidity of thirty-five million people. Pastors warned that God's hand would smite the Republic. And yet, the more numerous and grosser sort continued to admire the "smart" man.

Because this book will deal with a sizable number of men who were termed smart by their contemporaries, it is proper to know what the adjective meant. In early New England "smart" was not an unqualified compliment. It was reserved for the peddlers of wooden nutmegs, and later applied to lightning-rod salesmen. In time some of this primitive meaning was sloughed away, although "smart" was offensive enough to cause an action for libel as late as 1858. There was something a little wrong with the smart man as the Civil War came to an end.

The most notoriously smart figures of the postwar period in the United States were three characters who without too much exaggeration were also known as the men of disaster. They were Daniel Drew, Jay Gould, and Jim Fisk.

It would be difficult to find three men more dissimilar from each other than these. No one of them quite fits the character of the American mogul of business or industry. They were shrewd enough and ruthless enough; but unlike Commodore Vanderbilt and the great industrialists who followed him, such as Carnegie, Rockefeller, Hill, and a few more, these three smart men were not builders of anything. Many called them wreckers. "Foul hyenas," said an editorial writer of the time, "who when their prey was full rotten came to sink their slavering jaws into the carrion." That editorialist was trying hard and his simile was not too farfetched, yet his knowledge of wild animals was at fault. No hyena, not even the best hyena, had the bold courage of Drew, Fisk, or Gould.

Drew was the eldest. He was also first on the scene. Born in 1797 on a farm near Carmel, New York, he got his start with a hundred dollars received for serving as a substitute in the militia during the War of 1812. This made him unique: of all the early great American capitalists, Drew alone served in the armed forces of his country.

With his military bonus, Drew bought cattle which he drove to New York and sold, mostly to butcher Henry Astor, a brother to the fur trader and real estate shark. He extended his tours into Ohio, where he found he could buy more cheaply. He roamed over all of the inhabited portions, sleeping in barns, often by the wayside. Once as he sat his horse under a tree, lightning struck and killed the animal, leaving Drew unconscious. It was perhaps from this fairly close contact with the finger of God that stemmed Drew's lifelong pose of being a devout Christian, though it in no manner tempered his smart dealings. He seems never to have denied his most celebrated piece of knavery, which he used in his cattle business for many years. As a big herd of anywhere from six hundred to a thousand head of Ohio beef approached New York City, Drew had his drovers salt them well, then, just before reaching the market place, let them drink their fill. Cattle were sold live-weight. Drew's processing with salt and water added many tons to the average herd. "Watered stock" soon became a term in Wall Street.

Drew made money every trip. In 1829 he opened a cattle yard at Third Avenue and Twenty-fourth Street in New York. He also operated the Bull's Head Tavern, a favorite hotel of drovers. Money rolled in. Noting the success of the Vanderbilt steamboats, as related, he bought a shaky old tub, painted her, and called himself a steamboat line. He also advertised that he would carry a passenger from New York to Albany for a quarter of a dollar. Drew knew as well as Vanderbilt the value of a good nuisance, and made the Commodore buy him off the river at a smart price. Then he went into Wall Street.

Daniel Drew must have been young once, though none of his contemporaries seems to have mentioned it. In Wall Street he was remembered from the first as a tall, lanky, and "elderly" rustic, his face tanned and deeply lined from the suns and storms of his cattle-buying excursions until it looked like old leather. His eyes were never still. He was as bland as an undertaker. He was good-natured and insinuating. Despite the "catlike tread of his gait," he was often taken for a country deacon.

Drew liked to spout quotations from the Old and New Testaments. He was almost, but not quite, illiterate. Even when he was rated worth several million dollars, he kept his accounts in his head; he always knew just how many "sheers," as he invariably called them, of this or that stock he held. The whole paraphernalia of bookkeeping, he declared, was a confounded fraud. In a day when silk or beaver hats and gold-headed canes were a part of the wealthy man's getup, Drew had neither. Winter or summer, he wore a dilapidated drover's hat and carried an old umbrella. The bucolic title of Uncle Dan'l fitted him perfectly.

Drew found Wall Street to be far more remunerative and no more difficult to understand than the cattle or the steamboat business. "I got to be a millionaire," he liked to say, "afore I knowed it, hardly." He enjoyed telling how the good Lord had always blessed him in money matters. Yet when prayer failed to soothe him, he got himself a jug of whiskey, retired to some obscure hotel, and went forthwith to bed, there to remain quietly if completely drunk and covered with four layers of quilts, the window shut tight and the room stifling. He was never known to drink in company, and observed great caution that his solitary binges, which lasted as long as four days running, should not become public knowledge.

Unlike Daniel Drew in almost every respect was Jay Gould, another country boy come to town. A descendant of Nathan Gold, who arrived in Connecticut in 1647, Jay was born at Roxbury, New York, in 1836, to become a frail, undersized man with sad

COMMODORE CORNELIUS VANDERBILT

JOHN JACOB ASTOR
(From a painting by Alonzo Chappel)

E. I. DU PONT

dark eyes and the face of a frustrated poet. He was not given to talk, idle or otherwise, and there was absolutely no pose about him. He had cunning, but no hypocrisy. And if man ever called Jay Gould friend, the record of it is lost; and he was not guilty of a like softness.

After work as a surveyor, Gould bought into a tannery in Pennsylvania, then went to New York for financial aid in getting control of the business. A leather merchant there named Leupp was the unfortunate man who supplied it. Once in the saddle Gould soon brought about Leupp's financial ruin, followed by suicide; then set himself up as a leather merchant in New York. He began to speculate in railroad stocks, an occupation that Daniel Drew had long since entered.

The third of these smart fellows was neither so brainy as Gould nor so foxy as Drew, but he was just as smart as either, and nigh incredible as a personality. He was Jim Fisk, all solid brass, who came in good time to be known as the Prince of Erie, Jubilee Jim, the Barnum of Wall Street, and Admiral of the Fall River Line. Born the son of a tinware peddler in Pownal, Vermont, he left home early to travel with Van Amberg's circus and thus acquired a thorough education in regard to the best methods for treating easy marks, as suckers of the period were known, and learned at first hand of their great number and virtually unlimited credulity. With this valuable knowledge he returned to his native Green Mountains to become a partner with his father in the peddling of tinware.

Jim Fisk was a genial, handsome fellow who slapped men on the back and often pinched the girls elsewhere. Both men and women liked him. He could sell them stuff they did not want before they realized they had bought it. He advertised his tours in the country papers and by posters as though he were a three-ring circus. He decorated his vans like circus wagons. Business boomed to such extent that Eben D. Jordan of Boston took notice of the large amount of goods ordered by Fisk from the Jordan, Marsh wholesale department. He invited young Fisk to join Boston's biggest store, which he did in 1860. Then the country erupted in war.

The North needed things for its troops, among which were blankets and of which at that time Jordan, Marsh had a huge oversupply. Fisk went to Washington, saw the right people, and unloaded the lot on the Army at a nice profit; and later sold more Jordan, Marsh merchandise to the government. Mr. Jordan did not fail to mark these bold new talents. He made Fisk a vice-president of the firm.

When New Orleans fell into federal hands, Fisk took off to buy cotton for a Boston syndicate, which made a mint of money quickly. But when Fisk set up in Boston as an independent broker, things did not go well. Nor did they when he went to New York to play the stock market. The smart boys took him, and he lost what little cash he had brought from Boston. He didn't mind too much, but good-naturedly charged his losses to the cost of a postgraduate course in stocks and bonds.

It may have been Jim Fisk of whom somebody said the harder he falls the higher he bounds. Broke though he was, Fisk bounded into a nice office in Wall Street with "Fisk & Belden" in gold leaf, or at least gilt, on the door. Knowing that Daniel Drew, already a great figure in the Street, controlled a small and useless railroad, the Stonington in Connecticut, he approached Drew with a plan to unload the line on a group of Boston speculators. Drew was interested. He told the roly-poly young man to go ahead.

With methods not unlike those he had used in his circus and tin-ware days, Fisk proceeded to unload the railroad at a good profit in jig time. Fast money. Uncle Dan'l was delighted. He gave Fisk a big commission. He recognized in Fisk just the sort of a front he wanted for a number of undercover operations in stocks. The new and obscure little house of Fisk & Belden forthwith became the agency through which Drew bought and dumped stocks without the knowledge of rival speculators.

From the day it opened, Fisk's office was open house for anybody who cared to drop in. A bottle of whiskey and a box of cigars were always on the desk, and Fisk was free with them. He soon was known as the jolliest man in Wall Street.

It was through Drew that Fisk and Jay Gould first met. The sinister day is remembered as October 8, 1867. Drew, then past seventy, was girding his loins for the biggest fight of his long career. His opponent was none other than seventy-three-year-old Commodore Vanderbilt. Knowing the Commodore of old, Drew felt the need of help from "the two smartest young men in New York," a description that probably fitted Fisk and Gould. The Commodore would have to fight alone. It was against his nature to do otherwise. He could and did have allies, but never anyone who could have been called a partner or a lieutenant.

The struggle, which went into the history of crime and of finance as the "Erie War," was like nothing before or since; and though it involved the control of several railroads, and, on occasion, of at least two legislatures, to say nothing of courts and various officials, its name derived from the New York & Erie Railroad company, surely as unfortunate a line as ever operated in this or any other country.

When, in June of 1851, and after eighteen years of heartbreaking struggle, the Erie at last pushed its tracks from New York City to Dunkirk in western New York, it was declared by the Board of New York City Aldermen a gigantic and stupendous job worthy to be officially known as "The Work of the Age." The aldermen issued a statement saying as much which was embossed on vellum paper and decorated with a maze of scrollwork and seals.

Daniel Drew cared little what the road was called but he bought heavily of its stock. It seems worth knowing that this tragedy occurred in the identical year that a Mrs. Silas Horton, who lived near the Erie tracks at Owego, New York, saved an Erie train from disaster. Just before the train was due, Mrs. Horton noted that a large tree had been blown down across the rails. Even then, the whistle was sounding for the blind curve. There was no time to lose. Grabbing the first thing that came to hand, good Mrs. Horton dashed out of the house and on down the track, flagging the cars and becoming beyond doubt the first such heroine in railroad history. Her flag was a pair of her own red woolen undergarments, vulgarly called drawers. Out of her brave deed must have come the countless stories, poems, and ballads about the flagging down of the Fast Mail or the Lightning Express by waving a pair of red flannel drawers, women's, that have become a rich piece of our folklore.

One is made glad to know that the Erie Railroad did the right thing. Its president wrote Mrs. Horton his thanks and enclosed with his letter a life pass each for Mr. and Mrs. Horton. If only she could have warned the Erie of the incomparably greater danger to its peace and well-being in Uncle Dan'l Drew. . . .

It was shortly after this heart-warming incident that Drew began to buy Erie shares very quietly. Then, almost without warning, the eminently respectable officials of Erie discovered to their horror that Drew was on the board. It was as if a case of leprosy had appeared in the directorate.

Such was the reputation of Uncle Dan'l Drew. Yet he bought heavily. Three years later he became Erie treasurer—and the road was in for desperate times, the way it was with anything on which Drew laid his hands.

His first major operation was to advance the company three and a half million dollars, taking 28,000 shares of unissued stock and three million dollars of convertible bonds as collateral. Simultaneously he went short on Erie in a rising market, then suddenly unloaded 58,000 shares. The stock sank from ninety-five to fifty. Drew took enormous profits.

It was at this period that Commodore Vanderbilt began to take notice of Erie affairs. He sensed in the Erie Railroad a possible competitor to a system of rails he had in mind. He had been slow getting into railroads, possibly because of an understandable prejudice. Back in 1833 he had been seriously injured on the Camden & Amboy line when a train was derailed and rolled down a bank. All in his car save Vanderbilt had been killed. The memory had dimmed, however, and in 1860, or a little before, it had occurred to him that railroads might supplant steamboats. If so, then some line or other surely would want entrance to New York City.

Vanderbilt thereupon investigated the condition of the New York & Harlem, which had been a plaything of speculators and politicians ever since it was chartered in 1832. He also looked into the New York & Hudson line. The Harlem had got as far as Chatham to connect through another short line with Albany. The Hudson tracks had progressed as far up the river as Poughkeepsie. Beyond Albany ten separate roads had recently been combined to form the New York Central and connect Albany with Buffalo.

The Commodore saw possibilities. He first went to work on the Harlem. By subtle machinations that are not, almost a century later, quite clear to historians of stock and bond operations, he pounded Harlem down to nine dollars, then took control. To buy control of the Hudson cost him twenty-five dollars a share. But getting control of the New York Central was to call for much greater effort.

It had been the Central's practice to give freight and passengers to the Hudson road at Albany only when the river was frozen and the boat lines, with which the Central had an "understanding," were unable to operate. The Commodore did not like this arrangement. He felt that his Hudson should get all the business, summer and winter. It appears, too, that the Central had refused to give him a "bonus," which the Commodore thought was his due, though on what grounds is not clear. To make things worse for the Central, one of its officials had treated the Commodore in a brusque manner.

Treating Commodore Vanderbilt in a brusque manner was no way to run a railroad, any railroad. So, one bitter day in winter, the Hudson train stopped short at East Albany, almost two miles from the Albany depot, its usual terminal. If the Central's passengers waiting in Albany wanted to get to New York before spring and the river boats, then they could begin their trip by slogging through snow and across the bridge to East Albany. And if the Hudson's passengers were heading for western New York, or even for Albany, they might start by walking the two snowy miles to the Albany depot.

As indignant cries arose from press and public, the Hudson Railroad's officials announced that henceforth Hudson trains would run only as far as East Albany.

The alarmed New York Central demanded that the legislature take steps. A committee waited upon the Commodore and demanded to know why he refused to run his trains across the river as in the past. The old man appeared to be just waiting for someone to ask him that question. He took a good bite of the rich black Lorillard plug he favored, cleared his throat, and let them have it. He showed the committee, much to its astonishment, an old law that had never been either invoked or repealed, and by then long forgotten, which specifically prohibited the Hudson Railroad from running its trains across the river. Vanderbilt had no hand in making this law; it had gone onto the books before he had taken an interest in any railroad. It had been passed by the influence and at the instigation of the New York Central Railroad company in its formative days expressly to prevent competition west of Albany.

The Commodore thoroughly enjoyed meeting the committee. With mocking humility he expressed regret that the Hudson had been unwittingly breaking the law lo these many years and gave maddeningly pious assurance that it would not do so again.

When the committee had regained speech, one of its members could think of nothing better to say than to ask the Commodore where he had been when his railroad so suddenly refused to run its trains across the river. The old man replied, jovially enough, that he had been at his home, 10 Washington Place, New York City, engaged in playing whist, a game, he went on to explain, that required one's undivided attention. It was one of the vital old pirate's many remembered remarks.

The trains of the Hudson continued to stop at East Albany,

"according to the law"; and almost immediately the stock of the New York Central started to slide. When it had fallen to what Commodore Vanderbilt considered a reasonable price, he bought eighteen million dollars' worth of it and became president. Two years later, by some expenditure among legislators, he combined the Central and the Hudson into one system, which he was pleased to call the New York Central & Hudson River Railroad. He retained the Harlem in the Vanderbilt family, leasing it to the larger road at a good stiff price. He now had a railroad from New York City to Buffalo on Lake Erie. It was high time to do something about that other road to the lake, the Erie. . . .

But first things first. The Commodore wanted a fitting freight terminal depot for his new New York Central & Hudson River system. (A new passenger station must wait.) From Trinity Church he bought property in St. John's Park, along Hudson Street, and erected a huge three-story building. On its façade was a pediment 150 feet long and 31 feet high, which culminated in a central niche wherein stood the heroic figure of the Commodore himself, fur-lined overcoat and all, in bronze.

Scattered around the imposing metal Commodore, as if shot from cannon, were bronze steamships, locomotives, anchors, railroad cars, sea gulls, forest trees, and other lesser objects, the whole forming a hideous group of molten images—or so thought George Templeton Strong, who saw it on November 15, 1869 and was quite appalled. "A work of art that is bestial" is the way he summed it up.

A thing like the Vanderbilt bronze was not to be unveiled without a few remarks, and Mayor A. Oakey Hall of New York was ready to accommodate. Looking up at the gleaming likeness of the city's first citizen, the mayor cried: "Stand there, familiar image of an honored man! Stand there and breast the storms or glitter in the sunshine of coming centuries . . ."

The fur-lined Commodore was to stand right there for another sixty years, or until 1929, when he was removed and placed before Grand Central Station at the top of the ramp by which Park Avenue traffic reaches the elevated roadway around the station. And there he stood in 1952, still staunch and without blemish, after breasting the storms of eighty-three years and glittering in as many suns.

Chapter 4 THE WARS OF THE TROGLODYTES

IT was as obvious to Commodore Vanderbilt as it was to less shrewd men that Drew was not interested in the Erie Railroad as a transportation system. It was a piece of property to be manipulated for his own profit. From the day he became a heavy stockholder, he had by various means caused flurries, then depressions in its shares, taking his gains with each fluctuation. Both Gould and Fisk were now acting as his agents, and old Uncle Dan'l was about to learn exactly how smart his young men were.

The native bucolic flavor that adhered to Drew throughout his lifetime was one of his greatest assets. The old drover's hat, the rusty antique clothes, the umbrella used as a cane, and the nasal drawl of a bumpkin, these were valuable props and he knew it.

Many other men in Wall Street contrasted their own city sophistication with Drew's crudities and felt quite superior—almost always to their cost, if they were dealing with Drew. Lunching one day in a club frequented by speculators, Drew pulled out his well-known red bandanna handkerchief to mop his brow. A slip of paper fell to the floor, apparently unnoticed by the old man. Some trader saw and promptly covered it with his foot until chance let him read it. It was an order in the old rustic's illiterate scrawl to buy Erie stock. The smart trader shared the wonderful find with friends, and they hurried to the Exchange to purchase Erie. The price plummeted almost at once, and Drew added a few thousands to his millions.

Such tricks were not for Commodore Vanderbilt, who had methods of his own for stock manipulations. But he knew well enough that the Erie was basically a sound railroad, one that could become stiff competition for his own New York Central. This was a condition to be averted if possible.

The possibilities must have looked favorable to him. In forming the Central the Commodore had voted himself six million dollars in cash and twenty million more in new stock as a sort of bonus for his good work. He always liked the idea of a bonus. And he could hardly be blamed if he considered twenty-six million dollars a sum sufficient to remove any competitor.

Once his mind was made up, the Commodore announced publicly that he was going to buy control of Erie. His agents began to purchase its stock. Drew was unhorsed at a directors' meeting.

This was all very well, but suddenly there appeared on the market a lot of new and unsuspected stock of the Erie Railroad. It came from some mysterious source. The ink on the certificates appeared to be scarcely dry. Suspecting what was afoot, Vanderbilt obtained, or perhaps bought is the better word, an injunction from Judge George C. Barnard, a notorious tool of New York's "Tweed ring" of grafters, preventing Erie directors from issuing more stock. Jay Gould got a counterinjunction from another judge. Then Gould started his printing press to changing ten million dollars of Erie's happily convertible bonds into Erie stock and threw 100,000 shares into the market.

These unsuspected shares "exploded like a mine," said a contemporary writer, and the so-called "Erie Panic" ensued. ("Erie went down like a dead heifer" was the way Uncle Dan'l described it.) Wall Street filled with shouting mad men, for not only Erie but other stocks tumbled. Above the tumult "sounded the mad roars of Commodore Vanderbilt." Another war among troglodytes was getting under way.

Vanderbilt went headlong into action by having his creature, Judge Barnard, order the arrest of Drew, Gould, and Fisk. The puppet judge also issued an order pronouncing the Erie Railroad bankrupt and named a receiver friendly to Vanderbilt.

The three men of disaster worked even faster than the Commodore. At the Erie's head office in New York, they gathered some six million dollars in greenbacks, the funds from sales of their printing-press stock, tied them into bundles, tossed them into a hack, and drove like mad to the Jersey ferry. Here they were received by a small army of thugs who, Fisk said, were Erie detectives and whom he had thoughtfully engaged to protect the getaway.

They were needed, too, for close after the careening hack containing Fisk, Drew and Gould, and the greenbacks came other hacks loaded with deputy sheriffs set moving by Vanderbilt. But the clubs and brass knuckles of the Erie gang permitted escape of the three men, who were determined that the Erie Railroad should not become a mere means of transportation. Drew, Fisk, and Gould ferried safely across the Hudson to New Jersey. It was fine melodrama. Even better was to come.

In Jersey City the Erie men took over Taylor's Hotel and renamed it Fort Taylor. Jersey City itself was pleased to supply a detail of its police as guards. To these Fisk added the thugs he liked to call detectives. Three small cannon were mounted on the waterfront near the hotel. Four lifeboats, each holding twelve armed men, served as a shore patrol.

While Gould labored within Fort Taylor to reorganize the Erie as a New Jersey corporation and acted as operating head of the doomed railroad, Fisk was in his glory as "admiral" of the Erie navy and coast guard. From New York he fetched Josie Mansfield, the pretty mistress who was to prove so fatal later, and installed her in a gaudy suite in Fort Taylor.

Fisk also acted as a sort of public relations counsel, a job he enjoyed immensely. He served champagne to the press, who had followed the exodus from Manhattan, and was always good for a drink, a cigar, a loan, or a suitable quote for the papers.

"Commodore Vanderbilt owns New York," Fisk now told the young men of the *Herald,* the *Post,* the *Times,* and the *Tribune.* "He owns the Stock Exchange. He owns New York's streets and railroads. We are ambitious young men. We saw there was no chance for us to expand in your city, so we came over here to Jersey to grow up with the country."

The public loved it. To most Americans the Erie War was simply a good free show, perhaps the funniest farce to be seen outside the theater, and maybe inside. Fisk continued to regale the press with ribald announcements, and occasionally relaxed from his labors by taking Miss Mansfield for an airing.

It was Jay Gould's nature to say little at any time, but now from his lair in the Erie fastness came a statement. "The Erie Railroad," said he, "has reduced its passenger rate between Buffalo and New York from seven to five dollars." It caused New York Central stock to shed a few points. It is probable that by this time the Commodore realized his adversaries were smarter men than he had been accustomed to deal with. Gould was about to emerge as a master operator in the comparatively new field of railroads.

After several weeks of enforced exile in New Jersey, Jay Gould packed a big valise with half a million dollars in greenbacks and secretly took off for Albany, the New York State capital. Here he

assiduously cultivated members of the legislature, urging them to
legalize what he had already done in converting Erie bonds into
stock.

Getting wind of the business, Vanderbilt managed to have Gould
arrested, though the prisoner kept out of jail and, in the mild
custody of a friendly deputy, continued his machinations from a
hotel room. Boss Tweed of New York City, here in the guise of a
state senator, conducted matters for Gould with customary dispatch.
It mattered not at all to Tweed which side won the war, and he
made certain that his confreres, the elected representatives of the
people, received maximum bribes from both the Gould and the Vanderbilt agents.

What the mendacious legislators cost Vanderbilt that session
seems not to be known, but Gould paid them no less than one million dollars, give or take a few thousand. Gould won, too, when
the well-paid tribunes of the sovereign people passed an act pro-
viding that the conversion of bonds was legal in the state of New
York. In effect, the act meant that Gould, Fisk, and Drew could
continue to hold over the hoary head of the old Commodore the immeasurable threat of unlimited issues of Erie stock.

Mr. Gould now turned his attention to relations with the public.
He wanted his fellow Americans to know that he, together with the
judges he had bribed and the legislators he had bought, were really
friends of the people. To justify his and their actions he invoked,
or perhaps invented, the whipping-boy character of the arch-
monopolist. If he did invent the character, it was one of Gould's
great contributions; the arch-monopolist has remained a favorite
ogre of the American public.

To typify the ogre Gould of course selected Commodore Vanderbilt, and shuddered publicly to think what might, nay surely, would
have happened if Vanderbilt had not been prevented from getting
control of the Erie. Why, the Commodore would have made the
price of flour every day in New York and New England a dollar
less or five dollars more, as he wished; the poor man wanting only
a ticket to Buffalo would pay whatever exorbitant fare the Commodore cared to charge. The possibilities in such a heinous monopoly were limited only by the greed of such arch-monopolists as
Vanderbilt. It was a dreadful thing to contemplate.

No amount of abuse could cause Commodore Vanderbilt to haul
down his flag, but the threat of that Erie printing press, now
legalized, was something to be feared. The old man was suddenly

tired of the Erie War. He sent a secret message to Uncle Dan'l: "Drew, I'm sick of the whole damned business. Come and see me."

Drew appeared at 10 Washington Place one night soon, and began at once to ramble sentimentally about the value of old friendships, of the days when he and the Commodore were friends in the shipping business. The Commodore brought him up short. "Drew," he said testily, "if you'll wipe that tobacco off your chin we can get down to business." He also remarked that his trouble with Erie "has learned me it never pays to kick a skunk."

With these amenities out of the way, the Commodore proposed terms of armistice, if not of absolute peace. These were based on the premise that the Erie crowd should pay him back some four and a half million dollars that he said had been stolen from him by means of the printing press. Old Drew replied that he would have to see the other boys about it, then left.

A few days later Gould and Fisk, now the real bosses of Erie, having neatly ousted Drew from control, came to the Vanderbilt residence. A sort of agreement was made. Fisk said that the aged though still rambunctious Commodore had threatened "to keep his bloodhounds of lawyers after us if we didn't take that Erie stock off his hands." They did so. Even then Vanderbilt had lost more than a million dollars in the war.

It was typical of Jim Fisk that even during such a momentous conference, he noticed that the Commodore "was wearing a pair of four-buckled shoes such as I had never seen before." Fisk made up his mind that if men like the Commodore wore that sort of shoes, then he wanted a pair too.

Jay Gould had himself elected president of Erie. Fisk was made vice-president and comptroller. Continued tragedy for the Erie was assured.

The press began to refer to Fisk as the Prince of Erie. He loved titles like that and worked hard to deserve them. He bought Pike's Opera House at Eighth Avenue and Twenty-third Street, christened it the Grand Opera House, and set a horde of workmen and artists to making its interior fit for the head office of the New York & Erie Railroad company, including a gorgeous suite where the Erie's vice-president could, in his new and secondary role of impresario, interview and entertain such opera and musical comedy stars, female, as he thought would please the fashionable audiences he planned to attract. Fisk and Gould had the opera house property recorded in their own names. They bought it with money dipped out of the Erie treasury. They leased it to the Erie Railroad at the immodest rate of $75,000 a month.

Nothing better symbolized the era than the Erie offices. A dazzling staircase led to the second floor and its huge doors of elaborately carved oak. Beyond these was a marble hall surrounded by stained-glass partitions, gilded balustrades, chandeliers tinkling with cut glass. Frescoes and carvings and *objets de vertu* were everywhere. In the center of the main hall were a bronze bust of William Shakespeare and a set of bronze numerals—1869. These of course had reference to the year in which Gould and Fisk, with Drew looking on, took Erie in their strong hands.

A visitor to the office, an awed reporter from the *World,* noted that the ceilings were done in blue, carmine, lilac, and gold; and had "Pompeian designs of intertwining vines and flowers hiding naked cupids and rosy nymphs." There were also portraits of Franklin the electricity man, Morse the telegraph man, and Watt the steam-engine man.

Fisk's own office was a proper setting for the Prince of Erie. His walnut desk sat on a raised dais. His chair, so the openmouthed *World* reporter noted, was studded with gold-headed nails. The ceiling here was of delicate blue and fawn, except for ovals of startling crimson on each of which was lettered *Erie.* "In solid gold," Mr. Fisk explained. The minority stockholders of Erie might and did complain, and in vain.

The gaudy, ribald offices of Erie were nevertheless in perfect accord with the taste of the era. What was more, in combining the offices of America's second-greatest railroad and New York City's Grand Opera House, Jim Fisk, the smart Yankee peddler gone wild, achieved a wedding of business and the arts that had not previously nor since been seen in the United States. For the next half dozen years, Fisk was to play two leading parts in the shabby gilt show of the Gilded Age—that of a sinister conspirator and that of chief clown to the nation. He played both to perfection.

Riding as a passenger on the Erie Railroad, however, was becoming increasingly dangerous. Its employees were badly demoralized, and little wonder. One day in 1868, when Pike's Opera House was being prepared for its new owners, a New Yorker wrote in his diary: "Another accident on the Erie. Scores of people smashed, burned to death, or maimed for life. We shall never travel safely until some pious, wealthy, and much beloved railroad director has been hanged for murder, with a conductor on each side of him. Drew or Vanderbilt would do to begin with." The diarist might better have suggested Fisk and Gould, but they were not yet so well known as they were a twelvemonth later.

The greatest American hero of the time had just been elected President of the United States. Vicksburg had given Grant a reputation. Other battles added luster to it. "This man *fights!*" is what Lincoln had said. Then, too, the simple direct phrase Grant used at Appomattox fixed his character in the popular mind of the North. There was something veracious in the man. He had integrity. He also disliked braid. He was as common as an old shoe. . . . Go look again at Brady's photographs. Here a group of officers pose in the sunlight under scrubby pines. They are erect. Their shoulder straps are clear and in place. Their hands rest on their swords. Their boots reflect the sun. And there, somehow lonely on a bench, is a lounger you would expect to see on the steps of a crossroads store, a disreputable hat drawn over a bearded face, a cigar, a baggy coat unbuttoned, a pair of dirty boots. That is *Grant,* a man, but also a legend.

Now he was President of the United States, and "his commonplace figure gained in contrast to the windy, noisy creatures on paper stilts who surrounded him in Washington." He was also utterly naïve in all save military matters, a fact known to the political leaders who wanted Grant's great reputation under which to hide. They had put him into the White House with almost no effort at all.

Grant the President was tired. Decades of failure and four years of war had eaten out of this man most, but not quite all, of his native strength. When he had said, "Let us have peace," it was no political sugar-teat. It was a personal prayer. He was weary.

Whether or not Jay Gould contributed anything toward Grant's election isn't known and doesn't matter. Gould meant to use him, anyway. Grant was less than two months in office when Gould began paying his respects to Mr. and Mrs. Abel Rathbone Corbin of New York. Gould had known Corbin as a successful lawyer, speculator, and lobbyist, a handy man to have around. Now at the age of sixty-seven, Corbin had married a sister of President Grant. He was believed to be very close to the President and was said to have no little influence on him in regard to matters of government policy.

Running the Erie and several lesser lines into which he had bought, in no way taxed Gould's energies. He needed something more to keep his mind occupied. In his restless brain had developed an idea that other men had thought of, in their wilder moments of ambition and cupidity, only to dismiss it at once as beyond all reason, namely that of cornering the gold market in the United States.

It did not seem beyond reason to Gould. He thought he could lay hands on sufficient cash to buy all loose gold in the open market. But that, he knew, would not corner gold unless a means was found to get government "co-operation," that is, a certainty that the United States Treasury would not release any of its own large stocks of the metal and thus break the attempted corner.

This obstacle of the Treasury had patently appeared insurmountable to all men who ever had considered the task of a corner. They merely lacked imagination. Jay Gould had imagination. On his first social visit to the Corbins, early in May of 1869, he started to use it. One should bear in mind that Gould had known Corbin in Wall Street and perhaps in circumstances that gave Gould reason to believe the man, who was now brother-in-law of the President of the United States, was not above turning a more or less dishonest dollar.

With soft-spoken eloquence, Gould now went to work on Corbin, and without much difficulty persuaded him of the great benefits that would bless the country if gold were made scarce. The greenback dollar, suggested Mr. Gould, was too close to gold parity; gold's price must be raised; the dollar must fall and be plentiful; inflation would cause western grain crops to move rapidly and be sold in Europe. Did not Mr. Corbin recall that farmers and merchants had never been so prosperous as when, during the recent war, it had taken $2.50 to buy one dollar's worth of gold?

Yes, true enough, agreed Mr. Corbin, adding that Mr. Gould's plan was indeed noble. It should be carried out. Casually Gould went on to indicate that Mr. Corbin himself might well benefit somewhat, and quite legally, from a rise in the price of gold. For instance, Gould would be happy to purchase, in Mr. Corbin's name, a matter of one and a half million dollars of gold at 133—without any payment on Mr. Corbin's part. The President's brother-in-law sat right up in his chair. He was more certain than ever that Mr. Gould had the right idea as to national prosperity. He was also extremely grateful about everything.

A month later Grant arrived in New York on his way to attend a great Peace Jubilee in Boston. He stopped over at the Corbins'. He and they were taken in tow by Jim Fisk and sat with that impresario in his box at the Grand Opera House. Next day the Grant party, which included several notables, was put aboard the elegant SS *Providence,* flagship of the Narragansett Steamship Line, of which Fisk was president and a sort of admiral.

The *Providence* was gaily decked with flags and bunting. At the head of the gangplank, to welcome the distinguished party, stood a figure as dazzling as could be imagined. It was Fisk in his self-designed admiral's uniform, a splendid getup of spectacular vulgarity. On the deck near by Dodsworth's Band was playing. "Admiral" Fisk led the way to install the President in the wondrous ship's bridal suite, already well stocked with strong cigars and champagne in ice buckets.

During the voyage Fisk acted as master of ceremonies, while Gould went quietly to work sounding out Grant in regard to the Administration's policy on matters of gold, inflation, and so forth, none of which held much interest for the old soldier. Grant sat stolidly through the sumptuous dinner. For another four hours he smoked one cigar after another, also stolidly, and drank glass after glass, just as stolidly. Gould meanwhile kept the conversation centered on the dangers of unemployment, poverty, and panic, which he prophesied would soon make their appearance unless money was made easier.

In all that long evening Grant apparently made but one remark. He took the cigar from his mouth and mumbled something to the effect that there was "a lot of fiction in this talk about prosperity."

It wasn't much, it wasn't clear, but such as it was it did not sound to Gould as favorable. As soon as the vessel docked at Boston next morning, he hastened to a Western Union office and telegraphed his brokers in New York to unload certain of his stocks. For the moment he must be patient about the gold affair.

President Grant appeared and spoke briefly at Boston's gigantic Peace Jubilee, though history recalls little about the event save for one feature which was as characteristic of the times as the offices of the Erie Railroad. The remembered item was Patrick Gilmore, bandmaster extraordinary, heading a host of 1,000 musicians *and* 10,000 choristers, massed on the Common, in a noise that rocked the stout iron gates of the Old Granary burying ground and all but raised the dead patriots from beneath their weathered slabs of slate. Jim Fisk loved it.

Although Gould had as yet nothing to encourage his plan, he continued to buy moderate amounts of gold during June, July, and August. He also had several long conferences with Mr. Corbin about a proper man to fill the post of Assistant Treasurer of the United States, the result of which was the appointment by Grant of General Daniel Butterfield, another gallant old soldier. Mr. Gould was happy to purchase, in Butterfield's name and without any payment from that gentleman, a "substantial amount" of gold. Gould was a man thorough in all things.

Much of the press of New York City, and of other towns, soon broke out with well-written articles about the myth of the complexities of finance. The message was that sound finance was in reality a very simple matter and was based on "easy money," or greenbacks supported by a minimum amount of gold reserve. The articles were prepared by Dominick Henry, an English expert of good reputation. They were secretly paid for by Jay Gould.

"Admiral" Fisk was not idle. In August he arranged an excursion for Grant and the Corbins, who were taken to Newport, wined and dined, and the President heard Mr. Corbin and Mr. Gould expand again on the simplicity of bringing prosperity to the nation. Autumn was nigh, along with a bountiful harvest. The crops of the honest farmers must be protected. Gold should be put up to 140, or even higher, and be kept there. Grant said nothing that is remembered other than to remark that "Admiral" Fisk was indeed a good judge of tobacco in the form of cigars.

Gould continued to purchase gold. It rose to 137. Gould wrote a check for $25,000 which he casually gave to Corbin as a portion of his "profits to come." This is what confidence men call the "convincer," the barb in the hook that holds the sucker fast until the kill. On Corbin it acted as a sort of refresher to his mind of the enormous profits to be taken when gold should hit 180—or even higher.

Grant visited the Corbins again on September 2. As soon as he had returned to Washington, Corbin hurried to see Gould. He had good news. The President, he said, had changed his mind and had come around to the sensible viewpoint held by Gould and Corbin. And in Corbin's presence, he said, the President had written and dispatched to Secretary of the Treasury Boutwell an order to sell no government gold without specific orders from him, U. S. Grant.

The trap was ready. Only then did Gould take Fisk fully into his confidence. Fisk naturally knew that Gould had not wanted to entertain Grant just for his company, but he had not quite fathomed the real reason for it—and anyway, Fisk was no man to worry needlessly. Gould now needed Fisk's participation to help the plot along. Fisk did so with consummate cleverness.

In Wall Street, in the Gold Room of the Exchange, on Broadway, and in the Hoffman House and other haunts of speculators, the jolly, genial, hospitable Fisk made the rounds, dropping hints of great things brewing in the gold market.

Gold began to rise. Early in September it had reached 137. With funds supplied him by the Tammany-controlled Tenth National Bank, Gould increased his buying. Gold went to 141. In the *Tribune* Horace Greeley raised his voice against the Goldbugs, and demanded that the United States Treasury sell gold.

By September 22 Gould had bought forty millions of gold, or about twice as much gold as was ordinarily in circulation; and on that day, too, he got a shock: Corbin came in haste to show him a letter from Mrs. Grant, in which the President's wife told Corbin he must withdraw at once from his speculation. Corbin was frightened. He also wanted Gould to pay him that $100,000, his "profits," and take the gold off his hands. Gould refused.

The letter from Mrs. Grant could not be ignored. The President might be wavering again about the best method to get prosperity for the country. Gould must watch closely. But he said nothing to Fisk about Mrs. Grant's letter. That gambler continued to buy gold on the twenty-third. The price mounted to 142, then to 144. On the night of the twenty-third, Fisk and a number of Goldbugs who had been following his lead met to congratulate each other on the way things were going. Next day, they agreed, they would press the price again until gold should hit two hundred. Then they would unload.

On that same evening, too, according to evidence uncovered much later, General Butterfield, in charge of the Subtreasury in New York City, sent word to Gould that Grant had disavowed all connection with Brother-in-law Corbin. He had at last become suspicious. Gould had best be prepared for anything. Gould thanked General Butterfield, but failed to say that he, Gould, was already unloading. Gould was a man who did not get up early in the morning; he stayed up all night.

That the next day, September 24, was a Friday has ever been of the greatest comfort to the superstitious. It was to be *the* Black Friday of American financial history. Gold opened at 145. No one offered to sell. Wildest excitement followed the price up to 162. In Washington, Secretary of the Treasury Boutwell was being deluged with "tornadoes of telegrams" demanding the government sell gold. The entire American world of bankers, brokers, speculators, and even merchants was in agony, wrote an observer. Railroad and industrial stocks generally slipped, then skidded toward the cellar.

The President of the United States happened to be playing croquet when a message from Boutwell reached him; and suddenly the weary man who had been unable to make up his mind, and had vacillated for many weeks about the complexities of money matters, roused himself and acted. As at Shiloh, Grant roused late but when he roused he acted with all his strength. No halfway steps. He ordered Boutwell to start selling gold at once and continue to sell until the near corner of it was completely demolished.

The effect was immediate and dramatic. Buying bids on the New York Exchange ceased. There was a mad rush to sell. The price of gold tumbled. A man from the *Herald* saw the suddenness of the debacle. As the bells of Trinity Church started to peal the hour of noon, gold on the Exchange indicator stood at 160. Before the echo of the bells had died away, gold stood at 138, and soon fell another three points.

The man from the *Herald* sensed the great drama. He watched as "over the pallid faces of many speculators stole a deathly hue." They gazed on vacancy, he said. Others rushed madly through the streets, hatless. At least half of Wall Street was "involved in ruin."

There was more or less ruin to speculators from Boston to San Francisco. It was never clear whether Gould and Fisk came out of this "cyclone of disaster" with nothing lost and nothing gained; or with great losses, especially for Fisk; or if the two men made a profit of somewhere between nine and eleven million dollars. What is certain is that crowds of ruined speculators in New York set out to find the two leading Goldbugs with the idea of hanging them. Nothing came of it.

In the first days of despair, Fisk was the chief object of abuse, which was only natural because he was the one who made the most noise about buying gold in the first place. Gould as usual remained behind the scenes. But the ensuing Congressional investigations had the effect of making Gould, and not Fisk, the symbolic figure of evil incarnate, "unmitigated by any discernible decency." More than eighty years later Gould's name is often used to conjure up the character of any crafty, enigmatic master of financial trickery. We like our villains like that—crafty, enigmatic. We like them too, to be bold. Gould was all of those things. And we shall see what a real master of financial trickery he showed himself to be in the years after Black Friday.

As for Abel Corbin, brother-in-law of the President, he was thoroughly tarred by the scandal. General Butterfield was permitted to resign without disgrace. In later years his old comrades of battle-field and bivouac presented him with "a sword of superb workman-ship, set with emeralds" and a "5th Corps Badge, set with dia-monds"; and even later Congress presented him with a Medal of Honor for heroism at the Battle of Gaines's Mill. His brief career as boss of the Subtreasury just before Black Friday was soon for-gotten. A statue of him stands today, looking everlastingly, as historian Claude Bowers remarked, at the tomb of his old com-mander, General Grant, on Riverside Drive, New York.

Neither Black Friday nor the investigations left any mark on Jim Fisk. Obvious scoundrel that he was, he was a genial, open-handed and altogether "human" being. "Nothing is lost save honor," he said in regard to the Congressional investigations. And when the trail to Black Friday indicated a taint had spread through both houses of Congress, and even "approached the parlor of the White House," Fisk was delighted. "Let everyone carry out his own corpse," he told the committee of investigation.

Chapter 5   HE WAS ALWAYS KIND TO THE POOR

FISK was quite right: He and Gould had lost noth-ing save honor, and neither was of a nature to be troubled by ab-stractions.

They had broken no law. What they had conspired to do, and had nearly accomplished, violated no act of state or federal govern-ment. If a private individual had the whim to buy gold, it was his own affair. As Jay Gould's sole apologist pointed out, Gould was no more bound to be a high moralist than were those whom "he baffled by his superior adroitness." Of Fisk, another writer re-marked that historians have painted him blacker than need be on the wise theory that blackening a black sheep tends to make gray sheep paler; and besides, Fisk left no acute descendants to specialize in the destruction of testimony against him.

At the time of Black Friday, Gould was thirty-three years old. Though wracked by tuberculosis, he had many years of furious activity ahead of him.

Fisk was thirty-five. His days were numbered. Possibly he sensed as much. During the twenty-seven months left to him after Black Friday he enjoyed public and private lives such as few men have managed. Not even the expensive vulgarities of the sons of wealthy men, playboys like Jerry Vanderbilt, Charlie Gates, and Harry K. Thaw, were to merit the notice that has been devoted to the prodigies of Fisk.

It was the Barnum in him. Even his death was spectacular. Most moneyed men die of physical ailments. Fisk died virtually in his boots, and one can hope they were of the special four-buckled sort he had so admired in the dress of old Commodore Vanderbilt. If anything more were needed to make Fisk a unique character in his class, he achieved it not long after his death, when he became the hero, not the villain, of a popular ballad that is still, eighty years later, to be occasionally heard.

For a period after Black Friday, Fisk and Gould remained barricaded in the Grand Opera House, which Fisk now liked to call Castle Erie.

Gould kept busy enough, mapping new campaigns, in and out of Erie, but there was just then nothing calling for Fisk's peculiar talents in business. Inaction wore him down. Even worse was isolation from the public, of which Fisk was ever conscious. Thus he was overjoyed when some politician or other came to urge him to give aid to the 9th Regiment, New York National Guard, which was in a bad way. Interest had sagged. Equipment was worn out or obsolete. Less than three hundred men constituted its strength.

Fisk turned money and his great energies to the 9th. He bought fine new instruments for the band, and rumor had it he engaged a first cornet player at a salary of $10,000 a year. He offered cash prizes for recruiting efforts. The ranks filled quickly. The regiment forthwith elected him colonel. It now mustered more than seven hundred rank and file.

Colonel Fisk, attired in the most gorgeous uniform ever seen in the National Guard, took his command on an excursion to Long Branch, New Jersey, which turned into a monumental week-long drunk, winding up with a grand ball that was reported in the police court news. Fisk paid all expenses, including the drunk and disorderly fines.

Colonel Fisk staged an even greater event on Bunker Hill Day, June 17, in 1871, when he loaded the 9th onto one of his Fall River Line boats, took them to Boston, where they were refused a permit to parade on the Boston Common but did manage to give a grand concert in a theater Fisk hurriedly engaged. All costs were paid by Colonel Fisk, and one might wonder what stockholders of the battered Erie Railroad, of which Fisk was still comptroller, thought of his military doings.

Colonel Fisk's next appearance was unfortunate. It was on the twelfth of July, a day sacred to street and other fights among Protestant and Catholic Irishmen, of which New York City had large numbers. Orangemen had announced they would observe the anniversary of the Battle of the Boyne with a parade down Broadway.

The mayor called out five regiments of the Guard to keep the peace. The peace was broken before the marchers had moved two blocks. Bricks and stones, then bullets, mowed down the marchers, and also the Guards. The Guards used their guns. Colonel Fisk was knocked down and injured. Carried into a bakery, he soon fled through back yards to pause briefly in the Hoffman House, from where he took a cab to the ferry, and finished the day in a hide-out in New Jersey.

Only once more did Colonel Fisk appear with his regiment. This occasion was the visit to New York of the Grand Duke Alexis of Russia. Fisk had the 9th's wonderful band serenade the royal visitor, then invited him to "a good show in my Opera House."

In October 1871, when news came that all of Chicago was burning, Fisk acted effectively, and with characteristic ostentatiousness, to raise aid for the stricken city. He made a big cash donation, then got into his six-in-hand coach and drove it himself around New York, collecting load after load of food and clothing in his gorgeous drag. Response was most generous, and Fisk put everything aboard a special Erie train and sent her off, all tracks clear, heading for the scene of disaster. This was the incident that was to make Fisk the hero of a ballad.

Gould and Fisk continued to milk the Erie. Fisk used his share to play impresario. He leased the Academy of Music, the city's largest theater, and produced an opera, *Lurline,* which did not draw. He bought the happily named Boudoir Theater and staged several burlesques. But his only success as a producer was something called *The Twelve Temptations,* teeming with large, robust girls in tights, which had a good run at the Grand Opera House, or Castle Erie.

Meanwhile Fisk was "keeping" four or more beauties of the chorus, but finally began to concentrate attentions on Helen Josephine Mansfield, sometimes described as an actress, though she seems to have been devoted to a more equivocal profession.

Fisk lavished on Miss Mansfield a sumptuous home on West Twenty-fourth Street, with a ménage of maids, butlers, and other retainers sufficient to have supplied Commodore Vanderbilt's mansion. It was through her that Fisk met the exquisite Edward S. Stokes, an elegant playboy seven years Fisk's junior. Stokes's mother had given him an oil-refining business in Brooklyn, which the young man was managing so badly that he was about to lose it, when Miss Mansfield urged Fisk to take charge. He did so, and quickly put the business on its feet, becoming in the process a partner. Details of the affair are clouded, but the record shows Stokes felt Fisk had slickered him, which is a possibility; and the matter got into court by way of a statement Fisk had given to the press and which Stokes said libeled him. He sued.

The trial indicated that no matter what Fisk had done to Stokes in the refinery deal, Stokes had replaced Fisk in the fickle affections of Josie Mansfield. The press did not overlook this feature, and so the courtroom was filled to overflowing at every session.

The *Herald* reported that the "exquisite Stokes" appeared in a "swell new Alexis overcoat of dull cream color, while on a finger a huge diamond shone like a glowworm in a swamp." Fisk came into court wearing "a strange kind of blue naval uniform that fitted him wretchedly." It had double rows of great brass buttons. His mustaches bristled "ferociously," and a large diamond shone out from "his fat chest like the danger light at Sandy Hook Bar," according to the *Herald* man, who had a good stock of similes that day.

The evidence presented was in character with the startling attire of the principals. Fisk declared that the suit against him was nothing more than the end of a desperate attempt at blackmail: Miss Mansfield and Stokes, working in concert, had threatened to sell Fisk's letters to the pretty harlot to the press if he did not buy them for $15,000.

Fisk had paid that sum, he said, but had failed to get the letters. Instead, the blackmailers had demanded another payment, no less than $200,000. Fisk had refused to pay it.

The court dismissed the libel suit against Fisk; and a grand jury indicted Stokes and Miss Mansfield for attempted blackmail. The libel suit had been sensational enough, for Fisk's lawyers made it plain that Stokes was in reality nothing more than a fancy man, as pimps were known, who was living with and being supported by Miss Mansfield who, in turn, was living on Fisk's bounty.

On the very day of the grand jury's action, which was January 6, 1872, Fisk worked until after three at the Erie offices, then took a cab to the Grand Central (later Broadway Central) Hotel on lower Broadway, where he was to meet a Mrs. Morse, said to be the widow of an old friend.

A little after four o'clock John Redmond, a handyman at the hotel, was engaged in cleaning the plate-glass windows at the ladies' entrance when Colonel Fisk, resplendent in a cloak lined with bright vermilion silk, arrived. He passed the time of day with the handyman and started up the stairs to the parlor. He had almost reached the top when Stokes suddenly appeared above him, revolver in hand, and started shooting.

Fisk was hit twice, and collapsed on the stairs. A bellboy, who witnessed the incident, followed Stokes as he ran down the main stairs to the lobby, and out by a back door into Mercer Street. There he called a policeman who arrested the man.

Jim Fisk died next day. His body lay in state at Castle Erie. It was viewed by a procession of thousands, said the press, then given a grand send-off by the 9th Regiment, complete with band and Colonel Fisk's horse, with spurred boots turned backward in the stirrups, and attended by platoons of city policemen.

The band struck up a dirge and the procession moved across town to the New Haven depot on Fourth Avenue, where a draped funeral car was waiting to take the body to Brattleboro, Vermont. At every station along the line to New Haven was a crowd "waiting in silence to watch with bared heads as the train passed." (Was it a clown they were bidding good-by, or a personage?) Then the train wound up the starkly beautiful Connecticut River Valley, and near midnight arrived in white-blanketed Brattleboro, where "the whole population was waiting to meet it." Officers and men of the 9th Regiment set up an honor guard in the Baptist church, while the body lay again in state. An hour or so later a special

train arrived from Boston, bringing Fisk's old employer, Eben
Jordan, and many other prominent men of the Hub.

What was there about this dishonest vulgarian, notorious both
for his business dealings and his flagrant loves, to bring thousands
of "respectable" people to his bier in a bitter Vermont January?
It could not have been wholly morbid curiosity. Perhaps Chaplain
Pratt of the 9th Regiment guessed why. Having said bluntly that
as to Fisk's faults he would not speak of them, for a censorious
world "will do them ample justice," he mentioned that here lay
no mediocrity but a man of strong faults and strong virtues. He
remarked that "there is a crabbed meanness in rich men generally,
which is contemptible. But Colonel Fisk was generous to a fault
. . . he was always kind to the poor."

A sophisticated New Yorker—who considered Fisk's death to
be no loss, yet confided to his diary, "What a scamp he was, but
what a curious and scientifically interesting scamp!"—he said that
Fisk had a certain magnetism that attracted to him people who
were not particular about their associates. He felt that Fisk's influence on the community was bad in every way, but it was also
certain that "many people, more or less wise and more or less
honest, sorrowed heartily at his funeral . . ."

Surely there was a warm feeling for Fisk in Brattleboro, for
those uncommonly careful people collected $25,000 in order that
another local boy who had made good, Larkin Mead, might carve
in imported marble the elaborate monument that marks Fisk's
grave and which, eighty years later, is still one of the most popular
tourist attractions of the neighborhood.

Not all his fellow Yankees, however, felt that way about Jim
Fisk. From his pulpit in Brooklyn, the Rev. Henry Ward Beecher
let go with purple damnation. Terming Fisk the supreme mounte-
bank of fortune, the astounding event of the age, he said that
Fisk with one great leap had arrived at the very summit of power
in New York; he had held the courts and the legislature in his
hands; and had ridden his hour in glaring and magnificent prosperity—shameless, vicious, criminal, "abominable in his lusts and
flagrant in his violation of public decency."

Beecher's elegy to Fisk was delivered only a few years before
he himself was to go on trial for certain abominations in his own
lusts.

In the *Nation,* the humorless Godkin was appalled that there
was no elevating moral to be drawn from Fisk's death. no chance

to demonstrate that crime and sin did not pay. "The only end that would make Fisk's career a warning instead of a model," he wrote, "would be his death in old clothes, and in penury and neglect."

But Jim Fisk, alive or dead, was no man to supply material for moralizing, and Godkin went on, horrified at the spectacle. "But to be struck down in the Grand Central hotel," he wrote, "in his velvet and his diamonds, and with his gorgeous coach at the door, and to die with a dozen physicians round his bed, and a hundred reporters outside, and leave an enormous amount of property in a will drawn by a leading member of the Bar, was not, to the children of mammon, a very dreadful way of quitting the world. . . ." Godkin believed that a majority of Americans thought it a very fine way to leave the earth. Fisk had died a bit early, to be sure, but had he tarried longer, said Godkin, his figure would have grown more corpulent and his digestion more feeble. No, there was just no decent moral to it.

The editorialist then went on to reveal a most singular plan to recoup those "helpless stockholders of Erie whom Fisk has swindled." They had been reduced to hoping for succor from an unusual source, namely, that the publication of Fisk's letters to Josie Mansfield might bring some small return on their investment in a railroad property.

Miss Mansfield disappeared from her New York haunts shortly after Fisk's murder. (She turned up many years later in South Dakota where, in 1901, the press reported her to be seeking admission to a Catholic home for indigents.)

Public opinion was divided as to what should be done with Stokes. Perhaps George T. Strong expressed widespread feeling when he wrote that though he thought Stokes well deserved hanging, yet "I would hang him on a silken rope as having rid this community of one of the worst and most dangerous scoundrels that ever disgraced it." After three trials and heroic efforts by attorneys Stokes was put away in Sing Sing for four years. He died in 1901, still living on the bounty of women. During his last illness he was cared for by his sister in New York City.

The ultimate accolade came to Jim Fisk less than two years after his death, when Billy Scanlon, the popular singer and song writer responsible for "Peek-a-Boo," "Molly O," and other favorites, published "Jim Fisk, or He Never Went Back on the Poor." The maudlin ballad airily ignores those "helpless stockholders of Erie" and much else, to concentrate on Fisk's unbounded generosity

with other people's money, including the incident of the Chicago
fire, relating that "when the telegram came/ that the homeless
that night/ were starving to death slow but sure/ the lightning
express/ manned by noble Jim Fisk/ flew to feed all the hungry
and poor."

It matters little what events in Fisk's life were left unmentioned;
after all, a popular song can have but one theme. The song was
instantly popular and it tended to make hash of such ill-natured
epitaphs as those provided by Beecher, Godkin, and others. When,
years later, Carl Sandburg came to publish his *American Songbag,*
he included the Fisk ballad, properly enough, in the section devoted to "Bandit Biographies."

The death of Fisk prompted the long-suffering stockholders of
Erie to make one more effort to drive Jay Gould from his buz-
zard's nest in the Grand Opera House. They engaged the redoubt-
able and cantankerous General Daniel E. Sickles, a hero of
Gettysburg who had left one leg there, and had also shot and killed
on a street in Washington a man suspected of intimacy with the
general's wife. Sickles was a savage fighter wherever he was, and
for aides in the Erie mess, he lined up three more fighting men:
General John A. Dix, General George B. McClellan, and the noted
lawyer William R. Travers.

Sickles demanded of Gould that he call a meeting of the Erie
board of directors. Gould did not reply. He merely barricaded
Castle Erie and stationed a gang of those surly Erie "detectives"
around the place. Sickles, however, outsmarted the besiegers and
got a crew of *his* surly men inside. Then, while more than two
hundred city police kept the peace, a new Erie board was elected.
General Sickles was then pleased to give Gould a piece of sound
advice. "If you will resign," he said, "it will send the price of Erie
up fifteen points. You might make a million dollars."

Gould did resign. Erie stock rose not fifteen but twenty points,
and Gould left Erie with much more than a million dollars.

As for the melancholy Erie Railroad, during the Drew-Fisk-
Gould administrations, its funded debt had risen by sixty-four
million dollars. It was left so crippled with this enormous load that
the line did not pay a penny of dividends on its common stock
for another sixty-nine years.

Chapter 6 WRECKAGE

THE looting of the Erie Railroad was accomplished with the help of the easily corruptible legislatures of only two states, New York and New Jersey. It was a fairly simple business. But to loot the immense federal project of the Union Pacific Railroad required far more sophisticated talents. This monumental piece of thievery involved United States representatives and senators. It involved cabinet officers, the Vice-President of the United States, and a future President. The loot ran to approximately forty-four million dollars. It was removed almost painlessly from the Union Pacific's coffers by a trick outfit with a fancy French name, the Crédit Mobilier.

The Crédit Mobilier was put together by George Francis Train, a man of many parts and many eccentricities, acting as agent for T. C. Durant, vice-president of the Union Pacific Railroad company. The Union Pacific was sponsored and financed by the United States. The purpose of the Crédit Mobilier was to take over the contract for building the road.

Stockholders of the two companies were identical. They proceeded to contract with themselves to build the road at a cost calculated to exhaust the resources of the Union Pacific. The so-called profits were to be divided among Crédit Mobilier stockholders.

Prominent in Crédit Mobilier were Oakes and Oliver Ames, brothers of Easton, Massachusetts, who had inherited a business that manufactured the Ames shovel, a tool of so high and so standard a quality it was declared generally to be "legal tender in every part of the Mississippi Valley, and in the gold regions of California, Australia, and South Africa." The Hon. Oakes Ames was a representative of the old Bay State in Congress.

From the day it was whelped, the double-jointed money-making machine worked perfectly. As the tracks of the Union Pacific pushed onward across the Great Plains, the Crédit Mobilier collected the enormous bounty granted to the line from the public purse and domain. Mile upon mile the railroad was systematically stripped of its cash, which reappeared almost simultaneously as dividends for the happy stockholders of Crédit Mobilier. It was, as the Hon. Oakes Ames told his comrades in the House, "a diamond mine."

Mile upon mile, thousands of working-stiffs sweated beneath the great cruel sun of the Plains and were frostbitten when the skies turned gray and winter came down from Canada. Mile upon mile, many of them died in accidents, and others died of brawls in the jerry-built Sodoms that followed the end-of-steel across Nebraska into Colorado, into Wyoming, and so into Utah. Meanwhile, Crédit Mobilier paid their wages; and for every dollar in wages, collected almost two dollars from the government. It was the same with all supplies and equipment; they went into Crédit Mobilier at one price and emerged in the cost statements of the Union Pacific at double their original value. Mr. Ames did not exaggerate; few if any diamond mines had paid off so handsomely.

Yet, the gentlemen-thieves of Crédit Mobilier had a falling out when two factions fought for control; and the warfare gave those senators and congressmen who were not involved the courage to demand an investigation of the Union Pacific-Crédit Mobilier situation.

In an effort to forestall just such a possibility, the Crédit Mobilier officers had been distributing free stock in the House and Senate, and elsewhere. But Congress was at last forced to act, and the revelations of its investigating committee, headed by the incorruptible Senator Luke Poland (R. Vt.) were so appalling that "all decent men trembled for the honor of the nation."

No one was more hopelessly involved in the scandal than Vice-President Schuyler Colfax of the United States, except, of course, Representative Oakes Ames of Massachusetts, who, because his testimony was both direct and honest, was made a popular whipping boy for the entire gang, along with Representative Brooks, also of Massachusetts, who was well drubbed because he was a Democrat and thus deserved drubbing.

Although the Congressional investigation resulted in an almost complete official whitewash, it did leave strong doubt in many minds regarding the character of such eminent men as James A. Garfield, James G. Blaine, and almost a score more. One and all they had been well tarred before the whitewash was applied, with the tar of Crédit Mobilier. It was a pretty thick coating. The tar showed through.

But Oakes Ames was selected as the chief villain, repudiated and scorned by the very men who had been glad to own a few (free) shares of the Union Pacific's bastard subsidiary. "I am," Ames told reporters, with probably as much truth as humor, "I am like the man in Massachusetts who committed adultery, and the jury brought in a verdict that he was as guilty as the devil, but that the woman in the case was as innocent as an angel. These fellows are like that woman."

The Crédit Mobilier scandal did more than to reveal to the country at large the devious ways of the elected tribunes of the people. It brought on, or at least hastened, the panic of 1873 and turned the greatest American financier of the era into a bankrupt. This was Jay Cooke. At the time of the crash he was engaged in financing the second transcontinental railroad, the Northern Pacific.

To be "as rich as Jay Cooke" had been a byword for almost a decade. Cooke had reached this eminence without the least tinge of anything irregular in his affairs. He had on the contrary become something of a banker-patriot, honored above the run of wealthy men in the fields of real estate, railroads, and manufacture. Because we have had nothing like him since, there is no simile, no comparison to indicate his status during and just after the Civil War.

Cooke spent much of his youth in a Philadelphia banking house, where he showed great talents in his quick recognition of counterfeit currency and the bills of doubtful banks. Both were then commonly in circulation. He showed fine judgment in his promotion of canals, then of railroads. He did well with loans to the government during the Mexican War. Then the Civil War gave him his big chance and he took it famously.

In 1861, the state of Pennsylvania wanted to sell a large bond issue to finance its war effort. No banker but Jay Cooke would touch it. He sold the issue quickly, with a rousing appeal to patriotism. It was the first bond issue ever sold in that manner in the United States.

Noting his success, the federal government asked Cooke for his help. Moving his office to Washington and setting up shop across the street from the Treasury, Cooke organized a spectacular country-wide campaign to sell federal war bonds to the public. He used full-page advertisements in the press. He engaged brass bands. He hired spread-eagle speakers. He caused hundreds of thousands of flags to be displayed at his bond rallies. His salesmen worked on commission and were not turned loose until they had been thoroughly indoctrinated with the equivalent of pep talks and had learned at least ten ways of making nonbuyers look and feel like traitors. Jay Cooke, in short, set the American, or rather the Union, eagle to screaming for money. He disposed of the bond issue of 1861, and of many more that followed. They amounted in four years to nearly three billion dollars.

What Cooke had done was to invent and bring to the management of national finance a wholly new technique—the drive. With little modification it has been used ever since. Parrington said of Cooke that in certain aspects he could be reckoned the first modern American. The boys in blue must be supported by fighting dollars. He who bought bonds was as much a soldier as the lad with a Springfield on his shoulder.

From his immense commissions on bond sales and his many other activities, Cooke emerged at war's end as the greatest banker in the country. "On the day that Richmond fell," says Parrington, Cooke marked out the lines of a pretentious country house that was to cost one million dollars. This was a fifty-two-room palace named Ogontz. It contained a theater, several fountains, three hundred paintings and statues, a large conservatory, and an Italian garden facing a wall built to resemble "the ruined castle of some ancient nobleman." Here he entertained, among others, President Grant, on whom he showered fine cigars and a plenitude of whiskey and wine. To make sure that his cellar should not suffer, it was Cooke's habit to buy the pressings of entire vineyards, and cases of wines flowed in a rich, enchanting stream to his strategically placed friends.

Cooke dazzled Grant as he dazzled most contemporary Americans. He exemplified, said a critic, all of the substantial upper middle-class virtues of a people "newly given to the worship of a sterile money economy." One might call him also a vulgarian of money; placed in his own era, being a rich vulgarian merely made him a genuine great man. More than once, editorial writers and speakers coupled Cooke's name with those of Lincoln and Grant.

When the Civil War bond sales had run their course, Cooke began to look around for another large project suitable for his talents as America's most successful salesman. In 1869 he found it in the newly projected Northern Pacific Railroad. For this second transcontinental, which was planned to span the country between

Lake Superior and the Pacific Northwest, Cooke set forth to sell a hundred million dollars of bonds.

Cooke's buoyant temperament was fired anew as he contemplated the empire he would create in the great Northwest that reached from Duluth, that zenith city of Minnesota, clear to Puget Sound and the mouth of the Columbia River. He would lay open to the poor man the rich wheat lands of the Dakota country. He would put other men in position to free the Rockies of their fabulous mineral treasure. His rails would thread even the gigantic wildernesses of Idaho, Washington, and Oregon, remote and silent since time out of mind and where timber as thick in diameter as railroad water tanks stood waiting the ax and saw of the lumberman. . . . It was a magnificent dream, pure American, and Cooke threw himself into the project with all his characteristic enthusiasm. He proposed to sell the Northern Pacific as he had sold government bonds.

The first thing was of course proper publicity. To aid with this important item Cooke engaged Sam Wilkerson, something of a journalistic genius, whose prose soared into the rarefied regions usually inhabited only by poets. Well, Wilkerson was a poet too. He started promptly to fill daily and weekly papers, and numerous pamphlets, with descriptions of the lands along the Northern Pacific. Here, he sang, was a "vast wilderness waiting like a rich heiress to be appropriated and enjoyed," surely as fetching a comparison as any land shark ever conceived. He properly ignored the remark of General William T. Sherman, who knew this vast wilderness at first hand and said it was in large part "as bad as God ever made or anybody can scare up this side of Africa." Anyway, General Sherman had never been in Africa.

Poet Wilkerson's enthusiasms were such that it somehow got around that the Northern Pacific lands included wide expanses of orange groves and banana plantations, complete with fauna like monkeys. So, "Jay Cooke's Banana Belt" of the Dakota snowbanks became a piece of sophisticated repartee among cynical Wall Streeters—but not so with the schoolteachers, the farmers, the ministers, clerks, widows, small-town bankers and businessmen all over the United States. These people would not have dreamed of participating in the usual Wall Street financing of the era. But Jay Cooke was apart. He was still one of the heroic figures of the war period, this tall, handsome, kindly, and serene honest man, who now said that the Northern Pacific was an enterprise which had

never before been equaled. . . . *They believed him,* Jay Cooke,
and out of sugar bowls and from under bedticks, and even from
cast-iron kettles buried in back yards, came an all but incredible
total of money in small amounts. This money was to be one of the
long-remembered tragedies of the financing of the Northern Pacific
Railroad.

Yet it was not nearly the hundred million Cooke wanted, so his
agents went to Germany, where, to help matters along, thirty newspapers were subsidized in the interest of Northern Pacific bonds.
Cooke's men set up for business in ducal palaces to mingle with the
moneyed Junkers and barons who wanted to get richer.

Sales of large blocks of the bonds were being made when suddenly the Franco-Prussian War broke out. Many of the bond
purchases were immediately repudiated. It was a severe setback.
Cooke redoubled his efforts in the United States. He also drew
up a plan for revision of the generous terms of the Northern Pacific
charter which, if agreed to, would almost double the land grant
to the railroad. Cooke had already "loaned" money to Senator
Blaine, to Vice-President Colfax, and others who could be of
assistance in getting the charter revision through Congress.

At this critical moment the subterranean rumblings of the Crédit
Mobilier affair took a mighty heave and became a Congressional
earthquake, and all the rats began to hide. The grossest corruptible
politician dared not now raise his voice in support of Cooke's new
charter bill. Now too Cooke's overdrafts amounted to five and a
half million dollars. Northern Pacific bonds were selling, when
they could be sold at all, at a heavy discount. At this precise
moment a powerful new force became apparent. It emanated
from a new banking firm styled Drexel, Morgan & Company.

John Pierpont Morgan, almost thirty-four years old, had been
invited to join Philadelphia's Drexel & Company, a banking house
second only to that of Jay Cooke's. The austere and powerfully
built young Yankee with blazing black eyes was known, if at all,
only as the son of Junius Spencer Morgan, a Connecticut native
who had become an international banker in London.

The Drexels had long been envious of Jay Cooke's virtual mo-
nopoly of government financing. Among Drexel & Company's
many assets was an influential newspaper, the Philadelphia *Ledger.*
The *Ledger* had just announced the forming of Drexel, Morgan
& Company. The *Ledger* now brought heavy guns to bear on Jay
Cooke. It said that the Northern Pacific was certain to bring Cooke

DANIEL DREW

JAY GOULD

JAY COOKE

JIM FISK

to insolvency; that his efforts to get a new charter for the railroad were being put forth because of the fact that his own money and that of his bondholders had been exhausted. By these and even less subtle items the credit of Jay Cooke & Company was quickly and thoroughly undermined.

All was now ready for the great crash.

What history calls the panic of 1873 had been in the making since the Civil War started. It came to a climax when the house of Jay Cooke & Company, that very Gibraltar of finance, closed its doors at a quarter past noon on the eighteenth of September. Thirty-seven banks and brokerage houses in New York City closed during the afternoon. Trading on the New York Stock Exchange was halted by the board of governors.

Within forty-eight hours, railroad construction ceased not only on the Northern Pacific, but on roads in California, Texas, Iowa, Maine, and elsewhere. In the nation's capital angry crowds surged around the First National Bank demanding their cash or the hides of the bank's officials. The whole great bubble of expansion and inflation was coming down in water. Even nature co-operated. A reporter of the New York *World* saw hundreds of frantic haggard men lurching in Broad and Wall streets while rain came down in torrents.

Up in the backwoods of Michigan, sawmills ground to a halt on the Saginaw and the Muskegon. Blast furnaces on the Monongahela were banked. Five banks in Chicago closed their doors. So did other banks all the way from St. Paul to the west coast. When they could, men and women the country over withdrew their funds from banks, city and rural, solid or shaky (and were to keep their cash at home for years to come). Thousands of the less fortunate stood in line to stare at the grimly closed doors of empty banks and trust companies. No matter the weather, a pall of gloom seemed to settle down over everything. For the first time in their stark lives, millennial prophets were happy. Chaos and Old Night were here. The end was nigh.

President Grant and his Secretary of the Treasury hastened to New York, where they took a suite of rooms at the Fifth Avenue Hotel and summoned Commodore Vanderbilt and other financial leaders to offer advice. Little came of it, save for a remembered remark of the aged Commodore. "Building railroads from nowhere to nowhere," he observed between placid puffs of his cigar, "is not a legitimate business."

By the end of 1873 more than five thousand commercial enterprises had gone under; and though the worst of the panic soon passed, the country would not wholly recover for another five years.

After Jay Cooke, probably the most widely known victim of the crash was Daniel Drew. The old man had taken one beating after another from Gould and Fisk in the Erie War; and another from Gould in assorted railroad stocks. The panic found Drew loaded to the hilt with stocks, and when the water stopped running out of them, his liabilities exceeded a million dollars. His total assets were listed as follows: Watch & chain, $150; sealskin coat, $150; other wearing apparel, $100; Bibles and hymnbooks, $130.

For a short time the old man, now eighty, rusticated in his native Putnam County, but he soon returned to live with a son in New York City, remarking that he couldn't stand the visitors who had called to see him in the country. "Some of them fellers," he told a reporter, "said I had bought cattle from 'em when I was young. They was now one hundred years old or thereabout, and they wanted their pay. I never kept no books, and how was I to know I owed 'em for the critters?" Then he added reflectively, "It was dull outen thar," meaning Putnam County. Old Drew lived long enough to help bury Commodore Vanderbilt, but he was never again in Wall Street.

In the melancholy debris of the 1873 crash a few energetic men were moving about, finding opportunities not only for survival but to increase their fortunes. Among them, of course, was Jay Gould. He was watching the downward progress of Union Pacific stock. He and Fisk had tried to get in on the ground floor of the Crédit Mobilier scheme but had been rebuffed. Now, as Gould watched, Union Pacific shares were slipping a few points daily. They could not support the heavy burden of Crédit Mobilier.

Gould knew that the Union Pacific had been stripped of its cash, but it still had some twelve million acres of land. On some of this land, as Gould and only a few others knew, were extensive coal beds. There were also other possibilities, if one happened to control the Union Pacific. For one thing, a man could pick up a few worthless and now, thanks to the panic, bankrupt railroads. These would do to peddle to the larger line at exorbitant prices. All one needed was control of the UP.

Gould would need help in getting control. His old partner Fisk was dead. But Gould found an abler if less entertaining ally in

Russell Sage, who had made a lot of money in the stocks and bonds of various railroads. Together the two men now stepped in to buy Union Pacific at rock bottom. Panics indeed had their points.

It is likely young Henry Clay Frick thought so too. He had been building and operating coke ovens near Pittsburgh. At the age of twenty-four, and during the worst period of the panic, he had expertly negotiated sale of a short-line railroad for a commission of $50,000. Adding to this sum a few thousand dollars borrowed from his grandfather's Old Overholt Distillery Company, Frick put it all into more coke-coal lands, which he got at panic prices. He weathered the bad years to stand forth as the King of Coke.

In Pittsburgh, too, thirty-eight-year-old Andrew Carnegie saw opportunity in the bleak years after 1873. He bought here and there to expand the iron-making business he had started with a few associates and almost no capital. When the bad times had passed, Carnegie found himself well along toward becoming the first ironmaster in Pennsylvania, a region of ironmasters.

Even more indicative of things to come, of a new way of business and industry, was organization of the Standard Oil Company, in Cleveland, Ohio, by John D. Rockefeller and associates. This modest effort of a group of outlanders, capitalized at one million dollars, survived the panic which helped to remove at least twenty of their competitors and gave the Rockefeller group courage, had they needed it, to go ahead and incorporate a second company called Standard Oil of Pittsburgh.

To John Davison Rockefeller the panic of 1873 was just one more piece of evidence of the dangers, even the futilities, that lay in competition. Competition was wasteful, disorderly. Competitors, at least those of Standard Oil, must be tamed and brought in, or crushed.

Mr. Rockefeller himself much preferred that competitors should join him from preference. In any case, he was convinced that the competitive system by which the world had been doing business since Biblical times was a great and tragic mistake.

Although his contemporaries did not know it—yet—Rockefeller was a new kind of industrialist, an original. Beside him Commodore Vanderbilt and others of this primitive era were troglodytes in caves, Piltdown men with clubs—savage fighters, true enough, but antiquated in their thinking.

PART TWO

RISE
OF
THE COLOSSI

Chapter 1 ROCKEFELLER I

THE most reviled and in many respects the greatest of American moguls was born John Davison Rockefeller in 1839, in the hamlet of Richford, New York. God was to grant him a full ninety-eight years of life, and to bless him, too, with marvelous faculties which were faulty in one respect only—that public opinion was something he ought to consider never entered his mind.

Life was periodically hard for the numerous family of William and Eliza Rockefeller. The father's somewhat mysterious occupation took him away from home for many months at a time, during which the rent often lapsed and the cupboard was bare. Then the old man would suddenly appear from out of the vague world beyond Richford; the rent would be paid, food became plentiful, and the children got new clothes. But William's absences gradually grew longer. At last he ceased to come home at all.

William Rockefeller's business was a topic for speculation at the village general store. What did he do? Mrs. Rockefeller never said. The youngsters seemed not to know. Their father was a big and handsome and somewhat flamboyant man. His personality was described as breezy. Perhaps it was not much of a surprise to the curious citizens of Richford when one of their number, traveling in Ohio, came across a lurid poster in a hotel announcing that Dr. William Rockefeller, the man who cured cancer and all other ills, was coming to town. He would be available for free consultation.

Not even by the careless standards of the time could William Rockefeller have been properly termed a doctor; but the title was assumed in that day by anyone who wanted it; and hundreds of "doctors," some with shows, some without, ranged the country with impunity, often to their great financial gain. The senior Rocke-

feller must have had his good years, for in 1858, he was ready
to lend his son John $1,000, at ten per cent; and he said, moreover,
that if the interest was paid regularly, the principal was to be considered as a gift when the lad was twenty-one.

The loan was made when John was a mere eighteen but already
launching the commission firm of Clark & Rockefeller, at 32 River
Street, Cleveland. John had come to town two years before, to
work in a commission house for $3.50 a week and attend Folsom's
Commercial College. It is worth knowing that even then the young
man was putting out $1.80 a month, every month, for religious
purposes, which included sums to his Baptist Sunday school, gifts
to his Sunday school teacher, a few pennies to the Five Points
Mission in the New York slums, and a few more pennies for a
religious paper. Though young John wore the same shabby coat
winter and summer, the contributions continued.

The new firm of Clark & Rockefeller was successful from the
first. At the end of a year the books showed a gross business of
almost half a million dollars. One wonders if his elders in the
business world of the Ohio metropolis knew what kind of young
man had entered their circle. Though his native modesty never
permitted him, then or later, to boast of his accomplishments, it
must have early become apparent to Cleveland's commercial leaders
that here was an unusual young man, this tall, thin, polite and
pious fellow who said little and attended to affairs. It was he,
anyway, whom these businessmen chose, in the spring of 1860,
to go to the new oil fields of Pennsylvania to judge whether or
not they should invest in what looked to be the greatest piece of
mass insanity since the days of 'forty-nine.

Rockefeller was then twenty years old. He went to the oil fields
and returned to tell the Cleveland men that the producing end of
oil was something to shun. Money might be made, he said, in refining, though even that was a gamble. Keep an eye on it, however;
and above all keep out of the chaos of production.

The excitement young Rockefeller was sent to investigate had
been touched off by a few men working independently of each
other in a new field. This was a substance variously known as
rock oil, Seneca oil, and petroleum.

For at least two generations a branch of the Allegheny River
in Pennsylvania had been known as Oil Creek. From its surface
the farmers roundabout had collected the greasy stuff and used it
to oil their wagon axles. Medicine-show men had gathered and

put it into bottles, added a gorgeous label claiming cures beyond knowing, and sold it throughout eastern United States.

One of these medicine men was a minor Barnum, Doc Samuel M. Kier, who advertised his wonderful product with posters looking like bank notes for four hundred dollars. Close inspection showed reference to "The *Bank* of the Allegheny River," while the figure had to do with the *"Four Hundred* Feet Below the Earth's Surface" from where the magic oil was pumped by means of derricks. Derricks were pictured in woodcut on the poster, along with a benign-looking Indian chief and Columbia herself, complete with the shield of the Union.

Although the petroleum was a by-product of Kier's salt manufactory near Tarentum, Pennsylvania, he soon made it his main business, putting fifty red and gilt wagons on the road, their sides ornamented with paintings of the good Samaritan ministering to the afflicted under a palm tree.

In Pittsburgh, too, Doc Kier rigged up a still which was actually the first oil refinery in the United States. Here he succeeded in getting a wine-colored distillate which he named carbon oil. He invented a lamp burner that would consume this carbon oil and give a fairly good light. But it stank horribly, and sales of both the oil and the burner ceased almost as soon as they began. Neighbors complained about the stench and the dangers of his still. Doc Kier moved out of town and erected another still, but got nowhere. He was a good man, he was trying hard, but he was ahead of his time. Ten years were to elapse before refiners who followed his lead were able to remove the objectionable odor from refined petroleum, as the substance had come to be popularly known.

In the later fifties, George Henry Bissell, a graduate of Dartmouth College, when on a visit to Hanover, New Hampshire, was shown a bottle of petroleum on which his old professor of chemistry, Dr. Alpheus Crosby, had been experimenting. Dr. Crosby thought "there was something good in it." The two men discussed possibilities. Bissell, a man of imagination and enterprise, forthwith went to the oil region of Pennsylvania and leased a tract on which one of the so-called oil springs was located. He then sent a specimen of oil to Benjamin Silliman, Jr., at Yale. Silliman devoted seven months to the most complete analysis the stuff ever had. His report, which a century later is still considered one of the classics of literature about oil, indicated that petroleum could be refined to make a splendid illuminant, and also would yield valuable by-products such as paraffin and naphtha.

Bissell lost no time. To build and set up the first oil drill ever made, he sent Edwin L. Drake. Drake's training for this job had been taking tickets for many years as a conductor on the New Haven Railroad. He knew nothing of oil, of land, or of ordinary business procedure. But he had invested his life's savings, which ran to two hundred dollars, in Bissell's venture, and now something had to be done for him. So, away went Drake to Titusville, Pennsylvania, and undying fame.

After almost unbelievable difficulties in boring and derricking, Drake, one day in August 1859, brought in the first gusher of American history. The well started producing at the rate of twenty-five barrels a day.

From an old photograph in the Titusville *Herald,* Edwin Drake peers forth dreamy-eyed above a grizzled beard like some prophet of the new era, the era of kerosene which was merely the forepart of the age of gasoline. That Drake had neither any idea of the potential value of petroleum, nor any realization of what he had set going by bringing in the first well, does nothing to remove the aura of the prophet. What James W. Marshall of Sutter's Creek was to gold, Drake was to oil.

Drake's spouting fountain of oil was of far greater importance than the discovery of gold in California. He had uncovered a wholly new substance which in time was to change the lives of men all over the world. For the present, it simply changed western Pennsylvania from an undeveloped backwoods region into an industrial jungle teeming with activity. Hideous towns named Oil City and Pithole and Petrolia and Babylon crawled up and down the slimy creeks. Titusville overnight became the oil metropolis with a daily paper and a population of 22,000 wild-eyed men and women. Railroads built madly to tap the region, and tote roads hurried from the new wells to meet the rails. Long before the end of the Civil War, the western Pennsylvania wilderness was spotted with derricks, laced with pipe lines, stinking from small refineries, and echoing with the cries of stockjobbers, calling the suckers to them. The region had already suffered its first great oil-well disaster. It had produced its first oil millionaire in a dim-witted youth named John Washington Steele, known wherever American newspapers were read in 1864 as Coal Oil Johnny.

Young Rockefeller's advice seems to have been accepted by the Cleveland businessmen. None invested in the oil region. But Cleveland was quick to open refineries. Within the next two years Rockefeller saw their scum on the Cuyahoga River within the city, and could smell them day and night. One of these small plants was owned by Samuel Andrews, a man who understood machinery. He told Rockefeller that if only he had a little more capital, he could make his oil refining very profitable. Rockefeller and his partner Clark gave Andrews "a few thousand dollars."

In 1864, John Rockefeller married a girl from Massachusetts named Cetty Spelman. He sold his interest in his commission house, bought Clark's interest in the refinery, and went wholeheartedly into oil with Sam Andrews. Rockefeller already possessed two advantages over most of his competitors; he had a sizable bank balance, and partner Andrews had devised methods of refining far in advance of those common at the time.

Now appeared the first of the many remarkable men with whom John Rockefeller was to surround himself. This was Henry Morrison Flagler, born near Rochester, New York, in 1830, a bold, fearless, and some said unscrupulous man, who had married a neice of Stephen V. Harkness, the whiskey-distilling king of Ohio. Harkness had made a fortune almost overnight by knowing, in advance, that the federal tax on spirits was to be increased. He bought every barrel he could, and when the new tax levies went into effect, unloaded at an enormous profit.

Nephew-in-law Flagler wanted to make a fortune too, but had been in too much of a hurry. He attempted it first in the salt business at Saginaw, Michigan, but lost everything, then was obliged to return to his wife's home in Bellevue, Ohio, where for lack of anything else, he engaged in selling grain through John Rockefeller's commission house.

Now Rockefeller proposed that Flagler get his wife's uncle to invest in Rockefeller's new refinery. This was done and the firm became Rockefeller, Andrews & Flagler. With its new capital and reenforced, says one of Rockefeller's biographers—John T. Flynn— by the dynamic and imaginative Flagler, the new oil concern "set upon that extraordinary career in which it made vast fortunes for all its managers and allies," and also created a new era.

Rockefeller next brought his younger brother William into the firm and opened a new refinery under the style of William Rockefeller & Company. The refinery was in Cleveland, but William went to New York as selling agent. There he was to remain for the rest of his life and to the further glory of what was soon to become Standard Oil. William differed greatly from his brother. Those who knew old Doc Rockefeller thought William, Jr., was a chip off the same block. He was jovial and of small or no piety, a hale fellow generally liked, at home in any company, but as sharp as they came, usually sharper.

It was John, however, who dreamed up the plan. It was not a modest plan, say, of a monopoly of railroads into and out of New York City, which had been Commodore Vanderbilt's idea, but the monopoly of a whole industry and business, complete and world-wide. Rockefeller's vision of this monopoly may have occupied his mind as early as 1869, for in that year he took steps toward creating a monopoly of refining in the Cleveland area, which was then the center of refining in the United States.

To accomplish the monopoly he first went to the Lake Shore Railroad, which brought the crude oil from the producing fields to Cleveland, to demand a secret rebate of fifteen times that openly allowed the other and smaller refiners. (Rebates were kickbacks, paid by railroads to large shippers.) He got it. Within a short time Cleveland's thirty refineries were reduced to ten. The others had done one of two things: they either joined Rockefeller and associates, or went out of business.

On January 10, 1870, Rockefeller and associates incorporated the Standard Oil Company of Ohio. The stock issued was for one million dollars. Flagler was the dynamo of the new outfit. William Rockefeller was the genial front and fixer, though much more than the term implies. John Rockefeller was the mastermind.

The master plan of the mastermind called, first, for an end to refining competition in Cleveland. Next, the big refineries in the other regions must join Standard—or be eliminated. The railroads must make more favorable rebate arrangements with Standard and its allies than with others. The railroads also must refuse shipments of crude oil for export, for Standard planned to refine oil for the world. Lastly, there were those wild fellows, the oil producers. They had no sense of order, much less of the dangers of unrestrained competition. They would have to be educated. This might call for harsh measures. Producers were pigheaded men of no vision.

In 1870, when Standard was formed, John Rockefeller was considered one of Cleveland's successful businessmen, but no more than that. He took no part in politics or in civic affairs. His wife had no social ambitions. He belonged to no clubs. Then and for many years to come Rockefeller constantly cautioned his associates against any display of wealth. It did not do to call attention to one's business success.

The master plan of the mastermind of Standard Oil moved ahead with certainty. In retrospect it appears as remorseless as fate. One after the other the biggest and the best refineries of Cleveland, then of Pittsburgh, New York, and Philadelphia came into Standard. Their directors and managers had just caught sight of something coming over the horizon that bade them to join Rockefeller before it was too late.

The threat seen was a corporation innocently named the South Improvement Company, the work of Standard's Henry Flagler, who proceeded to make contracts between it and the Erie, the Pennsylvania, and the New York Central railroads by which those lines should grant rebates on all Rockefeller shipments of oil *and* on all oil shipments of independents or non-Standard Oil companies. By the contract the rail lines also agreed to supply Standard with copies of all waybills of the independents, a method by which the Rockefeller group could learn the prices, the discounts, and even the very names of the customers of their competitors.

The South Improvement Company was surely the boldest, the most naked effort at dry-land piracy that had been conceived. It was also quite legal. But when the press made clear just what the South Improvement Company had been organized for, there was a great outcry. The oil-well men formed the first of many protective associations. They refused to sell a gallon of crude to Rockefeller. They refused to ship any oil over the offending railroads. They started to lay pipe lines to independents in the refining centers.

In Titusville, John Rockefeller was hanged, then burned, in effigy. A hurriedly organized Congressional investigation termed Rockefeller's attempt to bring what he liked to call order into the oil business "one of the most gigantic and dangerous conspiracies ever conceived." The Pennsylvania legislature met and rescinded the South Improvement Company's charter.

John Rockefeller was shocked at such violent reaction. He had only wanted to eliminate competition, the same thing as waste, from the oil industry. Well, there must be other ways . . .

Possibly the ablest of Rockefeller's competitors in the oil fields was John D. Archbold, a native of Ohio who gained local fame as

Standard's most aggressive opponent. To battle the Standard monster Archbold worked furiously to lease the twenty-odd refineries still left in the producing regions. With these he formed the Acme Oil Company. The producers cheered.

The ink of Acme's stock certificates was no more than dry before it was clear to all that Acme was merely a subsidiary of Standard. Archbold had sold his group of independents down the river. He didn't mind the curses heaped upon him by the producers. He became a vice-president of Standard, and later president of Standard of New Jersey. In these capacities he was more than once referred to publicly as Standard Oil's arch-corruptionist, though one of his biographers put it another way. Archbold, he wrote, was "a corporation officer who had no hesitancy in calling upon men in the government to do his bidding." He was a mighty handy man to have around.

John Dustin Archbold was a man of short stature with an overly large head. He said he was a good Baptist, and looked not unlike a preacher. He loved to play poker. Early and late he was a truculent battler. All enemies were blackmailers or scoundrels of some sort. He was filled with righteous indignation, and often ran over with horrible threats. It turned out, too, that Archbold had a genius for putting legislators, judges, congressmen, senators, and governors in the state of mind that was of benefit to the Standard Oil Company.

In Flagler and Archbold, Rockefeller now had two outstanding men. He soon got two more, Henry H. Rogers and Charles Pratt, when by polite suasion, and not force, he brought their large Brooklyn refinery into Standard. This plant was turning out, under the trademark of Pratt's Astral Oil, the finest illuminating oil in the United States. It was an excellent product and a welcome addition to Standard's own line of goods. One may readily believe, however, that it was of less value to Standard than the two men who joined the firm as vice-presidents.

Born in Watertown, Massachussetts, in 1830, Pratt had dealt in oil from 1849 onward, and with Rogers had recently built a refinery more efficient even than the best Standard could muster.

Pratt's junior partner, ten years younger and also a Massachusetts Yankee, had been reared in small Fairhaven, across the harbor from New Bedford. Rogers' first business deal was consummated when he was a fourteen-year-old newsboy. One early morning, when his batch of papers arrived, he noticed a report saying that a vessel loaded with five hundred barrels of sperm oil, and consigned to a local dealer, had been sunk. Instead of delivering or selling his papers, Rogers hurried to the local sperm oil magnate, showed him the item, and proposed to sell him all his papers, thus suppressing news of the disaster and permitting the merchant to rustle around to buy up and corner the limited supply of whale oil in the neighborhood. Young Rogers calculated that his supply of papers, which may have cost him a total of fifty cents, was worth about two hundred dollars. The merchant agreed and the deal was made.

Rogers was the kind of quick-thinking young man John Rockefeller liked to have in Standard, not because he liked Rogers personally, which he did not, but because of sheer ability. Rogers was a profane man, and otherwise was the opposite to almost everything in Rockefeller's nature.

In the business world, so an observer wrote, only the elder Morgan had an eye so terrifying as that of Rogers, but among friends he was generous and warmhearted. Even Ida Tarbell, queen of the muckraking journalists, liked Rogers. He was a pirate, she wrote, but he was not a hypocrite. He flew his black flag and made no bones of it.

Almost as soon as Rogers joined Standard he was made head of its manufacturing department. This turned out to be a wide field. One of his first jobs was to help in Standard's biggest and hardest battle to date, a savage attack on a refinery and pipe-line outfit organized as the Empire Transportation Company by the able and aggressive Tom Scott, head of the Pennsylvania Railroad.

Rockefeller went to see Scott and politely asked him to cease and desist. Scott refused. Young Mr. Rogers went to see the Erie and the New York Central people to say that Standard expected their help in a oil war that was about to break. The freight rates on Standard's products, Mr. Rogers suggested, must be radically lowered for the duration of the war. They were. Standard announced new and lower prices of kerosene, not everywhere but in all districts where the come-lately Empire people were operating.

A few months of the price war served to appall Tom Scott and his associates. They were virtually giving away their kerosene. Just then came the railroad strikes of 1877. Anarchy gripped the Pennsylvania Railroad. In August, hardly before the smoke had cleared from around the burned locomotives and rolling stock and depots and roundhouses of the Pennsylvania road, Tom Scott went to Cleveland to make peace with Rockefeller.

Mr. Rockefeller never gloated, nor did he gloat now. He assured

Mr. Scott with the greatest cordiality that peace could be had in a most reasonable manner. Standard would buy Empire Transportation Company's pipe lines, refineries, tanks, cars, everything, and pay $3,400,000. What Mr. Scott thought of the price is not on record. He accepted the offer, anyway. Empire's pipe lines were put into Standard's subsidiary, United Pipe Lines, into which, too, presently went another independent, the National Conduit Company. This latter concern had been built into a success by a man whose name was to be seen on barns, covered bridges, billboards, and even on boulders in the fields and pastures of agricultural United States. This was Dr. David Hostetter, originator of Hostetters Bitters, the base of which was *not* petroleum.

The absorption of Empire and of National Conduit into Standard helped many other independent concerns to make up their minds, among them the several large refiners in Maryland. These were now gathered tidily into a new firm, Baltimore United Oil, a subsidiary of Standard.

The few remaining holdouts among refiners in the New York City area also asked to join what was coming to be known as the "Rockefeller alliance." The time was 1878. Rockefeller was thirty-eight years old. His "alliance" controlled ninety-five per cent of the pipe lines and refineries in the United States.

John Rockefeller now started raising a mustache, which was of reddish tinge, and he began to wear a silk hat. There was no perceptible change in his manner of living. There was also no lessening of his sharp interest in anything that concerned the Standard Oil Company. There, for instance, was the matter of bungs.

In going over a batch of monthly "competitive statements" from his various refiners, Rockefeller one time noted a discrepancy. He sat down and wrote the plant's superintendent. "Last month," said Mr. Rockefeller's letter, "you reported 1,119 bungs. Ten thousand were sent you at the beginning of the month. You have used 9,527 this month. You report 1,102 on hand. What has become of the other four hundred and ninety?"

Bungs cost a fraction of a cent apiece; and in the economy of Standard Oil, a fraction of a cent was something to be cherished.

Up to this point John Rockefeller and associates had worked their wonders with little if any harassment from the federal government. But now it was 1878, and the viewpoint of government was changing. In a few western states, it is true, the Grangers had agitated for legislation to control railroad tariffs. State laws had been passed here and there, and all of them were soon seen to be weak and ineffective. But railroads excepted, all industry had been operating as it would. The strikes of 1877 had changed all that.

Now there arose in the House of Representatives at Washington a congressman from Pittsburgh, Pennsylvania, to introduce a bill to regulate commerce *and* prohibit unjust discrimination by common carriers, by which was meant railroads. The bill passed—though not before the Congressional committee to investigate and recommend had undergone a slight change in its personnel, adding, as its chairman, the Hon. Frank Hereford of West Virginia, whose close adviser in all legislative matters was J. N. Camden. Mr. Camden was president of the Camden Oil Company. The Camden Oil Company, as somebody pointed out too late, was owned by Rockefeller and associates. The new act was not sent to the Senate. It was stuffed away in some House pigeonhole.

Yet, the times really had changed. Within the year another bill to regulate pipe lines was introduced in the House. It passed. It was promptly killed in the Senate where, so the public learned too late to protest, John D. Archbold enjoyed a great deal of influence. Mr. Archbold was a prominent Rockefeller associate.

The men who drilled for oil and brought it forth were becoming increasingly desperate. Standard controlled the pipe lines. Standard set the price of crude. Again and again the producers tried to organize themselves, and failed each time. They were, said one of their number, "a cowardly, disorganized mob." Too many mavericks, determined to get rich quick, were among them. Now, in 1878, they made another effort, their greatest to date.

It began with a monster meeting, the doors guarded against spies of Standard. Speakers declared this meeting to be the "Parliament of Petroleum," and oratory went forth from the most accomplished rabble rousers the oil men could assemble. When speakers had heated the great meeting to high temperature, and had damned Standard Oil and John D. Rockefeller properly, it got down to business. It was voted with ringing cheers to combine their resources and build a producers' own pipe line from the oil fields to the seaboard; meanwhile, it was agreed, drilling should be restricted until the new outlet was ready.

A bill granting right of way to the proposed pipe line was introduced in the Pennsylvania legislature. While Standard Oil's John Archbold stood by, and not idly, to watch the legislators, Standard's

United Pipe Lines announced it would accept no more crude oil for storage. There was no more room in its tanks, Standard explained.

Panic struck the producers. Oil was flowing from their wells in floods. There was no space to store it other than in the unnumbered tanks of United. At Bradford, huge crowds collected, then surrounded United's head office to jeer, then to threaten violence.

A grand jury met in Clarion County to indict Standard Oil, John D. Rockefeller, and others, for criminal conspiracy. The indictment said that those named were attempting to secure a monopoly of the oil industry; to oppress other refiners; to injure the carrying trade of the Allegheny Valley; to extort unreasonable rates from railroads; and to fraudulently control prices of crude and refined oil.

It is probable no truer indictment was ever made. It happened to catch several of Rockefeller's associates in Pennsylvania, and they were arrested. Rockefeller was in New York. He refused to return to face the indictment, and Standard's efficient corps of fixers managed to get adjournments of the trials of the associates, who were loosed on bail.

John Rockefeller sent for the chief attorney of the aroused producers, who were still calling themselves the Parliament of Petroleum, and proposed a settlement. Standard would agree to most of the things the producers desired. It would agree to store all oil offered—though here Mr. Rockefeller stipulated certain restrictions. As for the matter of railroad rates, Rockefeller, never in gentler voice, agreed that the same rates should apply to *all firms shipping the same quantity*. What this meant in effect is that Standard, far and away the biggest shipper, would continue to receive, as in the past, the lowest rate.

Although the producers of the Parliament of Petroleum could hardly see that Standard had made much of a concession, they disgustedly accepted the agreement.

With the indictments against him and his associates withdrawn, Mr. Rockefeller now turned his attention to another danger. This was the new Tidewater Pipe Line Company, a huge project, well financed, that was laying pipe over the Alleghenies to Williamsport. This was a considerable engineering feat in its day. It was completed in 1879, and it worked. Rockefeller's spies were there to see, and they spoke enthusiastically of its efficiency.

John Rockefeller admired anything that worked efficiently. Never in his long life, it is said, did he destroy a really successful business. He immediately offered Tidewater 10,000 barrels of Standard Oil a day. The offer was refused. After all, Tidewater had been built specifically to encourage independent refiners.

Well, said Mr. Rockefeller brightly, it was Tidewater's right to refuse.

Shortly thereafter, a stockholder of Tidewater Pipe Line Company applied to the courts for a receivership for the company, alleging gross mismanagement. The court investigation indicated that the distressed stockholder had bought into Tidewater with $7,500 loaned him by Standard Oil. The receivership was denied.

A little later, as it happened, Tidewater wanted to borrow two million dollars from a New York bank. Almost at the same moment, a large group of Tidewater's stockholders held a meeting, tossed out the company officials, and elected some of their own number in place. Tidewater, in short, had apparently changed its mind. It was now happy to sign a contract with Standard to divide the pipe-line business in its territory. The division is interesting because it makes clear who was to run Tidewater thereafter; 11½ per cent of the business was Tidewater's; the remaining 88½ per cent belonged to Standard Oil. The agreement was signed in 1881.

In 1881, Rockefeller had just passed his forty-second birthday. In eleven years Standard Oil had risen from the stench of two refineries in Cleveland to become supreme in the national field. Along its trail, as Allan Nevins has said, were strewn ruined men and abandoned plants. Ahead, on its course, lay unquestioned control over tremendous sources of wealth.

Yet, Standard's rise had come about so quietly, indeed with stealth, that almost nobody except those who had had dealings with it had any idea what a monster Standard Oil Company had become.

Mr. Rockefeller, however, was in no way content with Standard as it was. Its future, he thought, could best be shaped from the center of finance, and not from Cleveland. He moved with his family to a home at 4 West Fifty-fourth Street, New York City. It was a modest enough house, not to be compared with the baronial mansions either already established or just going up along Fifth Avenue.

John D. Rockefeller himself was unknown compared to the Astors, the Lorillards, and Vanderbilts. But William H. Vanderbilt, the Commodore's son and heir, was not unacquainted with young Mr. Rockefeller and his group of young associates. "They are mighty smart men," he explained earnestly, when pressed to give his reasons for granting rebates to Standard, and added, "I guess if you ever had to deal with them you would find *that* out."

At this period Standard's offices were in a modest building on Pearl Street. Its board met there daily, always behind closed doors that were also guarded. Mr. Rockefeller was conjuring up a plan to make Standard more magnificent than ever. This was to take form as the first American trust.

We shall come later to the Standard Oil trust. This is the place to consider the works of other men who labored in various fields, often in far places, and had more effect on life in the United States than any number of presidents, senators, generals and statesmen combined.

Chapter 2 CARNEGIE

ONE of the many thousands of speculators who failed to strike it rich in the oil rush to western Pennsylvania was a small and sprightly immigrant from Scotland named Andrew Carnegie who was to become King of the Vulcans, a title most pleasing to his supreme vanity. His one speculation in oil was small and little came of it, otherwise John D. Rockefeller might well have had a competitor to remember, for Carnegie could not have become a mere Rockefeller associate. He must be No. 1 man or nothing.

The honor of first taking notice of the future steelmaster of America belongs to the Pittsburgh *Gazette*. On November 2, 1849, that newspaper printed a heart-warming little story about messenger boy Carnegie of the O'Reilly Telegraph Company, who had found in the street a draft for five hundred dollars and, "like an honest little fellow, promptly made known the fact and deposited the paper in good hands, where it awaits identification."

The honest little fellow was almost fourteen. Within a few more months he went to work for the Pennsylvania Railroad, whose operating genius, Tom Scott, made Carnegie his private secretary, and later superintendent of the road's Pittsburgh division.

While employed by the railroad, the young man invested what

cash he had saved, and more that he borrowed, in a firm that made iron bridges, a healthy business in an era when railroads were expanding rapidly. Carnegie also got to know the Kloman brothers of Pittsburgh, whose plant was turning out the finest railroad-car axles on the market. The Klomans were doing very well, but they needed more capital. With the help of his brother Tom, and two friends named Tom Miller and Henry Phipps, Carnegie supplied the needed cash. The four men became partners of the Klomans.

The iron business was booming. Carnegie resigned his job with the railroad. He combined the iron-bridge firm with his Kloman interest to form the Union Iron Mills, which was prepared, at exactly the right time, to roll the huge beams needed to span the western rivers over which the Union Pacific must lay its tracks.

The partners in the Union Iron Mills each had certain talents of great importance. Miller, who just happened to be a railroad purchasing agent, could throw a good deal of business to Union. Henry Phipps was known in Pittsburgh as the man who could float a check in thin air until one came to believe that levitation was more than an illusion. The Kloman brothers had few peers at the making of good iron at low cost. Andrew Carnegie knew little about iron, then or later, but he was possibly the greatest traveling salesman of his time. He may have been also the smallest, for he stood five feet four inches, weighed 130 pounds, and was extremely vain of his number five feet.

There was nothing small, however, about the orders Carnegie brought in. The Union Iron Mills roared and thundered constantly. They had been roaring and thundering no longer than two years when Carnegie felt it was time the most gifted of the partners should take absolute management.

Carnegie proceeded typically to deprecate the company's future, telling partner Tom Miller that the good days had passed, that larger outfits such as Jones & Laughlin and several more were increasing their orders and were making much better profits than Union. After emanating pessimism for a good while, and even talking of trying to sell his own stock, Carnegie discovered a naïve person named David A. Stewart who said he wanted to buy into Union. He did so, buying the shares owned by Tom Miller. Only after the sale had been consummated did it become clear that no matter who David A. Stewart was, the new and real owner of Miller's interest was Carnegie. From this point on, there was no question as to which partner in Union Iron Mills was boss man.

The classic Pittsburgh of smoke and cinders had by now taken form. The perpetual half night in which the city has lived most of its life fell over the town as early as 1749, when John Frazer erected a forge there and began manufacture of flintlock muskets. The place was originally Fort Duquesne, a French outpost. The British drove out the French and renamed the fort for statesman William Pitt.

Fort Pitt was by nature a paradise for ironmongers. Two big rivers met there to form the Ohio, leading west in the direction of what orators said, rightly for once, was America's destiny. The hills round about held ore, and a vast amount of coal. There were sizable limestone deposits in the neighborhood. There was a forest from which charcoal could be made, until men learned that coke made from coal was better. Ore, coke, and limestone are the things iron is made of. Steel is refined iron.

As early as 1805 the Fort Pitt Foundry Company was in business, and a bit later it cast some tough cannon balls for the use of Commodore Perry on Lake Erie. General Jackson blew some of the same product into the British at New Orleans. In 1814, the government thought well enough of the new town of Pittsburgh to establish an arsenal there.

German immigrants, with their genius for metals, were naturally attracted to the place, among them the remarkable Schoenberger family, the able Christopher Zug, and the Klomans.

A pair of native Americans, Benjamin F. Jones and James Laughlin joined hands to establish an iron firm which a century later is both large and prosperous. There were others, too, and in 1867, when Andrew Carnegie came to dominate Union Iron Mills, he saw that if his company was to grow into the biggest ironmaker in the United States, as he intended it should, then it must continuously get more and larger orders.

The one incomparable place to obtain orders was New York City. With his widowed mother, who had made him, her oldest son, promise never to marry so long as she lived, Carnegie moved to the metropolis and took living quarters in the St. Nicholas Hotel. In Broad Street he opened an office on the door of which was no notice of the Union Iron Mills. The sign said: *Andrew Carnegie, Investments*. Carnegie was no man to have one iron in one fire.

A year after arrival in New York, Carnegie set down specific plans for his future. They appear so radically different from the ambitions of other rising young men of the era, and so equally different from what actually happened, that they are worth knowing. The memorandum set down to guide Carnegie's future was made at the St. Nicholas Hotel one evening in December of 1868. First noting that he was thirty-three, he next wrote, "and [have] an income of $50,000 per annum!" (The exclamation mark probably indicated more pleasure than astonishment.) He tells himself he must so arrange his business as to secure $50,000 every year, but "Beyond this never earn." He will go to England, "settle in Oxford and get a thorough education." He will make "the acquaintance of literary men." He will then go to London and buy a controlling interest in some newspaper or review. He will also take part in public affairs, "especially those connected with education and improvement of the poorer classes. . . . No idol," he remarks twice in the memorandum, is "more debasing than the worship of money." Therefore, he "will resign business [in two years] at thirty-five." (Carnegie's abdication of business came not two but thirty-two years later.)

The *Investments* sign Andrew Carnegie put on the door of his first office in New York was not for effect. He knew that the Union Iron Mills could not begin to use all his energies and he meant to occupy his spare time in a variety of ways. One was as a bond broker. A good bond broker. Within the next four years he placed thirty million dollars' worth of American securities in England and on the Continent, many with the London house of Junius S. Morgan & Company.

Carnegie was not neglecting Union Iron Mills. His increasingly large orders began to exceed Union's capacity. At this period a group of Pittsburgh ironmasters proposed to build their own blast furnace, on a co-operative basis, and thus save a portion of the forty dollars a ton they were paying to local manufacturers of pig iron. The Union Mills was invited to join the group. Carnegie thanked the group but said Union did not care to join. He then proceeded to build a furnace for Union. It was named the Lucy for Tom Carnegie's wife.

An early incident in connection with the Lucy furnace shows the kind of bosses Andrew Carnegie liked to have at his points of production. This was the Lucy's boss, foreman Skelding. The Lucy worked well for several months, then came down with a chill, which meant that through some breakdown of the furnace's machinery, the mixture being treated had cooled and formed a solid mass inside the tall brick stack.

The usual procedure to clear a chill was a long slow job, by which the mass of metal and flux was dug out by hand. Foreman Skelding of the Lucy swore horribly at the laggard progress made by his men; and said if he only had a cannon, he'd shoot all hell out of the chill.

Well, the United States Arsenal was only a few blocks distant; and either Tom or Andy Carnegie, both charmers of men, went to the officer in charge and talked him into loan of a small siege mortar. Skelding whooped for joy. He loaded the powerful stubby gun to the muzzle, pointed her straight up from the base of the Lucy's stack, and let her go.

The ball brought down a good hunk of the chill, and two more shots brought down more; yet much of the mass remained in place. Skelding had powder left but no more cannon balls. He loaded the gun again, rammed her near full of cotton waste, and on top of this put a fifty-pound hunk of hard iron ore that had come from the famous Republic mine in upper Michigan. He touched her off. Down came ton upon ton of chill. The Lucy was clean again.

Skelding's feat went into the legendry of Pittsburgh. Skelding himself was the first of a long line of notable technical men who, with the goading of America's greatest taskmaster, Carnegie, were to make almost incredible production records.

Andy Carnegie had a few blind spots. One of these was his stout opposition to the new process of making steel from pig iron in ten minutes. The process had been invented, almost simultaneously, by William Kelly of Ohio and Henry Bessemer of England, and had taken the latter's name.

Tom Carnegie and Henry Phipps had seen a Bessemer converter at work in Johnstown, Pennsylvania, and another in Cleveland. They urged adoption of the Bessemer process. Andy Carnegie demurred. This meant no. So Tom Carnegie and his father-in-law, William Coleman, who had often aided the brothers with both cash and sound advice, decided to go ahead without Andrew. They bought land twelve miles up the Monongahela, where General Braddock was defeated by the French and Indians, and interested several well-to-do Pittsburghers in putting up a new plant to make steel by the Bessemer process. The panic of 1873 caused the work to be dropped temporarily.

The troubles of '73 gave Andy Carnegie a chance to freeze the Kloman brothers out of Union Mills. The business survived and flourished chiefly because of the liquid capital William Coleman had at his command. Andy was most appreciative, and now, he said, he had changed his mind about the Bessemer process and asked to buy into the new steel plant to be operated by the newly incorporated Edgar Thomson Steel Company. The firm's name stemmed from the $100,000 in bonds taken by the president of the Pennsylvania Railroad.

The Thomson mill at Braddock was the largest and finest in the world. It was designed by an authentic genius named Alexander Holley. To operate it Holley brought to Braddock a first-generation Welsh American, Captain Bill Jones, who had been working in iron or steel since the age of ten. The title of Captain stuck to Jones after his gallant record as a soldier in the Civil War.

As a steelmaster Captain Bill Jones was fully fifty years ahead of his time. Convinced that men should not be driven twelve hours at a stretch in the little hells of steel manufacture, he installed three eight-hour shifts at Braddock. His men made one production record after another.

No matter in what form great ability appeared, Andrew Carnegie recognized it. In Captain Jones he had the peerless steelmaster of all, and he sought to have Jones buy stock in the company. Jones knew nothing of stocks and bonds except that he did not wish to be bothered with them. "But I tell you what you can do for me, Andy," Captain Bill shouted above the thunder of the rolling mill. "You can pay me one hell of a salary." Andy did so, too, giving him $25,000 a year, the same salary paid to the President of the United States. Captain Bill was content.

Amid the soot and the roar of Pittsburgh, where flames belched from scores of Bessemer converters, thousands of peasants from half of Europe sweated like gnomes and lived in rows of shacks clinging to the steep hills. Among them walked Captain Bill Jones, a hero to his working-stiffs, and to his employers the king of iron-masters.

Captain Bill could be temperamental, too, and every little while he resigned and swore he would work no longer for that oat-eating, son-of-a-bitching Scotchman. On these occasions, little Andy would hurry from New York to placate his manager, the only man to whom he was ever known to apologize.

Jones was one American who made a great impression on the English celebrities Carnegie now began to import and to display in New York and Pittsburgh. Herbert Spencer, Carnegie's revered mentor in intellectual matters, looked at Pittsburgh and was appalled. A month there, he remarked, would justify anyone in committing suicide.

Yet Spencer was honored to shake hands with Captain Bill Jones; and prevailed on him to prepare a paper for reading before the Iron and Steel Institute of Great Britain. The paper created something of a sensation there, for it showed the average American worker to produce 555 tons of steel a year, compared to 420 tons, the best that either Birmingham or Sheffield could show.

In May of 1889, too, Captain Bill gave dramatic proof of his ability to command in even a wider field than the immense plants of what had become the Carnegie Steel Company. A dam had broken near Johnstown, Pennsylvania, one of Captain Bill's old stamping grounds, and let go a flood, causing one of the greatest disasters of modern times. When news of it reached Braddock, Captain Bill waited for orders from nobody. He blew the big whistle and called for volunteers. Hundreds of his men climbed aboard a special train, already loaded with supplies, and away they went to the scene of the tragedy. In the stricken city, Captain Bill and his devoted men did heroic work in rescue and relief, and were later commended by Johnstown citizens.

But Captain Bill's end was near. On the twenty-eighth of September, in the year of the flood, one of the great furnaces at Braddock got to acting badly. It had a "hang." The molten metal was not flowing as it should. Captain Bill went to see about it just as the furnace exploded with a roar that was heard in Pittsburgh twelve miles away. Six helpers were turned to cinders where they stood. Captain Bill was blown backward and died from burns and a fractured skull. It was the proper way for death to call for Captain Bill Jones, in a slag pit, and with his boots on.

There was only one man to take the Captain's place. That was his trusted assistant, young Charlie Schwab, who was put in charge at Braddock.

Steel rails were rapidly supplanting the iron product, a fact recognized by a group of ironmasters who in 1881 had organized the Pittsburgh Bessemer Steel Company. They erected a plant across the Monongahela from Braddock at a place named Homestead.

Homestead, for some reason or other, had labor troubles from the start. These included strikes and sabotage. The price of shares in the new company dropped dangerously. When they were low enough, Carnegie bought control. The little Scot may have been backward in recognizing the importance of Bessemer rails. Now he meant to dominate the market for them.

No sooner had he taken control of the Homestead mill than another competitor built still another big mill on the banks of the Monongahela just above Braddock and started rolling Bessemer rails as the Duquesne Steel Company.

Duquesne had a most efficient plant. Within a few months the Duquesne rails were underselling the Carnegie product. Yet, in a few months more the Duquesne people discovered that their customers were dropping away—swiftly, like leaves in autumn after a frost.

It *was* a frost, too. It came in a letter composed by Andy Carnegie himself and sent out to the trade under his signature. Without mentioning names, Carnegie warned railroad presidents and purchasing agents the country over that rails "made by the direct rolling process" were dangerous. The letter more than intimated that derailment of trains and consequent loss of life and property were to be expected wherever such rails were used.

Without going into technicalities, it may be said the direct rolling process was that in use by the Duquesne and several more concerns. It was new, revolutionary, and cheaper than the older method still being used at the Union, Braddock, and Homestead mills of the Carnegie Steel Company. It also made better rails; and that, in Carnegie's mind, was the real trouble with the direct rolling process.

Yet Carnegie's influence was so great in regard to railroad steel that his letter was generally accepted as gospel; and uncounted tons of rails piled up in the Duquesne Steel Company's yard. Pretty soon, too, the Duquesne people were glad to sell out to Carnegie. The arrangements for adding Duquesne to the Carnegie group were in the hands of Carnegie's new manager, Henry Clay Frick.

Frick was to be more than a manager of the Carnegie Steel Company, more than a mere associate. He was already a millionaire and notable as the "king of coke" before he accepted Carnegie's invitation to consolidate the various Carnegie properties into a single and smoothly running corporation. He was also to be the one man in the company to whom Carnegie and all others granted the honorific "Mister." He was that sort of man.

Henry Clay Frick was born in the year of the California gold rush in Pennsylvania, where he worked on his father's farm, got a little, though not much, schooling, and spent a year as a bookkeeper in the distillery of his maternal grandfather, who was none other than Old Overholt himself. While still retaining this job, he and a few carefully selected associates built and operated coke ovens in the Connellsville coal region.

When he was twenty-one, Frick borrowed $10,000 from Judge Thomas Mellon of Pittsburgh to buy coal land. The panic of 1873 looked to Frick like an unparalleled opportunity. With still another loan from Mellon, and additional cash from his own family, Frick bought all the coal land and coke ovens he could.

Throughout the next three desolating years of depression, Frick managed to keep his ovens going. He also increased their number. He bought more coal land. By then, the steelmasters of the Pittsburgh district had learned that Connellsville coke was far superior to any other substance for the manufacture of finest steel. They also found that H. C. Frick & Company controlled about four fifths of the coke output; and that Mr. Frick was a cool, taciturn young man who slapped no backs and told no drummers' stories. He wasn't exactly unfriendly, but his cold eyes and rather distant personality were in contrast to the hot red glow of his many hundreds of blinking ovens.

Whether or not they liked Mr. Frick, the steelmasters bought his coke. By 1879 more than a thousand men were digging Frick's coal, then baking it for forty-eight hours until it turned into gray lumps. Ninety-odd carloads a day were being shipped to the hell-brewing furnaces along the Allegheny and the Monongahela. On December 19 of that year, when he had turned thirty, Frick spent a few hours with his well-kept accounts (he "hated messed-up figures and sloppy writing all his life") and learned that he was worth a little more than one million dollars.

The Carnegie plants required a major portion of Frick's output of coke. And for once, the Carnegies learned that neither threats nor flattery had any effect on the price they had to pay for this necessary material. Mr. Frick was as impervious to cajolery as he was to tough talk.

Tom Carnegie considered this king of coke as a young man of great abilities. He urged brother Andrew to buy into the coke monopoly. Andrew listened to Tom, and was permitted to buy a modest amount of Frick & Company stock. He learned too that Mr. Frick planned to run his company as he had run it in the past, the way he thought best.

Frick had announced an increase of a million dollars in capitalization of the coke company. Andrew Carnegie didn't approve, and wrote Frick a peremptory letter. Mr. Frick promptly wrote Mr. Carnegie, "I do not like the tone of your letter." Then he put through the capitalization as planned. He also added another 3,000 ovens, approximately one third of which was acquired from the Thaw family of Pittsburgh. The product of these many ovens was never to bear the Carnegie name. It was Frick coke.

Frick was obviously a man who was going somewhere. Mr. Carnegie proposed that Mr. Frick become general manager of all the Carnegie properties and a stockholder in the company. Mr. Frick thought it over and casually accepted. One of his first jobs, as related, was to buy the fine new plant at Duquesne. From there, he went on to assemble this and other mills into a solid, compact, harmonious whole, whose every part, declared Andrew Carnegie's public relations counsel, "worked with the ease and silent motion of the perfectly balanced machine."

This machine was the Carnegie Steel Company. It is of interest to know that all of the mills of the group were soon making steel rails by the same direct rolling process as that pioneered at the Duquesne and which, only a couple of years before, had appeared to little Andy to be a hideous menace to the railroads and an even greater danger to the life and limb of the traveling public.

The future held great things for Mr. Frick. It also held many trials, and the greatest of these was the "Battle of Homestead." This savage affair had its inception on April 4, 1892. On that day, from his mansion in New York, Andrew Carnegie wrote, signed, and sent to Mr. Frick a "Notice to Employees at Homestead Works," which said that no members of the Amalgamated Association of Iron and Steel Workers, a labor union, would be employed. Mr. Carnegie then took ship for a vacation in his native Scotland, feeling no doubt that he had done his part in preparation for the wage cuts planned for the Carnegie and other steel mills of the Pittsburgh district.

Mr. Frick did not post the notice. Instead, he had his plant superintendent inform a workmen's committee of employees of "the necessity for a cut in wages." Frick knew that the union was weak in every Carnegie mill except that at Homestead.

At Homestead, in the days before Carnegie took over, the Amalgamated had achieved a fairly strong membership and had even got several minor concessions from the management. It was now time to wipe out the union for good.

Mr. Frick gave notice that June 24 was the day on which the union must accept or reject the wage cut. It was rejected. On that day Frick asked Pinkerton's National Detective Agency to send three hundred guards "for service at our Homestead mill."

The Homestead mill had been closed by Frick's orders; and around it had been erected a high fence—a fence with small holes, just about the right size for a Winchester barrel, bored in it.

On July 6, two great armored scows, contents unknown but guessed at, were seen being pushed up the dirty yellow water of the Monongahela by tugs. It was still early morning. Just as the flotilla of trouble came abreast of Homestead, a long moan came from the whistle on the City Electric Light Works. It had been blown by the alert chief of the union's forces, Hugh O'Donnell, to arouse the sleeping working-stiffs.

The dreadful stark town back of the steel mill leaped to sudden life. From hundreds of shacks came men, shouting and running for the docks. As the scows came in and tied and gangplanks were let down, somebody's nervous forefinger pulled the trigger of a rifle. And all hell broke loose.

Captain Hinde, in command of the three hundred Pinkerton men, went down in a welter of blood. Rifles crackled all along the Homestead shore. On shore, too, four men were seen to throw up their hands and go down to stay.

Women came out into the streets screaming in twenty-two languages and dialects, then grabbed their kids and took to the near hills, the better to see their men shot down.

The Pinkerton men were hopelessly outnumbered. Perhaps about ten to one was the ratio. They did the only thing they could; they stayed in their armored scows, taking potshots through the portholes.

To get them out of their battleships, union men hurried across the river to Braddock, entered the G.A.R. Hall, and rolled out the old cannon, a relic of Antietam. But she was still in working order, and soon a ball tore a ragged hole in the side of one of the Pinkerton scows. A second shot went over and sheared the head clean off young Silas Wain, a good union man, who was crouching above the docks.

A raft of lumber was doused with oil, set afire, and sent to drift against the scows. When a tug came in, possibly in an attempt to get the scows loose, gunfire broke out from behind pig-iron and ingot breastworks, and in another moment there wasn't a whole pane of glass in the boat's ports or windows.

Word spread among the union men that a big load of dynamite had just arrived from the coal fields. Willing hands made sticks of it into bundles, lighted the fuses, and heaved. Spumes of water shot up close to the scows. One package fell smoking to the top deck of one scow, then exploded, blowing planks all over.

The battle raged around the scows until almost night, then Hugh O'Donnell walked alone and unarmed to the scows to parley. The Pinkertons asked only for safe conduct out of Homestead. O'Donnell promised them as much. He was an honest man, but overly optimistic. As the thoroughly cowed Pinkerton men were being escorted to an old skating rink, boys stoned them. Women clawed at them, and one harridan ran the sharp end of an umbrella into a Pinkerton's eye. Then, large infuriated men hauled Pinks from the line of march and beat them unmercifully.

Forty-odd Pinkertons, reduced to pulps of flesh, had to be dragged or carried to the skating rink.

For another five days mobs ruled Homestead. State troops moved in on July 12 to take charge. Fourteen men had been killed. The seriously wounded numbered 163. The Homestead works of the Carnegie Steel Company soon reopened with a wholly nonunion crew.

When the smoke of Homestead had cleared, public opinion may not have been wholeheartedly with the employees, but it was wholeheartedly against Mr. Frick. He was damned by press and pulpit. Then, an alleged friend of downtrodden workers committed a piece of idiotic violence that set public opinion to swinging the other way.

On July 23, as Frick sat in his office in the Hussey Building in downtown Pittsburgh, a slight, dark man entered the room, pulled a revolver from his pocket, and shot the steelmaster twice. One bullet lodged in Frick's neck. The other took off a part of his left ear.

Blood poured down over Frick's well-trimmed beard as he arose and grappled with his assailant, who thereupon drew a wicked knife and stabbed Frick again and again. Office workers collared the thug. Frick was bloody, though still game. "Hold him up," he said. "Let me look at his face." He pointed to the fellow's mouth.

"What is he chewing?" Frick asked. The man was choked and a small capsule taken from his mouth. The melodramatic pill "contained enough fulminate of mercury" to have blown up the office. The young man chewing it was Alexander Berkman, a Polish-Russian immigrant who had come, said he, to help the workers. His idea of helping the workers was to kill Henry Clay Frick. His one contribution served to set the public against unionism. It also hardened the steelmasters to make up their minds to run their mills as they pleased with "no union interference."

Henry Frick did not die from the bullets or from the knife wounds. With determination that matched his nerve, he remained in his office, bound with bandages, until the day's work was done, when doctors came to remove the bullet from his neck. He refused anesthetic. "I can help you probe better without it," he said. And that night, from his home in Homestead, Mr. Frick issued a statement. "I do not think I shall die," he said, "but whether I do or not, the Carnegie Company will pursue the same policy and it will win."

Frick was right. Not for another forty-five years would a steelworkers' union amount to anything in the United States.

Many a blast-furnace and rolling-mill man cursed, not Frick, but Berkman, the adolescent who fancied himself a hero-martyr.

What had been a hostile press changed overnight in admiration for the superb courage of H. C. Frick. "Those who hate him most," said the New York *World,* "admire the nerve and stamina of this man of steel whom nothing seems to be able to move." The *World's* reporter had found Frick back at his desk, looking a little paler and behind one ear "a hole stuffed with cotton."

Mr. Frick, who had never in his life posed as a friend of the workingman, came out of the Homestead affair with his reputation as an ironmaster enhanced. The Pinkerton agency, however, suffered an obloquy that was epitomized in the doggerel of a popular song, "Father Was Killed by the Pinkerton Men."

But it was Andrew Carnegie on whom the wrath of a nation fell in volume. The press charged that Andy had hidden away in Scotland in order that Frick should have the blame for Homestead. The Scot returned home to a country contemptuous of him. But it was also a country endowed with an acutely brief memory. Within a year or so, it is probable that only the battered survivors of the Homestead battle could recall where Andy had been when the shooting started.

Mr. Frick acted with fine judgment to control the seething unrest that pervaded Homestead after the great upheaval. He moved the Braddock manager, Charlie Schwab, to Homestead. His coming had an instant effect. Schwab's warmth, his easy genial ways, and the fact that he had risen by slow stages from laborer to manager and knew every job in the mill better than almost anyone else—these things made him the perfect man for this difficult post. He was soon put in charge of both Braddock and Homestead.

Up to this time, the steelmasters of Pittsburgh appear to have given the matter of ore little thought. They were content for the most part to buy their ore from the mining companies of Michigan. Mr. Frick believed it would be a fine thing if his company should own or lease a large area of ore lands. To this end he listened attentively to a caller, Henry W. Oliver, a pleasant immigrant from County Tyrone in Ireland, who had dabbled in steel and had also been West to investigate the newly discovered ore beds in Minnesota. This was of course the famous Mesabi Range. From the seven Merritt brothers of Duluth, Oliver had got long-term leases on an immense tract of Mesabi land. The ore, he told Mr. Frick, appeared most suitable for the making of Bessemer steel.

The brief panic of 1893, which had little effect on the Carnegie Steel Company, had wiped out the Merritt brothers; and one day Henry Oliver found out they were his landlords no longer. That place had been taken almost overnight by John D. Rockefeller and associates.

Oliver owed his new landlords some forty thousand dollars in long overdue rents. He hastened to New York, got an audience with John D. himself, and talked so charmingly, or perhaps it was convincingly, that the king of oil and much else extended Oliver's notes. Oliver next went to Mr. Carnegie, with whom, incidentally, Oliver had been a fellow messenger boy many years before. But Carnegie would have none of Oliver's ore. He could do better buying his ore, he said.

So, here was Oliver talking to Frick. He quickly convinced the steelmaster that his company could save half a million dollars a year by joining Oliver in the Mesabi venture. Carnegie still said no. Frick nevertheless joined Oliver, then staked him to cash with which to buy out three competing ore concerns. The entire group was then formed into the Henry W. Oliver Iron Mining Company, which held control of two thirds of the greatest ore range in the country. By this time, Carnegie had changed his mind, and was even heard to say that the new move was "the only element needed to give us an impregnable position."

It was high time little Andy had come round to Frick's way of thinking about ore. Great things were in the making. The Mesabi ore deal was completed only a short time before a notorious character named John W. Gates, together with an eminent character, who was J. Pierpont Morgan, and an Illinois lawyer, Elbert H. Gary, who looked and acted like a Methodist bishop, were beginning to assemble the first real threat to Carnegie's kindom of iron and steel. They called it the Federal Steel Company.

Chapter 3 THE FIRST HARASSMENTS

ROCKEFELLER'S near monopoly had brought "order" into the oil business. Carnegie controlled two thirds of America's steel production. These two men seemed to be leaders of a trend.

Newspaper editors began to use words like consolidation and amalgamation in discussing commercial affairs. Tobacco companies were merging. The same was true of sugar, of meat, flour, and much else, including street railways. In each industry or business, a few concerns grew larger by consuming the small, the unfortunate, and the weak. Consolidation had not reached its peak. This was to come a little later with the trusts.

Professors had by now brushed acquaintance with the theories of Charles Darwin, even with the classic exposition of social Darwinism that had been stated so clearly and startlingly by Herbert Spencer eight years before Darwin's book appeared. Spencer remarked that life was lived in a jungle, that it was governed by jungle laws. Only the fittest could survive. All progress was due to the evolutionary process that removed the unfit. There was nothing moral or immoral about it; it was an immutable law. There was no escape from it; poverty was the reward of the incapable and the imprudent. The reward of the idle was starvation.

Although there was little enough hope in this outlook for the great mass of Americans, it did not seem to dismay them intolerably, chiefly because the great American dream was still powerfully in the national consciousness—the dream that every native had a right, even a chance, to become President of the United States. What was more, the dream assured one and all, no matter where born, the opportunity to become as rich as Commodore Vanderbilt or Jay Cooke. Horatio Alger, Jr., an author of boys' books, wrote the identical story over one hundred and nine times to prove that the American dream came true in real life. Between the end of the Civil War and the end of the century, Americans bought approximately two hundred million copies of Mr. Alger's books. These books constituted the most influential literary tripe ever published in our country.

There were of course few intellectuals among American captains of business and industry, but they did begin to hear mention of Spencer and his remarks about survival in the jungle of life. This theory they were quite happy to accept as gospel. It was welcome balm to their impaired consciences to be told they enjoyed their riches simply because of the working of natural laws over which neither they nor anyone else had control.

Not all of the great industrialists were in agreement. Though he was a devout disciple of Spencer and a skeptic in religious matters, Andrew Carnegie believed that his great fortune was derived from no laws but from his own instinct for survival. The devoutly religious John D. Rockefeller credited his wealth to nobody but the Baptist God. In either case, the result was the same. Neither Rockefeller nor Carnegie could have prevented it, or at least that was the accepted proposition.

There was another proposition even more strongly held than that of Spencer's. It did not stem from a professional philosopher, but had grown into American folklore from some far place and distant past, most probably from Old Testament times. It was the proposition that the son or sons of all great or wealthy men were certain to be incompetents, weaklings, wastrels.

The idea is apparently the product of envy. Its fallacy has been exploded countless times and through generations of families of merchant princes. In our own times, to cite an example, it was made hash of by the career of William H., the son of Commodore Vanderbilt.

When the elder Vanderbilt died in January of 1877, as related, the management of his immense properties, including the New

York Central Railroad, was taken over by William Henry. The old man had wanted it so. Long before his death he had discovered that this son of his was not the weakling he had once thought. In his youth, young Vanderbilt had committed the grievous sin of marrying a daughter of poor parents. That she was also of good family and quite charming had nothing to do with it: Commodore Vanderbilt, the newly rich ferryboat man and oyster-scow operator, wanted no alliance with the impecunious.

William was also in poor health. The old man bought a small farm on Long Island and packed the newlyweds off to run it. William did run it, and made money. He even got the best of the Commodore in a deal involving horse manure, much to the elder's delight. He was glad to find that he had a "smart" son; so encouraged, in fact, that he made William receiver of the bankrupt Staten Island Railroad, sunk hopelessly in debt.

In less than two years, William H. had brought the road out of the depths, had paid all its bills, and was paying dividends. When the Commodore bought the Harlem Railroad, he made his son vice-president. Young Vanderbilt had the road double-tracked, and otherwise increased both its efficiency and its earnings. So, when the old man put together his New York Central & Hudson River consolidation, William went in as manager. He went methodically to work to learn the smallest details of every department. He crawled into and under every locomotive on the line. He figured coal consumption per mile. He "carefully scrutinized every bill" to the New York Central. He looked over vouchers. He checked reasons for delays of passenger trains. He answered much of his huge mail in his own hand.

To the end of his days, William H. Vanderbilt was disposed to settle all misunderstandings by reason and arbitration. He seems to have had no inclination for fighting in the roaring, brawling manner of his father. He could be generous enough on occasion, but in business matters he was close. He became noted for striking out items he had not ordered but were included in luncheon checks.

It has been said of the Commodore's son that he was not overly given to worry. This element of his nature must have been of the greatest comfort during 1877, which was the time of his sorest trials. The Commodore died in January, and the obituaries were scarcely done echoing when his heirs girded for battle to break the will; and the railroad workers of the United States staged a strike such as had not been seen before (or since).

The fight over the Commodore's will was the usual squabble of heirs, only it was on a titanic scale. It involved $105,000,000. Its outcome was to leave William the chief beneficiary, just as the Commodore planned it. The hearings ran for months and were popular with the newspaper-reading public; many family secrets were aired in detail. An interesting side issue concerned the pretty sisters Tennessee Claflin and Victoria Woodhull. To Tennessee the old man bequeathed the Aurora painting, already mentioned, and nothing else. But he also had set aside "certain large sums" to be used for advancing the noble work of spiritualism—under the trusteeship of Tennessee and Victoria.

The far from backward sisters told the press they were much disappointed. The certain large sums, they said, were in no way sufficient to promote spiritualism on the scale intended. They just happened to remember, too, that the Commodore owed them quite a little money—the residue, they said, of a deal in the stock market. They would be quite willing, however, to accept the certain large sums in lieu of the debt.

The New York papers reported that one of executor W. H. Vanderbilt's greatest trials was the presentation by Miss Claflin of a claim on the Commodore's estate for an indefinite amount, rumored "to be more than $100,000." No suit was ever brought. It seems to have been more or less amicably settled out of court. This much is certain: though the two sisters were known to have been virtually penniless early in 1877, in the summer of that year the girls sailed for England, taking a crew of newly hired servants and engaging six double first-class staterooms for the voyage. Once in England, they rented "a mansion in the fashionable West Brompton, a suburb of London."

Meanwhile, the railroads had exploded with violence. Because it had a tremendous and lasting influence, not only on the Vanderbilts and other railroad kings but on moneyed men in every field, this is perhaps the place to take notice of the violence of '77. It shook the country as nothing, the Civil War excepted, had shaken it since its founding. It flared first along the line of the Baltimore & Ohio Railroad in July, when, in protest of a wage cut, firemen and brakemen suddenly climbed down from their cabs and cabooses, leaving the trains where they stood.

Two days later, nearly a hundred B&O trains, a total of thousands of passenger and freight cars, were stalled. Militia and

federal troops were called. Rocks were thrown. So were switches.
Cars started to burn. Rifles and Gatling guns began going off.

Thousands of the Pennsylvania Railroad's employees struck,
along with thousands more of the Erie, the New York Central, the
Lake Shore, and many others.

Troops moved into Pittsburgh, where they were quickly driven
into a Pennsylvania roundhouse and besieged by 15,000 completely maddened men and women, many of whom were armed.
Soldiers attempting to flee the fort were shot and killed. Mobs went
about everywhere in the city, raiding hardware stores for guns and
ammunition.

Willing hands turned oil over a gondola piled high with coke,
set it afire, then rammed it head on against the roundhouse fort.
Out came the desperate soldiers, shooting their way through the
mobs and dying in the process.

Fire broke out in the long lines of cars in the great yards. It
spread rapidly to destroy five hundred boxcars and passenger
coaches and 104 locomotives. It leaped to the fine Union Hotel
and Depot. It spread to the Pennsylvania's office buildings. Smoke
rolled in clouds to bury the city, though flames lighted it here and
there. Ashes fell thick for miles up the Monongahela and down
the Ohio. Down on the cinders of the Pennsylvania's tracks lay
dead soldiers and dead strikers, strung out like so many loose ties.
Next day an editorial writer on a Pittsburgh paper looked at his
city and found it a scene of desolation and melancholy.

It was much the same elsewhere, in Altoona, in Easton, Johnstown, Bethlehem; and in Reading, where General Winfield Scott
Hancock and 3,000 regulars had to shoot and kill at least ten
civilians, and to wound as many more.

It was much the same in Buffalo, where Lake Shore strikers
were tearing up tracks, raiding saloons, and fighting with 1,600
militiamen and 1,800 members of the Grand Army of the Republic
who had been sworn in as deputies.

It was worse in Chicago, the great rail center. Several thousand
militiamen were called out there and aided by 5,000 armed deputies. They could do little against the mobs that stormed the
Chicago, Burlington & Quincy roundhouse and yards; and other
mobs at the Michigan Central terminal. Within a few hours not a
train could enter or leave Chicago.

Even the Sioux, far out on the Plains, knew that something had
happened, for General Phil Sheridan, who had been castigating

them, was obliged, on orders from Washington, to dispatch a full regiment of his troops to embattled Chicago in command of Lieutenant Colonel Frederick Dent Grant.

The wave of violence, traveling with the speed of epidemic, struck St. Louis, where there were many serious street and railroad-yard disorders. It flared in St. Paul. Locomotives and cars were fired and wrecked in Omaha. In frightened San Francisco, where the upheaval of the striking railroad men was quickly turned into the special California pattern and became race riots against the poor coolies from Canton, no longer needed by the Central Pacific, which had fetched them in the beginning.

William H. Vanderbilt met this great crisis of his career with a masterful stroke of public relations. He announced that the sum of $100,000 was to be divided, immediately, "among the loyal men of the New York Central & Hudson River Railroad." It was so divided, too, and it put W. H. Vanderbilt on the side of the angels in public opinion.

The railroad strikers of '77 did not win their demands. They were defeated on all lines. Yet they won much more than restoration of the wage scale which they had asked for and had not got. Out of their battles of 1877 came the brotherhoods, in many respects the most successful labor unions in the United States.

When the smoke of violence had cleared too, the press began to look at what had happened and to inquire about the reasons why. One great editor wrote in the Chicago *Daily News* that the public had little sympathy for the rioters, and even less for "the Vanderbilts, the Jay Goulds, and the Jim Fisks who have been running the railroads and have ruined one of the finest properties the world has known." Another editor remarked that the railroads had been run "wholly outside the United States Constitution," that they had corrupted everything they touched. Still another wrote of the railroad kings that, "having found nothing more to get out of stockholders and bondholders, they have commenced raiding not only the general public but their own employees."

In retrospect it seems odd that no editor pointed out a contributing cause, possibly the greatest of several causes, that touched off the near revolution of 1877, namely, that workingmen had begun, not long since, to read the daily papers. They had read in their papers, for instance, that the New York Central paid eight per cent in 1874, ten per cent in 1875. The Pennsylvania had done almost as well. So had other lines. In their reading, they could not well have overlooked the item that told of the $105,000,000 Commodore Vanderbilt of the New York Central had left. Then, four months after his death, these same men read that their wages were being lowered because the railroads were in hard straits. It was then they rose and tore things loose.

The wholly untrammeled morning of American moguls of finance was nearly over. The bright serene noon of their days began to pass in 1877. From then onward, capitalists and industrialists of all degree had to use more ingenuity than before. They had to fight harder. They were watched more closely. They were harassed infinitely more. And the most successful of them quickly developed new abilities of survival amidst the new complexities, complexities that might well have been too great for pioneers like Commodore Vanderbilt, Daniel Drew, and others of their comparatively simple era.

Having brought the New York Central unscathed through the terrible dangers of '77, W. H. Vanderbilt was prepared to defend it against other threats. One of these threats, called the New York, West Shore & Buffalo, had been built purposely to crush the Central. When it had at last reached Buffalo and started to accept freight to New York City, Vanderbilt slashed the Central's rates to ridiculous lows; and in other ways so harassed the new line that the passage of two years found it in the hands of a receiver and, almost overnight, in the far from palsied hands of W. H. Vanderbilt.

During his war with the West Shore, Vanderbilt felt urged to aid a nuisance railroad that was trying to threaten the Pennsylvania system, and thus gave the Pennsylvania warning it had best withdraw its support of the West Shore. It did so. It is of interest to know that the arbitrator of this affair was the still young J. Pierpont Morgan, whose fee for his trouble, said his biographer Hovey, was somewhere between one and three millions of dollars.

W. H. Vanderbilt took into camp another threat named the Rome, Watertown & Ogdensburg. He acquired the Boston & Albany to siphon New England for his major road. To get entry into Cincinnati and St. Louis, he got control of the so-called "Big Four" lines. Simply to get it off the Central's flank, he took over the Nickel Plate. In less than the eight years left to him after the Commodore's death, the younger Vanderbilt more than trebled, said a Wall Street commentator, the value of the Vanderbilt lines.

For all his unquestioned ability one cannot find that William Henry had any popular appeal to the public. He was just not, as the old Commodore was, a man in the heroic mold. He is recalled chiefly because of two things—he owned a famous race horse and he made a celebrated remark. The horse was Maude S., and for her private pasture Vanderbilt fenced the city block where the Biltmore Hotel was later to stand. From his office in Grand Central depot he could keep his eye on her.

The famous remark was, "The public be damned!" It was made on October 8, 1882, somewhere between Michigan City, Indiana and Chicago, in Vanderbilt's private car, while reporters were interviewing him in regard to a new rate war between the Pennsylvania and the Central. Vanderbilt remarked that the Central could not make a profit on a fifteen-dollar fare from New York to Chicago but was maintaining the fare because forced to by the Pennsylvania. "Otherwise," said Vanderbilt, "we would abandon it."

"But," said a free-lance writer, Clarence Dresser, in what seems like a stupid question, "don't you run the train for the public benefit?" Mr. Vanderbilt let him have it. "The public be damned!" he said. He was running the New York Central, he observed, for the benefit of the stockholders.

These were perfectly clear statements. They should have brought the unfortunate man public gratitude for their obvious honesty. Instead, once they had appeared in the Chicago *Daily News* and in most daily papers the country over, they brought down on Vanderbilt the wrath of "the incapable, the imprudent, and the idle," which was to say, the "unfit," and who numbered many millions of men.

When Vanderbilt sought to deny he made such statements, claiming them to be malign misrepresentation, he made things much worse by bringing the Commodore's name into the business. "That is not my way," he said, "nor was it my father's. I never use profane language." This merely added mirth to the nation's scorn, for William Henry was forever telling people how much like his father he was—a father whose profanity was so monstrous and pungent as to cause envy along the docks of New York and New Jersey.

"The public be damned!" was manna for the critics of capitalism. Every anti-monopolist, every city working-stiff, every member of the bucolic Patrons of Husbandry; every soapbox orator from the

Boston Common to Portsmouth Square in San Francisco, and almost every newspaper editor, raised their voices to cry aloud that Vanderbilt had summarized the attitude of capitalism in general and the railroads in particular. They went on to shout that Vanderbilt's remark epitomized the policy of Standard Oil, of Carnegie, of Chicago packers, Pennsylvania coal barons, western mine owners, New England textile manufacturers. They recalled, to a man, what a queen of France had said about the poor eating cake—just before the walls of the Bastille came tumbling down.

Nothing happened, of course, though the remark was used by radical organizers who were preparing to stage the uprising that was to go into American history, three years later, as the Haymarket Riot.

The significance of William Henry Vanderbilt was not realized until after his death which, as a prominent stockbroker pointed out with warm appreciation, occurred "after board hours," thus giving an overnight opportunity for Wall Street dealers to regulate their breathing. The significance was in W. H. Vanderbilt's estate. It exceeded two hundred million dollars.

Henry Clews, the Wall Street diarist, marveled at the size of it, and lost no time to take paper and pencil to translate its meaning into gold, finding it to weigh five hundred tons. Clews next applied horsepower to it and figured that the labor of five hundred strong horses would be required to move the fortune from Grand Central depot to the Subtreasury in Wall Street.

The estate of this second Vanderbilt, said Clews, showed many living men who considered themselves to be wealthy, that they were mere ciphers in the shadow of this golden pile. "They seemed to themselves," he wrote, "to be financially blighted, and miserably poor in contrast to the colossal magnitude of the Vanderbilt possessions as exhibited in the surrogate's court."

Not exhibited in the surrogate's court, but standing like some sinister monument of black granite fair in the public domain, remained Vanderbilt's one remembered remark. Generations of editorialists, cartoonists, and politicians were to use "The public be damned!" as a battle cry. The paradox here is that the second Vanderbilt was really a man who had great respect for public opinion, who had genuine pride in his railroad system, yet he went into history as the classic ogre of capital, the cruel, bloated character who delighted in flaunting his disregard for humanity, for common decency. One must be content to charge the paradox to the whims of the gods, whose sense of humor is often heavy-handed.

A more logical candidate for place of chief whipping boy for capital was surely Jay Gould, who earned it by the most ruthless and spectacular career imaginable and left a huge fortune but no remark fit to curse his kind. Gould was an uncommonly silent man, anyway.

It will be recalled that Jay Gould was at last forced out of Erie and used his loot to buy into Union Pacific during the 1873 panic, when stocks were paper-cheap. Now he was launched on the most brilliant part of his career, a career that was to "transcend the rational probability allowed in the latitude of fiction."

By 1874, Gould was a director and in virtual control of Union Pacific. Meanwhile he bought into the Kansas Pacific, and went on to take over the Denver Pacific, the Missouri Pacific, and get control of the Central Pacific.

Then, before fellow directors of the Union Pacific had an inkling, Gould said he had a good mind to extend the Kansas Pacific to Salt Lake City, connect there with the Central Pacific, and thus form a new transcontinental to compete with the Union Pacific, of which, it should be kept in mind, he was still a stockholder and a director. Neither the pleadings nor the threats of his fellow UP directors moved him in the least; he demanded that the UP be consolidated with the Kansas Pacific at par. It was done, and Gould sold his Kansas Pacific holdings for ten million dollars.

Gould had retained the Missouri Pacific. Now he bought control of the Texas & Pacific, and several smaller lines, and merged them all into a system of more than seven thousand miles to become the only real competitor to the Atchison, Topeka & Santa Fe.

He had other interests, too, one of which was the New York *World,* which he bought and proceeded to use with great talent as a means for the manipulation of stocks. First, he turned the *World's* guns on Western Union, the largest of the many telegraph companies. Readers of the *World* were soon learning that Western Union was an expensive and un-American near monopoly that was sucking the lifeblood of business. In the same paper, readers also saw that a new concern, the Atlantic & Pacific Company, was laying telegraph lines along the railroads which just happened to be in the control of Jay Gould.

Within twelve months, the business of Western Union declined by approximately two million dollars, and the company made up its mind it would be best to pay Gould's blackmail: Western Union purchased Atlantic & Pacific for a sum variously reported as "exceeding ten million dollars."

Within weeks, the New York *World* was describing in most favorable light another new telegraph outfit, the American Union, sponsored by Jay Gould. Western Union bought it, paying considerably more than its worth. Whereupon, Gould prepared to take Western Union itself into camp.

Calling his able henchmen, Russell Sage, James Keene, and Addison Cammack, Gould set the *World* on a campaign to wreck Western Union's credit, while his hatchet men used all the tricks of manipulation they knew so well to depress the stock still lower. It was a savage war and brief. In 1881, when he was forty-five, Gould had control of Western Union. "The methods of acquiring the control and possession of other people's property," wrote an admirer, "have been raised to the dignity of a fine art by Mr. Gould."

Moving his office into the massive Western Union Building, Mr. Gould issued a thumping great dividend of 38¼ per cent and raised Western Union's capitalization to eighty million dollars, a quarter or more of which was water.

Although transportation and communication were to remain his favorite speculations, now and then Gould turned his attention briefly to something else. When he learned that his old friend James Keene was trying to corner wheat, Gould stepped in with his newspaper and his buying and selling tactics, to quickly turn the stock market into a shambles. Keene emerged shorn of seven millions of dollars and "was turned adrift, a bankrupt."

Hosts of Gould's enemies became allies in efforts to plow the man under. Once, it is told, a pair of brokers kidnaped Gould's messenger boy and substituted another lad as a spy. For several days the spy brought all of Gould's letters and telegrams to the enemy to be copied, then sent on their way. When Gould caught on to the deceit, he said nothing but made mental note to ruin the brokers in good time. Perhaps he did. The story stops there and one doesn't know.

Gould was often in physical danger. Not counting the angry mobs of his days with Erie and his Black Friday affair, he was twice attacked on the street and knocked down. He thereupon employed a private detail of guards who were with or near him day and night.

Physical disabilities harassed Jay Gould almost from birth, and at forty-five he was aging fast. His beard was streaked with gray, his hair almost gone. His dark and somehow sinister face had hard, deep lines. His whole body had shrunk. Orchids were his passion, and his great gingerbread mansion at Irvington-on-Hudson was of less pleasure to him than the attached conservatory in which he grew the rarest species of his favorite flower. His town house at Fifth Avenue and Forty-seventh Street, standing until 1953 though molting brownstone chips, was conventionally sumptuous, but neither here nor in the quiet of his country place could he find sleep.

Wracked by chest pains, often spitting blood, Gould often paced the night away on the sidewalk before his Fifth Avenue home while one of the guards stood watch. Possibly the guard came to believe that wealth was not all.

During these night watches, the incredibly restless mind of the frail little man made plans for the next day, or the next, and so on. It is likely that he never knew peace of mind or of body. His mind now conceived the idea of getting control of New York City's newest form of transportation, the Manhattan Elevated Railway Company.

Gould started his attack through the courts, and supported it with editorials in the *World*. These called for annulment of the elevated company's franchise. The *World* was of the opinion that the company was corrupt, inefficient, and insolvent. This news, manufactured by Gould, was carried to the rest of the United States by the Western Union wires controlled by Gould.

Price of shares in Manhattan Elevated Railway started to skid. Gould and Russell Sage bought in. Just as soon as the gang had control, the *World* discovered that the company was not only solvent, but a pretty decent outfit.

Into the new regime as president of Manhattan went one of the most distinguished Americans, Cyrus W. Field of Atlantic cable fame. Field was also socially prominent, an intimate of the financial old guard, and of political leaders. Manhattan Elevated issued more stock. The shares were manipulated upward. The fare was doubled, to ten cents.

The *World* found all this to be benevolent, but not so the New

York *Times*, which began to refer to Gould as a pirate and a scourge. Such name-calling meant nothing to Gould or to his partner Russell Sage; but president Field, whom the *Times* chided for association with disgraceful stockjobbers, found it most unpleasant. Field seems to have developed a notable public conscience, and out of it came a thing disgusting to Gould and Sage: Field cut the elevated fare to five cents.

Now, Gould had made his several fortunes not by catering to the public, but by deliberate mismanagement of whatever he touched. He must get rid of Field, who seemed to be no better than a crazy reformer playing for public applause. With characteristic indirection, Gould urged Field to buy more Manhattan Elevated; and when Field was carrying a heavy overload of it, Gould and Sage staged a raid on the market which cut the price of Manhattan almost in half. Field was ruined.

Jay Gould was to undergo ferocious attacks throughout his later years. Once or twice it seemed as if his enemies had at last taken his measure. But no, he rallied and continued both active and successful almost to the day of his death, which came in 1892, when he was fifty-six. He left a fortune formally estimated at only seventy-seven million dollars, though his estate was probably worth twice that figure. At his funeral was an impressive phalanx of money lords, including J. Pierpont Morgan, a man noted neither for convention nor sentiment.

Not at the funeral was a man whose early career has often been likened to that of Jay Gould's. This was Edward Henry Harriman, born on Long Island in 1848, and probably the most precocious operator Wall Street had known. (Dime novels dealing with fictitious boy wizards of Wall Street seem to have been inspired by Harriman's youthful prodigies.) Entering the Street as an office boy at fourteen, he was a grave, silent and rather frail lad who became fascinated with the marvels performed with Erie Railroad stock by Drew, Gould, and Fisk. He was astute enough to see Black Friday coming in 1869, and was ready for it, selling the market short and clearing $3,000. He used the stake to buy himself a seat on the Stock Exchange.

One of the boy wonder's first efforts was a raid on coal stocks that brought him $150,000 and a reputation. The reputation brought him customers, among them the Vanderbilts and Jay Gould. Having married Mary Averell, daughter of the president of the Ogdensburg & Lake Champlain Railroad, he prevailed on his father-in-law to let him try to make something of the impoverished Lake Ontario Southern. Young Harriman reorganized the road, then improved the property and set the New York Central and the Pennsylvania railroads to bidding for what both of those lines knew to be a nuisance railroad. Harriman unloaded it at a top price on the Pennsylvania.

Harriman returned to Wall Street, but only briefly. He had liked what he had seen of the railroad business. He began to buy into Illinois Central, one of the most prosperous lines in the country, and perhaps also the most "respectable." It had known no scandalous management. Its officials and directors were "eminently reputable people."

At this period young Harriman's reputation was none too good. He was believed to be a younger Jay Gould, a ruthless, cold-blooded, and clever gambler who bought things to make money through wrecking them. The young man astonished everybody in Wall Street when the Illinois Central's directors made him vice-president. He went on to display a remarkable knowledge of how to run a railroad. The line flourished better than ever before. It began to expand into Iowa. Here Harriman had his first clash with J. Pierpont Morgan, who, on behalf of the Vanderbilts, was trying to take Iowa for the New York Central. Harriman fought the Morgan-Vanderbilt crowd to a standstill and won.

His next venture was with the Union Pacific. This portion of the first transcontinental had been battered and abused almost from its completion. Track was poor. Rolling stock was in terrible condition. Maintenance had been neglected. Grades were heavy. Curves were many and too short. In 1893 the road surprised almost nobody by going into receivership.

His years with the Illinois Central had an influence on Harriman. He had gone to that road with the reputation of a stock operator. A dozen years as executive vice-president of the IC had revealed high abilities as an operating head. Now he joined a syndicate formed to take over the foundered Union Pacific, of which he was made chairman of the executive committee.

Harriman immediately set forth on a firsthand inspection of every mile of the great system. Managers and superintendents were without exception amazed at the sharp technical knowledge displayed by this ex-stockbroker who looked like a bookkeeper. He took in everything all along the line. Before the trip was over,

Harriman had wired his directors for authority to purchase rolling stock, rails, and much else to the extent of twenty-five million dollars. He got the authority.

On a second trip, he repossessed for the Union Pacific the Oregon Short Line it had lost and gained control of the Oregon Railway & Navigation Company, giving the UP a Pacific port at Portland. Near the turn of the century he bought control of the Central Pacific, along with a heavy interest in the Southern Pacific. He went ahead to build the Lucin cutoff across the Great Salt Lake, which most engineers said was impossible, and otherwise improved the lines under Harriman management.

There is not room here to more than indicate the brilliance with which Harriman worked on the Union Pacific and allied lines, but by 1901 the whole great system was known simply as the Harriman lines. By then eight years of life remained to him. These were to be spent largely in war with James Jerome Hill, who turned out to be the only railroad man who could hold his own against Edward Henry Harriman. We shall come to the Hill-Harriman war in a later chapter.

Chapter 4   RULERS OF CHICAGO

IT is time to look at Chicago. Giants had appeared there. They were to be seen moving about in the murk of their factories, their packing houses, and railroad yards, while their women learned to pronounce *porte-cochère* properly and aped the more or less grand dames of New York, who were aping the duchesses, or at least the countesses, of England and Europe.

The phenomenon of Chicago had risen with incredible speed in the stinking wild onion swamp at the foot of Lake Michigan. In 1833, when it was incorporated as a town, a census showed 180 persons who lived in forty-three shanties and cabins. The population was made up almost wholly of real estate operators and the keepers of saloons and dives.

Michigan City, Indiana, was then the incomparable metropolis of the region. It contained almost twenty times the population of

Chicago. Milwaukee was double the size of the two-by-four settlement in the dismal marsh around old Fort Dearborn. Cincinnati was already a venerable town and was coming to be called Porkopolis because of its great meat-packing houses.

The one great commodity of Illinois of the 1830s was real estate, and it was immediately apparent there were enough suckers in the eastern states who would buy, sight unseen, all the cheap land put up for sale in almost any part of the Midwest. The United States was on the crest of its greatest land craze. It was this universal madness that fetched him on the scene who was to become Chicago's first great magnate of business.

This was William Butler Ogden, thirty years old in 1835 when he arrived by stagecoach in the hope of salvaging some part of the $100,000 which his sister's husband had, in an unhappy moment, invested in Chicago real estate. Young Ogden spent his first night in a vile two-storied shack called a hotel which was teeming with "confusion, filth, and racket." Next morning he went forth to stand, ankle-deep in water, and gaze westward. As far as the eye could reach was desolate swamp marked with cattails, high coarse grass, and the pungent wild onion. Bullfrogs conversed in the reeds. Gulls screamed overhead. That night Ogden wrote his brother-in-law back in New York City: "You have been guilty of the grossest folly."

But Ogden was going to try to unload, anyway. He worked indefatigably at platting the immense acreage; and when summer had dried the swamp somewhat, he held an auction. Excited men, cash in hand, stormed his little office and all but wrecked it in their urgency to buy a lot, or ten lots, or twenty. The astonished Ogden took their cash as fast as he could—and put the buyers down as lunatics, made so by some strange disease due to the miasma hanging over this worthless swamp country. Within a few days, he had sold barely one third of the tract, yet for it he had taken in a little more than a hundred thousand dollars, its original cost.

Ogden returned to New York with the money for his kinsman and intimated they were a couple of crooks. "There is no such value in that land," he said, "and there won't be for a generation." Yet, only a little later, when he went back to Chicago to sell the rest of the tract, he saw how wrong he had been. During the few months of his absence Chicago had not only built along half a dozen new streets, but the prices of real estate had tripled. Ogden sold the remainder of the tract at a huge profit, then went into business for himself. He survived the panic of 1837, and so did Chicago. In that year the place was incorporated as a city, with Mayor William B. Ogden at the helm. He was the first of the Chicago giants.

A decade later hundreds of big wagons rumbled over plank roads into Chicago daily; and fleets of ships docked to load or unload produce and merchandise. On Randolph Street was a vast camp, set up by the city itself for the convenience of the teamsters who brought wheat and corn from the prairies and returned thence with the goods the farmers needed.

Ogden, now the town's foremost capitalist and all-around dynamo, felt the place should have a railroad. He was opposed by most local merchants and businessmen, who believed that Chicago's future lay in being strictly a retail town, a place where farmers came in person to trade; and that if farmers could ship their produce, they would not trouble to come to town at all.

Ogden told the merchants they were a pack of myopic dullards, and set out with horse and buggy to sell $250,000 worth of stock in his Galena & Chicago Union Railroad. He built it, too, and in November of 1848 a train steamed into Chicago with a carload of wheat—the first of a host of such carloads. The Galena road was a success from its first day of operation. Ogden went ahead to expand it, changed its name to the Chicago & North Western, and became its president.

Magnate Ogden found time for other things than railroads and banks and real estate. Into his office one day came a fringe-bearded man from Virginia who said he was Cyrus Hall McCormick. He had, he said, invented a practical reaper for grain. He had sold a number of them, and now he wanted to settle here, on the very edge of the wheat lands, and manufacture the reaper in large volume. He needed a little capital to get started. Chicago's richest citizen talked briefly with the powerfully built inventor. He must have been pleased at the clear vision of this man who had selected Chicago as the right place. In any case, Ogden knew another giant when he saw one. He gave McCormick $25,000 and took a one-half interest in the new firm of McCormick, Ogden & Company.

When he came to Chicago Cyrus McCormick was nearly forty. Both he and his father had inventive minds. The old man had devised a hempbrake, a gristmill, a hydraulic machine. Both father and son had puttered off and on with a reaper. Then they dropped all their inventions to get rich from an iron furnace.

The furnace soon failed. Cyrus turned again to the reaper, improved it, got a patent, then made and sold a few of them locally. His next move turned out badly. He went through the Midwest and arranged for manufacture of his reaper in a number of cities, a sort of license agreement. But two years of this showed McCormick his mistake; the licensed makers of his machines did shoddy work. The reapers did not perform well. McCormick's reputation was injured. It was then he went to Chicago.

Cyrus McCormick's invention revolutionized farming. His business methods had a salutary effect on manufacturers in other lines. Up to the advent of McCormick, Ogden & Company, business had generally been conducted on the principle it was best for the buyer to beware. A seller got the highest price he could, no matter what his product was. Sharpness that went as far as dishonesty was prevalent. Cyrus McCormick had never been a businessman, or a trader. He had been and he still was, in 1848, a poor inventor given to dreams.

Now he told Ogden, who agreed, that every McCormick machine should be sold at a fixed price, $120, and no haggling. A farmer could have one for thirty dollars down, and pay the rest in six months. But, if the crop was poor or hard luck came, McCormick wanted to give the farmer more time. Then or later McCormick never employed lawyers to collect from farmers. His competitors, and industrialists in other lines, thought McCormick was insane. All of them maintained batteries of attorneys specifically for scaring the daylights out of the tillers of the soil, who were likely to be slow about paying. And they told each other that McCormick was certain to be left holding the bag. They were fantastically wrong.

From the first, McCormick reapers were sold and went out of the new plant as fast as they could be made. Three years later they were mowing and binding grain in every state where grain was grown in any volume. Competitors to the number of at least thirty had tried to get in on this good thing. McCormick mowed them down as neatly as his machines laid the wheat.

When, in 'forty-nine, it seemed as if every footloose man east of the Mississippi was on his way to the gold fields of California, and ten thousand of them left Illinois alone, McCormick hurriedly got out big posters warning the farmers to order their reapers early if they wanted one; labor was going to be scarce, come harvest time, and one McCormick machine did the work of ten strong fellows.

Orders continued to roll in. McCormick now set up nineteen assembling plants at strategic places in the Mississippi River Valley. Farmers, he knew, were slow to make up their minds about buying a machine. More than half of them were prone to wait until the grain was almost ripe before ordering one. From these regional warehouses, McCormick machines could be assembled as needed and roll into the nearby fields without delay.

And to demonstrate to farmers *who* made the best machine, McCormick staged a Field Day in every district—a sort of fair at which all makers of farm equipment were invited to display their wares in competition, in a field of ripe grain. It is to be supposed that McCormick reapers commonly won, for the firm continued to finance Field Days for many years, or until they had degenerated, as was the case with Muster Days of the militia, into monumental mass drunks.

There was no degeneration in what had become McCormick & Company. (Ogden had dropped out.) Brothers William and Leander had come to help Cyrus run the plant and sell the machines. In view of later events, it is of interest here to know that the Chicago *Tribune,* edited by chin-whiskered Joseph Medill, often attacked Cyrus McCormick—as an inventor, as a manufacturer, and charged him in Civil War days with being a Copperhead. One of Medill's daughters presently married one of the McCormicks, to found the dynasty represented later by Colonel Robert R. McCormick, publisher of the *Tribune.*

Cyrus McCormick's anti-abolition stand caused him much trouble during the war period, yet his thousands of reapers then at work in the fields of the North permitted the Union to feed itself and even to export large amounts of grain, while maintaining an army at the front.

The McCormick brothers also were quick to adopt any new device to improve their machines—first, a wire binder; then because bits of wire occasionally got into the threshed wheat, a twine binder; self-raking devices; anything at all that would make the McCormick machine better. Cyrus himself went abroad to arrange for showings at expositions in London, Paris, Vienna, and Melbourne. France made him a Chevalier of the Legion of Honor. The London *Times* remarked editorially that McCormick's reaper "will amply repay England for all her outlay connected with the Great Exposition." By the mid-seventies, McCormick machines were at work in every country on earth. By 1880 the company was shipping 50,000 machines annually.

Wealthy from manufacture, Cyrus McCormick speculated in gold, silver, and copper mines with great good fortune, and invested in many railroads. He built a fair-sized mansion on Rush Street, though it was never a show place; and "gave liberally to almost anything connected with the Presbyterian Church." He died in 1884, less than two years before Chicago police and McCormick's Pinkerton guards shot and killed six strikers at the entrance to the harvester works.

Cyrus McCormick was perhaps unique among wealthy industrialists of his era in that he was a genuine inventor, a creator who also had business ability such as almost no other inventor, until Thomas Edison, displayed.

Little of McCormick's fortune had come from investment or speculation. It had been acquired comparatively slowly over a period of thirty-five years, a glacial period when put beside the "killing" that made one of his contemporaries, Philip Danforth Armour, a rich man almost overnight.

Armour made two million dollars in ninety days. He was able to do this because he read the newspapers closely, with special attention to the reports of battles between the Union and the rebel armies; and though he was no military man and, like all others of the time who were to gain great wealth, never thought of enlisting as a soldier, Armour saw victory for the Union at least three months sooner than most other gamblers in commodities. Shortly after the battle of Gettysburg, when pork was quoted at forty dollars a barrel, Armour went to New York City and offered to sell pork for future delivery in any amount. Hundreds of traders who thought they were very shrewd fellows, bought pork futures from Armour by the thousands of barrels.

Pretty soon came the great string of Union victories, one after the other, as Grant started slugging. The price of pork sagged with each new victory. Armour was able to buy for eighteen dollars what he had agreed to deliver at from thirty to forty dollars. Many traders were ruined. Armour's profits permitted the brand-new firm of Armour & Company to begin business with no loans from banks and no mortgages.

Armour was born in 1832 at Stockbridge, New York, right next to the celebrated or notorious Oneida Community, which his father had said was "for people whose dreams hadn't come true." Young Phil Armour's dreams, whatever they had been before, turned by 1852 to concern California, where he went in an overland party and so to mining. Though he uncovered no bonanza, he returned East three years later with "several thousand dollars" and soon went to Milwaukee and into the wholesale grocery and commission business. His coup in Civil War pork was used to finance himself and brother Ossian in the meat business, in Chicago.

At this period Nelson Morris was the dominant packer, though pressing him for first place was Libby, McNeil & Libby. And in this same year, 1875, the trade was invaded by Gustavus Franklin Swift, a butcher from Cape Cod. These firms and Armour & Company were within the next decade or so to become known as the "Big Four" of meat packing.

Which of the Big Four took the lead in this or that new method, which was first to improve curing of meats, to adopt refrigeration, and to start packaging and at last to achieve almost complete utilization, is now beyond knowing because of the claims and counterclaims of three quarters of a century. What matters is that competition among them was so savage and continuous that long before the century's turn, meat packing was Chicago's first industry and one of the wonders of the world.

Philip Armour found Nelson Morris his most dangerous competitor in the early years. It was Morris's custom to arrive at the stockyards before daylight in order to get the pick of the hogs and cattle. So, one midnight Armour called all his buyers, gave them each a nice new lantern, and all hands made the rounds of the pens, hunted up the owners of the stock, and bought what they wanted.

Morris responded by sending his buyers into the country to buy and ship whole trains of stock. Swift concentrated on getting more out of each hog, utilizing what had been refuse to make soap, fertilizer, and other things. Armour was not left behind; his plants started making buttons from bones, glue from feet, combs and ornaments from horns, curled hair from tails, felt from wool. Hair was cured for plaster material. Blood and scrap went into fertilizer.

These barons of beef and pork were gluttons for work. Even after he had arrived at the silk-hat and frock-coat stage, old Swift, dressed like a wealthy undertaker, prowled his immense plant, prying around the sinks, looking for traces of grease on the water. This was waste, and when old man Swift found waste, somebody got the very devil.

For many years Armour, no matter his millions, was at his plant before seven, often at 4 A.M. Eight was the hour the office opened, and Armour always watched to see who got in before eight.

Often he presented some astonished clerk who showed a consistent urge to arrive early with a new five-dollar bill. News like that got around. In time the office of Armour & Company was fully manned an hour or so before it formally opened for business.

Armour had great respect for Germans, many of whom came to work in his company's research department. He told his secretary that "if a man calls who looks like a genius or a fool, wearing long hair, whiskers, and spectacles, treat him kindly." These German immigrants were the men whose efforts were bringing Armour, and other packers as well, more profits from "refuse" than from meat.

In good time, the Big Four discovered that though competition had done their business enormous good, it could be carried too far. Gentlemen's agreements ended virtually all competition, save perhaps for research; and the packers, as Matthew Josephson has remarked, "faced consumers with the compact organization and fixed price system . . . and on the other hand, they confronted the disorganized producers, the farmers, with the same concealed unanimity."

There was no perceptible conspiracy; only a fortuitous harmony of minds. To bid on cattle and hogs, only four buyers would appear at the Union Stock Yards. "The first offers a low price," wrote Charles Edward Russell, "the second is not interested, the third is not interested, nor is the fourth in a hurry to make a purchase. The next day, another sets a price and the other three refuse to buy." Stock growers might howl all they would. Their howls had no effect on the Big Four's informal yet adamantine front.

All of these great packers piled up fortunes. The fortunes were tarnished late in the century by the "embalmed beef" scandals, and again, a little later, by a novel entitled *The Jungle*. Neither had any effect on the individual fortunes of the big packers.

The first scandal had to do with the condition of meat bought by the Army during the Spanish-American War. To say that the condition of much of this meat was "bad" was arrant flattery. It was rotten. At a training camp at Chickamauga, for instance, wagonloads of beef arriving from Chicago could be trailed through the camp by the live maggots that were shaken off and fell to the ground. A typical American uproar was followed by a typical American inquiry. It was almost, though not quite, a whitewash. Perhaps it was a gray-wash. It satisfied nobody, neither the Army, nor the public, nor the packers.

This scandal was believed by friends of Armour to have contributed indirectly to his death. He denied complicity or even knowledge of the bad quality of the meat. There were many who believed him. Elbert Hubbard performed in characteristic fashion to link the American meat packer with an English poet. "Armour's years," wrote Hubbard, "were shorted by the stab of a pen—the thing that killed Keats—the tumult of wild talk concerning embalmed beef." Hubbard held that the meat scandal was concocted by the government itself to "divert attention from the unpreparedness" of the Army to take care of the health of its volunteers. But Hubbard's superb record for inaccuracy of statement clouded any of his positive remarks with a fog of doubt.

Philip Armour died in 1901, too soon to have seen the rise of one of his bright young men of Armour & Company to the position of the mogul of periodical literature in the United States. This was George Horace Lorimer, whom Armour had hired and advanced to the job of a department manager in the Chicago plant. Lorimer did his work there well and found time to utilize a by-product of Armour & Company that was unsuspected. He set down in notebooks, over the years, the "epigrams, phrases, orphics and symbols" ejaculated by Philip Armour himself.

When his notebooks were full, Lorimer left Chicago to take charge of the anemic *Saturday Evening Post,* which he transformed into a financial success of such magnitude that even capitalists came to hear of it and to pay it respect. Lorimer's first successful serial in the *Post* was the anonymous "Letters from a Self-Made Merchant to His Son," which he distilled from the philosophy of Philip Armour and which may well have had more influence on young America than the Armour Institute of Technology, bequeathed by the generous packer to posterity.

If Armour did not live long enough to know the success of his protégé's serial and book, he did die in time to escape *The Jungle.* This novel of the Chicago stockyards, by Upton Sinclair, published first in the Socialist weekly, *The Appeal to Reason,* shook the country as no book had shaken it since Mrs. Stowe's. Mrs. Stowe played upon the higher emotions. Mr. Sinclair hit the American stomach. With great relish he escorted the reader on a round of the stockyards and plants in a city he called Packingtown, only too recognizable as Chicago. The grunts, the groans, the agonized squeals of animals being butchered, the rivers of blood, the steaming masses of intestines, the various stenches, these were displayed along with the corruption of government inspectors. For a few pennies per animal, these wretches turned their heads when cholera-ridden hogs and tuberculous cattle were going through the mill to be processed into deviled ham, corned beef, and what not.

There was a story, of course. This dealt with a Bohunk immigrant who was a victim of every American with whom he came in contact, a victim not only of his callous employer and brutal bosses, but of his landlord, and of every storekeeper, employment agent, and politician in his ward. Even the beer he drank had been watered. Sinclair, never a man to do things by halves, poured it on. Scarcely a solitary American influence which this poor immigrant working-stiff met, failed to cheat, exploit, and brutalize him.

The irony of *The Jungle* was this: Author Sinclair's intent was not to attack the meat packers as such, but to attack capitalism. What *The Jungle* did, however, was not to make converts to socialism, but to convince the great mass of literate Americans it was time they did something to protect their stomachs from the poisons being concocted and fed to them by the Big Four of packers in Chicago. The novel's impact was immediate. There was an uprising of the press all over the nation. The favorite columnist of the era, Mr. Dooley, remarked that he had been unable to "ate annything more noorishin' thin a cucumber in a week."

There was uproar in Congress, too, and an even greater uproar in the White House. President Theodore Roosevelt knew a good safe menace when he saw it; and now he charged head on at the accursed meat packers of Packingtown. The hullabaloo probably speeded enactment of new laws in regard to food.

In all the rumpus about tainted meat in tin cans, George Horace Lorimer did not forget his late friend and employer. The *Saturday Evening Post* quickly began publication of a series of articles, at least signed if not written by J. Ogden Armour, son of the pioneer packer, which attempted to ameliorate the quakings of stomachs other than those of the vegetarians who, incidentally, were having a wonderful time.

Along with Chicago's Big Four of Packingtown were four other men who turned out to be giants of sorts. All four were merchants. Three were orthodox if well above the general run. The other was a heretic of merchants. The three were Potter Palmer, Levi Leiter, and Marshall Field. The maverick was Aaron Montgomery Ward, who never used his first name.

Palmer was first on the scene, being one of the 1852 men who arrived the year railroads established contact with the east coast. On Lake Street he opened a dry-goods store. In little more than a decade he had become one of the city's richest citizens, ready, he thought, to retire. He sold his store to young Field and Leiter, the one from Massachusetts, the other from Maryland. But Palmer did not retire. Instead, he changed the whole business geography of the city.

Business from the first centered on Lake Street. Palmer bought a solid mile of property along the east side of State Street, a district of straggling false fronts. He widened State by twenty feet, then at the corner of Washington erected the finest structure in the city. This he rented to Field and Leiter for their store. He built the first of three Palmer Houses. When the fire of 1871 made a shambles of the town, and seemingly had destroyed Palmer's fortune, he worked furiously to recoup. He put up new and even larger buildings along State Street, and a new Palmer House, a massive thing of Victorian elegance tinctured with pure American whim, such as a barbershop with floor of marble set with silver dollars.

Chicago boomed after the fire as never before. Potter Palmer gained a fortune far larger than his first, and changed the city's geography again by building what some esthete described as the damnedest mansion ever imagined on the North Side, a couple of miles from the great houses of Field, Armour, and other wealthy men who lived on the South Side. The South Siders began at once to move north, possibly because Mrs. Potter Palmer was the ac-knowledged leader of Packingtown's society.

Levi Leiter had neither Field's vision nor his boldness, yet he was a prodigious worker and the two partners made such a success of their store that Leiter was already wealthy in 1881, and did what so many of Chicago's wealthy citizens had done—he "retired" and went into the real estate business. He did very well. One of his daughters married Lord Curzon, viceroy of India. That cost some-thing, but the Leiter fortune was still stout enough to pay off the $9,750,000 loss made by son Joe, when he attempted to corner wheat, and leave enough for Levi to accumulate a notable collec-tion of early American history and literature.

Levi Leiter's partner, of course, became Chicago's greatest mil-lionaire, its "Big Business incarnate," as Lloyd Lewis called him. Few of Horatio Alger's heroes started lower in the scale than Marshall Field, and none of them achieved his wealth. He left home at seventeen to clerk in a village store in Massachusetts. Five years later he arrived in the brawling town in the wild onion bog beside the Chicago River.

Field's first store job in the West paid him four hundred dollars a year. He managed to save half of it by sleeping nights on a straw tick on top of a counter. Then came the partnership with Palmer and Leiter, which Field dominated from the first. He was a one-price merchant. All sales, in the early years, were for cash. Goods were not misrepresented. Unusual courtesy to customers was a strictly enforced rule. Another strictly enforced rule, as Chicago soapboxers took delight in pointing out, was to pay the exact and minimum subsistence wage to employees. One biographer of Field put it this way: Field himself was a fervent advocate of low wages.

Mr. Field had perceived that the storekeeper who depended on jobbers and manufacturers was often at their mercy. They also made profits on what they sold to the merchant. So Field started early to provide his own factories which, in time, were to be found in Spain, Germany, Italy, and Middle Europe. He owned woolen mills in Australia. He controlled silk mills in China, Japan, and India. And he did not ignore products nearer home such, for instance, as the fine lace made in nearby Zion City, Illinois.

Zion City had been founded by John Alexander Dowie as a heaven on earth for his fanatical followers. The cult bloomed for a few years. One of its chief industries was the making of lace. From Nottingham, England, Dowie imported machinery and workers, and the fine product they made was in great demand. But internecine strife followed Dowie's death. Sales of lace slumped. Field bought the Zion plant, commissioned artists of Cluny to create new designs, and soon the industry was turning out not only lace but lace curtains, tablecloths, handkerchiefs in 150 designs.

No middleman, if Field could help it, was to take toll of Field merchandise. Yet, even with this advantage, Field could scarcely have amassed the fortune he did had it not been for his real estate operations and his large interests in other Chicago enterprises such as McCormick reapers, Pullman cars, and the Chicago & North Western Railroad.

Marshall Field was known to comparatively few of his fellow citizens. He may have been the least known of the city's giants. He was almost pathologically shy. More often than not he walked from his home to the store. When he did take his carriage, he always had the coachman drop him off a few blocks away. To drive up at his place of business behind high-stepping horses struck him as ostentatious. He was never known to speak in public, and did not talk much in private.

"Marshall Field," wrote Henry Justin Smith, who was not given to panegyrics, "was the merchant of merchants, the grave, formidable, supremely able citizen who passed fifty years of his life in this rude city and never acquired its rudeness."

The rude city had been very good to him, a fact he recognized in many ways, including nine million dollars for the Field Museum. But the sum was no great injury to his estate. This amounted to something more than one hundred and twenty million dollars, bequeathed to his two grandsons, one of whom, Marshall III, survives in 1953.

In the employ of Marshall Field in the sixties was a lad from New Jersey, Aaron Montgomery Ward. Ward wanted to be a drummer, as traveling salesmen were called. He achieved his ambition with a St. Louis concern for which he ranged the Mississippi Valley, selling goods to country stores.

It happened to be a hard time for rural folk. Young Ward listened to their complaints and was convinced that they did indeed get too little for their produce and paid too much for what they bought. He joined their lodge, the Patrons of Husbandry, or Grange; and joined their discussions of the conditions that gave farmers fifteen cents a bushel for corn and permitted railroads to charge exorbitant rates from farm to market.

By 1871, Ward had accumulated a modest stake and with it set out to open what he called a mail-order house. The great fire of October swept away his small stock of goods. A year later, largely on eight hundred dollars' capital from a bank, he rented the hayloft of a livery stable on Kinzie Street in Chicago and said that Montgomery Ward & Company was open for business. No heed was paid to city trade. In a one-page "catalog" he said that the firm was founded expressly to "meet the wants of the Patrons of Husbandry." It was perhaps the first store to open to so circumscribed a group of customers.

Ward pointed out that he did not pay enormous rent. He would not sell his goods to country merchants. He would have no agents or middlemen. He would buy strictly for cash and he proposed to sell the same way.

The Grangers were quick to patronize Montgomery Ward. Four

years later the Ward catalogue required 150 closely printed pages to describe the Ward merchandise. As an extra service, Ward was selling grain for farmers at the startlingly modest commission of one cent a bushel. He also encouraged Grangers to start their own co-operative stores.

Ridicule, then ferocious attacks met Ward's idea of merchandising direct to consumer by mail. His was not the first mail-order house in the country; Thompson of Connecticut had had the same plan many years before. But Ward was the first to appeal specifically to the rural trade. He was a success from the start.

Ward did not turn the other cheek to the attacks on him by the conventional merchants. He used both catalogue and newspapers to brag that he had saved millions of dollars to consumers who had never spent a penny with Ward. This he had done by forcing country merchants to sell *their* goods "at fair prices." The rest of the Ward story is one of the great legends. Ward had started a trend. His success spawned a host of mail-order houses both great and small. A majority of the larger houses set up shop in Chicago.

Montgomery Ward seems to have had but one interest other than business: he was the watchdog of the lake front. His passion was to keep buildings off the shore of Lake Michigan that sweeps around Chicago. Over many years he spied out and stopped every effort to erect any structure there tall enough to be called a building. It is largely to his efforts, which were patently disinterested so far as gain was concerned, that the city owes its magnificent frontage, including Grant Park. It is a heritage, wrote a historian of Chicago, not "of the privileged few, but of the mass of the people, for whom Ward seems really to have cared."

The lake front was a fine thing to leave Chicago. To it Ward's widow added other gifts, including nine million dollars to Northwestern University, proving, if proof were needed, that selling things to Grangers by mail was not so ridiculous a business as it had seemed to many back in 1872.

It was in Chicago, too, where another fantastic idea materialized into a huge fortune. This was the sleeping car. George Mortimer Pullman did not dream it up originally, but he came to build sleeping cars in such quantities, and to operate them, that his company was a monopoly and "Pullman" a generic name for the product.

Pullman arrived in Chicago from Albion, New York, where he had worked as a cabinetmaker. He had also done well as a contractor, moving many of Albion's brick houses in order that the Erie Canal could be widened there. His first undertaking in Chicago was to raise by several feet the new city's four-story brick skyscraper, the Tremont Hotel. With 5,000 jackscrews and 1,200 men he accomplished the job so well that not a window was broken, a brick displaced, or a drink spilled in the busy bar. The press cheered. People marveled at the feat. Another giant had come to Chicago.

Railroads were the new dynamo of America. They had captivated the imagination, and many young men were inventing things to make travel on them swifter, or safer, or more comfortable. One of these inventors had planned a sleeping car as early as 1829. Another had patented a sleeping car in 1838. The Erie Railroad had tried sleepers in 1843. Now in Chicago, George Pullman wanted to build one. The Alton Railroad gave him two old coaches and told him to see what he could do converting them.

On the night of September 1, 1858, one of these primeval Pullmans made its first run, between Bloomington and Chicago. It was in charge of J. L. Barnes, who had been hired by Pullman himself. Barnes, this first of thousands of Pullman conductors, recalled that he had to compel the passengers to take off their boots before they got into the berths.

The Alton sleepers proved popular, and another was added. But the idea did not spread immediately to other lines. George Pullman was disappointed. Away he went on a mine rush to Colorado. He did not drop the idea, however. In 1864 he applied for and received two patents—one for a hinged upper berth, the other for hinging the back and seat cushions so they could become a part of the lower berth. Both devices remain unchanged in principle to this day.

Pullman returned to Chicago and there spent $20,000 to build a quite gorgeous piece of rolling stock he named the Pioneer. It was a truly imposing sleeping car, with plenty of plush, mirrors, fancy panels, and comfortable berths that could be folded up during the day. The whole rode on improved trucks with springs reinforced by solid rubber blocks. It was also a good foot wider and two feet higher than other cars.

Tradition has it that Mrs. Lincoln requested the Pioneer be attached to the President's funeral train at Chicago. Crews had to work day and night to alter platforms and bridges on the railroad to Springfield to permit its passage. From this incident, so Pullman history has it, came publicity that helped to make a quick success of Mr. Pullman's elegant sleeping car.

George Pullman built more sleeping cars and put them on the Alton, the Michigan Central, the Burlington, the Grand Trunk. He built a combination sleeping and dining car, which he called a Pullman hotel car. A year later he designed the first diner, which he named the Delmonico. In 1870 he staged an event of magnitude, when a complete train, the Pullman Hotel Express, carried a group of Bostonians on the first transcontinental trip to San Francisco —and to the acclaim of the nation. From this point onward there would have been little doubt but that George Pullman was destined for great things.

Most of the early Pullman cars were made in Palmyra, New York, then in Detroit. In 1881, George Pullman founded his own satrapy, the model town of Pullman on the lake shore just south of Chicago. (Some of the capital to build this huge plant came from Marshall Field.) The model community of Pullman was hailed as the start of a new era in the lives of working people.

Somewhat later, however, Pullman rents were seen to be too high, the public services too costly, and the wages of Pullman employees too low. Praise of Pullman ceased. It was now a "company-dominated serfdom operated for company profit."

Pullman was also the headquarters of a monopoly. One after the other George Pullman had either bankrupted his competitors or bought them out. Knight, Woodruff, Flower, Mann, even Wagner, he of the original Palace Car, which was highly successful in the East—they all went down before the Pullman car.

Pullman town grew. So did Chicago. Pullman in time became a part of the big city. George Pullman himself, for all his great contribution to railroading, was in many ways stupid. For one thing, he had lost all sense of time and of proportion. He fancied himself living still in the Middle Ages, a king, almost a god, worshiped by his 20,000 working serfs and their families. This was a mistake. His employees had learned to read the daily papers. Year after year they read that the Pullman Company had paid eight per cent on its stock. Having read which, they asked, one day in 1894, that a recent wage cut be restored. Pullman refused even to discuss such a heresy. The men struck.

Before the Pullman strike, and the supporting strike by members of the American Railway Union—led by Eugene Debs—was done, thousands of federal troops were sent to "keep order" in Chicago.

They were in command of General Nelson A. Miles, who took up his headquarters, significantly, in the Pullman Company Building.

There was a great deal of violence, in Chicago and elsewhere. George Pullman "won" his strike. He died three years later to leave a great fortune and a vastly impaired reputation. His stupidity in 1894 had been of immense, if costly, help in making clear to labor and to the public that the aura of omnipotence which many had believed to surround men of great wealth was somewhat of an illusion.

Chapter 5   MONARCHS OF THE FAR WEST

Because business enterprise on a suitably large scale cannot well operate in a void, notable moguls appeared on the west coast of the United States, two thousand miles beyond Chicago, many years before the vast loneliness of the interior plains and mountains had been eliminated.

Within less than a decade, migration to the Oregon country, and the gold rush of 'forty-nine to California, had attracted a population sufficient to encourage the best efforts of energetic promoters. Henceforth there were two frontiers—the original frontier, still pushing west from the Mississippi, the other pushing east from the Pacific slope. Both California (1850) and Oregon (1859) were admitted as states even before such midwestern commonwealths as Iowa and Kansas, and many years before half a dozen far-western states were formed. Sacramento had a railroad almost as soon as Chicago.

This phenomenal development of a civilization on the far edge of the nation, while the middle of it was still largely a battleground for army troops and Indians, created favorable conditions for acquisitive men of vision.

Among all of the thousands of acquisitive men who came in the rush of 'forty-nine to the new region were four who quickly developed an amazing vision when it was revealed to them by a true prophet. The true prophet was born Theodore Dehone Judah in 1826, the son of a Connecticut clergyman at Bridgeport. The four

ANDREW CARNEGIE

J. P. MORGAN, SR.

disciples were named Huntington, Hopkins, Stanford, and Crocker. These were to become the "Big Four" of authentically western exploitation.

Judah arrived in Sacramento in 1854, as chief engineer for a railroad modestly projected to run from the California capital into the placer mining country of the Sierra foothills. Its twenty-one miles were completed and in operation by February of 1855. It made money from the first.

Judah next engaged in laying the route for a proposed wagon road over the mountains to tap the new silver towns of the Comstock Lode in Nevada[1]. He returned to his base fired with enthusiasm for building not a wagon road but a railroad, and a railroad not just to the silver mines only, but on across the great void to the Atlantic coast. He dropped everything and set about rousing all California to see and share in his vision.

Judah first organized a Pacific Railroad Convention in San Francisco. He went around the Horn to Washington to ask the aid of Congress. Here he was so persuasive that, had it not been for the issue of slavery, which held Congress in thrall, he probably would have got his aid as early as 1859. But the matter was pushed aside and Judah returned to Sacramento.

The young man resumed his survey of his proposed railroad; and one day, just as soon as he had found the mountain pass he wanted, he spread out a sheet of paper on the counter of Dr. Strong's drugstore in Dutch Flat, and there and then composed "The Articles of Association of the Central Pacific Railroad of California." This was the genesis of the western half of the first transcontinental. It was also the genesis of a greater gold mine than any placer in the Sierra hills—though not for Theodore Judah.

Getting capital to begin work on his great project proved difficult. San Francisco's capitalists would have nothing to do with it. In Sacramento, no more than a dozen men attended his meeting. By now he had become wiser; he had seen that his idea of a railroad across the nation was far too big a dream for the local moneyed men. So now he talked about the road as merely one to the Comstock, one, naturally, that could hold a monopoly of the traffic with the booming silver towns of Nevada.

Judah's Sacramento audience could grasp the idea of a monopoly of traffic to and from Nevada. Every day Sacramentans were seeing

---

[1]The story of exploitation of the Comstock will appear in another book of *The Mainstream of America Series*.

the tons of freight starting for Virginia City and the wagonloads of bullion coming out. When the meeting was over, Judah had promises of capital sufficient to permit starting work on the line.

"In later life," wrote Oscar Lewis, "four of Judah's listeners that evening accepted easily the roles of men of vision, who had perceived a matchless opportunity and grasped it with courage. It was a role that none of them deserved." Yet these men, who were the aforesaid Huntington, Hopkins, Stanford, and Crocker, did possess enough sight to follow the path prophet Judah laid out for them, and also had the abilities to create a monopoly not of a jerk-line railroad to the Comstock, but a monopoly so immense and so prehensile as to merit the name given to it later in a famous novel, *The Octopus*.

With his Central Pacific organized on paper, Judah turned again from prophesy to surveying, and spent a year driving his location stakes up through Donner Pass and so into Nevada. Then he went again to Washington to lobby for the Pacific Railroad bill and to open an office in the capital which he called the Pacific Railroad Museum. On July 1, 1862, President Lincoln at last signed the act making the government sponsor of a railroad to be built simultaneously from its two ends, namely the 100th Meridian and the Pacific Coast. Judah sent a joyful telegram to his associates in Sacramento: "We have drawn the elephant. Now let us see if we can harness him up."

The true prophet, having now completed what his associates considered his usefulness, was soon eliminated; and the men who could congeal dreams into reality took charge. Let us consider them briefly.

They were a unique quartet. No other four American men of business worked so closely, if not always harmoniously, to achieve their ambitions. They were distinguished by intelligent co-operation. They recognized the value of specialization; and lost not a moment in assigning to each other the duties to which each seemed best fitted. Charles Crocker weighed 250 pounds, much of it muscle developed over many years as a sawmill laborer, farm hand, and blacksmith. He had come from New York State in 1850, leading a group of young gold seekers across the Plains. But Crocker did not dig long in the ground for gold. He opened a store in Sacramento and operated a freighting outfit. The money rolled in. Crocker had no sign of intellectual interest. He had no nerves whatever. He might have made a great soldier. Instead, he became the

Big Four's construction boss. It is doubtful that any railroad ever had better.

Leland Stanford, son of Yankee emigrants in upstate New York, had practiced law in Wisconsin with no great success. In 1852 he arrived in California broke. His brothers staked him to merchandise, and at Michigan Bluff he opened a store with miners' supplies. Being a lawyer he naturally turned to politics. In 1861 he was elected governor of California, in which position he was able to influence legislative acts that brought at least $825,000 of public money into the meager coffers of the Central Pacific, of which Governor Stanford was president. Stanford was just the man to handle the manipulation of politics and law in the best interests of the railroad, to act as a front man at ceremonies for the driving of golden spikes, and as a deliverer of sonorous platitudes in regard to honor, success, and even honesty. He weighed a full twenty pounds more than heavyweight Crocker. Stanford was also as vain a man as could be found in California.

Mark Hopkins, who should not be confused with the famous educator, was at forty-seven the eldest of the Big Four. Tall, scrawny, and long-bearded, he had a native rustic flavor. He spoke little, and that little mostly in monosyllables. He was a saver of string, a blower-out of lamps, a good man, so it turned out, to have charge of the books and the offices of the Central Pacific. But Hopkins was more than a glorified clerk. His mildness and calm, no matter what happened, made him the keeper of the peace of the quartet, a job he managed with great sagacity.

Collis Potter Huntington was the Big Four's dynamo. Forty years old in 1861, a native of Connecticut, Huntington came West in the van of the forty-niners. Having thoughtfully brought with him several kegs of miners' supplies in the form of whiskey and rum, he sold them at an enormous profit, then got himself a pick and pan and went into the hills he had heard were lined with gold. One day's work devoted to this silly project was enough for Huntington. He sold his equipment and went to Sacramento, where he opened a miners' supplies depot. Mark Hopkins became his partner.

Huntington was indomitable, and notoriously vindictive when crossed. One of his biographers, Stuart Daggett, remarked that Huntington was interested in nothing whatever outside business, and that he was "disposed to resist the idea that his railroad enterprises were to any degree burdened with public obligations." He was the financier of the quartet. He also spent a great deal of time in Washington where, so it has been noted, possibly with under-statement, "his task was well performed." If the Big Four could have been said to have a leader, it was Huntington. He was a man of large stature, well over six feet, who kept his beard well cropped to permit display of a chin of remarkable aggressiveness.

Like the group building the Union Pacific west from Omaha, which let its contracts to the Crédit Mobilier, the Big Four organized their own trick outfit, the Contract & Finance Company, and made a contract with themselves to build the Central Pacific Railroad. Through this convenience, the quartet siphoned off "several millions of dollars" to their personal profit in a short time; and much more later, though the amount was never known because the Central Pacific's books happily disappeared at about the same time a government inquiry got under way.

The overall agreement with the government stated that the Union Pacific should build from Omaha to the California line. The Central Pacific was to build that portion of the line which lay within the state of California. But, said the agreement, whichever outfit should first reach the California line was to continue to build westward or eastward as the case might be.

Land grants and government bonds were to go to each company on a basis of miles of road laid. It was a prize worth making an effort for, and Charlie Crocker, a roaring bull, drove the thousands of Chinese coolies to feats of labor that astounded everybody but Crocker. Up over the Sierras, through terrain that has never ceased to trouble operation of trains, Crocker pushed the grade, then laid the rails. He drove long tunnels for the blasting of which one Swanson, a Swedish chemist, manufactured on the spot a new and eccentric but powerful explosive called nitroglycerin.

By the middle of 1868 Crocker's gangs had reached and passed the state line and were heading across the Nevada desert. The rails met sixty miles west of Ogden, Utah, and whiskey and oratory flowed in equal amounts, while president Leland Stanford picked up a sledgehammer and took a swipe at the alleged golden spike. He missed, but the Central Pacific had missed no opportunity anywhere along the line—not even the opportunity for destroying all records of the Contract & Finance Company. These went up in a fire reported by Central Pacific officials to have been of unknown origin.

The Union Pacific's Crédit Mobilier had displayed no such astuteness, and thus it stewed in scandal while the Central Pacific went gloriously and freely on to other things.

These included purchase of a strictly paper railroad in California called the Southern Pacific, whose title was used a little later to describe the grab bag of small lines the Big Four built or bought and combined with the gold-plated Central Pacific into one system. These "other things" also included getting and retaining control of the California legislature, whom Huntington complained "were the hungriest set of men who ever got together." The Washington gang was hungry too. Huntington made certain that both groups of hungry men got a little something in the way of sustenance, and the Southern Pacific went on from one success to another. And why not? The Southern Pacific's largess to lawmakers sometimes ran to half a million dollars for one session of Congress, and almost half that figure for a helpful meeting of the boys at Sacramento.

There were, of course, several railroads of the Midwest looking for an outlet on the Pacific. The Big Four fought them off, taking possession of all of the mountain passes. Then the Southern Pacific rails started east across Arizona. They reached and passed the Colorado River in spite of United States troops sent there specifically to stop them; and so on to New Mexico and Texas, heading for distant New Orleans, which in time was reached.

The Big Four also looked at the sea, and in the early seventies they organized the Oriental & Occidental Steamship Company, bought ships, and went into competition with the old and well-heeled Pacific Mail.

These four men, dedicated to the proposition that California belonged by right to the Southern Pacific, worked so swiftly that the people of the immense state found themselves bound hand and foot before they knew what had happened. The Big Four charged far and away the highest tariffs in the United States. They gave rebates to certain industries in which they had an interest. Scarcely a human being or a piece of freight moved in all the state that did not somehow pay blackmail to the Southern Pacific. The Big Four were also keeping close watch of events to the north, in Oregon, where a wild maverick named Ben Holladay was on rampage.

For some not easily accountable reason Ben Holladay has never received the attention he deserves in the history of the West. Here was one of the most energetic and adventurous men imaginable, a semi-literate backwoods character from Kentucky, who was not only born in a log cabin but married in one; and by the time he was fifty, required a mansion in Washington, D.C., a gaudily grand piece of architecture and landscaping on the Hudson named Ophir Place, an immense home in Portland, and a rambling great "cottage" at Seaside on the Oregon coast.

Holladay had faults aplenty but they did not include lethargy. After trading with Indians in Kansas, he supplied army troops in the Mexican War, at the end of which he bought a large lot of surplus army goods. Loading fifty big wagons with this merchandise, he led the caravan to Salt Lake City, where Brigham Young himself gave him every aid to selling the stock. With the profits, Holladay purchased a herd of cattle, hired a crew of cowboys, and drove the animals over the mountains into California, where he sold the lot at high prices. Now he had capital to lend to the overland freighting outfit of Russell, Majors & Waddell; and when the firm went broke, he took over their Central Overland California & Pikes Peak Express Company.

Taking direct charge, Holladay displayed genius in reorganizing and improving the property. Under him the overland stagecoach business probably reached its peak. He secured most favorable mail contracts, which paid him better than a million dollars annually. His line had virtual monopoly of passenger traffic between the Missouri River and San Francisco Bay. During the Indian uprisings of the sixties, Holladay suffered terrible losses from marauding warriors. So did the warriors, who died in number from the guns of the tough gang Holladay liked to have around.

Off and on, Holladay made trips to New York, Washington, and California and Oregon cities. He organized the Northern Pacific Transportation Company, operating ships from Alaska to Mexico.

In 1866, when he saw a railroad, the Union Pacific, heading for the west coast, he promptly sold his extensive stagecoach lines and presently turned up in Oregon where, so he had heard, a railroad war was in progress. So there was. The war was between two groups seeking to build south from Portland to the California line, there to connect with a line building north from Sacramento.

Holladay quickly allied himself with the group building up the east side of Oregon's Willamette River. The west-siders never had a chance once Holladay started his generous treatment to legislators and had begun to display his driving force as a construction boss. The rails may not have been well laid, and the bridges patently were not too good, since they were constantly collapsing; but sufficient track was laid to win the federal subsidy of land. To celebrate his victory, Holladay engaged the fine brass band of the Aurora Christian Colony and served an elegant lunch with champagne.

While his railroad pushed on southward, Holladay had time for other matters. He bought a Portland daily paper and used it to boost East Portland which, he said, would, because of his railroad terminus there, soon outstrip Portland itself. Yet, for Portland he built a streetcar line, the first in Oregon. He was a great one for giving free excursions on his steamboats. He was as generous with his own money as he was with the money he got from railroad bonds sold in Germany. Perhaps this was the reason for his downfall. Or possibly he failed because there was not enough traffic along his Oregon & California Railroad. Then came the panic of 1873, which staggered him; and after the panic came Henry Villard, representing the German bondholders who had begun to worry about the O&C. Villard took over the road's assets, which were nowhere nearly so large as its liabilities.

Villard managed to obtain funds to resume building of the Oregon & California, then attempted to sell it to the Big Four. They must not have considered the line quite ripe enough, for they said they were not interested in an Oregon railroad. Meanwhile, Villard, acting for bondholders of the Kansas Pacific, was made receiver of that line. He was beginning to show remarkable talents in the railroad field.

Villard next organized a steamboat and railroad company and started to lay rails eastward across Oregon. With fifty friends who loaned him eight million dollars, he bought control of the Northern Pacific, of which he became president. He finished construction of the Northern Pacific to tidewater at Tacoma.

But this second transcontinental was in financial trouble. Villard was forced to resign. His Oregon & California road went into the hands of a receiver. The Big Four of California were standing by. They saw that the O&C was now ripe with the ripeness of harvest time. It tumbled into their waiting hands on lease, to become the Oregon portion of the Southern Pacific, or "Octopus" railroad.

Well before the century's turn, the Southern Pacific not only dominated all transportation in California; it was believed by the mass of Californians to be indistinguishable from the state itself. It had eyes on everything. Whenever it saw that some new law was needed to further interests of the Big Four, it was promptly drawn up and passed by the well-tamed legislature. County and municipal governments, too, were abjectly ready to do the SP's bidding.

Throughout the 1870s there were minor revolts against this domination. These were put down with a hand so heavy that few newspapers cared to report the events. But in 1880 the people got out of hand. This was the Mussel Slough tragedy. Its inception was in the Southern Pacific's determination to remove those it said were squatters on its lands in the San Joaquin Valley.

The so-called squatters formed a Settlers Rights League to attack by legal means the railroad's alleged right to the lands in question. The effort was defeated at every turn in the legal maze of courts. The Southern Pacific thereupon demanded that a United States marshal dispossess the squatters.

One May day in 1880, the very day which the Settlers Rights League had chosen for a picnic and mass meeting, there came a federal officer with two deputies and one other man who has been called, and not lightly, an *agent provocateur* in the Southern Pacific's pay.

The first farmer to be dispossessed was one Brewer. At his place the marshal and his men were met by a group of farmers. The alleged SP agent started shooting. The farmers shot back. When the smoke cleared, five farmers and two officers lay dead. For this "murder," seventeen farmers were arrested, tried, and found guilty. They were sent to prison. Nothing was done about the five farmers who were killed.

Remember Mussel Slough! became a rallying cry for the farmers of all California. A farmer named Christopher Evans, whose wife's people had been dispossessed in the Mussel Slough affair, turned train robber; and with a partner, John Sontag, began holding up trains in the San Joaquin Valley. For more than four years, these two dedicated men stuck up and robbed one train after another, while an army of railroad police tried frantically to catch them.

Evans and Sontag were cheered on by virtually the whole population of the San Joaquin Valley, and by a great majority of Californians elsewhere. When at last they were taken by a posse that numbered 3,000 men, they were heroes, not because they were robbers but just because they were engaged in "robbing the biggest robbers ever known." Sontag died in his boots. Evans, shot full of holes but still alive, was sent to prison for life. He was paroled in 1911 by Governor Hiram Johnson, no lover of the Southern Pacific.

It was the Mussel Slough affair and many other cynicisms of the Southern Pacific that inspired Frank Norris, who had grown up in California, to write *The Octopus*. In this novel a railroad very much like the Southern Pacific is the overall villain. The most odious characters are the railroad's agents. By then (1901) California newspapers had taken courage. Many of them were attacking the Southen Pacific at every opportunity.

Of the Big Four, Hopkins died in 1876, a little too early to see the SP in fullest flower, yet managing to leave his widow fairly well fixed. At Great Barrington, Massachusetts, she had a little summer home put up for two million dollars, but continued to live much of the year in the big Hopkins mansion on San Francisco's Nob Hill. Charlie Crocker expired in 1888, leaving an estate estimated at forty million dollars. Stanford amused himself by election to the United States Senate where he was able, said Gustavus Meyers, to stifle any feeble attempt of the government to compel the SP to disgorge a penny of its extortions.

Senator Stanford still had a naïve idea of public relations. Tossing twenty-dollar gold pieces to Washington newsboys struck him as about right. But he and his widow did much better; some thirty million dollars of their pile went into the founding of Leland Stanford, Jr., University, dedicated to the memory of a son who had died in 1884.

One of the most enchanting sights of the Stanford campus for many years was a museum wherein were displayed mementos, or perhaps relics is the better word, of the deceased Stanford scion. These included a replica, done in finest china, of Leland Stanford, Jr.'s Last Breakfast. This effort, patently inspired by the Biblical Last Supper, consisted of a couple of eggs (fried on one side, an old alumnus recalls), some bread, a cup of coffee, and a generous portion of sausages. A regrettable change in the taste of university officials, however, resulted later in removal of the ceramic breakfast, and possibly of its destruction.

And another power took pains to do something about the university's dedication. This originally appeared in mosaic on the campus chapel as "To the Memory of Leland Stanford, Jr. and the Glory of God." When earthquake crumbled San Francisco in 1906, it also shook the mosaic work and its legend from the Stanford chapel, to make an imposing pile of shattered crockery. When new mosaic was laid in place, the legend was seen to have acquired new emphasis: the university was rededicated this time "To the Glory of God and the Memory of Leland Stanford, Jr."

Huntington outlived his comrades of the Big Four, and outlived the nineteenth century, dying in 1900. Clews, the Wall Street Pepys, recalled Huntington was a tall, well-built man with a square resolute jaw, a full beard tinged with gray, and keen blue-gray eyes. He wore a black skullcap when in his office. Though for some reason, Clews thought that a stranger "would hardly take him for one of the financial kings of the country," he somehow managed to leave an estate of seventy-five million dollars.

Huntington left no children. A son of his second wife, whom he married when she was thirty-one and he sixty-three, still lived in 1952, in Bethel, Connecticut, as Archer (Worsham) Huntington, an aged man and the last tenuous connection with California's great legend of the Big Four.

Collis Huntington's able nephew, Henry E. Huntington, outlived his uncle by twenty-seven years, during which time he took occasion to marry his uncle's widow. Henry E. sold his large bequest in the Southern Pacific Railroad to Harriman and engaged in collecting rare pictures and rare books to fill the white marble library and museum he caused to be erected at San Marino. These works will be considered in a later chapter devoted to the elegances and bequests of wealthy men.

PART THREE

THE ERA
OF
FRENZIED
FINANCE

Chapter 1 STANDARD OIL IN FULL FLOWER

IT will be recalled that when he moved to New York City, early in the eighties, John D. Rockefeller was all but unknown in the metropolis. Only William H. Vanderbilt of the New York Central Railroad seemed to have any idea about Rockefeller's abilities and associates; and because he did know, Vanderbilt, as related, was able to make a historic statement. "The Rockefeller crowd are mighty smart men," he said, and added, "I guess if you ever had to deal with them you would find *that* out."

John Rockefeller had moved to the big city from Cleveland because he was planning further glories for Standard Oil and thought that New York was the proper place to materialize them. The company was already dominant in its field. Mr. Rockefeller meant that it should flower into a gigantic combination as the first American trust.

The trust was the logical result of Rockefeller's whole philosophy of business. He was one of the few men who understood that the old way of business had passed, the day when purely local concerns, working from limited supplies and for a limited market, could survive. Rapid communication and transportation had changed that. The United States had been changed into a few vast regions bound together by railroads. In the cities, and even in small towns, businessmen saw rivals entering with goods that had formerly belonged to local industry alone. Were not refrigerator cars now permitting Chicago packers to sell their meat in Bangor, Atlanta, Houston, and Seattle? This was the efficient way; and meat was only one of many commodities that were produced in one city and then shipped to ten thousand cities.

John Rockefeller's ambition to found a trust-monopoly cannot be charged wholly to his appetite for money. The man's mind craved order and efficiency, so his several biographers agree, as the drunkard craves alcohol. Hence he sought to eliminate competition. Competition was disorder. Often it was anarchy.

The beginnings of the Standard Oil trust were to be seen in 1879, when stockholders of Standard and all affiliated companies turned their stocks over to three employees of Standard. These three men then legally owned the various companies. This legal fiction was the work of Samuel C. T. Dodd, John Rockefeller's attorney. Through the fiction, Rockefeller and his associates could swear all sorts of things in court and not commit perjury. One can believe, with or without cynicism, that the arrangement was a handy one.

Three years later certain improvements were made. All stockholders in all of the affiliated companies conveyed their stocks in trust to nine trustees, among whom was John Rockefeller. The trustees held in their hands absolute control and direction of the entire fabric. Henceforth, the production of oil would be controlled to meet the demands of the public; and the price the public should pay would also be controlled—from 26 Broadway, where the new offices of Standard Oil had been established.

This was the kind of order John Rockefeller had been working for ever since he bought his first refinery. Here was the first great monster of corporate law, born full-blown and mighty, and without a sound louder than the scratch of a pen.

So quietly was this first trust brought into being that the public scarcely knew of it at all until six years later when the terms of the trust were made known.

Meanwhile, other industries could not help but note and envy the smoothness of Standard Oil's progress from one acquisition to another. Whiskey had been suffering from "overproduction." So had sugar and meat, glass and tobacco. The producers of cottonseed oil were in such desperate straits that they paid Standard $250,000 merely for a copy of its seemingly magical trust agreement. It was the first time the document had been seen outside the board room at 26 Broadway, now become the most famous business address in America.

Not long after the terms of the Standard Oil trust became known, harassment began. Congress passed an act prohibiting combinations in restraint of trade. This was the Sherman Act. The Supreme Court of Ohio declared Standard to be a monopoly. It ordered the Standard Oil Company of Ohio to withdraw from the agreement. On March 21, 1892, Standard's trustees complied. They not only voted Standard of Ohio out of the trust, but dissolved the trust itself. This was done with the best grace in the world. Standard's lawyers had learned about a new law in New Jersey.

Enacted in an effort to bring the state new revenue, the New Jersey act permitted companies incorporated in that state to hold stock in other corporations. This "extension of the privileges of property," to use Frederick Lewis Allen's happy phrase, not only brought many fat fees to New Jersey, it also whelped the first great holding company. This was Standard Oil of New Jersey. Into it went the stocks of all of Standard's constituent companies. The holding company was substituted for the trust. The capital of Standard Oil of New Jersey increased overnight from ten million dollars to a hundred and ten million.

Reflective men had watched the growth of Standard and other corporations with apprehension, and set about to let others know of the dangers they had sighted. Henry George's *Progress and Poverty* suggested that the more we had of the one, the more we seemed to get of the other; and Edward Bellamy's *Looking Backward* described a Utopia that contained no capitalists. Each book was something of a sensation. Both caused hundreds of thousands of Americans who in no manner could be called radicals to question the actions of industrialists and capitalists. Then came Henry Demarest Lloyd's *Wealth Against Commonwealth,* which had a good deal to say about John D. Rockefeller.

The reformers were loose, and S. S. McClure, who meant to be a mogul of magazines, set young Ida Tarbell to writing a history of the Standard Oil Company. This he ran serially in his magazine. It brought the story of big business and monopoly to that large public that did not read books. Out of it, and accompanied by many other attacks, emerged the great whipping boy of capital. He was John D. Rockefeller. He became and remained almost until his death, half a century later, the favorite ogre of the United States.

It seems likely that John D. was selected for the chief villain's part mostly because he was the most consistently successful of all his kind. Surely it wasn't because of his mild personality. It could not have been his aggressiveness, which was never obvious though often felt. Rockefeller was not cocky, like Carnegie. He was not bluntly forthright, like Mark Hanna. He was not assured, in the manner of Gould and Harriman. He was not imperious, like the elder Morgan. All these men were variously assailed and cursed in text and cartoon. Yet to none of them, not even Hanna in the dollar-mark suit of clothes invented for him by cartoonist Homer Davenport, was devoted the barrage of personal abuse that was heaped on the egg-bald head of John D. Rockefeller.

An old-timer of the oil fields, John J. McLaurin, summed it up by saying that every man who failed in the oil business had a tale to tell of how John D. had crushed him. "If a man anywhere in Oildom drilled a dry hole," said McLaurin, "or backed the wrong horse, lost at poker, dropped money speculating, stubbed his toe, ran an unprofitable refinery, missed a train, or couldn't maintain champagne style on lager-beer income, it was the fashion for him to pose as the victim of a gang of conspirators and curse the Standard Oil vigorously and vociferously." Standard Oil automatically conjured up the figure of one man, Rockefeller.

The editor of the *Arena,* a critical magazine, wrote that though there were worse men than John Rockefeller, there was not one who in the public mind so typified "the grave and startling menace to the social order." He had become a symbol. The symbol was a bald-headed, sly-looking, and cadaverous figure, dressed in sinister black, grinning like a death's head, and always performing some cruel act. Stealing money from pretty weeping widows appeared to be among his lesser abominations.

John D. "retired" in 1896. He bought land near Tarrytown, among the Pocantico Hills of New York, and there established the estate upon which he was to live most of the rest of his long life. He still got sustenance chiefly from milk and graham crackers. He neither smoked nor took liquor or wine. He read little. His favorite authors were Artemus Ward and Ella Wheeler Wilcox. He played considerable golf, and had the reputation of never cheating on his score. He once told George Harvey exactly what, more than any other one thing, had contributed to Standard Oil's success. "We never," said he, "deceived ourselves."

Rockefeller also said something else that is remembered, when he told his Sunday school class, "It is wrong to assume that men of immense wealth are always happy."

The attacks on Rockefeller continued after his retirement, and became so bitter and numerous that John T. McCutcheon of the Chicago *Tribune* was moved to give the old man a break. He drew a cartoon that showed Rockefeller standing before a large news-stand that displayed nothing but two score different magazines and papers all bearing either John D.'s name or his likeness. In the caption Rockefeller is asking plaintively of the newsdealer: "Have you got something to read that is not about me?"

His son, John D., Jr., entered the office at 26 Broadway in 1897, fresh from college. As quiet and modest, and as pious as his father, young Rockefeller began his business life with both the prestige and the curse of his father on his shoulders. It seems agreed that John D., Jr., as he came to be known, was quite ap-palled at the continuous war on the old man, and on Standard, too, and from the first worked to bring it to an end.

When he retired in 1896, John D., Sr.'s personal fortune could hardly have exceeded two hundred million dollars. It had been made mostly from kerosene. Amassing it had taken some thirty years. In the next fourteen years after 1896, the old man's fortune was more than quadrupled because of the internal combustion en-gine, which burned gasoline. Both kerosene and gasoline have their sources in petroleum.

The so-called retirement of John D. Rockefeller caused no per-ceptible change in the affairs of Standard Oil. All of its several helmsmen were competent. William Rockefeller, Rogers, Flagler, Archbold, these and lesser-known Standard men could steer a true if not always a direct course. Indirection was necessary, anyway.

Then, there was James Stillman, often called the Rockefeller banker. He had been born in Texas of well-to-do Yankee parents who for seven generations had engaged in maritime trade. The Stillmans of Texas moved to New York in 1855, when James was five. He went to work for a mercantile house. At twenty-one he was head of the family in charge of the million-dollar estate left by his father. He first met William Rockefeller as a fellow director of a railroad. (Both of his daughters were to marry Rockefeller's sons.)

At the urging of William Rockefeller, Stillman accepted the presidency of the National City Bank, one of New York's smaller institutions. Within a short time, Stillman had brought it to first place in the city, and later to first place in the United States.

James Stillman was a small, elegant man, like Carnegie vain of his small feet, who perhaps had the largest wardrobe of any of the masters of capital. He was coldly handsome. Though allied from the first with the Rockefeller crowd, he was spiritually closer to J. Pierpont Morgan. The two became fast friends and both, who had inherited wealth, seemed to look with disdain upon their associates, who had merely worked to earn *their* money. Both men were good haters. Morgan hated, among others, John D. Rockefeller. Morgan and Stillman both hated Carnegie. Yet it was said of Stillman that he was never rude to a man of importance.

Stillman was perhaps the perfect banker. He was a chilly character both in business and socially. He was shy, reticent, as detached and abstract, said his biographer John K. Winkler, as a force in nature. He had a genuine hatred of personal publicity. The public knew him not at all, and it was left to a son and a daughter-in-law to put the Stillman name on the front pages of American and Canadian newspapers by way of a divorce action that made favorite reading in the 1920s.

Stillman's right-hand man was even less known. He was John W. Sterling, Yale 1864, who entered the bar in New York and became chief counsel for National City Bank. His office was a shabby affair. It contained only a small table, two chairs, and a hatrack; yet in these unlikely premises some of the biggest Wall Street deals were planned.

Sterling himself was a crotchety little man. He was fanatically precise. Clients who were one minute late had to return another day. His sole vice, he said, was membership in the Union League Club, an institution he often boycotted for weeks at a time when he had happened to find a chair out of place in the club's library, or had been served an inferior meal. He never married. He was believed by many to be the foremost corporation lawyer in the country. James Stillman seldom made a move without first consulting him; and it happened that Stillman's moves never failed to make National City more powerful than before, or Stillman richer. Sterling himself accumulated a fortune of twenty million dollars, which he left to Yale.

It was the Rockefeller crowd, rather than John D., that was closely allied with James Stillman. The crowd did not operate as Standard Oil, and only on occasion did John D. himself take part in its activities. At the crowd's disposal were the vast stores of "idle" capital of Standard Oil, and other stores of capital in the National City vaults. Idle capital to men like Henry H. Rogers and William Rockefeller and John Archbold and Henry Flagler meant dollars that were sweating no more, say, than six per cent. To them idle capital was as revolting to contemplate as empty freight cars were to a Harriman or a Vanderbilt. Hence the entry of the Rockefeller crowd into fields other than oil.

Wall Street's Henry Clews began to notice the crowd early in its career. He called it the "Standard Oil combination," and remarked that into their stock market operations they had introduced "the same quiet, unostentatious and resistless measures that they had always employed theretofore in the conduct of their corporate affairs." This was merely Clews's orotund way of saying that you could never tell where the Rockefeller crowd would strike.

Clews admired the crowd's power and ability even while he feared them. With them, said he, the manipulation of stocks ceased to be mere speculation. "Their sources are so vast," he commented, "that they need only concentrate on any given property in order to do with it what they please." This utter absence of chance was what made the Rockefeller combination so terrible to contemplate. Beside this group, Clews explained, every other man or combination of men that had ever operated in the Street was "belittled in comparison."

The Rockefeller-National City gang were indeed powerful. Their investments and speculations were many and complicated. Among them were the Mesabi iron ore properties, public utility outfits in many states and cities, Amalgamated Copper, of which more later, and numerous railroads, including the Everett & Monte Cristo, in northern Washington, which the group built to tap a mountain said to be almost wholly composed of gold. It wasn't, and this particular speculation had to be charged off as twelve million dollars' worth of experience.

This is perhaps the place to give some notice to the extracurricular activities of these Standard Oil magnates. William Rockefeller, as indicated earlier, was almost the opposite of his brother. Bill was known favorably as a regular guy. He knew and told stories about the drummer and the farmer's daughter. He used tobacco. He drank well. He raced horses. There was not an ounce of piety in him. Most everyone preferred to deal with Bill rather than John.

Bill Rockefeller and Henry H. Rogers got along famously together. These two probably had as much to do with running Standard Oil after John D.'s retirement as anybody, save perhaps for Henry Flagler. Flagler, who continued active almost to the end of his life, was believed by many to dominate the company after John

D.'s departure. It will be remembered that Flagler was one of the old man's first partners. It was he who had conceived things like the fantastic piracy of the South Improvement Company and also thought up other ways to make Standard impervious to competition—or, rather to eliminate competition.

Flagler's enormous interests in Standard Oil, and his occasional fliers with the crowd, were not enough to keep him occupied. In middle life he embarked on a project in Florida, where on a visit he had been charmed with the scenery and the climate and appalled at the poor hotels and the worse railroads. He organized the Florida East Coast railway, which he extended from Miami to Key West, one of the great engineering feats of the time. He built a string of big luxury hotels. He built schools, hospitals, and churches. His investments, and donations, in Florida came to exceed forty million dollars. He was at least the godfather of Florida as a winter playground.

Flagler was filled with energy, and with virility, almost to the end of his days. At seventy-one he was named corespondent in a divorce case. In 1901, possibly at Flagler's urging, the Florida legislature passed an act making incurable insanity a cause for divorce. Flagler thereupon divorced his wife, and ten days later married a much younger woman. Flagler's old partner, eating graham crackers in the Pocantico Hills, must have found these latter-day doings of his cherished friend most unseemly.

John Archbold, of course, continued to handle judges, lawyers, legislatures, and Congress, all to the end that Standard Oil should be permitted to increase and multiply. One of his most helpful creatures in Congress was Representative Joseph Sibley of Pennsylvania, who posed as a reformer yet seemed more often than not to champion the harried trusts. Senators Quay, Penrose, and Foraker were also good friends of Archbold.

Archbold's only weak spot, it turned out, was one of his messenger boys, Willie Winkfield. Needing cash, Willie and a file-clerk accomplice stole a batch of Archbold's letters which they thought might be of interest to some newspaper or another. Hearst's New York *American* was glad to pay Willie and his chum $20,500 for the loot, but did not print the letters. Mr. Hearst kept them secret for a few years, then published them to drive Senator Foraker out of office.

The letters proved that John Archbold of Standard Oil bought congressmen and senators and paid them moderately well. "My dear Senator Quay," he wrote on one occasion. "Not because I think we should, but because of your enticing ways, I enclose your certificate of deposit for $10,000."

Throughout the nineties and into the new century, Archbold had his hands full, for the war on Standard increased in ferocity. Standard usually won its battles, even when it technically lost them, as, for instance, the Texas affair. The state of Texas became indignant about a local oil firm operated under style of Waters-Pierce Company, charging it was no more than a sheep in the coyote's clothing of Standard. Criminal indictments were brought against John Rockefeller and a number of his associates. After much noise, a division agent of Standard was convicted. He was fined fifty dollars. Cynics thought it a good joke on the laws of Texas and of the United States generally.

Then the attorney general of Missouri started prosecution of Standard for violation of state laws, alleging it was operating bogus independents. Still another attack was directed at Standard of Indiana. Then came a dozen or more separate attacks. These continued without cease until 1911, when dissolution of Standard of New Jersey, the holding company, was affirmed by the United States Supreme Court.

The case had moved sluggishly through lower courts for many years. Now the highest court of all decreed that within thirty days, Standard of New Jersey must divest itself of all its subsidiaries. The many pages of testimony seemed to say that the holding company was a monopoly.

Most of the press was elated. For once, big black headlines were cheerful; the enemy, the arch-enemy of all decent men, had been defeated. Cartoonists went wild. The wizened figure of their favorite villain, old John D., complete with back skullcap, was shown *this* time being crushed by common people armed with the Sherman Anti-Trust Act. It was quite wonderful.

Standard of New Jersey went ahead and with no fuss divested itself, as ordered by the Supreme Court. When it was done, there were thirty-eight separate Standard Oils, or affiliates, each under management of its own board of directors instead of the directors of Standard of New Jersey.

It soon became quite clear, too, that there was no shadow of competition among the thirty-eight companies. The major stock in them all belonged to a small group of men. The same men who had controlled Standard's empire through the New Jersey holding company, now controlled it through absolute control of the several companies.

The net result of the interminable war was to raise the stock market valuation of Standard Oil's empire from $663,000,000 to $885,000,000. The cynics laughed again. Yet, as John T. Flynn pointed out, the increase in value was wholly within reason. Unlike so many enterprises, which increased their size with watered stock, Standard Oil had been capitalized *under* its real assets. There was no water in Standard. It was all oil.

Among Rockefeller interests outside the oil business was the profitable Colorado Fuel & Iron Company operating twenty-four mines in the Rockies. During the summer of 1913, miners sent the company a demand for certain reforms in working conditions. The company did not deign to notice it. In September the miners struck. A county sheriff and more than three hundred deputies, most of whom turned out to be employees of the Baldwin-Felts Detective Agency, noted for its strikebreaking activities, moved in "to protect company property." The strikers had set up their camp at Ludlow, just off company land.

Clashes between the opposing forces began and continued through October, when the governor of Colorado called out the National Guard. Order of a sort was restored. But nothing had been settled.

Police filled the filthy jail at Trinidad with strikers, including the celebrated Mother Jones, a rebel dating back to Haymarket Riot times. Writs of habeas corpus were denied on the grounds of military necessity. The winter wore on, marked by more clashes. Spring came, and with it a determination of the strikers to make a major effort.

On April 20, 1914, an all-day battle took place. Militia staged a raid on the strikers' camp, a collection of tents and jerry-built huts, and set it afire. One of the strike leaders was shot and killed. When the smoke cleared, strikers found their camp in ruins and in the ruins the charred bodies of two women and eleven children.

The striking miners went mad. A call to arms swept the district. Next day large mobs rushed through the region, burning and wrecking. The great Empire mine was set afire. Three mine guards were killed by strikers' gunfire. A day later, the Forbes mine started to burn. Nine more guards were killed. Another guard was killed later that day. Federal troops arrived and soon brought comparative order.

John D. Rockefeller, Jr., was a director of the Colorado Fuel & Iron Company. When press and public exploded in anger over the "Ludlow Massacre," he was automatically singled out for denunciation. Editorials and cartoons pictured him as responsible for what it was agreed was "this odious survival of labor conditions supposed to be extinct."

John D., Jr., was stunned. It is unlikely he knew anything about the primeval working conditions at Colorado Fuel & Iron or had sensed that the company's attitude toward labor was outmoded. He was thoroughly shocked at the attack on him personally, and only a little less shocked at the fury of the attack on the company of which he was a director.

It was perhaps the first time the younger Rockefeller was made to realize the hatred engendered by his father and Standard Oil over a period of many years. It had been accumulating, and now John, Jr., saw the storm rise with acute horror.

Young Rockefeller was determined not only to change the feudal attitude of Colorado Fuel & Iron, but to do something toward removing the curse attached to the name of Rockefeller. He engaged a sort of genius, Ivy Ledbetter Lee, to advise him in regard to relations with the public. It is improbable he ever took a more important step. He took it strictly on his own initiative, too, for the old man was against it. The years that had rolled over John D., Sr.'s head had made no change in his social philosophy, which in 1914 was as antiquated as the kerosene lamp. But he put no obstacle in the younger man's way; if John D., Jr., could learn only by experience, then let him.

That public opinion was something that he ought to deal with had never entered the senior Rockefeller's mind. To him the public meant a customer. It was important to give the customer the best of oil and the best service. That ended the matter. When the public abused him, as it had almost since men could remember, he merely took shelter from it "in his scorn."

Any account of great corporations since about 1912 is inadequate without mention of Ivy Lee. He was born in Georgia in 1877, son of a Methodist minister who was also a man of great talents. (One of the elder Lee's several books, *The Earthly Footprints of Christ and His Apostles,* sold more than one million copies.) Ivy migrated North to attend Princeton, where he got his A.B. in 1898, together with a prize of five hundred dollars. This money he used for further schooling, at Harvard Law for a time, then at Columbia. He worked on New York City newspapers until 1903, when he took charge of publicity for the Citizens Union, a group that successfully backed Seth Low for mayor. Lee's propaganda work in this hot campaign is said to have been not only most effective, but subtle—something seldom before achieved in political literature.

In 1912 the Pennsylvania Railroad hired Lee for a new job, which Lee himself said was a public relations counsel. Here, according to his biographer, he advocated absolute frankness between company and the public. When a serious wreck occurred, Lee loaded a special train with newspapermen and took them to the scene, a bold step in contrast to railroad orthodoxy which held that the thing to do about a wreck was to "keep it out of the papers," or at least do everything possible to minimize casualties.

Lee's refreshingly original work for the Pennsylvania caught the attention of other concerns, and soon he was advising the boss men of Bethlehem Steel, of the Guggenheims, of Chrysler. Then, in 1914, Lee had come to John D. Rockefeller, Jr.

With angry cries of Ludlow Massacre still on the air, Lee engaged William Lyon MacKenzie King, a former Minister of Labor of Canada, to go to Colorado to study Colorado Fuel & Iron's difficulties. King did so, and drew up a plan for reform. John D., Jr., eloquently urged his fellow directors to adopt it. It was adopted, though with no approval from John, Sr.

In spite of the hostility of labor unions, MacKenzie King's plan worked out pretty well, and was copied by other corporations. King also successfully treated the still strong animosity of miners who had been in the Ludlow affair.

In due time MacKenzie King returned to his native Canada, which was soon to make him premier.

Ivy Lee continued his subtle work to erase from the Rockefeller name not only the stains of Ludlow, but the deep soot that had been accumulating since John D., Sr., had started to bring "order" into the oil business half a century before. To Lee has been credited the complete cleansing and refurbishing of the elder Rockefeller. One of his most effective contributions to this end was the shiny-dime idea. The old man was kept supplied with bright new ten-cent pieces. At decent intervals, John D. would present a shiny dime to some shrewdly selected person. The recipient might be some poor country boy with well-tanned cheek whose shoes, if a picture was wanted for the papers, had been thoughtfully removed for the occasion; or it might be some business magnate, or prominent newspaper editor, or actor, or any other character of some eminence.

Old John D.'s shiny dimes came to be cherished as souvenirs of America's richest man. Somehow or other, they were a homely touch, though exactly why they were so effective is not clear on any rational ground.

These dimes had something to do with old John D.'s steady rise in public esteem. Ivy Lee's carefully written and carefully planted magazine and newspaper articles also helped. They pointed out, and truly, that the old man possessed the characteristics of pioneer America, namely, frugality, piety, attention to business, and generosity.

Rockefeller's vast donations to religion, medicine and education, and even international relations, after 1913 by way of the foundation bearing his name, and which will be mentioned in the proper place, were also of incalculable aid in placing the Rockefellers, father and son, in a light other than that of public enemies.

And lo, even as the public watched, old John D. changed from the most villainous capitalist in history into a smiling, twinkling, genial, and simple old gentleman, given to patting little boys on the head and presenting them with new dimes. (I myself recall hearing discussion of this miracle in logging-camp bunkhouses, where old-time Wobblies, members of the IWW who had gone to Ludlow to support the striking miners, were still bitter. They were inclined to charge the entire metamorphosis to the idiocy of a public that could be so easily bamboozled by the sly efforts of "Poison Ivy" Lee, bullcook and dogrobber for corporate bodies.)

John D. Rockefeller lived ninety-eight years. He died in 1937, a time when all of the industrial giants of his youth, and even of his late manhood, had already departed. He was the last of his generation, almost the last of his species. How much he was "worth" is probably beyond knowing, for his fortune in later years piled up faster than he could give it away. Gustavus Meyers estimated that Rockefeller's personal fortune was somewhere around one billion dollars.

Biographer Flynn believed that Rockefeller's, of all the great fortunes, was the most honestly acquired. He had dealt honestly with his associates, his employees, his customers. His offenses had been committed "almost wholly against his competitors." (Well, competitors are people too.) Flynn also compared Rockefeller most favorably with "the group of stockjobbers like Morgan and Gates. . . ."

These stockjobbers must now be considered for the leading parts they played in organizing the first billion-dollar company, in the United States or anywhere else, under style of the United States Steel Corporation.

Chapter 2   THE STEEL TRUST

I N whose febrile mind was originally conceived the United States Steel Corporation will never be clear. It was the second great consolidation in American industry and, like Standard Oil, was termed a trust. At the moment of its birth, formally announced on April 1, 1901, it was capitalized at $1,402,000,000. It was thus a monster larger than the oil trust.

It seems quite possible that the success of Standard Oil would have sparked in many alert imaginations the idea of a similar merging of steel interests. But no matter the originator, it was Charles M. Schwab, Andrew Carnegie's manager, who first stated the proposition with an eloquence no other American industrialist could match.

Schwab's hypnotic yet energizing eloquence was delivered to an after-dinner audience of important bankers. It was directed specifically at one of their number, who was J. Pierpont Morgan. Morgan, fired by the vision Schwab had laid before him, thereupon "put together," to use the vulgar phrase of John W. Gates, the United States Steel Corporation.

Such is the popular account of the forming of a company which half a century later has 300,000 employees and does an annual business approaching three billion dollars. Like most such capsule accounts, this one contains truth but it makes the event far too simple and also misses the many instructive and entertaining events that led up to the historic after-dinner speech.

United States Steel was born of a war between men who have been called the Titans of finance and industry. It started in 1898, or perhaps a year earlier, and lasted three years. Much of the struggle was conducted submarine style. Only when a torpedo went off, to send spume flying in newspaper headlines, did the public know which side was staging a raid.

Perhaps the man most responsible for starting the war in the first place was that Falstaffian character, John Warne Gates, who was born of Yankee parents in 1850 on the Illinois frontier. Gates, said one who knew him, was a rollicking soul compounded of all the failings and all the virtues, a sort of latter-day Jim Fisk. "Bet-a-million Gates" was his popular nickname. He had earned it by his readiness to gamble on anything offered by the faro bank, the roulette wheel, the stock market.

Gates began to show his talents in 1878, when he went to Texas as salesman for barbed wire. The product was new. Texas cattlemen were skeptical. Gates wasted no time talking about his line. At San Antonio, he had a barbed-wire corral built, then issued a challenge to ranchers. Bring in your meanest, wildest longhorns, he jeered, and turn them loose in it. This kind of fence will stop and hold them. It is as light as air, stronger than whiskey, and cheaper than dirt.

The event turned into a sort of primeval rodeo. There was bull-dogging and roping, and a good deal of hard liquor. Bands played. Then forty big steers were herded into the Gates corral and stampeded. They bellowed and thundered in all directions. They also bounced off the barbed wire a couple of times. Then they stood still, and well away from the murderous barbs. Gates had brought a revolution to Texas. His only trouble thereafter was to get sufficient wire to fill the orders that inundated him.

John Gates was no man to be content with commissions on sales. He quickly set up a manufacturing plant of his own. It turned out a lot of barbed wire, too, even though he often had to move it across state lines to prevent closure because of court actions against Gates's infringement of basic patents. It survived, however, and Gates bought interest in other wire plants. In 1880 he set about "putting together," as he liked to call it, a sort of barbed-wire trust which, eight years later, became the American Steel & Wire Company of New Jersey, capitalized at ninety million dollars. This was the giant in its field, yet Gates was hungry for bigger things.

He next became president of Illinois Steel, which supplied some of the crude metal to Gates's wire mills. Here he thought he saw possibilities for a huge steel combination that would encompass everything from ore to the refined products of steel. Gates seldom thought long upon anything without acting. With the legal aid of Elbert H. Gary, a corporation lawyer of great ability and of almost unendurable sanctimoniousness, Gates proposed a merger of Illinois Steel, two smaller steel companies, the Minnesota Iron Company, and the Elgin, Joliet & Eastern Railway. This, he figured, would make an overall concern second only to Carnegie's empire. To handle the deal, Gary went to J. Pierpont Morgan.

Morgan was agreeable, but said that Gates must go. "I don't think property is safe in his hands," he said. Gates withdrew from activity in the merger, but retained his stock in the new outfit, Federal Steel, whose assets were approximately fifty-six million dollars and its capitalization almost four times its assets. Stock-rigging performed by agents of the House of Morgan sent Federal shares up sharply. Gates sold his stock for half a million dollars and turned to other things. Judge Gary, as he liked to be called, became president of Federal Steel.

Now came the brief war with Spain, during which both the Carnegie and the Federal concerns did a rushing business, having observed a gentlemen's agreement about prices. With the postwar lull, Carnegie reverted to character which, so far as the steel industry was concerned, has been likened to that of a hyena. The comparison is hardly apt. What it attempts to convey is merely that the little Scot ignored the gentlemen's agreement and cut prices of steel. In a short time he had broken the steel-rail pool by underselling the market.

Noting which, Judge Gary of Federal Steel urged his master, Morgan, to buy out Carnegie. Mr. Morgan, a good hater always, refused. He said he did not like Carnegie. He said Carnegie likely wanted to sell. He added that he did not want to give Carnegie the satisfaction of buying. But Mr. Morgan had come to like the steel business, and now he picked up several small concerns and made them into the National Tube Company.

Other consolidations were taking place. John Gates had added new firms to his American Steel & Wire. The Moore brothers, who had already formed National Biscuit and Diamond Match, now collected 265 tin-plate mills into a single corporation.

It was known in the trade that Carnegie and his great manager Frick were fighting an internal war. The falling out was variously reported to have come from the price of coke Frick charged the Carnegie plants, from the price of a piece of ground Frick had bought on Carnegie Steel account, and from the disease of greatness common to both men. Carnegie started to oust Frick. Frick sued. Carnegie sued. Frick prepared to present evidence in court that would have shown the *real,* not the published, profits of the Carnegie Steel Company. These were based in part on steel produced at twelve dollars a ton and sold for $23.75 a ton, behind a high tariff wall "to protect our American industry and our workers from cheap foreign steel."

The revelations promised by Frick would probably have been too much even for the comparatively crude sensibilities of 1900. The quarrel was patched up, though the two men never spoke again. Frick resigned as manager. Young Charlie Schwab was put in charge.

Andy Carnegie was enjoying his oatmeal and his bagpipers at his laird's castle of Skibo in Scotland, in the early summer of 1900, when the first subterranean rumblings of trouble were heard. Cables from Pittsburgh began to bring bad news. It appeared that the new combine, Morgan's National Tube, whose several component parts had always bought their billets from Carnegie, were about to erect their own blast furnaces and rolling mills, which would of course manufacture steel billets.

Next, John W. Gates, head of American Steel & Wire, who had bought much raw material from Carnegie, notified the Scot that henceforth he would manufacture his own steel.

Then came word from the Moore brothers' gigantic tin-plate trust that they would need no more Carnegie steel; they could get what they needed elsewhere.

It possibly struck Carnegie that "elsewhere" might have reference to the brand-new Federal Steel Company backed by Morgan.

In 1900 Andrew Carnegie was sixty-five years old, just the right age to protect his steel empire from the encroachments of these new enemies. The flag soon came down from atop Skibo Castle, for the laird had left his glens and was heading for Pittsburgh. And at Pittsburgh, even if only figuratively, the Carnegie battle flag went up. What followed in the next few months surely was war.

Sensing correctly that the strategy of the forces opposing him was first to ruin the Carnegie empire before moving in to force its sale at a bargain rate, little Andy told the press that the Carnegie Steel Company was due for a vast expansion, in keeping with the growth of the United States.

Soon Carnegie agents appeared at Conneaut, on Lake Erie, to purchase 5,000 acres of waterfront property. Contracts were let, or allegedly were let, to build a plant costing twelve million dollars. This plant, said Mr. Carnegie, would manufacture nothing except steel tubing, and the product, though of the finest, would be made so cheaply, due to improved processes, that it would break the vicious monopoly held by (Morgan's) National Tube trust. Ten thousand men were to have jobs in the Conneaut plant.

Within a short time, Carnegie called the newspaper boys of Pittsburgh to his office and said he would begin construction at once on "the largest steel-rod plant in the world, right in Pittsburgh." The Carnegie steel rods would naturally be the finest rods ever seen, and they would serve to break the unspeakable monopoly of rods held by an unnamed trust.

When another few weeks had passed, the American railroad world was astonished, and part of it alarmed, to read that Mr. Carnegie, through happy arrangements with George Gould's Western Maryland Railroad, was to extend Carnegie's own Bessemer Railroad from Pittsburgh to a junction with the other, and thus give Carnegie plants an outlet to the Atlantic seaboard other than those of the Baltimore & Ohio and the Pennsylvania railroads. These two lines, due to Mr. Morgan's "community of interests" idea, had recently worked so closely, and agreed so well on vital matters, that their identical freight charges to the Carnegie Steel Company had been almost doubled.

Mr. Carnegie referred to the B&O and Pennsylvania community of interests as strangulation of industry, and pointed out that soon the Carnegie-Gould line would carry Carnegie Steel products to market at much lower cost.

Seemingly as an afterthought, a sort of footnote to his other plans, Carnegie let it be known that "because present rates for transporting ore" were so villainous, he thought he should start soon to build a fleet of ore carriers for his own use.

All of this happened during a few months of 1900. It was big news. It sounded fine to the thousands of steelworkers. But to steelmasters and railroad operators, as well as to bankers who had heavy investments in steel and rails, it was madness. Wars between nations were all right; they brought "prosperity." But not wars between steelmakers or among railroads.

J. Pierpont Morgan, who had a great deal of money in steel, and even more in railroads, did not like the look of it. He was heard to complain that Carnegie was "demoralizing" both railroads and steel. Gates and Gary had long been urging the financier to buy out Carnegie and build a real monster of a corporation. By now Morgan had become sufficiently worried to ask Charlie Schwab, Carnegie's manager, to come and have a talk. Schwab ignored the summons.

Such were conditions along the hostile front when the Schwab Dinner was staged. It was an event worthy of the capitals so often used for it.

The dinner was held on December 12, 1900, in New York City. Charles Schwab, president of Carnegie Steel, was the guest of honor. The hosts are remembered as two bankers, J. Edward Simmons and Charles Stewart Smith. Why they should honor Schwab at this moment has been explained as an expression of appreciation. The bankers had recently visited Pittsburgh, where Schwab had taken them through the Carnegie plants and otherwise acted as a charming host. The dinner has also been credited, without any proof, to the desire of Mr. Morgan to meet Mr. Schwab. It has even been charged that Carnegie himself arranged the matter.

In any case here, gathered around the festive board at the University Club of New York City, were some eighty leaders of finance and industry. Mr. Morgan was placed next to the guest of honor, Mr. Schwab. When the dinner, which has been loosely described as a sumptuous collation, was done, Mr. Schwab arose to pass a few remarks. He opened his speech, as always, by saying that because he knew absolutely nothing about anything except steel, he would talk about steel. Then his organ-like voice wafted his listeners away from the coffee and cigars and took them high up on the mountain top.

Here on the mountain, Charlie Schwab, almost thirty-eight years old, spread before the assembled colossi the splendor of the universe of steel as he envisioned it could be. It was a dazzling prospect. It was a new one to most if not all of his audience. The young steelmaster showed that steel's future belonged to the United States. American ore resources could not be equaled elsewhere on earth. American methods of manufacture excelled all others. They had put the price of steel within the reach of all. Yet, he was sure, said Mr. Schwab, that the lowest possible price had not been reached. This being so, then how could further savings in manufacture be achieved?

For the life of him—Mr. Schwab went on—for the very life of him, he could not see how improved machinery or improved chemical processes could add much if anything to the technology current in the better plants. No, gentlemen, if cheaper steel is to be made, then it must come from something other than technology. (Mr. Morgan, right under the flow of Charlie Schwab's words, was seen to be abstractedly cudgeling his unlighted cigar.)

The speaker considered first one, then another possibility for lowering the price of steel, and dismissed them as visionary. But at last he came to a gleam of hope, a hope that grew magnificently, even as the bankers listened, into a full-blown opportunity. The thing could be accomplished by consolidation, then specialization. If all, or a goodly part of the whole American steel industry were merged into one great corporation, it could then make wondrous savings. Each mill would be a specialty mill—one for rails, one for tubes, one for beams, and the same for wire, nails, and every last product imaginable.

Why, gentlemen, the great company which the speaker had the honor to manage—this biggest maker of steel on earth had recently discovered its own incompleteness. It turned out vast tonnages of steel but was not equipped to transform the crude metal into articles of daily need.

(Mr. Morgan continued to gaze intently at the Morgan plate and to belabor his still unlighted cigar.)

On went the mellifluous voice that had soothed the riotous Bohunks of Homestead and had already hypnotized the masters of capital. Only a corporation infinitely larger than anything in existence, said Mr. Schwab, could place the steel industry on a really scientific basis. Such a corporation must *not* be a mere monopoly for the restriction of output and the increase of prices. No, a thousand times no! The ambition of this consolidation should be to put prices down to the lowest possible level.

Thus ended, on a note of high purpose, the most celebrated speech ever delivered by an American industrialist.

After the applause had subsided, says Carnegie's biographer Hendrick, it was clear Mr. Morgan was profoundly impressed. "He took Schwab by the arm and led him to a corner. For half an hour the two men engaged in intimate conversation." Mr. Morgan then left for home, and Mr. Schwab "took the midnight train for Pittsburgh." The viable germ of the United States Steel Corporation had been implanted in Old Money Bags.

THOMAS W. LAWSON

HENRY H. ROGERS

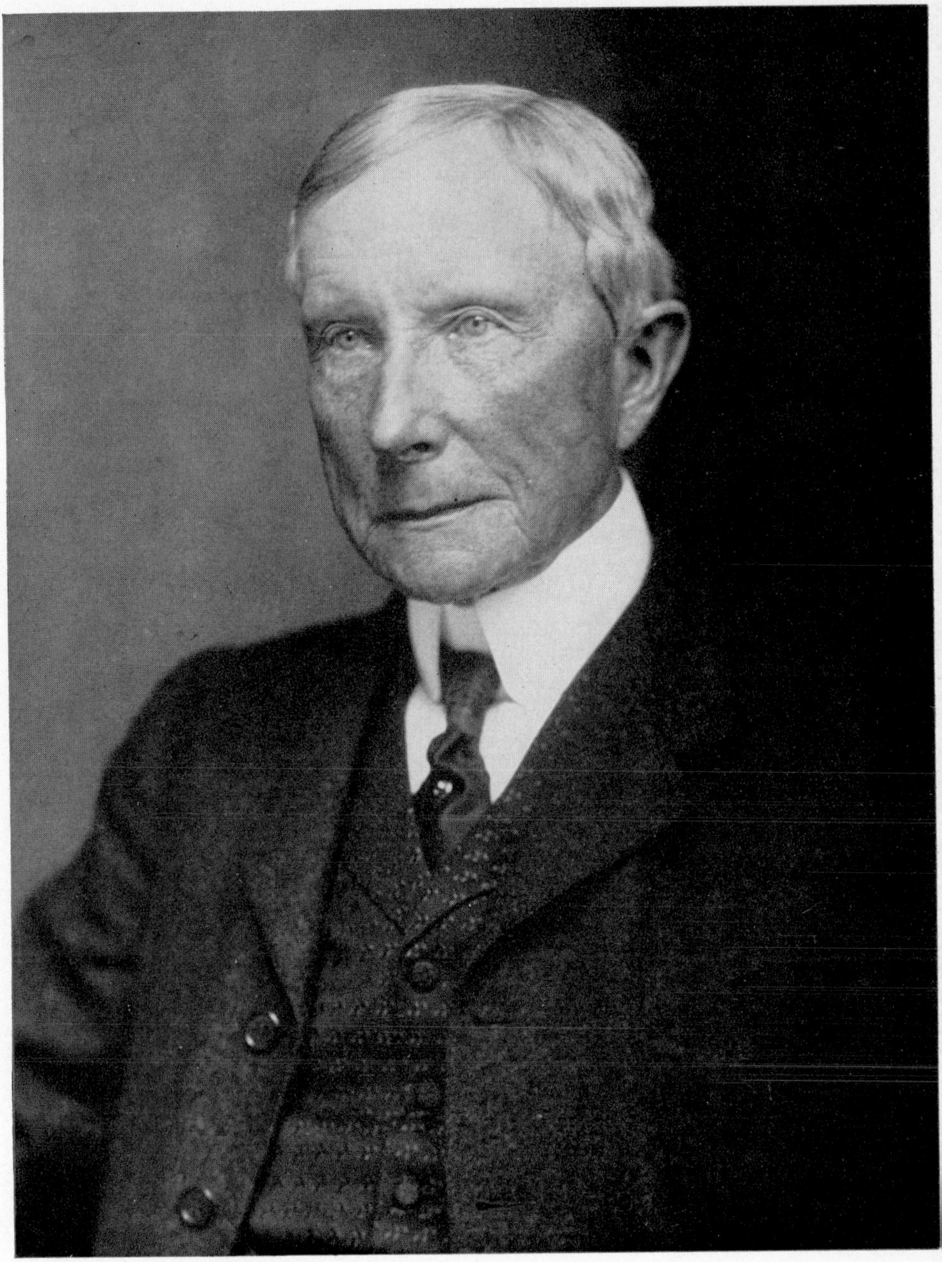

JOHN D. ROCKEFELLER, SR.

The enchanting vision revealed by young Charlie Schwab from the mountain top had indeed impressed J. Pierpont Morgan. For several days following the dinner he spoke often of it to his associate Robert Bacon; and finally he sent for John W. Gates. "Do you think the Carnegie properties can be acquired?" he asked. Gates said he did. "Then I think I shall take up the matter with Mr. Frick," said Morgan. Gates was aghast at this ignorance; Morgan apparently knew nothing of the Frick-Carnegie war. Gates spoke up bluntly. "If you see Frick about it," he warned, "you will never make a trade with Carnegie."

Gates suggested that he should arrange a meeting between Morgan and Schwab. Morgan agreed. Gates so arranged the meeting, and he and Robert Bacon sat and listened while Schwab and Morgan talked away the night. Morgan asked questions about this or that steel company, demanding production figures, costs, and so forth. Schwab seemed to have the answers at tongue's end. It was a remarkable exhibition of knowledge and memory, for the information given concerned not only the Carnegie plants but those of other large and small steel outfits. And on it, Morgan dismissed this or that firm as unnecessary for the corporation he was planning to assemble.

At dawn, Morgan told Schwab that "if Andy wants to sell, I'll buy. Go find his price."

While the Morgan-Schwab-Carnegie negotiations were going forward, Morgan set out to buy John D. Rockefeller's immense ore holdings on the Mesabi Range in Minnesota. Mr. Rockefeller, through his son, said he did not intend to dispose of his ore. This was bad news; if Morgan was going to build a giant of steel, he would need the biggest ore deposits to supply the mills. Morgan called Mr. Frick and asked him to see Mr. Rockefeller about the business. Frick did so, and came away with the Lake Superior Consolidated Mines for Mr. Morgan's new corporation.

It quickly became obvious, too, that Andrew Carnegie was ready to sell his steel company. With Charlie Schwab as intermediary, he let Morgan have Carnegie Steel for a sum usually reported to have been $492,000,000. There was no haggling. The deal was consummated with less fuss than commonly went into a horse trade of the era.

A few days after he had sold out, Carnegie booked passage for Europe, and on the way to board ship in New York stopped to see Morgan. The two men chatted a few minutes, then Andy shook the banker's hand. "Now, Pierpont," he said, "I am the happiest man in the world. I have unloaded this burden on your back and I am off to Europe to play."

Mr. Morgan was ready to shoulder the burden. Things began to happen at once. Morgan took over John W. Gates's American Steel & Wire. He took over American Tin Plate. He acquired American Steel Hoop, and American Bridge. He already had control of Federal Steel, National Steel, and National Tube; and as related, most of the Mesabi ore now belonged to the Morgan syndicate. On April 1, 1901, organization of the United States Steel Corporation was formally announced.

This behemoth was capitalized at $1,402,000,000—a figure to stagger anyone but an astronomer. The press broke out with editorials and cartoons. A favorite picture showed a schoolroom in which well-known men appeared as small boys. At the blackboard was a lad easily recognizable as J. Pierpont Morgan. He had just written a string of figures that reached away across the board. A little boy with Andy Carnegie's bearded visage held up his hand. "Teacher," he protested, "there isn't such a sum in my arithmetic." Said teacher: "But Pierpont has his own arithmetic."

A popular story had to do with a Sunday school teacher who asked one of her small fry: "Now, Johnnie, who made the world?" And Johnnie replied: "God made the world in 4004 B.C., and it was reorganized in 1901 by J. P. Morgan."

The House of Morgan came out of the deal with an estimated eleven and a half million dollars of profit. The reputation of the House and of Mr. Morgan for financial wizardry grew even vaster. No other house and no other man, after 1901, were to approach them. Perhaps they *were* mere stockjobbers, as was charged, but stockjobbing on the scale of a billion and more dollars is no shabby occupation.

The very idea of a corporation capitalized at close to one and a half billion dollars was enough to dismay men who still thought in terms of local banking, local industry, and all-around local enterprise. Standard Oil had started this new manner of business many years before. United States Steel was bigger than Standard. From the day U. S. Steel was formed J. Pierpont Morgan was the supreme symbol of massed wealth, recognized as such not only in Wall Street but in the far corners of the Republic. Three thousand miles away, on Puget Sound, a slick, frock-coated promoter, who was trying to unload a paper city on the public, began all his pitches with the remark: "The first time I met J. Pierpont Morgan . . ." It was most effective. Yet for some reason, few babies of the period seem to have been named for America's greatest man of money. "Dewey" and "McKinley" were still the favorite efforts of parents who hoped thus to transmit to their male progeny the abilities of outstanding men. In 1901, however, there was a grown man, a Russian-born anarchist living in San Francisco, who was often arrested at street meetings simply because he sported a beard of the type used by cartoonists to depict a bomb-throwing nihilist. His name was John Bielaski. Tiring of the harassment by police, and realizing he must either remove his whiskers or become an American, Bielaski chose the latter course. He was admitted to citizenship not as Bielaski but as John Pierpont Morgan, probably the only anarchist of that name on earth.

Before announcing formation of U. S. Steel, Mr. Morgan thoughtfully engaged James R. Keene, a noted freebooting manipulator, to "make a market for the new stocks." Keene did so. The market churned and heaved to Keene's unseen stirring, and both U. S. Steel common and preferred went soaring.

Despite the water in it, U. S. Steel was a good buy in 1901. One often overlooked reason this was so concerned a decision just then handed down by the United States Supreme Court in a patent case. The patent had to do with the steel mixer invented many years before by Carnegie's old plant boss, the incomparable Captain Bill Jones of Braddock. The Court held that U. S. Steel alone had a right to use the Jones mixer, and it cracked down with a cease and desist order on Cambria Iron Works and other concerns that were no part of the trust, for using the device. Henceforth, the use of mixers was subject to the license rights of U. S. Steel. The rights came high, too.

There was another inducement to buy U. S. Steel stocks. Heretofore rails had been selling at $23.75 a ton. The new trust announced a raise in the price, "due to increased costs of operation," to twenty-eight dollars a ton—thus proving that even so prophetic a man as Charlie Schwab could be wrong. Not only was his vision of cheaper steel thus scuttled, but rails remained at the new and higher price for another thirteen years.

Schwab became the first president of the United States Steel Corporation. He was to remain only three years. He did not get along too well with Judge Gary, chief counsel and much more than that, of the corporation; and besides, Charlie Schwab meant to have a big outfit of his own. We shall come a little later to his Bethlehem Steel consolidation.

Sale of Carnegie Steel had provided the main framework for the steel trust. It also made some thirty-odd millionaires overnight. These were the so-called Carnegie partners, young and middle-aged men who had served their master well and were now to be paid beyond their wildest dreams. Some of them still smelled a bit of burning coke, and a Penn Avenue barber in Pittsburgh reported that the first shampoo one of these newly rich men ever had brought out two ounces of fine Mesabi ore and a scattering of slag and cinders.

The "Pittsburgh millionaire" had arrived. In that city's expensive though hardly exclusive Duquesne Club, the new and newly rich members gamboled and learned that napkins were not to be tucked under the chin. Their throats, long used to the scalding of straight whiskey and gin, were soothed by fancy drinks mild in comparison and served by the club lackeys on silver trays. A steward recalled seeing one of the partners sprawled in a chair and covering page after page of the club's embossed stationery with figures. "I am trying," he said, as the steward fetched him another drink, "to find whether I am worth six million or if it is eight million."

At least ten of the Carnegie partners set sail for Europe with their families. Another went off alone except for a mistress who was described as "a show-actress." Still another moved his ménage into a New York City brownstone. Yet, a majority of the partners were loyal to Pittsburgh—or almost. They considered the Pittsburgh suburb of Sewickley Heights to be heaven. Onto the Heights they prepared to move, and their architects, making ready the new estates, shuddered. Shuddered but also obeyed; and there rose on the high bluffs near Pittsburgh some of the gaudiest monstrosities of the age.

One Sewickley job, done for a partner who must have read at least one book, and that *Ivanhoe,* carried the Baron Front de Boeuf motif right down to a moat with drawbridge. The attached sun parlor seemed to stem from the New York City Aquarium. There were a score of other new places, each presenting various horrors of design and décor.

Old Alex Peacock, who had been general sales manager for

Carnegie, did not move to Sewickley with the main crowd. Instead he built Rowanlea on Highland Avenue in Pittsburgh, a truly elephantine mansion encircled with a nine-foot fence that was entered through gates so massive they rolled upon wheels. From the top of each gatepost glared an iron figure of *Felis leo*. Marble columns stood everywhere there was room for a marble column. Inside the mansion the elegance continued. And when he heard that one of his old cronies of Carnegie days had installed two gold-plated pianos in his Sewickley home, Alex bought four gold-plated pianos.

The generous and good-natured Alex Peacock looked up old friends. If they were in straits, he paid their debts, paid for their operations, their babies, their funerals. He threw parties that are remembered with awe fifty years after. One can believe that perhaps he, of all the partners, got the most fun from his sudden fortune.

For the first time in history, heraldry bloomed in the murk along the Monongahela and the Allegheny. One expert of this arcane craft ran the line of a Carnegie partner clear back to Geoffrey Plantagenet, a man of substance in his time, and drew a quartered shield to dazzle a belted earl. Another partner had *his* crest embossed on his cigar bands.

In Pittsburgh the parties given by some of the new rich of steel occasionally got out of hand. One of the most celebrated began modestly on six floors of a downtown hotel, but the place wasn't large enough. The host, a partner, hired the Pittsburgh Natatorium and moved his guests there, all eight hundred of them, and there, so a guest remembers, all hands got good and drunk and the partner himself, and scores of his guests of both sexes, disrobed and went swimming au naturel.

Within two or three years after Carnegie sold to U. S. Steel, the term "Pittsburgh millionaire" was coming into circulation. It denoted freehanded and ostentatious spending that reached a new high point, or perhaps low point, in vulgarity. Though he was no Pittsburgher, Diamond Jim Brady, who sold Pittsburgh steel products, gave the term even wider circulation. He dressed like the king of three-card monte men, gave gold-plated bicycles to ladies of the stage, ordered champagne in hundred-case lots, and was seen everywhere.

Then came Harry K. Thaw to make Pittsburgh millionaires notoriously known the world over. Thaw was not a partner but came of a wealthy and cultured family of Pittsburgh whose money had been made in coal, coke, steel, and railroads. Lacking both brains and balance, Thaw thought it a splendid idea to shoot a famous architect, choosing Madison Square Garden in New York for the scene of the murder. The resultant trial was so lurid it has had few equals as a newspaper sensation. It also gave lasting durability to the symbol of the Pittsburgh millionaire.

No other metal was the source of so many millionaires' wealth as steel in one form or another. Yet an enormous amount of money came from copper. The wars for supremacy in copper were accompanied by a savagery beside which the struggles of oil and of steel seem a little pale. Violence is apparently inseparable from copper. The scene must now move to Butte, Montana, for the story of Anaconda, often known as the "copper trust."

Chapter 3   THE COPPER-PLATED KINGS

Sixty and more years ago, as it does today, Montana meant copper. Copper meant Butte. And Butte, so it turned out, was to mean long and bloody wars.

Aside from Wall Street, which doesn't count here because it deals with symbols like stocks and bonds and not with actual mines and ores, there has been no physical battleground in the same class with Butte, Montana. Butte stands a mile high, a mile deep, and it stands alone in the matter of violence.

All over the slopes of the long hill sprawls and rambles this old mining camp. Below the hill is a brief rolling plain, then the Rockies. It is a stark and fitting scene for what has gone on there these past seven decades.

Viewed at twilight from the high pass where the Northern Pacific's Limited emerges from the mountains, Butte presents a dramatic picture, twinkling with astonishing brilliance in the high thin air. Viewed closely at noon the big camp is as ugly as sin and just as fascinating.

Joe Howard, who loved and loathed it, called Butte the black heart of Montana, feared and distrusted. From the sixth floor of one of Butte's office buildings, he wrote, "go forth the corporate commands to politicians, preachers, and press, all the pensioners and servile penny-a-liners of corporate capitalism." Howard wrote that as recently as 1943. He was referring to the Anaconda Copper Mining Company, sometimes called the Big Snake. Anaconda is the empire that resulted from the war of three men who were rightly enough called the copper kings. There was more than alliteration in the title.

The three copper kings were Clark, Daly, and Heinze. Unlike the Big Four of California railroads, these men did not work in harmony, or even as a coalition. They were lone bandits, or lone geniuses of industrial enterprise, whichever way you want to put it.

William Andrews Clark was first on the scene. He reached Montana Territory in 1863, after studying law at Iowa Wesleyan and teaching school in Missouri. Montana then was a void into which were stampeding a few thousand men attracted by reports of a gold strike.

Clark opened a store at Virginia City. Tobacco was in short supply, worth half its weight in dust. Twenty-four-year-old Clark set out to locate some tobacco. He found more than a ton of it away over on the other side of the mountains, in Boise City, Idaho. He bought it all, then packed it muleback to Last Chance Gulch, later renamed Helena, where he sold it for a small fortune. Several other trading ventures turned out well. Clark opened a bank in Deer Lodge.

Nine years after he arrived, William Clark was the leading banker and all-around businessman in the Territory. He was physically a small man, starchy, tightfisted, humorless, and ruthless. Not even his enemies charged him with harboring the commonplace vices of drink, gaming, and harlotry. He was singularly attentive to the main chance. No dollar ever got away from him, it was said, except to come back with another sticking to it.

During the nine years Clark had been coming up in the world of Montana, the gold-mining camp named Butte came into being. It had known a first quick rush when the population rose to about five hundred, then it started to fade. The meager placers had played out. Beneath them was quartz containing a little gold, somewhat more of silver and of other metals. The problem was to separate the precious metals from the refractory ores. This called for considerable capital. There was no capital in Butte.

In 1872, when banker Clark visited there for the first time,

Butte was a ghost camp. Less than twenty of the hundreds of men who had flocked in to mine the placers remained. Here and there on the slopes of the desolate hill were the shacks and other relics of the departed, now homes for owls and magpies. The surviving few prospectors made banker Clark welcome and showed him the ledges which they assured him could make them all rich.

For all his plug-hat and slightly "eastern" or fastidious manner, banker Clark was no fit subject for salted mines and high-graded ore. With him when he first came to the Territory he brought a copy of Hitchcock's *Elements of Geology*, which he knew by heart; and he also knew a great deal more. He had grubstaked miners. He had inspected their claims. His bank had bought and shipped to the Philadelphia mint more than a million dollars in gold each year. So, the urgency and the sales talks of the Butte hopefuls made no impression on him. But he listened, and he also went down into the few shallow shafts. When he left Butte, Clark had in his pocket options on four claims for which he had paid a few dollars.

Now we come to a most significant and revealing incident in the life of William A. Clark. Turning over his banking business to underlings, he went to New York City and entered the Columbia School of Mines. If he were to turn from banking to mining, he wanted to know as much as possible; certainly he wanted to know much more than was usual, in the mining camps of the era, about the best methods to extract metal from ores. It was not incidental that he took with him to Columbia a goodly sack of specimens from the very ore in which he was most interested, just in case the professors might need something to use in the lessons on assay and analysis. A year later, ex-student Clark was back in Butte, this time to stay.

One of the most energetic of Butte's hopeful mine owners was W. L. Farlin, who had toted a load of his ore four hundred miles overland to have it refined at Corinne, Utah. The stuff ran to four hundred dollars a ton, which was just about the cost of transporting it from Butte to Corinne. This would not be a way in which to get rich. Farlin thereupon raised a little capital and in Butte put up a stamp mill and refinery. Construction had used up all his cash. He had nothing to pay for operation. Clark was pleased to lend $30,000 and take a mortgage. In a little while, Clark owned the mill and refinery. It was a way Clark had.

Simultaneously, Clark erected a much larger stamp mill, finished in 1876, and called the Centennial. He built another. The holes in the ground on which he had taken options were paying out big. Even with the crude and wasteful early stamp mills, four-hundred-dollar-a-ton ore returned a heady profit. The mining camp of Butte started to take on population. Within a year or so, it could muster close to five thousand people. Mine-operator Clark was its first citizen.

News of booming Butte spread over the whole West, and the Walker Brothers, leading bankers of Salt Lake City, looking for a speculation, sent an agent to investigate Butte mining chances. He was Marcus Daly, a proper man to investigate mines. Daly had been born in Ireland in 1841, and fifteen years later arrived at New York in the steerage, and so to California to wield pick and shovel in a quartz mine; then to the Comstock in Nevada to work for another Irisher, John W. Mackay. When he arrived in Butte, Daly was a good mine superintendent and also a pretty shrewd man when it came to assessing a mine's potential value.

Mark Daly's abilities were well hidden beneath the rough exterior of the type of Irish immigrant just then being satirized by Harrigan & Hart in *The Mulligan Guards* and other comedies. Ruddy-faced, short and stocky, Daly had a warming smile, a genial manner, and quite a bit of blarney on tap. He looked Butte over carefully, then for the Walker Brothers bought a small silver mine, the Alice, and erected a small stamp mill.

Near the Alice was a small, shallow hole which its owner, Mike Hickey, had named the Anaconda. Hickey was anxious to sell. Daly looked the mine over, found it to present certain possibilities, and urged the Walker Brothers to buy it. Why the Walkers should doubt Daly isn't clear; but they didn't say yes or no to his recommendation. Instead, they sent another expert to inspect Hickey's Anaconda. He was against buying. Daly didn't mind. He quickly sold his interest in the Alice and for $30,000 bought Hickey's mine.

Daly was now without funds to start operations. He knew where he could get funds. Back in the early 1870s Mark Daly had directed the attention of George Hearst and James B. Haggin of California to a mine in Utah. They had bought it on Daly's favorable report. And from it they had been taking out an average of one and a half million dollars a year. They were prepared to put money into anything Daly suggested and now, with another Californian, Lloyd Tevis, they supplied Daly with all the capital he wanted.

Mark Daly did not expand operations in the Anaconda. He closed down the pumps and shut up the mine. Rumors, which Daly himself probably set in motion, circulated to the effect that Mike Hickey had taken Mark Daly for a cleaning, that the Anaconda was worthless.

Working through secret agents, Daly used his new capital to buy a great deal of the hill surrounding his boarded-up mine head. It was bought very cheap. When this had been done, Daly sent big crews down his shaft to start work on what he had discovered at the three-hundred-foot level. This was an enormous vein of almost pure copper. The Anaconda Copper Mining Company was under way.

William A. Clark was still the dominant figure in Butte. His interests had spread to include forty-six silver and copper properties in the district. He and Mark Daly, suddenly become the No. 2 copper king, were good friends. Both were staunch Democrats; and Daly's marriage to a sister of Clark's brother's wife, seemed to cement the relationship.

Like many a wealthy man before him, Clark conceived the idea of a political career. He announced his intention to run as a candidate in the race to elect a territorial delegate to Congress. He went headlong into the campaign, spending lavishly for entertainment and the outright purchase of votes. He would have been elected, too, had he not made a slighting remark about Mark Daly. Daly, said Clark, was not only an uncouth man, but his discovery of the rich Anaconda had been dumb Irish luck.

Daly made no reply. He merely told his several thousand miners and smelter workers to vote for nobody but the Republican candidate, a book agent named Thomas Carter. Carter was elected by an overwhelming vote.

The war of the copper kings was on.

A year after Clark's defeat, Montana was admitted as a state. Daly, who had laid out and built a town around his smelter and named it Anaconda, wanted his city to be made the Montana capital. Clark declared for Helena. He acquired the Butte *Miner,* a moribund daily, brought in modern equipment, and hired a high-priced staff. The *Miner's* task henceforth was to make Helena the state capital.

Daly accepted battle readily. He imported John H. Durstine, a noted editor of Syracuse, New York, to take charge of a brand-new daily, the Anaconda *Standard,* which Daly financed and for which he erected a fine plant in his smelter town. The *Standard's* job was to bring the capital to Anaconda.

Helena won. Clark's efforts reputedly ran to $40,000. Daly was said to have spent more than two million dollars in his fruitless campaign. One incident indicates what could happen in Montana in a copper kings' war: On election day an enthusiastic citizen of Helena who did *not* want the capitol in his town strolled down Main Street shouting, "Hurrah for Mark Daly and Anaconda!" He was thrown into jail. Hearing of it, Daly charted a special train, loaded it with legal talent and his newspaper gang, and rolled over the hill to Helena. There he had the man released on a writ of habeas corpus and took him in triumph to Anaconda. Legend has it that Daly presented his supporter with a mining lease that netted him $60,000. It's a good story, and it gives an idea of the heat generated.

Clark's victory in the Anaconda-Helena battle gave him confidence to try again for office, this time for that of United States senator. The Daly forces defeated him. In 1898 Clark again became a candidate. This time, he told his heelers, he *must* win; and win he did after expenditures that are talked about sixty years later. These included the hiring of masked gunmen who, in an attempt to steal the ballot boxes in the Daly stronghold of Dublin Gulch, shot and killed one election official and wounded another.

Mark Daly's forces were defeated this time. But Daly was still fighting. He instigated and financed an investigation of Clark's campaign which resulted in revelations of scandalous bribery and Senator Clark's forced resignation from the United States Senate.

Two years later, Clark tried again and this time he made it. Through an alliance with F. Augustus Heinze he was elected to the Senate and took his seat without protest. Marcus Daly died soon after the election. His last great effort was to form his Anaconda and many other properties into the Amalgamated Copper Company, capitalized at seventy-five million dollars, far and away the biggest thing in Montana. His chief partner in this enterprise was Henry H. Rogers of the so-called Standard Oil crowd in New York.

Senator Clark's ally in his last and successful attempt to get into the United States Senate, the Heinze mentioned, was well on his way to becoming the third of the copper kings. His public pose was to be different from Clark's. Clark liked to be thought a dignified, plug-hat and gold-headed-cane type, a sort of standard conception of the big-moneyed man of late nineteenth century. Marcus Daly's pose, also characteristic of the period, was that of the honest workingman who had made good, the rags-to-riches figure who never forgot his pick-and-shovel friends and days and ways.

Heinze was neither of these. He set up shop as the gay desperado, a reincarnation of Robin Hood who would surely steal from the rich, and just as surely give it to the poor.

Frederick Augustus Heinze was born in Brooklyn of a Connecticut Yankee mother and a German father. He was given an excellent education for his future career at the Columbia School of Mines, from which he was graduated in 1889. From Columbia he went directly to the scene of the noisiest mining excitement in the West, which was Butte. Here for a hundred dollars a month he started work for the Boston & Montana Consolidated, and stayed just long enough to note possibilities overlooked by the copper kings Daly and Clark, and also to recognize certain shortcomings in his own education.

Heinze returned to New York to work a year on the staff of the *Engineering & Mining Journal,* a good place to fill the void left in his technical training. This was knowledge of the manner in which mining companies were formed and where best to look for capital for new ventures.

In 1892, Heinze returned to Butte and leased the Estella mine. A year later he organized the Montana Ore Purchasing Company and built a smelter for the small independent producers. This fitted in perfectly with the demagogic preaching he already had started against the big "monopolists" Daly and Clark. They were vultures. Small operators were saintly men. Jim Fisk had used the same pose years before. It was a good one.

Heinze next tried a diversion. At Trail, British Columbia, he put up a small smelter, got a charter and a land grant for what was obviously a nuisance or blackmail railroad, then permitted the Canadian Pacific Railway Company to buy him out.

With the blackmail money, Heinze returned to Butte. This time he was ready for his major effort, which he said was to put the "depraved trust," meaning the Daly interests, out of business. Heinze knew that in any attack on Daly he could count on the help of William A. Clark, whose influence spread through the courts, which Heinze was going to need on his side.

Now it so happened that a Heinze mine, the Rarus, adjoined the rich property of the Boston & Montana; and presently it was seen by the B&M management that miners of the Rarus were encroaching on the B&M's rich veins. The company sought an injunction. This was what Heinze wanted. He told his men to continue to dig ore. With them he stationed armed guards in every corridor. Then he went to court.

Heinze's trump was to cite the apex theory of mine ownership. This theory, made a federal law in 1872, held that the owner of land on which a vein of ore came to its apex could follow the vein downward, even under the claim of another. While the matter was still in the courts, the B&M became a part of the Amalgamated Copper Company organized by Marcus Daly and the Rockefeller crowd represented by Henry H. Rogers of Standard Oil. The Amalgamated inherited the suit.

One of William Clark's creatures was Judge William Clancy, a shyster lawyer who had spent many more hours as a saloon hanger-on than at any other bar. Now he sat on the bench in Butte specifically to do Clark's bidding, and the bidding of Clark's new friend Heinze. He closed the B&M mine by court order. Heinze, still playing his apex theory, next went into Judge Clancy's court to claim that the veins of three of Amalgamated's major properties, including the famous Anaconda itself, apexed in a small piece of land, 74 feet long by 10 feet wide, which just happened to be owned by Heinze. Clancy ordered the three big mines shut down.

The closures threw more than three thousand Amalgamated miners out of work. They held a mass meeting, then they marched down the long hill in a spontaneous threat to announce, in front of Silver Bow County Courthouse, that they had come for the purpose of lynching Judge Clancy. The judge had expected nothing like this. He hastened to dissolve the restraining order. The enraged miners marched back up the hill and returned to their jobs.

This was a technical victory for Amalgamated. But Heinze was not alarmed. He founded a newspaper, the *Reveille,* staffed it with talented men, and announced it was dedicated, as was Heinze himself, to freeing the honest, hard-working people of Montana from the domination and brutality of the copper trust, or Amalgamated.

Heinze also instituted more than a hundred suits against the trust. Judge Clancy and Judge Harney signed every decision written

THE AGE OF THE MOGULS

for them by Heinze's lawyers. Many of these suits enjoined Amalgamated from operating its own properties. The suits were of course appealed to higher courts, and while waiting for decisions, the Heinze miners drilled into the trust's properties and proceeded to lift a million dollars' worth of high-grade ore to the surface through Heinze shafts.

The *Reveille* played every tune conceivable on the theme that Standard Oil, in the form of Amalgamated, was trying to take over entire the state of Montana. Trusts, either real or imagined, were then an even bigger public menace in the West than in the East; and Standard Oil's highhanded methods in Pennsylvania were cited, and enlarged upon, to show Montana's common people what was in store for them, too.

Heinze continued to play his role as friend of the workingman. He always tried to pay his miners a little more than the trust paid theirs. He was paternal with the widows and children of miners. Holidays brought turkeys to the rows of shacks, crowded terracelike, on the steep slopes of the copper hill of Butte, where Heinze's men lived. Their picnics were flooded with free beer and whiskey and often flooded, too, with Heinze oratory. The orations reminded them who their great enemy was—the copper trust.

Heinze continued to raid mines of the trust through his own properties, and even incorporated a phantom Johnstown Mining Company, which had no assets whatever, to do much of his poaching. The Amalgamated caught on quickly enough. As fast as Heinze's crosscuts bore into one of their mines, the intruding spearheads were destroyed by blasts. In one case, Heinze's crews were ordered to drop their tools and get out just before a valve was opened and the corridors flooded. Heinze set the rumor going that the trust had "drowned scores of miners."

The rumor set going by Heinze had no basis of truth; but even without such a holocaust, the subterranean war was terrible enough. On one occasion, when Amalgamated investigators had broken through to one of Heinze's shafts, his men poured slaking lime into the fresh-air pipes and set the fans to going. The investigators retreated in face of the scalding flood, whereupon the Heinze gang quickly hoisted the disputed ore and filled the looted stopes with debris.

The Amalgamated men had retired only to get new weapons, and now they returned to the battle with hot-steam pipes and drove out the enemy. This particular engagement lasted for days and nights on end. It raged through miles of underground workings. Two miners lost their lives. Scores more were hospitalized.

The Heinze-Amalgamated war continued its pettifogging way in the courts, while hundreds of men fought almost personal battles in the hot steamy avenues half a mile and more beneath the streets of Butte. In their efforts to drive each other out, these natives of Cornwall and Galway fought underground with savage joy, and fought again on the surface. They fought in the saloons, the bawdy houses, and on holiday picnics. One of the latter jolly affairs, held on a July Fourth, resulted in a battle during which, so wrote a Butte reporter, the sun was obscured by the clouds of flying beer bottles.

One may ask what it is about copper that has so often inflamed the men who dig it? Does some inherent poison emanate from the handsome red metal that drives men mad and sends them running berserk along the corridors that are almost as hot as hell, slugging, shooting; and to cutting mine cages from their cables; and to dumping tons of rock down shafts—all in the hope of killing other miners? (I have heard talk of it in mine dryhouses by men who had suffered from this mental poison of copper. The reasons for it baffled them. All they could say was that the digging of neither gold, nor silver, nor lead, nor even coal, was done to the accompaniment of such violence as had attended the mining of copper.)

The death and injury of miners in the underground war brought more suits into the courts, usually against the Amalgamated. And at last, in the court of the old reliable Judge Clancy, the Amalgamated was declared an illegal combine, and its several subsidiary companies permanently enjoined from paying dividends to it. Heinze, the honest workingman's best friend, had won his great victory.

William Scallon, head of Amalgamated, recalled the effect that 3,000 out-of-work miners had had on Judge Clancy on a previous occasion. Mr. Scallon now prepared something that was to have greater and wider effect. On the day following Judge Clancy's ruling, every piece of industry, large and small, controlled by the Amalgamated was shut down, tight.

It was as if some unseen blighting paralysis had swept Montana. The many mines of Butte's hill, the huge smelter at Anaconda, the refineries at Great Falls, sawmills at Missoula, logging camps along the Flathead, the Bitterroot and the Kootenay, one and all they were closed.

Next morning was the most melancholy in Montana's memory. More than twenty thousand men had no jobs, and none in sight. The state's great industry had died. Within another two days, railroad men were being laid off, stores were closing or cutting their help in half. Barbershops, saloons, the girls of Butte's Venus Alley, all knew that something dreadful had happened. October had come. The peaks of the Rockies, even their slopes, had taken on mantles of new snow. Winter was coming down the mountains.

Three days after the shutdown, threatening crowds appeared on Butte streets. Their threats were directed, not at the monster trust of Amalgamated, but at F. Augustus Heinze. Somehow or other, he who had been their friend had now caused them to face a penniless winter. The miners' union called on Heinze and demanded that he act to undo the blight he had brought to Montana. He promised that he would explain matters next afternoon from the steps of the courthouse.

It was one of Butte's great days, remembered half a century later. Fifteen thousand men, women, and children assembled as near as they could crowd around Silver Bow County's fine courthouse. A bright clear photograph of this, Butte's moment of superb melodrama, survives. It shows a mass of humanity packing the street and overflowing into the yard, into vacant lots, mounting the high steps, hanging from porches, hanging out windows, clinging to telephone poles.

This angry crowd had come half determined to string up their double-crossing former hero. They had not rightly estimated the full forensic powers of F. Augustus Heinze. There he stood, above this vast mob, handsome, smiling, assured. Then he began to speak.

It was cold that October day high on the copper hill, but no man felt the chill two minutes after Heinze started speaking. He was to speak for more than an hour, and what he said held the crowd in thrall. What he said was demagoguery, but the demagogue was a master. One who heard Heinze that day likened him to Mark Antony, as quoted by the Bard. Heinze denounced his foes, piling one horrible charge upon another until the copper trust was plainly seen to be the greatest evil since original sin entered man. He called the copper trust by the name of the most hated corporation in America, Standard Oil, and he painted a hideous picture of what it held in store for Montana once its slimy coils had enveloped the state and all within it.

These people are my enemies, said Heinze, and they are fierce, bitter, implacable. They are your enemies, too. If they crush me today, they will crush you tomorrow.

Lo, said he, have you not already an example of what Standard Oil has in store for you? Is not this complete shutdown of all their properties in Montana a sample of their malignant power?

On and on went the golden voice, now husky with emotion, now ringing clear with defiance, now touring a moment into sonorous asides, but returning always to the business in hand:

"They will force you to dwell in Standard Oil houses while you live—and they will bury you in Standard Oil coffins when you die. . . ."

A low rumble in the crowd grew quickly into a full-throated roar. He had them now, these brawny men of the shafts and the stopes, these Cousin Jacks and Harps and Bohunks who dug the ore and fired the stinking smelters.

You and I are partners and allies, shouted Heinze. We stand or we fall together . . .

Now they were cheering. Heinze told them what he would do. He would submit the copper war to an arbitration board. They cheered him again. It looked like victory for Heinze, but it was not quite victory. His great speech had seemed to loosen the coils of the Big Snake, the outfit once called Anaconda and later was to become Anaconda again. It had really done no such thing. The coils even then were tightening.

Yet the copper trust had learned something from Heinze. It had learned that public opinion, to which it had never given much consideration, was valuable to have on one's side. But first, Montana must be properly conditioned; so, the Amalgamated properties were kept shut tight for another week, the better to show what a full winter without work could mean. Then Amalgamated proposed that the governor of Montana should call a special meeting of the legislature to pass a "Fair Trial" bill. This act provided that a judge, if charged with prejudice by a litigant, could be removed. The meeting was called. The bill was made into law.

On that same day the mines, the smelter, the refineries, the sawmills, and logging camps of Montana resumed work, and that night the saloons of Butte, Anaconda, and Great Falls were packed again, while impromptu bands gave street concerts.

The copper trust had won the last battle and the war. There remained, however, the substantial mine interest of Heinze, plus more than a hundred Heinze lawsuits against Amalgamated totaling about fifty million dollars.

John D. Ryan, successor to William Scallon as managing director of Amalgamated, was a man with all the charm of Heinze, and a preference for discussion rather than war. Heinze liked him. Heinze knew that his great speech on the courthouse steps had checked only temporarily the drift away from him of his friends the miners. The rank and file had been notably cooled by the Amalgamated shutdown.

Ryan and Heinze secretly got together. It would not do for Heinze, the No. 1 enemy of the trust, to sell out to Amalgamated. Nor was H. H. Rogers a man much given to arbitration. Rogers would not dream of paying blackmail to Heinze in order to get rid of the troublesome lawsuits. But Ryan had a plan to save everyone's face. He cooked up a trick company, which he happily named Butte Coalition. Into this went Heinze's Rarus, Minnie Healey, Nipper, Belmont, Hypocka, and Corra-Rock Island mines, together with his smelting and milling properties. Butte Coalition then paid Heinze ten and a half million dollars. Butte Coalition was directly taken over by Amalgamated.

To mark the occasion, Heinze staged a monster party in his Butte apartment, then chartered a special railroad car. Taking eight old cronies along, the party set out for New York City. The former workingman's friend, almost thirty-seven years old, who had come to Butte to work at five dollars a day, was heading for Wall Street.

Chapter 4 TOM LAWSON AND THE SYSTEM

IN the spring of 1906 F. Augustus Heinze, the hero of Butte's miners, arrived in New York City with ten and a half million dollars. The panic of 1907 was then not even a speck on the horizon. Yet there was a close connection between the event of Heinze's coming to New York and the coming of panic.

With the perspective of years, many writers on financial affairs have come to the conclusion that the sudden panic was precipitated by the struggle to get rid of Heinze. The struggle, as nobody doubted, was waged by the Standard Oil crowd, not company, headed by the indomitable Henry H. Rogers, with his close partner, William Rockefeller, and their financial aide, James Stillman of the National City Bank.

The war between Heinze and the Standard Oil crowd began, as related, on the hill at Butte and reached its frantic zenith when the Amalgamated Copper Company achieved a sort of victory by paying Heinze to get out of Montana.

There is another part of the Amalgamated story. Butte isn't in this portion. There are no mines in it, no copper, no underground battles, no speeches in front of the Silver Bow County Courthouse. This other story deals only with the symbols, the stock certificates of Amalgamated. It is a bitter story. To tell it we must return to the conception of the monster of copper, and consider Tom Lawson.

Amalgamated was born in the brilliant, restless mind of Thomas William Lawson of Boston, one of the most spectacular figures in stock market history. A native of Charlestown, Massachusetts, he went to work in State Street at twelve as an office boy. He started to speculate at once, and while still in his teens made something of a killing in a flurry of railroad stocks. This amounted to $50,000, and with it the lad Lawson plunged headlong into what turned out to be a thorough wringer. Lawson came out of the affair with exactly $157. To celebrate his first, though not his last, shearing the youngster invited a crowd of his State Street cronies to a fine dinner at Young's Hotel. He gave the five dollars left over, his last, to Horace the headwaiter. It was typical of Lawson's life.

Playing pretty much a lone hand, Lawson at twenty-one was one of the best-known plungers in Boston. He married and became the father of four handsome daughters and two strapping sons. At thirty he had made his first million. To celebrate this event, he wrote and had privately printed at his own expense a *History of the Republican Party*. Four copies of this work were printed on satin. This struck some people as eccentric. Possibly it was, but it was no more eccentric than that a wealthy American should write a book at all. Few conventional capitalists of the era, save for

Lawson and Carnegie, ever read a book, much less wrote one. Lawson's really effective book was to come later.

In the mid-nineties Lawson lent his great talents to a strange character out of nowhere named John Edward O'Sullivan Addicks, who was coming to be known as the "Napoleon of Gas." He had made his pile in Siberian railroads. His features were considerably adorned with a fierce sweeping mustache in the Cossack style. Addicks had also performed doubtful services to the public by his manipulation of gas contracts in Chicago and Brooklyn. Now he had come to Massachusetts to organize the Bay State Gas Company.

The Standard Oil crowd were interested in gas. They ganged up and drove Addicks out of Brooklyn. They hammered at his Chicago syndicate. Now they were bringing the war against him to New England. Looking around for help, Addicks saw in Lawson the sort of aggressive help he wanted. Lawson joined up. With compelling advertising and shrewd work with state and city officials, Lawson almost lone-handed soon had the Standard Oil crowd fighting a rear-guard action.

Henry Rogers, heading the Standard forces, recognized in Lawson a man who should be working with and not against Standard. The two men met. The gas war soon came to an end. Addicks left for other parts. His Bay State Gas was in the hands of Standard Oil.

Now comes the Amalgamated Copper Company. In 1897 Lawson conceived a plan he called simply "Coppers." It was a broad and comprehensive project, he said, having for its object the buying and selling of all the best copper-producing properties in America and Europe, and "the educating of the world up to the great merits of these consolidated copper properties as safe and profitable investments." Lawson broached the idea to Rogers and William Rockefeller. They liked it. It had the grand design that appealed to their sort of men. It also seemed to present possibilities of a fruitful nature.

Marcus Daly's Anaconda, under style of Amalgamated, became the first section of the Lawson-Rogers Coppers to be offered to the public. Its manner of birth has been described succinctly by John T. Flynn as follows: The Rockefeller group gave Daly a check for thirty-nine million dollars, on the National City Bank, with the understanding the check was to be deposited and remain uncashed for a stipulated time. The Amalgamated was then organized with a covey of Standard Oil clerks as dummy directors. These dummies, without flexing a muscle, transferred the Anaconda properties to Amalgamated for seventy-five million dollars. This was not cash, but stock. The Standard group took this stock to the National City Bank and borrowed thirty-nine million dollars on it—which paid for Daly's check.

The next step was to unload the seventy-five-million-dollar stock issue on that portion of the public who think of themselves as incipient millionaires. When this had been done, the thirty-nine-million-dollar loan from the bank could be liquidated and still leave a profit of thirty-five million, a tidy enough sum for a group which had invested only enough of its own cash to print a raft of handsome stock certificates.

Now came Lawson's part of the project, which was to "make a market" for Amalgamated shares. This he proceeded to do with the wildest success. Lawson had the confidence of a large number of Yankees who had taken his market tips in the past and had done well with them. New England was also well conditioned in the matter of copper stocks. They had been favorites of Boston investors since the early days of Calumet & Hecla, a gilt-edged outfit from the day it was incorporated. Half a dozen of Butte's copper mines had been financed with Yankee dollars. When Tom Lawson loosed his eloquence on Amalgamated, which he did in startling signed advertisements, old ladies on Beacon Hill, frosty patriarchs of Commonwealth Avenue, and chin-whiskered bankers in Hartford, Providence, Burlington, Bangor, and Manchester were ready to listen.

Writing later of the Amalgamated excitement, which he termed "dollar hydrophobia," Lawson painted a graphic picture of sheep in headlong stampede to the *abattoir*. On a Monday morning, following Lawson's advertisements, his office in Boston's State Street was the center of a mass of people all trying to get inside at the same time. It was much the same at the National City Bank in New York. All day the speculators fought for places in the buying lines. Lawson went to New York, where at 26 Broadway, Standard's headquarters, he might get reports from all sections of the country, and from Europe, too, for his advertisements and other promotions had not overlooked London, or Berlin, or the French bourse.

Tuesday the excitement seemed to mount higher. Cables and telegrams came flocking in, all demanding stock in Amalgamated. The smart boys of Wall Street, too, were buying. At the Waldorf, a favorite place for out-of-town brokers to congregate, the management had to add from two to four cot beds in many rooms to accommodate the crowd of quick-money men.

Lawson himself swung into the big hotel through the carriage entrance on Thirty-fourth Street to see what he called the rapt concourse of the dollar worshipers preening themselves against the plush, onyx, and gildings of the caravansary. Lawson always had an eye for stage settings and the appearance of the actors. He thought now he could see in the mirrors, on the walls, on the very buttons of the hotel's lackeys, the "universal crest of the twisted S with its two upright bars."

In the Waldorf's dining room Lawson was all but mobbed as soon as he was recognized. He found the whole business so entertaining that "I lost sight of the terrible seriousness of it, and I chuckled as one does when one sits on the cool grass under the apple trees and watches myriads of ants hunting and jostling and bumping over each other to get away with what to humans is but a tiny grain of dirt."

When Lawson had finished his dinner, the headwaiter came forward to lead him into a corner where his assistant and the head chef were waiting. One of them asked, "Is it safe, Mr. Lawson, for us to put our savings in Amalgamated?" A moment later the hotel's manager, Mr. Thomas, asked Lawson the same question. At the desk, room clerk Palmer said he was going to buy three hundred shares. The bell-captain wanted to know if Amalgamated was good.

"I would rather have lost a finger that day than have jeopardized their savings," Lawson said later. "For all of them I had but one answer: 'Go your limit.' "

The Lawson campaign with Amalgamated Copper was not only one of the most spectacular in the history of Wall Street; it was also one of the most successful. In a matter of a few days the stock issue was oversubscribed. In a matter of a few weeks the price went up to $130. Then it plummeted to seventy-five. "I did all in my power to prevent the decline," Lawson wrote of the debacle, "and lost millions of my own money in the effort. Some of the insiders made millions. The public was fleeced of millions."

At seventy-five, the stock was far from its nadir. It dropped again, this time to thirty-three. Now the Standard Oil crowd was glad to take it off the hands of the suckers. Lawson was "out" along with the little fellows. He turned his talents to other stocks, and sat down to compose one of the most celebrated attacks of the muckraking era. This was *Frenzied Finance,* which appeared first as a serial exposé in *Everybody's Magazine,* and was published as a book in 1905. The serial sent the magazine's circulation soaring to more than half a million, truly immense for the time. The book went through many printings.

Although author Lawson wished to appear as a champion of the people, he was honest enough to indicate his mixed motives for writing *Frenzied Finance.* Right off he informs the reader that his desire to write the story of the "Crime of Amalgamated Copper" is tinged with hatred for and revenge against "the system," a term he coined to describe the methods used by "colossal corporations for the incubation of wealth" from the people's savings in banks, trust funds, and insurance companies, and from public funds. His own part in the Amalgamated crime is excused on the plea that H. H. Rogers, William Rockefeller, and James Stillman had not told him, Lawson, the truth about the copper giant. He points to his own losses in that stock as proof of his good will in the enterprise. He has nothing but good to say of Rogers, Rockefeller, and Stillman in their private lives. They are turned into unconscionable ogres by the system, the dollar-making machine of manipulation and deception.

There was plenty of fact in Lawson's flamboyant narrative. "It is basically true" was the comment of one old Wall Street hand. It was also something of an eye opener. Whether or not it prevented congenital suckers from playing their predestined parts is to be doubted; but the book did have effect in one field, that of life insurance, and touched off the investigations that brought Charles Evans Hughes into the public eye as prosecutor of the big insurance companies. It also gave the public a new term, the system, to describe the use of roguery and corruption by large financial and industrial interests. The term has even been admitted to Webster.

Frenzied Finance made Thomas Lawson a national figure. The system was naturally bent on laying him low, but he was to ride high a few years yet. In the town of Egypt, on Massachusetts' south shore, he had built Dreamwold, a huge castle set in the middle of a thousand-acre estate. He built a yacht to compete for the America's Cup, which was excluded from preliminary trials on vague technical grounds. Lawson denounced the New York Yacht Club as an enemy of democratic processes and had his own yacht scrapped—to big headlines.

At this period Lawson presented a character and figure that endeared him to the press. Newspapermen found him a man "of piercing eye, bold manner, and fancy vest." He paid $30,000 to a florist for a carnation bearing Mrs. Lawson's name. His magnificent physique was garbed in the wardrobe of a fashion plate. He loved black pearls. His was an arresting appearance—dark-haired, blue-eyed, heavy-browed, with a square jaw. Energy radiated from him. One of his four handsome daughters married a son of Governor Samuel McCall of Massachusetts, and for the couple Lawson established a ranch in the wilds of central Oregon that is famous forty years after.

But the enmity aroused by *Frenzied Finance* eventually cost Lawson his fortune, estimated at thirty million dollars. He lost clients on both sides of the market. His later deals in copper and other stocks, especially a flier in Yukon gold for the Guggenheims, went sour. He had exposed the system and the system must have revenge. One blow followed another. He was to die a comparative pauper. But just before the end, Tom Lawson rallied once more. The effort was characteristic of the man.

Not long before his death in 1925, according to one of the family legends, Lawson took to his bed in his Dreamwold Castle. It was no longer his. It had gone to creditors, along with the rest of his estate, including his limousine. But houses costing six or seven million dollars are not to be sold overnight, at least not in Massachusetts; so the ill and aging man was permitted to live on there while the receiver looked for a customer.

Lawson had failed for something like six million dollars. One day an agent for the receiver was at Dreamwold, making estimates of its probable liquidation value, when he came across a small cashbox. In it were $550 in bills. Lawson didn't even know it was in the house, or when he put the money in the box. The receiver's agent, a kindly man who knew Lawson well, turned the cash over to him. "Tom," said he, "this sum is too small to do your creditors any good. Why don't you take it and buy yourself some comforts while you are ill?"

Lawson thanked the agent, accepted the $550, and with it had a direct wire to Wall Street from his bed installed. For six weeks, from what was his final bed, he played the market by telephone, coming out of a flurry $40,000 the winner. Thereupon Tom Lawson cashed his profits, gave the money to his children, turned his face to the wall, and died. He must have died fairly happy, too. That final foray surely gave him satisfaction, told him that he still had the gambler's touch.

Lawson's book was at the height of its sensational success when F. Augustus Heinze arrived in New York with the ten and a half million dollars paid him by the Standard Oil crowd to get out of Butte. What Heinze thought of Lawson and his book isn't known, and in any case, the hero of Butte probably believed that he needed no one to warn *him* about the Rogers-Rockefeller-Stillman gang. Had he not made them pay him well to go away and leave Amalgamated alone?

In New York, Heinze quickly set up two of his brothers in the stock exchange firm of Otto Heinze & Company. He allied himself with Charles W. Morse, a man from Bath, Maine, who had made a large fortune from the American Ice Company monopoly which he had organized and which he manipulated notoriously. Morse and Heinze together incorporated something Heinze named the United Copper Company, a "paper" concern capitalized at eighty million dollars.

Though there surely was not a great deal of substance to United Copper, it offered, as C. B. Glasscock, the writer on copper subjects remarked, "the opportunity Heinze sought." But Heinze also needed a bank. To this end he bought control of a New York institution, the Mercantile National. The manipulation of United Copper went forward. It rose from thirty-seven to sixty. The Standard oil crowd, still bent on dissolving F. Augustus Heinze, had accumulated a vast number of shares at rock-bottom prices. They now unloaded quickly. Banks, though not the Mercantile National, called all loans on United Copper. Heinze, Morse, and their associates, were forced to sell their stocks to meet the called loans. United Copper went down and almost out of sight.

A sudden run started on the Mercantile National. Otto Heinze & Company collapsed. The Mercantile National appealed for help to the Clearing House, whose officials replied that help could not be had—until and unless Heinze and Morse resigned from the bank's directorate. The two did so under strong pressure. It failed to halt the worried run on the bank. A day later, runs started on the Knickerbocker Trust Company and spread with panic swiftness to other houses. It *was* panic.

The Knickerbocker failed after paying out eight million dollars to depositors, who incidentally, did not include in their number Mrs.

Hetty Green, the wealthy old woman in rusty black taffeta whom the press called the Witch of Wall Street. Hetty Green never claimed to prophesy, but several weeks before the crash she had told a friend to get her money out of the Knickerbocker Trust Company. Hetty had done the same with her own cash. "The men in that bank are too good-looking," she explained. "You mark my words."

Having paid out eight million dollars, the Knickerbocker had nothing left to meet demands for another fifty-two million which it still owed to depositors. The panic of 1907 now went rushing ahead. From Bangor to Seattle, money went into hiding. Clearing House certificates became a medium of exchange. On the estates of the wealthy, so a commentator wrote, horses were sold and stablemen dismissed. Factories were closed. A few bread lines were formed, but lines much longer were queuing up at banks and other allegedly financial houses that seemed to have no money.

As the clouds grew darker, the top-level partners of J. P. Morgan & Company anxiously waited return of the old man himself, who just then was attending an Episcopal convention in Richmond, Virginia. Bishop Lawrence noticed that Mr. Morgan was receiving an unusually large number of telegrams. The bishop also read the newspapers and knew that not all was well. But when one of the Episcopal party casually remarked to the head of the House of Morgan, "You seem to have some bad news," the old gentleman shot his memorably fierce gaze across the table and said nothing. The subject was not mentioned again.

Then, and not until the convention was over, Mr. Morgan had his two private cars hooked to a train for New York, loaded them with bishops and minor clergymen, and started North. Next morning, Bishop Lawrence recalled, when the train was approaching Manhattan and the bishops went into break their fast, they found Mr. Morgan "sitting at a table, singing lustily some tune which no one could recognize." Once in New York, however, he hastened to his favorite place, the new Morgan Library, "like a general," says Frederick Lewis Allen, "arriving at the headquarters of a beleaguered army."

The most prominent financier in America spent the remainder of Sunday and well into Monday talking with partners and friends, including bankers and trust company people, about what to do to stem the panic. By daylight he was ready. He first sent his son-in-law, Herbert Satterlee, to get in touch with certain bankers, men able to make quick examinations of conditions of any bank which applied for aid. Then Morgan himself went downtown. He conferred with officials of Knickerbocker Trust. He decided it was in a hopeless condition. Let it fail. It ran out of cash, and did.

News of the failure came next day as a mighty thunderclap in the gathering storm. Secretary of the Treasury Cortelyou arrived from Washington. A run began on the big Trust Company of America. While two of Morgan's men were inside appraising the securities in its vaults, the line of depositors grew in the street until it occupied more than a block. Seven windows were paying out as fast as money could be counted.

A little after noon, the line grew in length. Morgan, sitting in his back room like a field marshal receiving reports from his generals at the front, at last came to a conclusion. "This," said he, "is the place to stop the trouble." Just before it would have been too late, funds arrived at the Trust Company of America. These funds were made available by a quick grouping of still solvent trust companies forced by Morgan. John D. Rockefeller also came forward with ten million to aid in damming the panic.

Another day of it saw the Exchange closed in Pittsburgh. The Westinghouse Company failed. Lesser firms went down. Stocks were tumbling faster than the ticker could record the events. By noon trading was all but stopped on the New York Stock Exchange; there was no cash to buy with. Exchange president Thomas crossed the street to Morgan's office. "Mr. Morgan," he said, "we will have to close the Exchange." Within a few minutes, says his biographer Allen, Morgan raised twenty-five million dollars to be lent on the Exchange, which remained open until the regular closing hour of three o'clock.

As October wore on, conditions began slowly to improve. The writers of financial news started to express a sort of optimism, well watered, to be sure, with conditional phrases. Just then a new crisis appeared. The prominent brokerage house of Moore & Schley had "overextended" itself. This is a euphemism for a condition almost indistinguishable from bankruptcy.

Moore & Schley had loaned money on Tennessee Coal & Iron stock, and then borrowed money, using the identical stock as collateral. The panic had come with its sudden demands for cash. Moore & Schley had insufficient cash. If they could not get it, they were going to collapse.

Some unknown party, who perhaps was not wholly disinterested, came to J. P. Morgan with an idea. Tennessee Coal & Iron, he pointed out, was a competitor of Morgan's recently organized U. S. Steel. Morgan had failed to include it in the trust because he thought its shares were too high. He also realized that the failure of so important a house as Moore & Schley might set off a string of other failures. The Tennessee shares were now to be had at a more reasonable price. Why not take this coal and iron company into the trust? It would be good for the trust. It would save Moore & Schley.

On November 2, when the panic seemed about to renew its original force, Morgan called another meeting, this time in his new marble library on East Thirty-sixth Street. Again a call went out for the captains of cash to assemble. Morgan would need twenty-five million dollars to swing the Tennessee deal. He had come to the conclusion also that the trust companies should put up about twenty-five million to support the newly besieged Trust Company of America.

Into the East Room of the Morgan Library were ushered the heads of banks and assorted financiers. Into the West Room went the trust company bosses. Morgan took up his headquarters in the small Librarian's Room, just off the entrance lobby.

It was to be quite an evening. Here sat or paced those whom the press called the money lords of the nation. They sat or paced amid the Morgan treasures, many of them ecclesiastical, while the stained-glass windows lighted up from the street lamps outside. There was the incredibly costly triptych that contained a sliver of the true cross; the gorgeous brocades; old masters; and shelf after shelf holding nothing but rare editions of the Holy Bible. And there facing the old man's desk was the Ruby Vase, worth a fortune, which was placed in a direct line with the Morgan chair—right where the blazing dark eyes above the famous ruby nose could cherish the ruby ceramic treasure.

The meeting lasted all night, with this banker, then that one, being called into the Presence in the Librarian's Room. When Benjamin Strong, of Bankers Trust, had made his report to Morgan, he thought he was done and might go home. He found the Main Library door locked. The key was in the old man's pocket. He went back to the East Room to sit on a lounge and contemplate the true cross, or to doze, until a quarter past five, when the conference was declared to be at an end.

By that hour the trust company heads had been bludgeoned into putting up twenty-five million dollars to support weaker concerns; and the Tennessee Coal & Iron merger had been arranged. One more thing needed doing: Morgan hesitated to put Tennessee into the trust without word from the federal government that the action would not bring prosecution. So, Henry Clay Frick and Judge Elbert Gary made a hurried trip to Washington, where President Theodore Roosevelt assured them he would not interfere. The deal was then consummated. Tennessee Coal & Iron went into the steel trust. Moore & Schley were saved from their "overextension." The crisis had been met successfully. By mid-November the panic was seen to have run its course and the undertakers were sorting out the debris of ruined firms to see what could be salvaged.

A part of the salvage operations included the indictment on charges of fraud of F. Augustus Heinze and his partner Morse. It appeared that they had committed "certain irregularities" for which they ought to be punished. The irregularities perpetrated by Morse and Heinze were probably no more heinous than the promotions and deals that had been going on daily in Wall Street for years and were protested only by the victims. Many believed that the crime of F. Augustus Heinze had been his defiance of Amalgamated Copper; and the crime of Morse was to be Heinze's partner.

A commentator observed that "the forcing of Heinze and Morse out of their banks" was the first sign that trouble had reached the acute stage; and that the closing of Knickerbocker Trust was the first consequence of a public frightened by the run on Heinze's and Morse's Mercantile Bank. Failure of the Knickerbocker was not a part of the plan, if plan there was, to remove Heinze and Morse. The matter had simply got out of hand, and suddenly the nation's prosperity was endangered. Whereupon, "Morgan and the Standard Oil joined forces to keep the fire from spreading any farther than necessary."

Morse was convicted of the fraud charge. Heinze was acquitted. The boys in Butte had followed the trial of Heinze as they followed a prize fight. When news of his acquittal came over the wires, reported the *Engineering & Mining Journal,* "Butte went wild with joy." In spite of his temporary removal as hero of the copper miners, Heinze had long since been reinstated. His hide might now be nailed to the door of 26 Broadway, New York City, headquarters of Standard Oil (or Amalgamated Copper). If so, then he was a greater hero than ever before.

Heinze, now fairly well cleaned of the ten and a half million dollars he had brought to New York, returned at once to the scene of his old triumphs on the copper hill in Montana. He was barely forty, but he was tired. The fighting spirit seemed to have left him. He had lived hard, perhaps too hard. There did not seem to be anything left in Butte that he could get his teeth into. He still owned a mine in Idaho, another in Utah; and his income was sufficient to encourage him to marry. The marriage was brief. It ended in divorce. F. Augustus Heinze died soon after, forty-five years old, still a hero to much of Butte.

Wall Street's punishment of Heinze precipitated the panic of 1907, wrote copper historian Glasscock. "It may not have been the cause," he said, "but it was the spark in the powder magazine. The Amalgamated wished to nail his hide to their door. It was nailed."

It would seem that both Heinze and Thomas Lawson were victims of the system, which both men understood thoroughly. One cannot find that either of them ever complained of rough treatment. Unlike as they were in most respects, these two men had two things in common. They were brilliant operators. They were complete gamblers.

PART FOUR

NEW GIANTS
APPEAR

Chapter 1 THE RISE OF CHARLIE SCHWAB

WHEN the liquidating winds of 1907 had cleared the financial scene of much of its debris, sharp observers might have perceived the rise of a new giant. This was the Bethlehem Steel Corporation. Its president, organizer, *and* owner was none other than Charles M. Schwab, who had been the first president of United States Steel.

Why Charlie Schwab left a job that in the previous year had brought him two million dollars in salary and bonus was a matter of considerable interest. The basic reason was probably Schwab's intense dislike for Judge Elbert H. Gary, chairman of U. S. Steel's board of directors. Gary, as intimated, was a man who wore his religion into the board room. He wore it as ostentatiously as Diamond Jim Brady, the notorious salesman of steel products, wore his headlights of jewels. Gary was filled, said one who knew him, with "pious mouthings," a prissy and tut-tut sort who enjoyed reading little homilies to his subordinates. He held playing cards to be a work of Satan and said that card-playing was "undignified," hence little short of a crime. Worse than all else, Gary had absolutely no sense of humor, which is to say, of proportion.

Such was the man with whom jolly, hearty, and earthy Charlie Schwab had to work in U. S. Steel. It is believed that Gary liked him no more than Schwab liked Gary; and Gary was old Morgan's right-hand man in the new corporation.

For two years, Schwab directed the production and marketing of U. S. Steel with brilliance. To do so he worked even harder than usual, which was very hard; and in 1903, his health failed. Physicians explained to him the facts about high blood pressure, heart attacks, and one thing and another, and must have scared him somewhat; for that summer he rented a yacht, at $22,500 a month, from one of the Drexels and set forth on vacation.

The soothing Mediterranean was indicated, and while cruising its pleasant waters, Schwab stopped off at Monte Carlo. The fancy gambling hell was then at its peak. Massed around its roulette wheels were crowned heads, prime ministers, and scions of international banking houses. Whether Schwab won or lost at the tables is not of record, which is of less importance than that he was seen and interviewed by a reporter for an American news-gathering system.

The American press came out with a fine, colorful story about U. S. Steel's president and his efforts to "break the bank at Monte Carlo." The story hinted also that J. Pierpont Morgan was none too well pleased. Schwab saw the story, and as soon as he returned home went with characteristic frankness to Mr. Morgan to ask if the old gentleman had been disturbed at the report of his gambling abroad. Morgan told Schwab to "forget about it." It was Schwab's own affair. "At any rate," said Schwab, "I didn't do anything to be ashamed of. I didn't do anything behind locked doors." Morgan shot his famed glance at Schwab and rumbled something to the effect that "after all, that is what doors are made for."

Eugene Grace, long associated with Schwab, is responsible for the story that the steelmaster resented certain encroachments on his authority made in his absence. Schwab told Morgan that unless he were to be completely free in his job, then he must leave U. S. Steel. Morgan, though urging him to stay, replied that in such a large enterprise it was proper to establish certain checks and balances of authority. The "checks and balances" were known to have come from suggestions by Judge Gary, perhaps by his explicit order. Charlie Schwab was not a man who worked well under any sort of check or balance. He walked out of United States Steel and into what was then the Bethlehem Steel Company, a small and sound independent concern.

Schwab was no stranger to Bethlehem Steel. In 1901, while head of U. S. Steel, he had "taken a flier on the side" and bought into the smaller outfit. But Morgan and the directors of U. S. Steel had objected, doubtless with good reason, to this diversion. Schwab had then sold his Bethlehem stock. Now that he was free, he again bought into Bethlehem, this time to achieve full control.

Bethlehem was in 1903 already an old firm. Founded in 1857 in an eastern Pennsylvania town named and settled by a sect of Moravians, it had been made into a successful business by the mechanical ability of John Fritz, one of the steel industry's all-time notables, and the organizing ability of Joseph Wharton of Philadelphia. It was still tiny compared to U. S. Steel, but Charlie Schwab had ideas for its future.

At about the same time Schwab moved over to Bethlehem, a group of fast-money promoters were putting together a conglomerate thing called the United States Shipbuilding Company. They planned to make of it a trust, like U. S. Steel. Or, at least, to unload a lot of its stock on the public. It had been inspired by general belief that the Republican Party was soon to pass a liberal ship-subsidy act in Congress. This would of course bring about a great and sudden revival in shipbuilding.

The subsidy did not pass. Shipbuilding was not revived. And the gigantic new piece of promotion had no more than come into being before it started to fall apart. The promoters had collected and put into it eight concerns, one or possibly two of which were sound properties. The others were largely junk yards, at least one of which was bought for less than $100,000 and immediately made to represent two million dollars' worth of stock in the United States Shipbuilding Company. "Then to the astonishment of everybody," wrote John Moody, who knew a good deal about financial matters of the time, it was announced "that the company [U. S. Shipbuilding] had bought the Bethlehem Steel Company [a sound concern] from Charles M. Schwab." The astonishment was due to the understanding that Schwab had been paid in bonds of the U. S. Shipbuilding Company which, said Moody, "promised to be worthless."

Schwab knew what he was doing, and presently, when the whole shipbuilding scheme went down with a crash, he was found in possession of the entire group of properties that had constituted the trust. The first mortgage bonds he had accepted for Bethlehem carried voting power. When the stock-selling outfit blew up and collapsed, he took back his Bethlehem Steel and all else in U. S. Shipbuilding. He then lopped off the junk yards, salvaged what he could from other components, merged them with Bethlehem, and lo there he was, master of the second-largest steel company in America. This he reorganized as Bethlehem Steel Corporation.

Before taking up the fantastic success story of the Bethlehem Steel Corporation, let us consider briefly Charlie Schwab's successor as president of United States Steel. There can be few so ironical events in American industrial history.

The second head of the world's greatest steel concern was William E. Corey who, like Schwab, had come up through the ranks. Among Corey's many contributions was an improved method of hardening steel. He had also made a fine production record at the Homestead Works. Now that he had arrived at the pinnacle, Corey felt the need of a new mansion and a new wife. The new mansion was simple enough for a man of Corey's means. A likely new wife appeared in the person of pretty Mabelle Gilman, whom Corey had first met as a star of the *Mocking Bird* company, a show troupe playing Pittsburgh.

First, Corey must free himself of Mrs. Corey, a woman who had married him when he was a common laborer in the mills at Braddock. The divorce was arranged. When Corey's plans became evident to his comrades of the high management of steel, they were shocked. These were crude men, mostly, and often kept a mistress or two, as even Mr. Morgan himself was reputed to do; but their homes remained intact. In 1907 divorce was not the commonplace affair of subsequent years. It somehow carried a taint that was not easily removed, if at all.

In 1907 the big men of steel were also touchy about the reputation for unlimited vulgarity they had achieved. They were no longer happy to be known as "Pittsburgh millionaires"; the term had changed into a fighting word. Thus, when the president of U. S. Steel's plans were made known, many of his lieutenants pleaded with him not to go ahead with the marriage. Divorce itself was bad enough. Immediate remarriage would be horrible. And that the bride-to-be was an actress made the thing too dreadful to contemplate. Corey, however, was not to be moved. The best his comrades could hope for was that the marriage would be discreet.

The Corey-Gilman wedding was discreet to the extent that it was not held in Madison Square Garden, where, incidentally, a playboy fairly accurately described as a Pittsburgh millionaire, had recently shot and killed America's most famous architect. It was held in Hotel Gotham, New York City, and with full benefit of clergy and press. The bridegroom was voluble about everything. He readily told newspaper reporters that the wedding breakfast cost $5,000, the flowers $6,000. He said his gift to the bride was a two-hundred-thousand-dollar chateau in France. He had also set aside $200,000 "for honeymoon expenses." These and a few incidentals the re-

porters added up to indicate the Corey-Gilman wedding and honeymoon had come to a good round $500,000—or exactly $499,995
more than the first Corey marriage had cost in Braddock, many
years before.

Half a million dollars was pretty elegant, even for the "Iron
Chancellor," as a part of the press liked to call William E. Corey
in a most inept reference to Otto Eduard Leopold von Bismarck.

Here was the man with whom Mr. Morgan and Judge Gary had
supplanted Charlie Schwab, allegedly because Schwab had played
roulette at Monte Carlo on holiday and because "gambling was not
conducive to respect in the person of the president of the United
States Steel Corporation." It was an ironic twist that must have irritated Mr. Morgan very much, and been almost too much for Judge
Gary to bear; but it tickled the underlings of U. S. Steel, and even
the workers in the plants, where Schwab was still something of a
heroic figure. Thirty years afterward, old-timers at Homestead often
referred to the Homestead Works of U. S. Steel as the Mabelle Gilman Works and told this writer that Corey had once attempted to
have the plant so named by official action.

Corey's relations with U. S. Steel, and especially with the chairman of the board, went into a marked decline. He soon resigned the
presidency. Divorce from the "show actress" came later. Mrs. Mabelle Gilman Corey lived on in her French chateau. The Iron Chancellor died in 1934. The obituaries devoted almost as much space
to Mabelle Gilman as they did to Corey himself.

When Charles M. Schwab took over Bethlehem in 1905, Eugene
Grace was merely superintendent of yards. "Even in the lower
rungs," Grace recalled in later years, "we could feel the breeze of
the new personality. He radiated vitality. He was tireless. He was
warmhearted and genuine. Not at all the type of the old-school
martinet."

Schwab set about at once to show doubters, who numbered most
of the wiseacres of steel, that eastern Pennsylvania could compete
successfully with Pittsburgh. Because mountains barred Bethlehem
from a cheap haul of Lake Superior ore, he developed iron mines
in Cuba with ore so cheap as to make up for the water-plus-rail
shipment to Bethlehem. Then he got the immense El Tofo mines in
Chile. He improved the shipyards he had got in the U. S. Shipbuilding deal, and for the Republic of Argentina built a whole navy,
complete with guns.

Schwab's daring had often cost him dear. Off and on he had taken fliers, as the phrase had it, in various things of which he knew little and which turned out badly. He joked of being an easy mark, and he liked to quote the advice given him by an even more daring man, who was John (Barbed Wire and Bet-a-Million) Gates. "Charlie," Gates told him, "if a card sharper comes to you and bets that he can call the Queen of Spades to jump out of the deck and also, as a part of the bet, he will make her spit in your eye, don't you take it. You will lose the bet and get your eye full of spit."

Yet, when the matter had to do with steel, Schwab seems never to have been far wrong. In his early days with Bethlehem, an obscure young Englishman, Henry Grey, came along with a new method for making structural steel. He had tried to peddle his method to U. S. Steel and other firms, and was turned down. Schwab not only listened to Grey but acted. He had seen that America had gone mad about steel-framed skyscrapers. He saw that Grey's design for wide-flanged sections would save a large tonnage of metal.

Schwab first had to promote the new idea to architects and engineers who were used to figuring on the standard shapes of the era. He did so with dispatch, for Schwab knew steel as well as any man and better than most. Then he set Bethlehem to erecting a big new plant specifically to make the Grey beams. Engineers estimated it would cost four million dollars. By the time it was half done, estimates soared to twelve million. Bethlehem put out a bond issue in that amount just when the panic of 1907 struck like an earthquake. Most of the issue remained unsold.

Schwab scurried around to raise the needed capital. New York bankers, who possibly had been warned by the House of Morgan, declined, courteously enough, to have anything to do with financing the new plant of a company not affiliated with U. S. Steel. Schwab did not falter. By his charm and enthusiasm he prevailed on the contractors building his own plant to accept notes ranging from $20,000 to $200,000. The excavating company was so taken with Schwab's magnetism that it agreed to complete nearly half a million dollars' worth of work on open account, that is, to charge it, then offered Schwab a loan. He got banks in Philadelphia and Bethlehem to take notes for large sums. He got the Lehigh Valley and the Reading railroads to accept Bethlehem freight on account.

Bethlehem pulled through its difficulties. The Grey plant was completed and it soon proved Schwab was right; the architects and the engineers of America's great contribution to world architecture, the steel-skeletoned skyscraper, demanded Grey wide-flanged structural shapes as fast as they could be made. Only Bethlehem was prepared to supply them. Second only to Bethlehem's munitions works, which came later, the Grey mill from the day it was built was Bethlehem's greatest money-maker.

Charlie Schwab never posed as a prophet, and it is improbable that he could see a world war coming as early as 1913. Yet in that year Bethlehem took over the ore and manufacturing properties of the Pennsylvania Steel Company at Steelton, Pennsylvania, and also the Maryland Steel Company at Sparrows Point, Maryland, a tidewater mill which Schwab immediately rebuilt and enlarged. By these mergers Bethlehem's capacity was much increased. It also had its own port for receiving ore from cuba and Chile and for shipping its products. Schwab and his Bethlehem Steel Corporation were now ready for the shot at Sarajevo, an explosion that touched off the greatest demand in all history for steel projectiles and steel cannon to shoot them.

In his book, *Masters of Capital,* Moody wrote that in 1914, when war broke out, there were only two American businessmen well known in England. One was J. Pierpont Morgan, the other Charles M. Schwab. Although Moody's statement sounds a little too exclusive, it remains that when Earl Kitchener was named England's Secretary for War in 1914, "one of his first acts was to cable Schwab," asking him to take the next ship to London.

A few days later, Schwab and Kitchener were closeted at the British War Office. How many shells could Schwab supply, a million? Yes. How long would it take him? Ten months. Could Schwab make guns? Yes, and quickly. Schwab also offered to sign an agreement that Bethlehem would not be sold to German, or any other interests, so long as it had British war contracts.

Schwab returned to the United States, and Bethlehem went furiously to convert itself for the business in hand. Within the next two years the company supplied Great Britain with approximately three hundred million dollars' worth of munitions. Although these were mostly guns and shells, Bethlehem also manufactured parts for twenty submarines which were sent to Canada, assembled there, and sent across the Atlantic as complete ships under their own power. This was a good year before the German submarine *Deutschland* landed on American shores, which were still neutral officially, and was heralded as an unprecedented exploit.

When in 1917 the United States entered the war, Bethlehem supplied it too with ships and guns and ammunition. Long before war's end it was the biggest maker of munitions on earth, bigger than Krupp; and its shipyards were turning out a bigger tonnage than all the shipyards of Germany combined.

All of which was both profitable and legitimate business. Bethlehem went on to grow. It bought Midvale Steel and Ordnance Company, which had been founded by the same William E. Corey ousted from U. S. Steel, and which included several small mills and the large works of Cambria Steel at Johnstown. Gradually it became common usage to group Bethlehem and United States Steel together as Big Steel. All others were Little Steel.

Schwab lived to the fairly ripe age of seventy-seven, and died September 18, 1939, in an apartment in New York City. He had recently closed what the New York *Times* referred to as "his stately granite chateau on Riverside Drive at 73rd Street." For many years Mr. Schwab had considered himself retired. During these latter days he was Uncle Charlie, noted as an after-dinner speaker and something of an industrial statesman. He may have been no greater a mogul than Andrew Carnegie, but surely he was one of the very few in little Andy's class, though he died far from wealthy.

Chapter 2   THE LAST RAILROAD WAR

T HERE was still time, after the century's turn, for one more bitter war for dominance between railroad moguls before the internal combustion engine should set Americans to rolling on their own wheels and otherwise change the nation's habits in regard to transportation.

This last great struggle has gone into railroad history as the Hill-Harriman war. It *was* war, too. It began in 1901 and lasted more than twenty years. Both principals were in their graves before the fighting was really done. In its first phase, only the polite and conventional weapons of stocks and bonds were used. The war soon turned savage, however. In one of its later campaigns, both sides reverted to the more primitive gunpowder and dynamite. In at least one engagement, the martial technique went back even further, to neolithic times, when the armies turned to artillery of heaved rocks and rolled boulders.

One of the principals was Edward H. Harriman, whose earlier career has already been traced. His ability in getting control of the Union Pacific, then revitalizing the run-down road and merging it with the Southern Pacific made him an outstanding figure.

The other principal was James Jerome Hill. Of his abilities an expert on railroad strategy wrote that "Mr. Hill's judgment has never been seriously at fault in any of his undertakings."

Jim Hill has been called the Commodore Vanderbilt of the West. The analogy is not sound. Hill was an original. In his lifetime he was called many things—the empire builder; the man who *made* the Northwest; the man who wrecked the Northwest; the scourge of Minnesota and the Dakotas; the curse of Montana; the Puget Sound pirate; the Oregon bandit. He was the true prophet of northern wheat. He was the Evil One of homesteaders, who named a particularly offensive weed Jim Hill mustard. That was him, Jim Hill, the barbed-wired, shaggy-headed, one-eyed old so-and-so of the great West.

Jim Hill began life with nothing. He came to be lord of an empire that reached from the Great Lakes to Puget Sound, from the Canadian border to Missouri and Colorado, and staked out provinces in China and Japan. He died worth fifty-three million dollars. This was only half as much as Commodore Vanderbilt left behind, but Hill won it in a region sparsely settled and believed by most eastern capitalists to be an intact and worthless wilderness.

Hill was born in Ontario, Canada, in 1838. At eighteen he was on his own in the raw new settlement of Pig's Eye, later christened St. Paul, on the upper Mississippi. It was to be his base of operations for sixty years.

After clerking for a river steamboat line, he set up for himself as a forwarding agent. About 1866 he contracted to supply fuel for the St. Paul & Pacific Railroad, Minnesota's chief source of revenue for corruptionists, lobbyists, and legislators. Hill also ranged out to see what Minnesota contained in the way of opportunity for an energetic young man.

The Red River of the North looked good. It flowed northward into Manitoba, and its traffic was cared for by a monopoly of the hoary old Hudson's Bay Company. Hill observed, correctly enough, that the United States and the Dominion of Canada were free countries, then put a boat of his own on the Red. He added another, and called himself the Red River Transportation Company. In a little while he had won a large portion of the river trade.

Jim Hill had lost an eye in a boyish game with bow and arrows. The handicap was never noticeable in business; and while running his river line, he could also watch the steady decay of the St. Paul & Pacific Railroad. If he could but lay hands on that streak of rust and corruption, he told his good friend Norman Kittson, agent for the Hudson's Bay Company, it could be turned into a profitable enterprise. Along came the panic of 1873 to add the final touch needed. The railroad went into receivership. Hill felt the time had come to act.

Hill had a little money. So did Kittson. To buy the St. Paul & Pacific, however, would call for several million dollars. Hill and Kittson went to Canada for the capital. Acting through Donald Smith, one of the Bay Company's big men, and George Stephen, head of the Bank of Montreal, six million dollars was raised. Hill and Kittson added $780,000 from their own resources. The four men then organized the St. Paul, Minneapolis & Manitoba Railroad and took over the bankrupt line. To get it so cheaply, Hill himself had taken the bondholders' committee over the road—or, so tradition has it, over the most worthless stretches of it and in the most decrepit rolling stock available; and had said behold your folly.

At $6,780,000 it was something of a bargain. The new owners promptly sold the greater part of its land grant for $13,068,887. They still owned the railroad, such as it was.

Partners Donald Smith, soon to be Lord Strathcona; George Stephen, soon to be Lord Mount Stephen; and Norman Kittson, to remain such, became officers. Jim Hill took charge of making a railroad that would pay its own way wherever it went.

Directing the job in person, Hill drove his construction crews at a furious rate. Across Minnesota went the rails, then north to the border to meet the Canadian Pacific, which had built a line south from Winnipeg. Two great harvests followed completion of this first Hill railroad, and the freight traffic grew heavy and profitable.

What had been a trickle of immigrants from Norway and Sweden turned to flood, for Hill's agents had been in Scandinavia singing the glories of the Red River Valley. Homesteads could be had free, or Jim Hill would sell some of the land grant still in his possession for $2.50 an acre. The lands along the way filled up rapidly.

Jim Hill's idea of a railroad was not a piece of track to connect the Twin Cities with Winnipeg. As early as 1879 he told his fellow directors he meant to push the road across the continent to reach Puget Sound. Some of the directors were agitated. No other concern had attempted to build a transcontinental without a subsidy from the government, in lands and often in loans. The Union Pacific, the Central Pacific, and the Northern Pacific each had been given millions of public acres. Hill could get no land grant, other than that the road already had in Minnesota and had largely sold.

Did Hill not realize that to reach Puget Sound he must cross the savage voids of Dakota and Montana and Idaho before even he got to Washington; and that Washington alone presented another four hundred miles and another rugged range of mountains before tidewater could be reached?

Did he not realize that even if by some sort of legerdemain he did manage to lay his rails to Puget Sound, he could not hope to compete with the Northern Pacific, subsidized with an immense federal land grant?

Jim Hill knew all this. He was still determined. His presumptuous plan, when it became public, was quickly labeled "Hill's Folly." Hill's Folly moved westward with great speed, though not so fast as to preclude short feeder lines being built as the main rails moved on, heading for the northwest shore. Hill knew much of this vast region at first hand. He seemed to know just where a branch would become a profitable feeder almost as soon as it was completed.

Soon the main line started the long haul across Montana, running well to the north of the Northern Pacific, which Hill pretended to ignore, other than to set his freight and passenger rates very low in territory where he could compete with the other road.

Near Great Falls, which Hill's Folly reached in 1887, Jim Hill showed what he could do to a stubborn community. He laid his rails in a graceful arc clean around Fort Benton, a miserable place that had rejected his demand for a right of way free of charge, and left the town a good mile from his tracks. Great Falls had been debating how much to charge Hill for a strip through the city. Seeing what had happened to Fort Benton, it dropped the debate and Hill was given a dandy right of way through the middle of Great Falls's city park.

Municipalities had to be educated, and often they could learn only by the hard way. At Wayzata, Minnesota, for instance, citizens complained of the noise made nightly by Hill's switching engines. Jim Hill sent a crew to Wayzata to tear down his railroad station and move it two miles to the east, then set it up again and call it Holdridge.

Hill never failed to protect the rear of his railroad, whose name was now changed to the Great Northern. His strongest defense was grain elevators, plus a continuous flow of immigrants to homesteads. Hill was ready to haul a good healthy peasant from Europe halfway across the United States for ten dollars if he'd promise to settle along the Hill rails. Hill did not, despite much loose writing to the contrary, seek to gouge the new settlers with high rates. He told his directors it was to the Great Northern's best advantage to give rates as low as possible to settlers.

At forty, Hill was already a grim old lion, a thickset man with massive head, gray beard, and gray hair, shaggy and long. He looked perfectly the part he played—the aggressive magnate, frontier style. Even when he felt that the amenities called for a silk hat and frock coat, total strangers sensed that beneath the hat and under the coat was a genuine frontier character.

Hill's temper was none too serene. Once he tore a telephone from its moorings and heaved it out through a window. Again, he fired an inoffensive Great Northern clerk who, when asked by Hill, replied that his name was Spittles. It *was* Spittles, too, and Hill fired him because of it. The man had many sides. Once when a Great Northern crew was working to clear the tracks of six feet of snow during a blizzard, along came Hill in his private car. The rugged old man got out to spell off first one man than another, sending the working-stiffs inside for coffee, while the head of the railroad wielded a big shovel with ease and expertness. No wonder he made a legend and that he *was* the legend.

The Great Northern reached Puget Sound at Everett, Washington, in 1893, a bad year for railroads. The Santa Fe went into receivership. So did the Union Pacific. And so, to the delight of Hill, did the Northern Pacific. Of all the rails that reached the west shore, only Jim Hill's Great Northern survived 1893 intact.

The Northern Pacific was the Great Northern's only real competitor west of Fargo, North Dakota. Hill had studied it closely. He was now ready to remove it as a rival. With his old associate of the Bank of Montreal, now Lord Mount Stephen, Hill made an agreement with NP bondholders: he would take over their railroad. Whereupon a Great Northern stockholder objected and cited a Minnesota law that prohibited the merger of parallel and competing railroads. An injunction halted the merger.

Hill and his directors were irritated at the foolish law; but there was no law to prevent them from buying copiously of Northern Pacific stock. This they did. The road was reorganized with the help of J. Pierpont Morgan. Henceforth the NP was for all practical purposes a second track of the Great Northern. The two roads became known as the "Hill Lines," and for them Jim Hill planned further expansion. The expansion Hill had in mind was a great mid-western property, the Chicago, Burlington & Quincy Railroad.

Hill wanted the Burlington for several reasons. It would give him entry to Chicago and St. Louis. The road met the Great Northern at St. Paul. It touched the Northern Pacific at Billings, Montana. It operated vast mileages in Iowa and adjacent states which together comprised America's great domestic lumber market; the far-west reaches of Hill's GN and NP had to rely largely on lumber for eastbound freight.

Then, too, the Burlington would give Hill contact with the cotton-hauling roads entering St. Louis and Kansas City; and with the smelters of Colorado and the Black Hills of South Dakota. It would bring the packing houses of Omaha into his orbit.

Hill and Morgan had met during reorganization of the Northern Pacific. Now, as allies again, they set out to buy the Burlington. They got it from under the nose of Edward H. Harriman, who also wanted it. Harriman's Union Pacific ran no farther east than Omaha; the Burlington had access to Chicago. The Hill-Morgan forces had outgeneraled him.

Harriman was one of the very few men in the United States who did not fear Morgan. Morgan in 1901 was at his colossal best. His and Hill's coup with the Northern Pacific had occurred in March. In April Mr. Morgan sailed for Europe, planning to take the waters at Aix-les-Bains. In April, too, Mr. Hill rolled across his own empire to Seattle to see how his affairs might be prospering on Puget Sound.

During the last few days of April, Mr. Hill, then in Seattle, was perturbed to note a sudden and sharp rise in Northern Pacific shares. It troubled him because the Hill-Morgan syndicate owned less than half of the NP stock. In most cases a strong minority interest was sufficient to hold control of a railroad. But not always. And this new activity in Northern Pacific shares struck Mr. Hill as considerably more than mere trading. He acted promptly. In Seattle he had his car hitched to a special train, had the tracks cleared, and started a fast run for New York City.

Arriving in New York, Jim Hill took a cab direct to the office of Jacob Schiff, of the banking house of Kuhn, Loeb & Company. He demanded of Schiff to know if his suspicions were correct. Was Schiff buying NP shares for E. H. Harriman? Schiff admitted as much. If the Hill-Morgan crowd would not let him have the Burlington, then Harriman was going to buy the Northern Pacific from under their feet which, Schiff said, were not planted firmly enough to hold it. Indeed, Harriman already had control. (This was not quite accurate; Harriman needed possibly another 40,000 shares.)

Mr. Hill hastened with the bad news to the House of Morgan to tell them they had been caught asleep in the old man's absence; that the enemy was buying Northern Pacific and probably even then had got control. When the stunned Morgan partners had regained sufficient poise to act, they sent a cable to Aix-les-Bains, asking Morgan for permission to buy 150,000 shares of NP common.

All of this had happened on a Friday. On Saturday, while the Morgan partners and Hill awaited a cablegram, Harriman decided to purchase another 40,000 shares of NP common; just to be on the safe side. He called Jacob Schiff's office and gave the order. It was never executed. The devout Schiff was at the synagogue.

By Monday it was too late. Trading had no more than begun on the Exchange when the House of Morgan poured buying orders into the market. Morgan brokers on Monday bought 127,500 shares of NP common. The price climbed from 114 to 127½. The buying continued. On Tuesday the price hit 149. By Thursday, though the Morgan forces had quit buying, the price rose to 1,000.

A brief sudden panic followed the fantastic boom. Many stocks went tumbling. But the Hill-Morgan crowd had reached an understanding with Harriman. In what was really no more than a sort of temporary and strictly regional peace, it was agreed that Harriman should have representation on the Northern Pacific board.

Control of all three railroads, however, remained with the Hill-Morgan people; and James J. Hill continued to run the Northern Pacific, the Great Northern, and the Burlington as he thought best.

The effects of Hill's strategy were soon to be seen. His agents in the Orient prevailed on Japanese industrialists to try a shipment of American cotton to mix with the short-staple article from India they were using. It worked well. From then on Great Northern cars carried a steadily increasing tonnage of American cotton over the Burlington, and the GN or the NP, rails to Seattle. It became big business. So did American export of New England goods to China. Minnesota flour started crossing the Pacific in huge amount. So did metals from Colorado. And they all went over the Hill Lines.

Hill kept his rates, not as high as the traffic would stand, but as low as the Hill Lines could stand. He liked to say that if the people of a single province of China could be induced to eat an ounce of American flour daily it would require some seventy million bushels of midwest wheat annually. The Hill Lines carried the flour dirt-cheap to Seattle, where, through inducements offered by Hill, the Nippon Yusen Kaisha sent its ships to take the product across the Pacific.

Jim Hill's campaign to populate the so-called wastelands between Minnesota and the Cascade Mountains was wildly successful, but the end results were in some degree tragic. In twelve years after 1910, forty-two per cent of Montana's vast area was settled by homesteaders, virtually all of them induced hither by Hill's agents and his continuous promotion through text and picture. They plowed this short-grass country deep. Erosion followed. The Montana wind, which never stops, blew the topsoil out of Montana and disaster into the region. By 1919 the average yield of wheat had fallen to 2.4 bushels per plowed acre. Abandoned homesteads became the most characteristic scene in Montana. They demonstrated that Mr. Hill's judgment, at least on one occasion, *was* "seriously at fault."

The so-called Hill-Harriman peace was made late in 1901. Four years later the war broke out again, this time in the Far West. Hill apparently was the aggressor. He had been nettled ever since Harriman had virtually forced his way into the Hill-Morgan Northern Pacific board. Nor did Hill enjoy contemplating the fact that Harriman through his Union Pacific and Northern Pacific considered all Oregon to be his domain.

In 1905, when the Oregon metropolis of Portland invited him to attend its Lewis & Clark Exposition, Mr. Hill was happy to accept; and while there took occasion to remark quite casually, to be sure, that he had a good mind to "help with the development of this great state."

Mr. Harriman knew very well that whenever Jim Hill planned to

help with "development" anywhere, it was best to be alert. Sure
enough, Harriman soon learned that Hill had already completed
surveys down the north bank of the Columbia River to occupy
a water-level route across the Cascade Range, which the Northern
Pacific had originally planned to use but for some strange reason
had been deflected to the south bank.

Harriman acted with his usual celerity. At about the same time
Hill's gangs started grading and laying track down the north bank,
they were met with injunctions and all manner of legal harassments.
What Harriman had done was to organize a couple of trick paper
railroads whose "rights-of-way" conflicted with the Hill locations
everywhere.

Most of this engagement was fought in the courts, though violence broke out occasionally in the field. Hill's tough crews set upon
Harriman's surveyors at least twice and drove them off. The Harriman men returned accompanied by armed guards. There were also
a few night raids, when Hill equipment was dynamited.

During this battle occurred one of the incidents that is retold
whenever the Hill-Harriman war comes up for discussion. Harriman
was stricken with appendicitis and was taken to hospital. Just as
soon as he came out of the ether, Harriman reached for the telephone and called Jim Hill long distance, to say that he, E. H. Harriman, was feeling fit as a fiddle and would soon be back at the
front.

Hill bested the legal and physical harassments and won the north-
bank fight; and his new line, later named the Spokane, Portland
& Seattle, went into joint operation by the Great Northern and the
Northern Pacific. He was not content. He now had a foothold in
Oregon and he wanted to "develop" the state on a much grander
scale.

Hill's new campaign was spearheaded in the greatest secrecy.
Into the wilds of central Oregon, one day soon, went a genial sports-
man who said he was John F. Sampson. He carried more poles and
reels and trout flies than was common along the Deschutes, one
of the state's famous fishing streams. Sampson also appeared to
be carrying more cash than was usual with sportsmen on vacation. He liked the country so well that he bought options on ranches
and unfenced wild lands all over the region. Said it was a sportsmen's paradise. Everybody liked him fine. One day he disappeared,
leaving no trace.

Quite soon the ubiquitous Sampson turned up in Portland, where lived one William Nelson, among whose souvenirs was a handsome charter for a nonexistent railroad, the Oregon Trunk. A little surveying work had been done for this road, long before, up the east bank of the Deschutes River. Otherwise it existed wholly on paper.

William Nelson was surprised to be approached by the somewhat mysterious Mr. Sampson; and astonished, a few days later, when Mr. Sampson asked him to come to a secluded place in one of Portland's many parks; and all but stunned with Sampson pressed upon him $150,000 in good legal tender in exchange for his stock and charter described as the Oregon Trunk Railroad.

On the heels of this astounding transaction, Mr. Sampson disappeared, this time for good; and John F. Stevens came onto the scene. They were one and the same. Stevens was one of the best-known engineers in America. He had served as one of the top men on the Panama Canal project, and for Jim Hill, his present employer, he had discovered a fine "Lost Pass" through the Rockies, the Marias, and through this pass had gone the Great Northern rails.

Engineer Stevens now announced that Mr. Hill was about to start construction of a railroad from the Columbia River up the Deschutes to a place virtually unknown, even to Oregonians, called Bend. Bend was 165 miles from the Columbia, set in a region given over to sagebrush, extinct volcanoes, and lava beds, yet hedged with a vast stand of virgin ponderosa pine.

The news of Hill's plan for developing central Oregon, where almost nobody lived, gave Harriman a start. He knew well enough that the hamlet of Bend was not the terminus Hill had in mind. Hill, so Harriman figured correctly, meant to build to Bend and right on through in a direct line to San Francisco. California was a Harriman province. It would not do for a moment to leave central Oregon to Jim Hill's alleged plans for opening up the country.

So, to parallel Hill's Oregon Trunk, Harriman hastily chartered a new railroad called simply the Deschutes. He moved surveyors and a huge gang of laborers into the neighborhood and they went directly to making grade and laying track up the west bank of the Deschutes River.

All of Oregon and much of the railroading part of the Far West watched with mounting interest while armies of the two great railroad generals massed to fight what turned out to be the last of the old-fashioned construction wars. It was a rouser. Both guile and violence came into play.

All supplies had to be toted in over rough country. Teamsters were made drunk, or doped, or removed bodily from their wagons. In the narrow Deschutes Canyon, little more than a mere cleft in high bluffs of rock, the opposing crews carefully placed dynamite charges, then exploded them at opportune times. Shovels, crowbars, and pick handles were used for close fighting. Men were killed. Several warriors narrowly escaped death when great boulders suddenly came rolling down the steep grade.

In more open places, the factions harassed each other's right of way with fences, barricades of dynamited rock, and court orders. Armed guards lay flat on the rimrock to shoot at any mysterious movements in the brush.

One crisis came at Mile 75. The Harriman construction boss, George W. Boschke, who had built the famous sea wall at Galveston, received a telegram, purportedly from the Texas city: "Come at once. The sea wall has broken." Boschke ignored the fake wire.

The campaign at last came to a head at the ranch of a man named Smith, who managed to prove his right to the claim, then sold the right of way to Harriman. There was no other route to Bend than through this particular ranch.

Hill decided to arbitrate matters. Harriman was agreeable. A truce was arrived at by which Hill agreed to build no farther than Bend. The truce applied only to central Oregon.

West of the Cascades, the Hill-Harriman war went on. Hill built and bought a number of electric lines to take local freight and passenger traffic away from Harriman's Southern Pacific. He bought an ocean terminal near the mouth of the Columbia River, put two fine steamers on the San Francisco run, and ran a special boat train from Portland, all to compete with the Harriman rails to California.

Harriman was not idle. He built a large number of feeder lines in western Oregon and laid plans for a new SP line from Weed, California, to Portland by way of Klamath Falls. This line was not completed until after Harriman's death in 1909.

Hill died in 1916, too soon to see the Great Northern's extension south from Bend to connect with the Western Pacific in California, over which GN trains could, at last, reach San Francisco. Only then could the Hill-Harriman war be considered as finished.

Harriman left an estate variously estimated at from seventy-five to a hundred million dollars. According to our rather quaint if conventional method of grading "great" men, that would make Harriman a much greater man than Hill, with his miserable fifty-three-million-dollar estate. Which man exerted a greater influence on the American West could be and often has been a subject for debate. The influence of both was very great. The difference between the two men would seem to have been chiefly in appearance. Harriman looked like an office man, some said like a bookkeeper. The craggy, shaggy Hill looked every inch the aggressive, hard-fighting frontier character that he was. Each was well paid for his efforts.

With Hill and Harriman passed the great era of the railroads, when rail shares were the favorite stakes of big gamblers and actual rails the sole path of continental commerce and transportation. The internal combustion engine was about to break rail monopoly. It is significant that at the very time Jim Hill's Great Northern was building the last link of its connection with San Francisco, elsewhere the Great Northern, and almost every other railroad in the United States, had started to pull up the tracks of their branch lines and to board up uncounted depots on their main lines.

Chapter 3   HENRY FORD'S NEW ERA

TWO unrelated events of 1909 marked the twilight of one era for Americans and the dawn of another. In the same year that saw the passing of Harriman, the great railroader, Henry Ford launched his Model T automobile.

Ford's announcement contained as little grace as the thing he was talking about. "I will build a motorcar for the great multitude," he said pompously. He went on to remark that the Model T was to be so low in price it would be within the means of everyone; and wound up with a reference to Deity and a resounding cliché. Everyone and his family, concluded Ford, could, with his new car, "enjoy the blessing of hours of pleasure in God's great open spaces."

The professional advertising men may have gagged, as well they might, but in the next nineteen years Ford made and sold fifteen million copies of his Model T and stamped his name indelibly on an era.

Ford had nothing to do with inventing the internal combustion engine, or even with the assembly-line method of manufacture, which was already old when Ford was born. What he did was to take both the invention and the method and tinker them into near perfection. He did more than that. His theory in regard to wages, which we shall come to presently, created, or rather forced, a new philosophy that Ford's contemporary manufacturers found hard to accept.

The great tinker or the "divine mechanic," as he has been called, was born on a farm in 1863. He did not want to be a farmer, though his gaunt face and angular frame were considered characteristically rustic and he did not like big cities or big-city people. As soon as he was able he left his father's acres, where his only interest had been farm machinery and cheap watches, and went to Detroit to work in a powerhouse. His spare time was spent wholly in tinkering, mostly with a gasoline engine of his own contrivance.

Other Americans were tinkering with similar engines which they were attaching to buggies. Still other Americans were applying electric power to buggies. And the traditionalists were using steam power for the same purpose. In the summer of 1893, Charles Duryea braved ridicule by running his little gasoline machine up and down the streets of Chicopee Falls, Massachusetts. A year later, a horseless carriage built by Elwood Haynes and the Apperson brothers, Elmer and Edgar, made the Fourth of July memorable at Kokomo, Indiana.

Meanwhile Henry Ford had put together a machine that would run pretty good. Only lack of money prevented him from taking it to Chicago in 1895, where an endurance run for horseless carriages had been sponsored. In that year there were approximately three hundred motor vehicles in the United States, mostly home-made affairs. (England had more than twice as many.)

Possibly the first motorcar made specifically for sale in the United States was a job by Alexander Winton, marketed in 1898. After that, things began to happen rapidly. The fast-money boys were quick to sense a new opportunity for stock issues. During the first four months of 1899, at least eighty concerns were formed, allegedly to make one or another type of motorcar. Their stock issues totaled $338,000,000, and though few of the companies made many cars, and some made no cars at all, the amount of stock offered for sale indicated that Americans, who had been bilked with canal stocks, bilked again with railroad stocks, were positively gluttons.

Then, on Christmas Day, 1900, occurred an omen of the great new age in the making, when in New York City, a "young woman was knocked down and fatally injured while crossing Broadway by an automobile vehicle." The Ford era had arrived, even though the Ford Motor Company was three years in the future.

Henry Ford tinkered on. Finally he put together a car that would run like the very wind and drove it himself in a number of the early races. In 1903, with twelve partners who put up a total of $28,000, the Ford Motor Company was organized in Detroit.

Parts for the cars were to be made under contract by several different companies. Space for an assembly plant was rented for seventy-five dollars a month. Ten men were hired at $1.50 a day. Ford thought that the outfit, of which he was manager and tinker general, could make ten cars daily.

There was plenty of competition. Buick had just been incorporated. Apperson, Franklin, Pierce-Arrow, and Stearns had been in business for two years or more. Cadillac, Overland, and Packard had been making cars for more than a year. The older firms, all dating from the 1890s, included Haynes, Locomobile, Oldsmobile, and Studebaker. There was also a host of others, possibly as many as five hundred, which came and went, most of them leaving stock certificates to go into attic trunks along with yellowing certificates of shares in canals that were never dug and railroads that were never built.

The new Ford Motor Company progressed steadily through the usual lean periods and hard times customary with most business enterprises. In five years it increased output about fivefold. During this time Ford had tried eight different models, which varied from two to six cylinders. Both chain drive and shaft drive were used. One model had the engine behind the driver's seat. The output had grown to one hundred cars a day. Ford himself was still the boss mechanic, seldom far from the bench and the drafting board.

Five of Henry Ford's original partners were afflicted with shortsightedness. They wanted to get out. Ford was glad to buy their stock, which gave him majority control of the company. Now he could go ahead with an idea that had been brewing in his mind, namely, to make one thousand cars a day. A car that would sell for no more than the price of a horse and a buggy.

Ford's remaining associates were solidly against 1,000 cars a day. They were "inexpressibly shocked" and even contemplated court action to stop the madness. But Ford went ahead to design, then to announce Model T, the one and only model that was to occupy him for the next two decades.

There may be Americans who have never seen a Model T, but they cannot be many and their lives have been singularly circumscribed. It was a stark, almost a grim affair, this black mechanical monster that was to change life in America in so many ways, this new god of Henry Ford's countrymen.

Its appearance interested Ford no more than did the nuances of grammar. He meant that this thing, this vehicle, should *run,* that its owner could repair it with haywire or, if seriously injured, with new parts supplied cheaply by Ford dealers all over the country. He meant that its first cost and its upkeep should be within the means of those who, just a little later, were to be familiarly known as the lower third or the "little people."

In 1909 Ford's idea was revolutionary. In that era motorcars were generally considered to be the ostentatious toys of the wealthy. Dr. Woodrow Wilson, president of Princeton University, saw the deepest social aspects in the automobile, and said publicly that the motorcar presented "a picture of the arrogance of wealth, with all its independence and carelessness." He felt that more than anything else it had "spread socialistic feelings" among Americans.

Henry Ford's Model T stopped any such socialistic feelings in their tracks. Within a few years the lowest proletarians were seeing America, or at least getting around, in Ford cars; and one-gallus sharecroppers had something besides procreation to amuse them. Yet, the motor era which Ford did so much to usher in also brought a new caste system that was founded on neither birth nor wealth nor brains, but simply the make of car a man owned. Vestiges of it are still to be seen half a century later.

Ford got Model T into production not a moment too soon. A promoter named William Durant was putting together what he hoped would be an automobile trust similar to U. S. Steel and Standard Oil. He called it General Motors. Into it went Buick, Cadillac, Oldsmobile, and lesser concerns. (Durant also wanted the Maxwell Company, and Ford, but failed to get them.) Durant tried to get capital from J. P. Morgan & Company, boasting to the bankers that half a million cars could be made and sold every year.

The House of Morgan dismissed Durant as visionary and otherwise unstable.

Promoter Durant at last got from the banking houses of Lee Higginson and J. & W. Seligman a five-year loan of fifteen million dollars. These bankers considered motor making so risky that General Motors had to pay them two and a half million in cash and some four million in securities. The loan not only came high, but the bankers also insisted on a first mortgage and forced Durant to surrender leadership of the company to the bankers' representative. The high-priced loan was used for plant expansion and to buy materials.

Henry Ford's Model T was meanwhile becoming the sensational gadget of the United States. Selling for a little under a thousand dollars in 1909, its price dropped spasmodically over the years to as low as $295. "Watch the Fords Go By" was more than a slogan. Almost every other car on the dusty highways was a Model T. It was the only automobile that went into folklore. Cartoonists, gagsters, vaudeville comedians, and the anonymous fraternity that invents off-color stories went to work on the Ford car with enthusiasm. It was the Tin Lizzie, and more things happened to Tin Lizzie than ever happened to the farmer's daughter of legend. The Ford Motor Company had a conventional advertising appropriation, though it was not needed. No American gadget ever received so much free advertising as Model T.

In 1914 approximately two hundred and fifty thousand Model T cars were made and sold. They accounted for forty-five per cent of all automobiles made in the United States that year.

Then, also in 1914, Henry Ford rocked all American industry with an announcement. He told the press that the Ford Motor Company had just instituted a wage scale based on a minimum of five dollars a day. What was more, the Ford day henceforth was eight, not nine, hours long.

The effect of this announcement cannot well be described to later generations. They will have an idea of its impact, however, if they know it created a sensation greater than the outbreak of World War I, and an intense interest, greater even than that attending the World Series.

The Ford wage of five dollars for eight hours for common labor was twice as much as the highest common labor wage in the United States. Millions of men were glad to work nine hours for two dollars.

Garet Garrett, then an editor on the New York *Times* recalls that "four kinds of ruin" were immediately prophesied. Detroit would be ruined by an exodus of employers; those who stayed and tried to meet Ford's fantastic wage would be ruined; the Ford Company itself would shortly be bankrupt; and Ford's employees would be demoralized by the sudden affluence.

None of these things came to pass, though Ford's announcement, unqualified by any warning, gave Detroit and thousands of witless working-stiffs a bad winter. It set off a tidal migration that brought men from Bowery slums, from Oregon logging camps, from New England farms, from Texas ranches. Textile Manchester and Lowell felt the surge. So did the packing plants of Chicago.

They came on the rods, the bumpers, and the blinds of railroad trains. They came in boxcars. Some few arrived in Model T Fords. Many arrived in shoes with soles flapping.

They came to see this sudden Utopia with their own eyes, and with the hope of sharing in its blessings. In 1914, a simple age, five dollars for eight hours' work *was* Utopia. Even the IWW was given pause, though its fiery speakers and editors caught themselves in time to warn that it must be some new trick of capital.

The Ford plant was then at Highland Park. Within forty-eight hours after Ford's announcement, 10,000 men milled around the plant gates, only to learn that all the five-dollar jobs had been filled before they got there. Police were called, and the great mob was scattered by the fire hoses of Utopia.

But there was no mistake about the wage. Inside the plant, while cops defended the gates, 15,000 men were at work assembling Model T Fords, and the least of them got five dollars.

"Industry must manage to keep wages high and prices low," Henry Ford told the press. "Otherwise it will limit the number of its customers. One's own employees should be one's own best customers." There it was in capsule form, the new theory, namely, that the wage earner is more important as a consumer than as a producer. Yet, he had better be up and doing; he had to *produce*. He had to produce a great deal more than ever before. Ford's assembly line saw to that.

The assembly line, as said, was not new. Eli Whitney with rifles, Eli Terry with clocks, Samuel Colt with revolvers, they and others had used it before Henry Ford was born. Ford's contribution was to study and to speed the line until men had no place in it if they needed to go to the toilet between shifts. Such weaklings were

weeded out as soon as discovered, and other men were paid to discover them. Nature and not the Ford line had to adjust itself.

To make more Model T cars Ford built the immense River
Rouge plant. It is probable that he had then no idea whatever of
making anything else, ever, than the Model T. The car was changed
slightly over the years, but it remained pretty much the stark, black,
ugly, efficient, and comfortless thing it had been since its birth.

Meanwhile the Dodge brothers, who had got rich making Ford's
engines until he started making them at River Rouge, had set up as
makers of automobiles. They brought out an efficient small car and
in their advertising suggested that many people might like to own
a *real automobile* by paying only a little more than a Model T cost.

General Motors, which had survived its inauspicious beginnings,
was also cutting into Ford sales with its low-priced Chevrolet, a car
designed by William Knudsen, who had been Ford's production
manager. The Chevrolet was a handsome thing compared to Model
T. Ford dealers the country over began to complain: Why couldn't
Ford give them something to sell that looked like a car and not like
a Model T?

Henry Ford blamed his salesmen. Then he blamed the American
people; they were running after false gods, which was to say, beauty.
He cut Model T's price to $295, but still the many Ford agencies
were clogged with unsold cars.

But that was not the least of Ford's troubles. His half dozen
stockholders were finding fault with the chief; he wanted to put
most of the company's profits into plant expansion, or otherwise to
invest it in the business. Instead of dividing ten million dollars
among the stockholders, as had been done for several years past,
Ford proposed they and he get along with $1,200,000. The stock-
holders went to court to force Ford to distribute the company earnings. They also asked the court to enjoin the hundred-million-
dollar expansion program Ford was proposing.

At the trial Henry Ford made clear that he was a new kind of
mogul, or capitalist, or employer. He displayed in court heresies
that would have brought quick apoplexy to a Vanderbilt, a Rockefeller, or a Carnegie. Ford told the court that the profits of the
Ford Motor Company were neither his nor the stockholders'. "After
they [the employees] have had their wages," he said, "and a share
of the profits, it is my duty to take what remains and put it back
into the industry to create more work for more men at higher

wages." He denied that either generosity or his conscience had anything to do with it. It was simply good business.

The opposing lawyers exhibited a Ford Motor Company statement showing profits of the year previous to have been a little more than fifty-two million dollars. Did he propose to give his stockholders a little less than one fiftieth of that amount? He did, indeed.

It was too much for the court, perhaps too much for any court; and this particular court ordered Henry Ford to declare a dividend of $19,275,000. "It is not," said the court, "within the lawful power of a corporation to shape and conduct its affairs for the merely incidental benefit of stockholders and for the primary purpose of benefiting others."

The stockholders forthwith got their dividend, which amounted to a matter of $688 for each dollar of cash originally invested, or 68,800 per cent. But the Ford Motor Company lost its president. Henry Ford suddenly resigned, though retaining his seat on the board of directors.

Ford's resignation was made public with a statement to the effect that he, Henry Ford, was leaving to devote his time to "other interests," which were not named. With that he went off to visit his friend, the naturalist John Burroughs, in California. He remained there several months; and because his resignation had created something of a stir comparable to the assassination of a President of the United States, newspaper reporters trailed him and Burroughs at their bird watching.

Now and again Ford was glad to meet the press and to hint mysteriously at what he might be thinking about. It is here that Ford appears to have adopted the foxy ways of Uncle Daniel Drew and other early masters of capital. For a moment, indeed, Ford becomes almost indistinguishable from Drew and Gould and Vanderbilt. He told the inquiring reporters that nobody, not even he, Henry Ford, had as yet built a really good automobile. He had half a mind, he said, to start a new company, a concern with no stockholders to harass him. With his experience and certain new ideas that had come to him he, Henry Ford, ought to go far.

All of this and much more of Ford's musings went directly into the daily papers, often on their front pages. What the Ford stockholders thought of it isn't of record. It seems safe to say that they were frightened. Harry Bennett, Ford's handy man of all work, says that Henry's musings about a new company put the directors into a panic and they were glad to "sell out to him pretty much on his own terms." In any case, the minority stockholders did sell out to Ford, and went their way, each a multimillionaire. One would like to know if they drove off in Model T cars.

Just when Ford himself came to the inevitable conclusion about Model T does not seem to be known. The stockholders did not drive him to it, for now he had no stockholders. The Ford Company had become and was to remain a Ford family property.

But when he did make up his mind about Model T, it was no halfway measure. He would not change Tin Lizzie. He would build a new car. It would be even better than Model T. It would be called Model A.

The vast plant at River Rouge, which had been turning out 1,800,000 copies of Model T a year, was shut down tight. It remained silent for many months, while Chevrolets were rolling in increasing numbers over the new highways with which the nation and the states were subsidizing the automobile industry, much as they had earlier aided the railroads with land grants. Mixed now with the Chevrolets and the Model Ts were the new products of Walter Chrysler's factory.

Then, one day in 1928, after a build-up which more than one newspaperman referred to as the "Second Coming," Ford's Model A went on the market. It cost a little more than Model T had, but times were flush, so good, indeed, that within thirty days after the first showing, Ford was making 6,000 cars daily. Henry Ford's reputation was such, says Harry Bennett, that "500,000 customers made a down payment on the Model A before they knew its price or had even seen it." New York City papers reported that Madison Square Garden was a bedlam on the day Model A was exhibited there, while in St. Paul some twenty-five thousand people turned out in subzero weather to gaze on the new wonder.

Model T had lasted almost twenty years. Model A lasted only five. Ford's competitors made it obsolete, not in performance but in appearance. Shrewd as he was in many ways, Henry Ford found it difficult to accept any fact that came from a source completely alien to his thinking. Hence fashion or style he dismissed with the same countryman's snobbishness that prevents a Georgia cracker from wearing anything but a "wool hat."

What had been happening, though Ford ignored if ever he knew it, was that most Americans wanted a new-style car not every twenty years, or every five years, but annually. Ford's competitors were largely responsible for this acquired taste. They had noted the manner in which the women's dress industry labored to make any gown or suit "old-fashioned" before it was quite a year old. So, the annual exhibitions of motorcars turned into fashion shows. Each year saw new models on the market. They might not, and seldom did, run much better, their owners were killed or maimed just as often in accidents; but they were killed or maimed while in the latest model, for the latest model was the only way in which a majority of Americans could show they had achieved Success.

Thus Model A went the way of Model T, only much quicker; and the Ford plant shut down again, this time to come out with the V-8. It was doubtless as good a car as any other at its price. The trouble was, all makes of cars were good. The Ford Motor Company had become one, and not the largest, of the so-called "Big Three" with General Motors and Chrysler.

By the time Model A made its appearance, Henry Ford's empire was generally believed to be the greatest industrial enterprise in the world. The River Rouge plant alone covered 1,100 acres. In it were employed more than a hundred thousand men, most of them robots. The company operated thirty-five branches in the United States. Thirty-one of these were assembly plants.

Then, because Ford must get his material cheap if he was to build good cars at low cost, his empire included his own timber lands, ore mines, smelters and mills, ships and a railroad, a host of subsidiary manufacturing plants, and a rubber-producing tract in Brazil of six million acres. He operated branches in at least thirteen foreign countries. These branches employed a total of 8,000 men. Ford's direct pay roll in the United States totaled 165,000 employees. Bennett estimated that approximately half a million men and women were directly or indirectly dependent on the Ford Motor Company for employment.

During its first quarter century the Ford Company profits came to one billion dollars. Henry Ford was in no manner astonished. He told his friend, Garet Garrett, that "a business absolutely devoted to service will have only one worry about profits. They will be embarrassingly large."

The Ford profits *were* embarrassingly large, yet of all of America's very wealthy men, Henry Ford almost alone seems to have escaped the charge of being a bloated capitalist, as the popular phrase had it. This may have been due in some part to the fact that he neither looked nor acted nor thought like a Morgan or a Rocke-feller, or even a Jim Hill. His was a bucolic figure, and at heart he was a rustic. He hated banks and bankers. He abhorred idle people. Again and again he denounced the profit motive, and for all his immense fortune, one is prepared to believe that Ford really did not care for money.

If he ever thought of himself as the champion of anything, it was as the champion of the man with the hoe, or the hammer. Far from being classed with the moneybags of the nation, Ford was considered a radical, perhaps a revolutionary. Archie Sinclair, an organizer and editor for the IWW, a crew not given to kind words for industrialists, hailed Ford above Marx. "Agitators from John the Baptist to Earl Browder have made a lot of noise," Sinclair wrote, "but accomplished little. Social change comes about by the acceleration of energy conversion. The man most responsible for social progress is Henry Ford. He eliminated distance and brought city and country dwellers into close communication."

Yet Ford was most implacable against the labor unions. They would interfere with his manufacturing methods. His was a mon-archy. He knew what was best for workingmen, and to defeat the new automotive unions he established a "service division" com-pared to which the old-time detective operatives were crude and inefficient. Ford also fought the so-called Wagner labor act through the courts, and lost each time. Though his son Edsel, and his ad-visers, pleaded with Ford to accept the unions, it was as difficult for him to understand that unions had come to stay as it had been years before to realize that Model T was outmoded.

When Ford did surrender, and signed a contract with the UAW, he gave the union everything it asked for and a lot it had not planned to demand. The Ford-UAW contract was said at the time to be the most liberal of any in the automotive industry.

Whatever Henry Ford's ultimate ambition may have been in the world of manufacturing, the unions defeated it. His ambitions seemingly were predicated on running his assembly line faster and faster to make cheaper and cheaper cars. When the unions stepped in to regulate the speed of the line, Ford could carry his basic idea no farther.

At the time of his death, which came in 1947, Henry Ford was eighty-four years old. The Ford Motor Company was still a family affair. What Ford himself was "worth" in money is impossible to know. Statements appeared in financial pages saying that a billion dollars would not be far wrong. To spend the Ford personal income he had long since established the foundation that bears his name and of which more in its place.

In his later years Ford devoted much time and a great deal of money to the collection of Americana. Whether or not this was a conscious effort to live down his most celebrated remark, namely, that "History is bunk," is not to be known. It may have come to him, over the years, that his Model T had done more than any other one thing to remove the America he had known in his youth, known even as a man of forty. It had eliminated the old-fashioned farm isolation. It had radically changed hamlets and villages. It had done something to large cities.

Nostalgia suddenly gripped Henry Ford, and held him. He set out to collect the past. He collected it with the same devoted intensity that had gone into the making of motorcars. It appears as Greenfield Village on two hundred acres in Dearborn, Michigan, headquarters of the Ford Motor Company, and it is one of the great local and tourist attractions in the state. The present and the future may have claimed Henry Ford's mind and imagination, but his heart belonged to the past.

It was most fitting that on the night Ford was stricken, a great storm broke over Dearborn, the powerhouse went out, and the last of America's three billionaires died in the light of a kerosene lamp.

Chapter 4   MR. MELLON

THE three Americans each reputedly worth a billion dollars were also granted lives well beyond the Biblical span. Henry Ford died at eighty-four, John D. Rockefeller at ninety-eight, Andrew W. Mellon at eighty-two.

None of these men could have been described even in their prime as of robust appearance. Ford was a lean, angular rustic of the Uncle Sam type. Rockefeller lived for many years chiefly on graham crackers and milk. Perhaps the best word picture of Mellon was that given by an anonymous writer, who remarked of the then Secretary of the Treasury that he "looks like a tired double-entry

bookkeeper afraid of losing his job; worn, and tired, tired, tired."
Others observed of Mellon that he was a wisp, or a shadow of
a man.

Possibly the richest of the three, and surely the least known, was
Mellon. Not even his name, much less his picture, had ever appeared in the New York *Times* until January 1, 1921, when he
was already sixty-six years old and an official or director of companies capitalized, as somebody took the pains to figure out, at
two billion dollars.

His name then appeared in the *Times* not because of his wealth,
which as yet was largely unknown, but because he was being urged
upon President-Elect Warren G. Harding for the post of Secretary
of the Treasury. Harding was not familiar with the name. "Mellon
—Mellon?" he muttered. "I don't know him." Neither did an overwhelming majority of Americans. Only in Pittsburgh and in a few
close financial circles had the man ever been heard of.

This was not exactly by chance. No other American fortune was
acquired with the stealth that attended the lives and the works of
the Mellons, father and sons. Railroad men said they worked for
Gould, or Hill, or Harriman, or Vanderbilt. The lowest laborer of
Standard Oil knew about John D. The image of Henry Ford was an
icon, even if an irritating one, to his hundreds of thousands of
robots. Yet only a very few top men in some three hundred large
corporations knew that Andy Mellon was their chief employer.

This seemingly mysterious condition of more than seventy years'
duration clears a little when you reflect that the Mellons were
primarily bankers; and that their fortune grew, according to Frank
R. Denton, a director of the Mellon bank, as "a sort of revolving
fund for the promotion of enterprises . . ." They liked to find a
man both honest and capable who had started a business and was
in need of capital. They gave him the money—if he passed their
thoroughly competent investigation. They took shares in the business and left the man to run it as he would, except that when and
if he got into difficulties, the Mellons were ready to offer advice,
and possibly more than advice. When the business became a going
concern and the loan was repaid, the money then went into some
other business in need of capital.

Yet, there was something more to the mystery than that. J. P.
Morgan was a banker, too. He financed many enterprises and was
widely known. Morgan was even more conservative in his banking
and financing than the Mellons. But there was nothing shy about

him for all his pretense of hating publicity. Often Morgan was grossly arrogant in public, as when he ordered his chauffeur to drive the Morgan limousine onto the sidewalk to pass obstructing traffic. Then, too, Morgan's famous ruby nose added to his personal fame, and with some humor he once said it "would be impossible for me to appear on the streets without it." His nose, he remarked on another occasion, "was part of the American business structure."

When Morgan faced a camera, the resulting picture more often than not showed a figure as if in headlong charge upon the photographer, the fierce eyes glaring with something like leonine fury. Andrew Mellon in a picture reminded many people of Caspar Milquetoast, a cartoon character. He looked like somebody who was just leaving the room. This fancy is not overdrawn, for Andy Mellon was so painfully shy that he fled college commencement exercises, says one of his biographers, "to escape the painful task of delivering a peroration."

The obvious conclusion is that if J. P. Morgan really did dislike personal publicity, he was singularly unsuccessful in avoiding it; while Andrew Mellon remained virtually anonymous for most of his long life.

Judge Thomas Mellon was not so shy as his son, yet he was a "cold, impenetrable person, hardly human" to most of Pittsburgh, and remained until his death a "granite-like figure."

The Mellons were of Ulster stock whose dominant family trait was the shunning of debts. They bought nothing they did not actually need and seldom, said Judge Mellon himself, anything they did need until they had the money to pay for it.

Thomas left his father's farm near Pittsburgh to read for the law in the city. His practice flourished. His income was notably increased by shrewd buying of mortgages and liens. Within five years he had accumulated and saved $12,000, a goodly sum at the time. He married. What he always referred to as the "transaction" was "consummated" on August 22, 1843. Even his courtship had been no heated affair. "There was no love making," he wrote of it. "Had I been rejected, I would have left neither sad nor depressed nor greatly disappointed, only annoyed at the loss of time." That is how stood such lighter things as matters of the heart with Judge Mellon.

Eight children were fruit of the transaction, among them Andrew,

JAMES J. HILL

WARD H. HARRIMAN

COLLIS P. HUNTINGTON

GEORGE HEARST

CYRUS H. McCORMICK

born in 1855. By then Judge Mellon was modestly wealthy by pre-Civil War standards in Pittsburgh. During the war, by which Judge Mellon's properties made a great deal of money, he abjured his sons not to join up. "It is only greenhorns who enlist," he said. The boys listened to him, and Son James managed a coal business during the war years, then sold out at a handsome profit.

In 1870, Judge Mellon felt the time had come, and in a rented store building he opened the T. Mellon & Sons Bank. The Mellon name carried integrity in an era when bankers were not universally known for that quality. Money could be let out at from eight to twelve per cent. Deposits flowed into the new bank. Almost at once it was obvious that the quarters were too small.

The Mellons bought property on Smithfield Street and erected a fine two-story structure more in keeping with an institution that was soon to survive the panic of 1873 and to emerge from the wrecks all around it as Pittsburgh's leading bank.

All the sons were put into banking or other business as soon as their schooling was done. Among the bank's clients was Henry Clay Frick, who used Mellon loans to purchase distress coal properties after the panic. He and Andrew Mellon became fast friends, and in 1879 they made the grand tour of Europe together. Frick was already a millionaire from coke ovens.

A year later old Judge Mellon turned his banking interests over to Andrew. The bank was in capable hands. Its assets increased steadily under direction of the wispy young man who, in 1889, was glad to advance, after suitable inquiry, a credit of $250,000 to a concern with a vague and to the layman an almost meaningless corporate title. This was the Pittsburgh Reduction Company.

The company had just been organized by Alfred Hunt and George H. Clapp, formerly metallurgists for Pittsburgh steel mills. They had little money of their own, and the main reason for their company, an inventor named Charles M. Hall, had none. Hall had devised a method for smelting aluminum. The light metal samples looked good to young Mellon. He advanced the capital in exchange for sufficient stock to control the Pittsburgh Reduction Company.

Many men had been working on aluminum processes ever since the metal had been isolated in 1827. Hall had started experimenting while a student at Oberlin College. His original contribution was the idea that aluminum oxide, dissolved in melted cryolite, could be electrolyzed. Using an old clay crucible lined with carbon and heated with a plumber's blowtorch for furnace, Hall made globules of aluminum in the family woodshed at Oberlin village.

At least two nearsighted capitalists, one in Boston, the other in Cleveland, refused to advance Hall any money to set up even a pilot plant. He then went to Pittsburgh, and so to Mellon.

Unlike most inventors, Charles Hall was not bought for less than a song and then cast off. The Mellons permitted him "a generous portion of stock" in Pittsburgh Reduction, which eventually became the "aluminum trust," and Hall accumulated a fortune, one third of which, one is glad to know, he bequeathed to Oberlin College, where "Chemistry Professor F. F. Jewett first interested me in aluminum."

Inventor Hall went happily about running Pittsburgh Reduction's plant. He cut the cost of production almost in half, or to a dollar a pound. But a market for this new and deceptively light metal must be made. To make it, the Mellons hired young A. V. Davis, something of a whirlwind, who engaged salesmen and set them to ranging with samples to show kitchen-utensil manufacturers.

The Mellons' legal battery had to work, too, for the Cowles brothers of Schenectady were soon making aluminum by what the Mellons held to be an infringement of Hall's patent. A bitter battle ensued. It was settled in the Mellons' favor by William Howard Taft, a federal judge in Cleveland. The decision, said Harvey O'Connor, biographer of the Mellons, was worth $100,000,000 to the Mellon family. After the decision, there was never any doubt about who made all the aluminum in the United States. It came from something referred to as the "aluminum trust."

Many of my generation first learned of the aluminum trust in 1917–18, when we were members of the American Expeditionary Force in France. Each of us two million soldiers possessed one aluminum mess kit, one aluminum canteen and holder used for a cup, one aluminum bacon can, and one aluminum condiment can.

Now, the canteen and cup and the mess kit were light, serviceable, and of use.

The other two items, which belonged to a day when soldiers carried and cooked their own rations, were absolutely worthless. They were worse than that; they were added burden and they took up space. But we lugged these two useless things over much of Europe. They had to be displayed on our bunks for daily inspection. We cursed them daily. We cursed the men who thought them up. We cursed the men who made them.

In time we came to use the bacon can to carry extra plug chewing tobacco. But the condiment can, a fearful thing of complicated design and several compartments, would hold nothing that soldiers had to carry. It was merely cute. The Mellons were of course not to blame for giving us obsolete equipment made from a new metal. The responsibility lay with some old cavalryman of the Army, still thinking of a muzzle-loading war when soldiers were their own cooks. Enormous profit, however, lay in supplying us with this needless stuff—impedimenta of the worst kind. We had not then heard of the Mellons, but most of us did know of something called the Aluminum Trust and we bellyached about it with the typical fervor of the set-upon enlisted man. I still recall the shock, delayed until about 1919, of learning that fortunes could be and were made during wartime.

The success of Pittsburgh Reduction set off organization of many stockjobbing aluminum concerns by fast promoters. One and all they quickly folded, including the fatuously named Aluminum Company of America, whose title was taken over later to rechristen Pittsburgh Reduction.

Working under a protective tariff of fifteen cents a pound, the Mellon trust went remorselessly ahead. A big plant was built at Niagara Falls. Another went up at Shawinigan Falls, Quebec. International "understandings" were made with the German, French, and British makers of aluminum, and the world markets partitioned by agreements. By 1898 the Mellons were manufacturing kits for every soldier in the Russian Army, and probably bacon tins and condiment cans.

The Mellon trust next achieved a monopoly of bauxite, the basic material of aluminum; and before long the metal was going into wire, radiators, castings, and hundreds of products theretofore made from other metals. Then came the mass-production automobile industry, which called for incredible amounts of aluminum. The Aluminum Company of America was ready to supply it in any amount and at a price set by the still unknown Andrew Mellon and his anonymous advisers.

If you did not want aluminum, the Mellons would sell you steel. When Frick and Carnegie had their falling out, as reported earlier in this book, the former and Andrew Mellon organized a fine and efficient nuisance called Union Steel Company and built a city around its main plant, Donora, Pennsylvania, named for the company's president, Donner, and Andrew Mellon's wife, who was Nora McMullen of Dublin, Ireland.

At Butler, Pennsylvania, Mellon built the Standard Steel Car Company to manufacture railroad rolling stock. He financed two young engineer graduates of Lehigh University to form the McClintic-Marshall Construction Company, retaining a sixty per cent interest in this outfit whose specialty was the building of steel bridges.

When Morgan was forming U. S. Steel, an attempt by his minions was made to force the Mellons to sell their Union Steel cheaply to the trust. But the Mellons did not "push" well, as one of big steel's attorneys put it. They held on, then merged Sharon Steel with Union, and announced plans for building a rail mill as large and much better than the steel corporation's plant at Braddock.

At last U. S. Steel decided to pay the Mellon price, which a United States commissioner of corporations later estimated to have been around $30,860,000. It was a complicated business at best, but the commissioner was sure of one thing: the price paid was fantastically more than the Mellon property merited.

It would be monotonous to list the accumulations of properties acquired by the Mellons over the years. For the most part they continued to practice the method of buying a heavy interest and often of control which they had found best suited to their business temperament.

The family showed consistent good judgment. A mention of some of the firms taken under their wing, and often their direction, will give an idea of their diversified nature. There was Pittsburgh Glass and several other glass concerns; the Pennsylvania and other railroads; the great Pittsburgh-Buffalo Coal Company; the Equitable and other insurance companies; and the already big Westinghouse properties. Shares in T. Mellon & Sons Bank, issued at $100, came to be quoted on the market at $2,000 each.

The Mellons also founded the Union Trust Company. Now, near the century's turn, they scrapped the old family bank and replaced it with the Mellon National. They also founded the Union Savings Bank. (They were fond of "Union" in a corporate title.)

In good time a building suitable for Mellon National was erected.

"It lifts its imposing Doric facade," wrote Silas Bent after a visit there, "above a whole block of Smithfield Street, and its spacious loggia gleams with granite and bronze and Ionic marble. Its ten thousand safe deposit vaults were the first to be fashioned of aluminum."

Andrew Mellon lacked even his father's condescending touch with the world. As the millions piled up, he drew further into the shell of his bank and ran his assorted empires through hired hands. He had no liking for either society or Society. He was seldom seen in the clubs to which he paid a member's dues. Before he was fifty he was a legendary figure in his own city and wholly unknown elsewhere.

A still younger member of the family was largely responsible for bringing into the Mellon orbit the great enterprise known today as the Gulf Oil Corporation. He was William Larimer Mellon, son of James, nephew of Andrew. During the 1890s William pioneered the West Virginia oil fields and, with family backing, built pipe lines and started refineries, even venturing into Pennsylvania. These the family sold in 1895, at a fine profit, to a subsidiary of Standard Oil. The Mellons were believed to have cleared two million dollars on the transaction.

Thus the family included a seasoned adviser when, a little later, they were called upon by Colonel James McClurg Guffey in regard to a certain proposition in Texas, a hog-wild gusher called Spindletop. W. L. Mellon knew Guffey. Guffey was not at all the Mellon type. For one thing he was a Democrat. For another, his getup reminded the bankers of a medicine-show man. Guffey never appeared without a broad-brimmed black hat and a flapping swallow-tailed coat. His sweeping white mustaches and bluff, hearty manner gave the added flavor of a "doc" who might at any moment start to lecture on the marvelous curative properties of Kickapoo Indian Sagwa.

But W. L. Mellon, who was the specific Mellon Guffey had come to see, knew him as one of the most successful drillers in the West Virginia and the Titusville oil fields. Naturally Guffey was a gambler, but up to now, which was 1901, a major portion of his chance-takings had paid off pretty well. He and his partner, John H. Galey, had rich oil leases in Kansas and elsewhere. Now, in the Mellon bank at Pittsburgh, Colonel Guffey told the Mellons of a new oil field beside which everything that had gone before was as nothing. Spindletop in Texas, he said, was quite incredible, and it was also a fact.

The gusher had just been brought in by a Yugoslav prospector whose Americanized name was Andy Lucas. He had searched for gold for years and had nothing to show for it. In 1899, he had turned to drilling for oil on an abandoned claim called Gladys City, not far from Beaumont, Texas.

For almost a year Lucas and his wife lived in a shack while the monotonous drilling went on, day after day, week after week. When his drill reached 575 feet, the sands brought up were most encouraging. Dr. W. B. Phillips, director of the state's geological survey, said so. Lucas should by all means carry the hole deeper, he advised.

The trouble was that Lucas had not a penny to buy more pipe. He and his wife had been living on short rations of even food and clothing. In his desperation Lucas sat down and wrote Guffey and Galey, the well-known oil men of Pittsburgh. They were known as long-shot gamblers. John Galey thought enough of Lucas's letter about his claim to go to Gladys City.

Galey looked the situation over, observed the sands recovered from 575 feet, then he made a deal with Lucas: Guffey & Galey took over a majority interest in the Lucas holding in return for a grubstake of pipe and other supplies needed. The drilling was resumed.

On January 9, 1901, Lucas felt the ground tremble and heard a deep rumbling. He fled to safety just an instant before a vast torrent of oil and mud roared up from the depths, ramming ahead of it some eight hundred feet of steel pipe as though it were a straw. The gusher crested two hundred feet above the ground, a black geyser that started blowing nearly one hundred thousand barrels a day.

Oildom, Colonel Guffey told the Mellons, had not seen the like. Drake's famous gusher of 1859 in Pennsylvania had astonished the world with its twenty barrels a day. The amazed John Galey telegraphed his partner, Colonel Guffey, for immediate funds and told him why they were needed.

On the day after the strike, said Galey, he had put hundreds of men and scores of teams, hurriedly recruited from Beaumont, to work throwing up dikes to hold the lake of oil. Thousands had come just to look and to wonder; and while Lucas and Galey and their crew were trying frantically to cap the gusher, some fool or ill-wisher tossed a lighted match. Hell broke out at Spindletop. Masses of flame took the air. Clouds of black smoke rose to plunge the whole region into semidarkness.

Before the fire had been conquered, oil possibly worth a hundred thousand dollars was consumed. The gusher was capped at last. The ground still shook spasmodically, but the fountain of oil was contained. Putting out the fire and getting matters under control had taken a lot of money, Guffey told the Mellons. He and Galey had used all their ready capital. It was clear, he said, that a great deal more money would be needed to meet the producing and marketing requirements of this hundred-thousand-barrel-a-day flood. Storage tanks must be built, a pipe line laid to tidewater, refineries established. And what did the Mellons think of it?

Acting on the advice of W. L. Mellon, the Pittsburgh bankers made three million dollars immediately available. They formed the J. M. Guffey Petroleum Company (later changed to Gulf Oil), gave Guffey a million dollars cash, another half million to be taken out of profits, and made him president. Even Andy Lucas came off better than well, considering that he was merely the man who had uncovered the oil Golconda. His rights in everything were bought for $400,000.

This time, the Mellons were in oil to stay. They went on to lease millions of acres in Texas and Louisiana, brought in several great wells, built a fleet of tankers, erected more refineries, and made Gulf Oil the largest independent, second in size only to Standard.

Indicative of Gulf Oil's proportions, thirty years after the Lucas gusher, were the titles of a few of its subsidiaries: Indiana Oil, American International Fuel & Petroleum, Gulf Petroleum Maatschappij van Nederlandsch Indie, Mexican Gulf Oil, Venezuela Gulf Oil, and Gulf Pipe Line of Pennsylvania. Such was the magic wrought by the money and brains of the Mellons on the gusher of Andy Lucas.

Six years after its incorporation, Colonel Guffey was no longer president of the company named for him. "They throwed me out" was the way he described what had happened to him. W. L. Mellon took Guffey's vacated seat. Twenty years later a jury awarded to Guffey, then aged eighty-six, the respectable sum of $348,695, which he had charged was owed him by the Mellons. The Mellons appealed, and won. Guffey died at ninety-one, a relatively poor man, says one of his biographers, Asher Isaacs, who rated the colorful colonel as a "personality endowed with the traditions of pioneer daring."

The Gulf Oil Corporation had walked unasked into the Mellon offices at Pittsburgh on the swallow-tail-coated legs of old Colonel Guffey. The Pittsburgh Reduction Company, reborn as the Aluminum Company of America, also had come hat in hand to borrow cash. from the Mellons. By 1914, these two concerns were the crown jewels of the Mellon collection. In that year a third gem, fit to cluster and dazzle with the other two, made its appearance. It did not come unasked. Andrew Mellon himself summoned it in the person of Dr. Heinrich Koppers.

Dr. Koppers was a native of Germany, inventor of the Koppers coke oven, who had recently come to Illinois to build a 280-oven unit at Joliet. From this type of oven Germany had built up a tremendous industry making explosives, aniline dyes, and many other products from the so-called waste gasses incident to making coke.

It was Henry Clay Frick who first told his close friend, Andrew Mellon, about these ovens. Frick said that they might well pay a bigger profit in by-products than the returns from the coke itself. Yet Frick's thousands of beehive ovens continued to desolate the country around about, as their gasses were loosed in a killing fog. American coke users had seen the Koppers coke and would not have it. It lacked the sheen of the beehive-oven product, and one of the strongly held myths of the industry was that the sheen contained some sort of magic qualities proper for the making of good steel.

Andrew Mellon may have listened to his friend Frick, but his active interest in Dr. Koppers came almost simultaneously with the outbreak of war in Europe in 1914. Through Frick and others, he knew that the gigantic guns of Germany were being fired by explosives derived at least in part from the by-products of coal gas. He asked Dr. Koppers to come to see him at Pittsburgh.

Dr. Koppers came to talk with the wispy and almost voiceless man in the big bank building. Possibly Dr. Koppers had a poor head for business. Maybe he was merely discouraged. Whatever the cause, he was glad to sell his plant and his patents to Mellon for $300,000, which he took as stock in a reorganized Koppers Company, and the promise of a ten-thousand-dollar-a-year salary. The offices of the new concern were established in Pittsburgh.

Over in Europe the war was growing. Andrew Mellon, no man to act impulsively, yet felt the need for haste on this occasion. He drew millions from the Mellon coffers to start at once the building of vast numbers of Dr. Koppers' by-product ovens. The Koppers Company built the ovens for others, but always on a profit-sharing basis. It also built many more ovens to be operated by its own subsidiaries.

Then, in 1917, the United States entered the war. The Koppers Company corps of engineers was doubled, and the whole crew of them often worked day and night to build still more batteries of ovens. A new such plant was completed every month or so during 1917 and 1918.

When it came to pass that Germany was an enemy of the United States, our alien property custodian demanded of American business and industry to know if they harbored any enemy aliens among stockholders. The Mellons truthfully reported that twenty per cent of the Koppers Company stock was owned by Dr. Koppers, who was then a resident of Essen. The United States government declared these shares to be confiscated, and they were put up at public auction at the Pittsburgh Stock Exchange. The sole bidder was an official of the Koppers Company and of the Mellon National Bank. He got the 3,000 shares of Dr. Koppers for $302,250, which was their value as of 1914, with accrued dividends, and they went into the Mellon vaults. They came cheap enough, for they represented in 1918 one fifth of the value of a concern worth about fifteen and a half million dollars.

The Koppers Company went on to new glories after the war. A subsidiary, Koppers Gas & Coke, came into being with a twenty-five-million-dollar bond issue. It was only one of the brood of fifty-seven companies hatched by the magic ovens of Dr. Koppers, plus the magic touch of the Mellons. The era of the holding company had come into its fantastic heyday, and pyramids of corporations arose.

It is instructive, though a dizzying experience, to contemplate the structure of the pyramid whose base was the Koppers Company of Delaware. Into it went eleven corporations, including the Koppers Gas & Coke, and Alan Wood Steel.

Koppers Gas & Coke controlled an even twelve corporations, including Eastern Gas & Fuel, Koppers Coal & Transportation, and American Tar Products.

American Tar Products controlled four companies. Eastern Gas

& Fuel controlled seven companies, one of which was Massachusetts Gas which, in turn, controlled Boston Consolidated Gas.

Koppers Coal & Transportation controlled twelve companies,
including New England Fuel & Transportation which, in turn, controlled six companies.

Alan Wood Steel controlled four companies, none of which, for
some reason or other, seems to have controlled any other concerns.

Still another Mellon empire, which had neither visible nor corporate connection with Koppers or the Aluminum Company of
America, was Pittsburgh Coal, a monster with twenty-four subsidiary provinces. A number of these companies had "Coal" in their
titles, but the empire included such unlikely sounding corporations as Interurban Realty, Valley Supply, and Elizabeth Marine
Ways.

The Mellon name was no part of any of the fifty-seven corporations referred to above, yet you were dealing with Mellon, even if
the business happened to be so seemingly remote from coal, or oil,
or gas, or aluminum, as the charmingly named Walloon Realty,
Massena Securities, Wood Preserving, and the Mystic Iron Works.

There were many, many more items in the Mellon "portfolio,"
as financial writers quaintly term a listing of acquisitions. These
included large interests in such well-known corporations as the
Pennsylvania Railroad, Bethlehem Steel, Pullman Company, Niagara Hudson, and Carborundum; and in pure holding companies
such as United Light & Power, United Light & Railways, Continental Gas & Electric, Duke-Price, and the Philadelphia Company.

What the Mellons were worth, or even what Andrew Mellon
was worth when his name appeared for the first time in the New
York *Times* as a possible Secretary of the Treasury, is probably
beyond knowing. In his study of the Mellons, Harvey O'Connor
wrote that the family controlled industrial assets alone valued at
$1,942,850,438, and controlled banking and financial interests of
more than half a billion dollars. In 1929, said O'Connor, the Mellon banking interests returned to the family $3,851,370 in divi-
dends; and their profits from industrial shares and bonds amounted
to $91,146,168. When Andrew Mellon became Secretary of the
Treasury he resigned from the boards of fifty-one corporations.

In 1909 Mrs. Andrew Mellon returned to her native Ireland.
She liked Pittsburgh no more than Herbert Spencer had liked it,

and he, it will be recalled, looked upon the place and remarked that a month there would justify anyone in committing suicide.

A year after Mrs. Mellon's departure, Andrew Mellon sued for divorce; and while the action was pending, the legislators of the state of Pennsylvania, possibly urged by their boss, Boies Penrose, thoughtfully passed a new divorce law that empowered a court to appoint a master who might hear evidence in private, thus precluding the airing of the details of domestic discord, often to the great disturbance of public morals.

The Mellons were divorced in 1912. The charges were simple desertion. Each parent was given custody of the two children, Paul and Ailsa, for six months of the year.

Divorce apparently brought no change in the life of Andrew Mellon. He continued to live, as in the past, in the imposing if somewhat gloomy mansion at Pittsburgh. Unlike Frick and Carnegie, and many another Pittsburgher of wealth, Mellon never let his home town down. He lived quietly there, and he conducted his affairs, just as quietly, at the Mellon National on Smithfield Street. The Mellon millions continued to grow as quietly as they always had. That there was such a person as Andrew Mellon was still unknown to his fellow Americans.

Why Andrew Mellon, surely the shiest of all American men of wealth, should have wanted to enter the hurly-burly of public life was explained succinctly by Frank R. Kent, the political columnist. Mr. Kent observed that there were men of large means who, on reaching middle age and having achieved remarkable success in finance or business, discovered there was no further thrill to be had in piling up more millions. To fill the void they developed a yearning for some sort of public honor and prestige.

Such men, said Mr. Kent, were known to practical politicians as "fat cats," and they were most welcome to Republicans and Democrats alike. Mr. Kent went on to say that "if Andrew Mellon is not the finest fat cat they have had in Pennsylvania since anyone can remember, then every sign fails."

What inspired Mr. Kent to his observations was the fact that the Mellon bank had just underwritten a little deficit of $1,500,000 in the campaign chest of the Republican National Committee.

Such was the manner in which Mr. Mellon's name was submitted as a likely candidate for a cabinet post under President Warren Gamaliel Harding. He was soon confirmed as Secretary of the

Treasury. The newspaper boys had the greatest difficulty writing about this man whom leading papers referred to as "one of the lesser-known cabinet figures" and "an unknown millionaire from Pittsburgh." Some papers gave him a *G* for a middle initial, others had it *D,* still others used either *J* or *A.* His name did not appear in a list of the one hundred wealthiest families in the United States. Nor was Mellon himself the man to help very much. He did let it be known that he was firmly against the League of Nations. Otherwise he had nothing to say. Nothing at all.

Of Mr. Harding's entourage, only Calvin Coolidge, the Vice-President, spoke less, and not much less, than Mellon. There was garrulity enough around the table anyway, what with Albert Fall, Edwin Denby, Harry Daugherty, James J. Davis, Will Hays, and Henry C. Wallace, ready to air their opinions. Charles Evans Hughes and Herbert Hoover were other members of the group.

President Harding and several of his cabinet members were quite awed as they gradually came to appreciate the immense wealth represented by their colleague. Not that he bragged of it, but now and then something slipped out of him, as casual and as subconcious as breathing, that sat them up in their chairs. For instance, when the cabinet was discussing the possible scrapping of a war plant, and Secretary of War Weeks asked Mellon's advice, the answer came in a voice almost too faint to hear. "I have not looked into it thoroughly yet," said Secretary Mellon, "but I had a similar case recently in one of my own plants to deal with. The amount involved was the same, or $12,000,000. I scrapped mine." He might have been speaking of giving an old suit of clothes to the Salvation Army.

Seven years after Mellon was sworn in as Secretary, Silas Bent remarked that he had withstood all the raking fire of professional sharpshooters and remained unruffled. Mellon, he said, had also "developed an unexpected expertness in rapier play." But there "was no political patronage in the Treasury while he headed it."

Mr. Mellon's long career as Secretary of the Treasury and his brief career as Ambassador to England are not within the province of this book. Sufficient to say that if he had wanted prestige, he got it in fabulous measure until the depression, when it waned in the misery and the bafflement of the American people. Then the fulsome praise of "the greatest Secretary of the Treasury since Alexander Hamilton" became a term of bitter mockery, along with the "two chickens in every pot" of Mr. Hoover.

Whether or not he originated it, one treasury reform in the Mellon administration was of lasting benefit. This was the new and small format for currency, only two thirds the size of the bills that had been used for decades. One of Mellon's biographers, Philip H. Love, said the new format represented an annual saving to the government of $552,520 in paper, $120,000 in ink, and a round million dollars in labor. "Inspired by his natural Scotch belief in economy," wrote Mr. Love, "these thrifty bills, which run from $1 all the way up to $10,000, are distinctly Mellonistic both in design and in size."

To present the remote Andrew Mellon as a human being is impossible from conventional sources. A score of books both good and bad have traced his life as a great financier and as a cabinet officer. Then there are the sustained attacks on him as the greatest villain of all American capitalists, John D. Rockefeller not excepted; and the pious and sirupy drivel put out by his fawning apologists both amateur and professional.

Such being the case, I appealed for help to an old friend, Lucius Beebe, who I knew had been on fairly close terms with the Mellons, and asked him if Andrew Mellon really was human. "He was much more interesting than you might infer from the record," said Mr. Beebe, "but he was extremely reserved, patrician, and shy of personal contacts. Like all rich men he was elaborately hedged by guards, servants, and underlings. I have heard businessmen say Mr. Mellon was harder of access than J. P. Morgan or Henry C. Frick. Even Paul Mellon was a little frightened of his father and spoke frequently of his 'ice-water smile.'

"Yet he was a most interesting old gentleman to talk with, and I spent hours on a park bench in Bermuda with him when he was Secretary of the Treasury, with only a British police guard at a removed distance, listening to him tell about his past. In his youth he had made the grand tour of Europe when it was known as just that. He used to put up at Brown's in London, an unbelievably conservative 'private hotel' favored by country squires and Bostonians such as my own family abroad, and one compared to which Claridge's, which was patronized solely by visiting royalty and earls and dukes, was flashy and fast.

"Mr. Mellon told me that his most persistent recollection of London was 'listening when I awoke in the morning to the clopping of horses' hooves on the wooden blocks which paved the street

under my window at Brown's. It seemed to me they were the ever-
lasting voice of London, those horses' hooves, and I thought, as a
melancholy boy will, that they would still be clopping on the pavements long after I, and perhaps my money, were gone. Now I've
outlasted the horses in the streets of London. It makes me feel
very old indeed.'

"That was the nearest to sentiment I ever heard him come,
though on the same trip to Bermuda he occasioned an incident I
shall never forget. There were quite a group of us boys along,
all friends of Paul, some of us with the Mellon party like myself,
others who had come down on the same steamer at reduced college
rates for Easter. We all went to Trimmingham's to watch Mr.
Mellon buy Paul a polo coat, at that time uncheapened by gangsters
and universality, and a very fine thing for a college boy to own,
though way beyond most of our means.

"Then, when Paul had been fitted and the old gentleman was
counting out the square English bank notes, he turned with his
timid frosty smile to a group of at least five of us and said hesi-
tantly: 'Wouldn't you boys each like a polo coat? I'd admire to
stand treat.' Of course we all swore we had polo coats at home
by the dozen (which we hadn't) and all wanted desperately to
have one, but the quaint old-fashioned remark stuck in my mind
because the treat wouldn't have cost him more than about a
thousand dollars—just as though it were a round of sodas!"

As Secretary of the Treasury, Andrew Mellon was obliged to
give lip service to prohibition, but he never had any sympathy
with the experiment noble in purpose, and though he himself was
little given to liquor, the Mellon portfolio had for many years
contained a goodly portion of the Old Overholt distillery. During
prohibition, Mr. Beebe recalls, the Mellon home at Pittsburgh
contained not only a gallonage of the family whiskey more than
sufficient to cover all needs, but gin, rum, wines light and otherwise, and malted beverages of foreign and domestic manufacture.

"The Mellon home," continued Mr. Beebe, "was guarded by a
night watchman, named appropriately Mr. Moon, a fine old gentleman, whom I guessed to be some sort of family retainer and who
wore a distinguished white beard, a dinner suit, and a watchman's
clock on a strap around his neck.

"I am an early riser, a circumstance which promoted me with
Mr. Mellon, and even after coming in at seven could take off my
dinner clothes and come to breakfast half an hour later in good

shape. (Those days are now past.) The old man was very fond
of thin little hot cakes and sausages, and their service was ritual.
One morning in the midst of their presentation, one at a time by
the day footman, another lackey brought in the telephone on a
cord and announced that the Minister of Finance of France wished
to speak with Mr. Mellon on the transocean. 'Not with the hot
cakes,' said the old gentleman testily, and then to me, who was bug-
eyed, 'These foreigners have no sense of propriety.' "

Mr. Beebe said he had heard that Andrew Mellon's philanthropies were very considerable but that the more personal ones
were kept hidden out of his "patrician hatred for anything savoring
of personal popularity or seeming to cater to good will." He had
understood, too, that Mellon's benevolences such as hospital care,
college educations, pianos for music students, and all sorts of
generosities, were shrouded with scrupulous secrecy; and that every
Christmas time, he had a sort of private celebration of his own.
This consisted of burning the notes of small creditors and telling
them to forget it.

For a man of such towering power and wealth, Mr. Beebe
thought Andrew Mellon had developed few eccentricities. "He
smoked a diminutive sort of cigar called 'Between the Acts' and
which came ten in a small tin box for fifteen cents," Mr. Beebe
recalls. "These he smoked in chain at all hours of the day and
night. He invariably wore white stiff linen collars and cuffs, never
acknowledging the soft shirt or sports-garb era. His clothes were
really beautiful but very subdued.

"He owned a 'Mellon' automobile of which he was humorously
proud. It was the only one in existence, and every part of it from
cylinder block to upholstery was made of some product dominated
by the old man. Largely, of course, it was of Mellon aluminum. I
heard it cost $40,000 to have it hand-built throughout. I remember
riding with him in it to the Mellon bank in downtown Pittsburgh.
It was not a particularly beautiful car, being somewhat angular,
but obviously it was Mr. Mellon's car, and traffic parted before it
as the Red Sea for the children of Israel."

It was in Pittsburgh, too, where Andy Mellon and a newspaperman whose name has been lost to history combined to make an
enduring legend. The Secretary of the Treasury was home for a
week end and was much put out to read a local news item which
said Son Paul was gravely ill. Mr. Mellon himself telephoned the
newspaper to deny the story as a canard. Somebody on the copy

desk picked up the phone to hear a faint voice say: "This is A. W. Mellon . . ."

"Well, hell-o, you old son of a bitch," shouted the copy desk man, "and how about lending me five dollars?"

It took a little effort on A. W. Mellon's part to convince the brash lad of the press that he really was talking to a character as remote and shadowy to him, and possibly as mythical, as Midas, King of Phrygia.

Chapter 5   INSULL THE FALSE MIDAS

O NE of the several supernatural powers of a genuine Midas is the ability to detect a false Midas. So, early in 1930 Andrew Mellon "prudently," says his biographer with the modest understatement characteristic of his subject, "prudently disposed of his holdings in Insull's Middle West Utilities."

Midas Mellon was then in his ninth glorious year as Secretary of the Treasury.

Midas Sam Insull was still believed by almost everybody to be the genuine article, the man who had built and now lived at the top of a pyramid of solid gold, or at least a reasonably good facsimile. Two years later he was horribly shown to be a false Midas. By then he was a fugitive in a small and aromatic tramp steamer which should have been, but wasn't, named the *Flying Dutchman,* seeking safe harbor in one port after another where extradition to the United States would not be operative. Many thousands of his countrymen wanted him returned to Chicago to tell them what had become of the $750,000,000 they had put into the slots of the Insull patented money-making machine. In addition, certain bankers wanted to know the same thing about $43,500,000.

The divination of the prudent Mr. Mellon may have come through the new science of electronics, or it may have emanated from some mysterious element inherent in the office of Secretary of the United States Treasury. In either case, the foresight removed the Mellon cash safely from the shadows of the Insull structure a good two years before it tottered and the walls came tumbling down in the crash of the century.

Yet for all that, Sam Insull contributed something more than the most stupendous financial failure of record. Before the resounding echo of his collapse had died away, there was new legislation afoot for regulating the issuance of securities, the outlawing of holding companies, the governing of stock exchanges, and in general giving assurance "to the shorn lambs and the lambs yet unborn that the same instruments would not be employed to fleece them again."

The legislation is now the federal Securities Exchange Act. It came higher than anything Jay Gould ever bought from lawmakers. If it does prevent congenital suckers from filling their predestined places, then it is more than a wonderful law. It is a miraculous law.

Among the American colossi of money Samuel Insull was unique in two respects. His was the greatest failure of them all, greater even than Jay Cooke's; and he was a native of England. Born in 1859 in a grubby part of London, his father was an obscure nonconformist preacher which, in England, is to say that he was a man of little standing and of even less means. Sam's mother aided in the family livelihood by operating Insull's Temperance Hotel. Hotels that were not pubs were notoriously meager in cash return, yet the Insulls' income permitted young Sam to attend a good private school and he seems to have made excellent use of his time there.

At fourteen he became a junior clerk for a firm of auctioneers. He learned shorthand and how to run the newfangled typewriting machines. Four years later opportunity knocked when a Colonel Gourard engaged him as secretary. Gourard was the London representative of Thomas Alva Edison, the American inventor and all-around wizard with electricity. Insull's quick intelligence impressed everyone connected with Edison's English interests. In 1881, aged twenty-one, Insull arrived in the United States with the promise of a job with the chief himself. He became Edison's private secretary, and was soon much more than that; he was Edison's most trusted adviser; and a few years more he was general manager of most of the Edison enterprises.

One of these concerns was a small outfit at Schenectady, New

York, the Edison General Electric Company. It was having troubles. Its output was slow and irregular. It was losing money steadily. Edison told Insull to go up there and run it. "Whatever you do, Sam," as Insull liked to tell the story, "either make a brilliant success of it or a brilliant failure. Do something!"

Sammy did something. When he took over, the plant employed 200 men. When he left, less than a decade later, it had 6,000 employees, Insull was in charge of both manufacture and sales, and his salary had risen to $36,000 a year. He was at this time, said one who knew him, a rugged, thickset Briton of the traditional rare roast-beef type, who radiated self-assurance and had "an iron jaw beneath a cushion of fresh, pink skin."

Fresh and pink, and assured, he arrived in Chicago in 1892, ready to head another small and dubious company. This was the infant Chicago Edison. He accepted the presidency at $12,000, a third of what he had been getting at Schenectady. He borrowed $250,000 from Marshall Field with which to buy himself a good hunk of stock in the new enterprise.

The Columbian Exposition of 1893 was to be the greatest demonstration to date of the wonders of illumination by electricity. Insull's little company helped to make the fairgrounds brilliant. Another was the small Commonwealth Electric Company. Insull convinced Commonwealth that the two concerns could grow faster and make more money if he, Insull, headed them both. He was promptly made president of Commonwealth, and ran both firms until 1907, when he consolidated them as Commonwealth Edison. Insull, of course, was president.

He had long since learned the methods by which legislators and assorted politicians are to be charmed, and proved it in 1907 by getting from the city of Chicago a forty-year exclusive franchise "to distribute electric power within the present or future limits of the municipality."

Insull had not overlooked the country surrounding Chicago. In the late nineties he began buying small electric properties in five counties, combining them into the Public Service Company of Northern Illinois. They were acquired in the usual manner, through issues of stocks and bonds, and the swapping thereof, a sort of legal legerdemain at which the young Briton was a master.

He was even better as an operator. Nothing in the mechanical line quite suited him. He wanted bigger energy for his many plants and longer transmission for their power. At about this time there arrived in the United States a sample of a new machine called a compound steam turbine. It had been invented by an Englishman, Sir Charles Algernon Parsons, but that wasn't why Insull wanted one; he knew that a Parsons turbine had already driven a ship faster than ever a ship had moved before. What would a Parsons turbine of enormous horsepower do for the generation of electric power? Insull had one built and it was a wonder of the time.

In 1903, on Chicago's Fisk Street, Sam Insull watched while his Parsons-type turbine produced 5,000 kilowatts. Nothing like it had been dreamed of, nor was the great day forgotten. A quarter of a century later, power men from all over the Midwest gathered at the Fisk Street station to place a tablet honoring its part in bringing light into dark places.

"This turbine," wrote Chicago historian Henry Justin Smith, "unknown to the crowd, had performed an immense feat. Before it, transmission reached only about 2,500 feet. With it, transmission became comparatively without bounds." It is remembered, too, that because Insull's directors showed reluctance to underwrite the cost of the turbine, he guaranteed the cost from his own pocket. Within a year the company had installed another big turbine of the same sort. So far as the Midwest was concerned, the two machines on Chicago's Fisk Street were the Adam and Eve. Turbines multiplied and grew in size—to 20,000 kilowatts, to 50,000 kilowatts, then doubled and tripled.

The great abilities of this assured young Englishman were quite apparent to other Chicago industrialists, including the discouraged officials of the Peoples Gas, Light & Coke Company. They needed help. The firm was a million dollars behind in taxes. There was no money to replace antiquated equipment. Bills for supplies were long overdue. Receivership was being contemplated when Insull went in as chairman of the board. He formed a separate By-Products Corporation, financed by sale of its stock; then proceeded to make and sell gas to the parent company cheaper than had been the case. Obligations were met. Peoples Gas was now a solvent and flourishing utility.

Was this man an Aladdin with lamp in his hand? The boss men of Chicago's battered traction companies believed so. They came to Insull with their difficulties, which were numerous. Insull took over. He combined the several shabby and conflicting and competing lines. He borrowed money, put out a bond issue. He got new equipment to improve the surface lines. He extended the elevated and suburban runs and restored the whole to comparative health, even though like much else in the city they continued to be graft-ridden.

Insull accepted graft as a condition of living in Chicago. Then and later he and his colleagues were always ready to aid whatever political party was in power. He was careful only that whoever was the dominating personality of the public utilities commission should enjoy the Insull generosity. Insull was also freehanded with all things described as "good causes" and no list of patrons of the arts, sciences, or charities was complete without Samuel Insull's name down for a fat contribution.

At suburban Libertyville, Insull established an estate, dressed in knickerbockers, and became a transplanted English squire, growing a sweeping mustache that turned white early and added a distinguished note to this mellow and affable country gentleman. Affable, that is, in his social life. In business he remained ruthless and dictatorial, and "his will seemed to dominate the affairs of Chicago."

Taking heed, long before most of his fellow power men, of the rising opposition to private utility companies, Insull began selling stock in his companies to employees and customers. These people, he thought, would create a bulwark against the mounting sentiment for municipal and government ownerships. Even more remarkable was Insull's attitude about "government interference," remarking publicly that if there was anything wrong about his business, he wanted to know it. He was generally courteous to critics. And once at least he said that if public regulation of private utilities failed, then public ownership would follow. But he did not want public ownership.

In 1912 Insull entered the phase of his career by which he is remembered, none too tenderly, forty years later. To raise more money with which to expand his operating concerns, he formed Middle West Utilities, the first of his many holding companies. The growth of this concern over the next twenty years, remarks Francis X. Busch, was astonishing, for it came to serve "over 1,800,000 customers in some 3,500 communities in thirty-nine states."

Although the several parts of Middle West Utilities were separately managed, all were directed by Insull himself. He was working harder than ever before, reaching his office before eight after the long drive from his suburban estate. He was dreaming bigger than ever. The time was the twenties, a period for monstrous dreams, a time for the whelping of stock-selling companies, of holding companies, the era when the common man was to become a minor capitalist, even though he carried a dinner pail to work.

This lush period could not have happened earlier than it did. It had to await the appearance of a vast congregation of speculators, or at least investors. The congregation developed in no small part because the years of World War I had created, through Liberty Bonds, a whole new class of investors, people who had never before owned a bond or a share of stock in anything. By the mid-twenties the demand for speculative opportunities had become great. Gifted men, among whom was Sam Insull, rose to the occasion. Within a brief time there appeared wonders like Giannini's Bancitaly Corporation, the pyramid of the Van Sweringens' railroad system, and Sidney Z. Mitchell's mountainous Electric Bond & Share Company. These were primarily stock-selling outfits.

So was Insull's newest creation, which he chose to call Utility Securities Company. This was merely a starter of what became known for a while as the Insull empire and later as the Insull bubble, or the Insull bust. It was an illusion composed of all of the concerns already mentioned as Insull properties, while piled on top were things like Insull Utility Investments, Inc., Insull, Son & Company, Insull, Son & Company, Ltd. (England), Corporation Securities Company of Chicago, and Corporation Syndicates, Inc.

The relation to each other of these and of still other and minor Insull mirages need not be mentioned here. Owen D. Young, the corporation lawyer, covered the matter in a couple of sentences. It is "impossible," he said after delving into the Insull disaster, "for any man however able really to grasp the real situation [of that vast structure] . . . it was so set up that you could not possibly get an accounting system which would not mislead even the officers themselves . . ."

During the wild seven years of the twenties, it didn't matter. Americans would buy any old stock just as they'd try a swig of any bottle plainly labeled whiskey. American business, so the prophets cried in the market places, was headed for new frontiers and a destiny undreamed of. It would carry with it to affluence all who possessed the wit to buy shares—shares in almost anything offered by these new and generous masters of capital who were inviting the man in the street, and even the street cleaner, along with the barber, the store clerk, the housewife, to join them in this golden opportunity.

Of these new-type masters of capital, surely the most potent was

Sam Insull. In eight months of 1929 stock in Insull Utility Investments went from $30 to $147 a share. His other paper enterprises
were almost as glittering, and the sun-crowned king of this incredible age was living regally up to his station. He scattered largess.
On Wacker Drive he promoted and helped to finance the twenty-
million-dollar Chicago Opera House, and in it installed the Civic
Opera Company, which he financed—briefly. It was believed that
Insull's wealth far exceeded the fortunes of Chicago's earlier capitalists like Field, Pullman, and Armour. A local newspaperman
said it was worth a million dollars to any man to be seen chatting
with Sam Insull in front of the Continental Bank.

In January of 1929 there was no one to look over the edge of
the cliff and note how far it was down to the bottom of the canyon.
Businessmen and their hired prophets said that the new high road
to prosperity was clear, so travel along the rosy thoroughfare continued. The traffic slowed briefly in April, when stocks seemed to
waver, but they quickly recovered. In August the sacred Dow-
Jones average for industrials hit a new high. In September it
went to 381, a point that still stands.

Yet, in September there came a break in prices, then a recovery.
Almost imperceptibly the market weakened until October 28, when
frightened speculators started really to unload. All stocks went into
a sharp decline.

The time had come. It was now the moment to perform the old
magic act that had been traditional with Wall Street since the
panics of the nineties. So the biggest big shots assembled in the
offices of J. P. Morgan and, to quote Thurman Arnold, "formed
a consortium to shore up the market." All the old reliable gags and
rituals were dusted off and presented in full dress. Richard Whitney, the Morgan broker—not quite but almost ready for Sing Sing
—bid heavily and ostentatiously for U. S. Steel. Old John D. Rockefeller was corralled on his golf course and urged to speak for the
good of the nation. "My son and I," quavered the old man, "are
buying stocks." Lesser figures rose like automatons all over the
United States to say that the country was basically sound.

It had all worked in the past. Similar incantations had appeared
to stem disaster in '93 and in '07. They were futile now, and they
were wholly drowned in the real crash, which came on October 28,
a Monday and thus a disappointment to the superstitious.

Sixteen and a half million shares changed hands that day, and the thuds you heard were said to be the bodies of brokers landing on the pavements of Wall and Broad streets; and on Chicago's La Salle Street, too, for the great pyramid of Insull shook with a mighty palsy.

Insull's collection of paper corporations had long since entered the regions of unreality. The system on which he had erected the structure depended on continuous growth, or rather a continuous sale of shares. He must have something with which to pay dividends. Money to pay them had to come from new issues of stock. Simple enough. But continuous sale was imperative.

Insull could not retrench. He could only go on, and on he went, showing profits, paying dividends, and selling stock. His brokers stimulated matters in the usual manner by buying and selling Insull stocks to each other. As late as 1931 Insull's brokers, Halsey, Stuart & Company, were managing to peddle shares in Insull securities, chiefly to small investors who would be more likely than the big fellows to hold on to them.

There is good evidence that Insull himself still believed devoutly in each and every part of his monstrous pyramid of what one dislikes to call "properties" and thus abuse one of the most worthy and highly respected words in our language. He borrowed wherever he could, using stock as collateral. It was of no use. The current of liquidation was not to be dammed—not even by the five million dollars Insull borrowed on his own personal account from the National City Bank of New York and turned into the empty coffers of his Corporation Securities Company; or by another million dollars borrowed from General Electric which he used to reduce the National City Bank loan; or by the half-million-dollar life insurance policy he turned in; or yet by the remnants of his own holdings in stocks and his four-thousand-acre estate. All of his personal property and that of his wife were turned over voluntarily to his creditors. It must have been a bleak time for the Insulls.

How bleak a period it was we can judge from the observations of Lloyd (Duke) Ryerson, one of the thirty-six personal bodyguards of the Insulls, father and son, who were engaged at this time because of threats from frightened speculators who were not getting any return from their shares in Insull properties.

By now, Sam, Sr., had given up his estate and moved into an apartment across the street from the Drake Hotel. Sam, Jr., lived in a co-op apartment on Lake Shore Drive, into which he had bought in prosperous days. The thirty-six guards were detailed in eight-hour shifts, twelve to the shift. They were hand-picked men, and paid a dollar an hour. They were armed.

"I soon learned," Duke Ryerson recalled, "that the Insulls were receiving an average of twenty threatening letters a day. Most of them were directed at Insull, Sr. A few were addressed to the son, and some to the son's wife. They came from all parts of the Midwest, with now and then one postmarked on the west coast. I think I read all of them. None threatened kidnaping of Sam, Jr.'s children, but they promised violent death in one form or another to all the Insulls. Bombing, stabbing, hanging, burning, and other variants of homicide, with shooting the most popular, were promised.

"The letters obviously came from several kinds of people with one thing in common—they owned shares in the Insull house of illusion. The number of letters increased steadily during the more than a year I acted as a bodyguard. And they got on the nerves of the Insulls. Both the old man and Sam, Jr., held up well for a long time, but they became jumpy. Mrs. Sam, Jr., was a nervous wreck."

Duke Ryerson remembered several attempts of strangers to get into one or the other Insull apartment. One of these came when Ryerson was on the graveyard shift between midnight and 8 A.M. Somebody piled a mass of boxes and rubbish in the alley, set it afire, and turned in an alarm. Half a dozen companies responded with sirens screaming. The Gold Coast awoke in the midst of the uproar. Doormen and elevator operators left their posts to go outside, leaving main entrances open. Ryerson remained in the Insull apartment-house lobby, and presently saw two men trying the entrance. But they saw Ryerson and fled.

There were many other alarms, but the close call came when Sam, Sr., was being driven to his office in the Opera House, and a bullet crashed through the limousine's window glass and lodged in the chauffeur's shoulder. The old man had felt the wind of a .38-caliber missile. Shortly thereafter, a 16-cylinder Cadillac arrived for Insull's use. It was armor-plated from radiator cap to rear bumper. The windows were of plate glass one inch thick.

As the depression worsened and it became increasingly apparent that the Insull stocks were to pay no more dividends, the most active duties of Ryerson and his fellows were in the Insull offices, where they stood just inside the main entrance. "I had to stop many callers forcibly," Ryerson said. "They were bound they were going to get in to see the old man. They wouldn't talk to anyone else. I'd try to reason with them, and if they didn't like that, I'd throw them out into the hall, frisk them for weapons, and let them go. I never found one armed and I don't think any of the other guards did. We didn't bother to have the callers arrested. They were too many."

Duke Ryerson did not claim to know anything about stocks, but he came to like all the Insulls. "I felt mighty sorry for them," he said. "They were kindly, considerate people, and I believe they were absolutely honest. Like many other unfortunates, they were the victims of circumstances. If the market crash had not come along just when it did, the Insulls would soon have ranked with the House of Morgan. Anyhow, living with the Insulls during their dark days cured me of wanting to be a multimillionaire."

We have seen how Samuel Insull avoided personal bankruptcy by turning over to creditors his stocks, his estate, and his life insurance. But the Insull empire had gone to pieces, and in April—it was now 1932—the man with the black hood called at the Insull offices. "Does this mean receivership?" asked the old man. (He had turned seventy-three.) He was told that it did. "I wish my time on earth had already come," he said. He was old, he was ill, he was mortally discouraged, yet somewhere in his tired and shrinking body remained a piece of the man's almost infinite energy; and because of this, Americans and the world at large were to be treated to a dandy cops-and-robbers chase on an international scale.

The saga of Insull the fugitive began quietly enough on June 14, 1932, two months after the receivership was announced. He and Mrs. Insull, with no protest from any quarter and with no great notice, sailed from Quebec for Europe.

In September the investigators of Insull's affairs got busy. It looked to them as if the losses to investors in Middle West Securities alone would run to more than seven hundred million dollars. Add eighty-five million dollars' loss to shareholders in Corporation Securities.

The investigators also reported certain "irregularities," to use the genteel euphemism employed in the bankers' trade to cover almost any conceivable crime. A "crossloaning" of collateral had taken place between Insull companies. Illegal preferences had been given to favored creditors. Millions of dollars had been removed from assets to pay "questionable" brokers' fees. Insull's inner-sanctum crowd had operated a secret syndicate list by which big profits had been secretly paid to some sixteen hundred favored participants. Relatives and friends of Insull were found in bulk on company pay rolls.

It was an election year, and one of the candidates, Franklin D. Roosevelt, had erected an imposing platform, one plank of which was a promise to put drastic curbs on corporations, with special attention to holding companies.

In Chicago, State's Attorney John Swanson was up for re-election. "He was quick," remarks Francis X. Busch, "to take advantage of the hue and cry against Insull and share in the front-page publicity." He set a staff of his catchpoles to working with the receivers of the Insull properties, and another crew to "study the applicability of existing state criminal laws to the anticipated evidence of wrong doing." Swanson warmed up the press by announcing there seemed to have been violations of the Illinois Blue Sky Law.

On September 25, Chicago papers reported that the federal department of Justice had begun a full-scale investigation of the Insull companies.

On October 4 a Cook County (Chicago) grand jury returned indictments against Samuel Insull and his brother, Martin Insull, charging embezzlement from two of the Insull companies.

The investigations continued, resulting in two more indictments. One charged Samuel Insull and sixteen others, including his son, Samuel Insull, Jr., and Harold L. Stuart, of Halsey, Stuart & Company, with using the mails to defraud. The other said that the Insulls, father and son, and Stuart, had illegally transferred Insull securities with intent to defeat the National Bankruptcy Act.

It was now June 1, 1933. And where were the three Insulls? Martin, Sam's brother, it appeared, had taken up residence in Canada. Sam, Jr., remained in Chicago. The old man, somebody suddenly recalled, was somewhere abroad. Over the cables went the news of the indictments, and in Paris an American newspaperman reported Sam Insull, Sr., and wife to be living in an obscure hotel there. But when called upon, the old man denied his identity and promptly dropped out of sight.

But there was no hiding place. A news dispatch from Athens said Sam Insull and wife had taken residence there. It was true. Friends in Chicago had advised him by cable to establish domicile in Greece, with which the United States had no extradition treaty. In Athens, the Insulls were living well though modestly. Until the indictments, Insull had been getting an eighteen-thousand-dollar-a-year "pension" voted by the directors of one of his companies. After the indictments, the refugee had to depend on the bounty of a few English and American friends.

Demands for arrest and extradition of Insull were made on the Greek government by the United States. Greece stood stoutly on its rights and refused to comply. The bickering continued by cable, while the Insulls remained unmolested and rather popular in Athens. But on December 5, 1933, the Greeks suddenly ordered Insull to leave the country on or before January 1. By fast work of Insull's Greek attorneys, who pleaded the old man's illness, the order of expulsion was extended to March 15. On that day police were sent to put Insull on a ship. They could not find him, not in Athens or elsewhere in Greece.

A new hullabaloo arose. By now Insull the refugee was something of an international celebrity. He was pictured as an old and broken man, "creeping around the back streets of Europe," with the cops gradually closing in. His secret departure from Greece piqued the Greek government, which immediately set afoot an inquiry. All vessels that had recently sailed from Greek ports were radioed to report a list of their passengers. Promptly came back a wireless from the captain of the small tramp steamer *Maiotis,* bound for Egypt: Mr. Insull was a passenger; his papers were perfectly in order; he had left without notifying authorities simply to avoid publicity. The ship had been chartered by "an English friend of the refugee."

The *Maiotis* was ordered to return immediately to Piraeus, the port of Athens. It did so. Both the ship's and Insull's papers were found to be in order, and after a brief detention, the *Maiotis* and its full complement of passengers set forth again.

The flight and chase now took front-page position as one of the wide world's favorite news stories. The press flashed daily rumors of wireless negotiations between the refugee and several Mediterranean and other countries, asking permission to land and establish residence. These included French Somaliland, Ethiopia, Yugoslavia, Albania, Rumania, and Turkey.

Where would this latter-day *Flying Dutchman,* the *Maiotis,* finally land? Conflicting reports continued, one after the other; and the affair turned into an exciting continued story, a cliff-hanging serial. No, Rumania would not give the old man refuge. Neither would Albania, nor Yugoslavia. While the little steamer rolled up and down and across the Mediterranean, the American Congress hurried a bill into law giving the United States the right to arrest Insull in any country in which by treaty it had extraterritorial rights.

For several more days the *Maiotis,* now the best known vessel afloat, remained hidden in the ocean mists. Then, on March 28, she put into Istanbul for provisions. The United States ambassador, on direct orders from the State Department, demanded of the Turkish government that it arrest Insull forthwith. It complied. Insull was taken from the ship and placed in Istanbul's house of detention.

The old man was still fighting. Attorneys, probably engaged by the same "English friend" who had chartered the ship, appealed the Turkish court's order. Bickering began. Meanwhile, Insull remained in custody, attended by a valet whom he paid twelve cents a day, as the press took pains to report, and spent the time writing letters and reading novels. He appeared in surprisingly good spirits.

Turkish officials held that no appeal could be made. On April 11, 1934, America's most celebrated refugee was transferred, "under heavy guard," to the American Export liner SS *Exilona,* bound for New York City. The great chase was over.

Arrived at New York, Insull was put aboard a Chicago-bound train. Next day he entered Cook County Jail a prisoner, while a photographer of the Associated Press recorded the event. The picture may never have won a prize for excellence, though it deserved one, not only because it proved hundreds of thousands, perhaps millions, of Americans mistaken: Sam Insull *could* be put behind bars; but also because the photograph is loaded with all the emotion that the great Gustave Doré got into his illustrations for the works of Milton and Dante and the Bible.

Here in stark half tone is the bolt-studded door of the Chicago jail, slit with an evil barred window, just as the turnkey slides it half open to admit Sam Insull. The old man stands in the aperture, or rather leans on the arms of two guards who are supporting him. His figure is no longer robust. His withered face looks pallid, and his white mustache droops with the drooping mouth. Behind his glasses, the old man's eyes peer questioningly at his welcomer, the blank-faced turnkey in cap and sweater, a bunch of long keys in one hand.

Here it is, caught for the subscribers of the always alert Associated Press and their millions of readers—Adam's Fall. Dives Enters Hell. The Wrongdoer Taken. The Capitalist Confined. The picture cannot record the clang of the closing door, yet countless Americans heard it plainly, and the also countless Insull investors enjoyed their first satisfaction since the last dividend from the illusions that had been known as Insull properties. This was Judgment Day even though, as it turned out, the judgment of Sam Insull by a jury of his peers, was not quite what had been expected and hoped for.

The case of the United States of America v. Samuel Insull *et al.,* for using the mails to defraud, came on for trial, as *Bench and Bar* quaintly put it, October 2, 1934. We need not go into it, other than to cite it as one of the most complicated of record. Gluttons for details will find them in the clear and careful account given by Francis X. Busch in his capital *Guilty or Not Guilty?*

One can sympathize with the federal prosecutor, especially in his struggles to arrive at some formula by which he could show the jury that the real value of certain Insull stocks was not what the Insulls had claimed it to be. When court attendants had brought in and hung on the wall a big blackboard, the attorney took chalk in hand and resorted to algebraic equations. This is what he wrote:

$$X = A + \left(\frac{a}{b} x' \right) \text{——} C$$

$$X' = A' + \left(\frac{c}{d} x \right) \text{——} C'$$

What the poor jury made of this and other matters of evidence was a cruel disappointment to the mass of Insull investors. Almost two months later, when everything had been said that either defense or prosecution could think of, the jury retired and in a little more than two hours returned with a verdict of not guilty for all of the defendants.

Then, in the following March, Sam Insull and his brother, Martin Insull, were put on trial for embezzlement of a mere $66,000 from Middle West Securities Company. The trial was brief. The jury said the defendants were not guilty.

As June 1935 came in, the federal government made one more

attempt to fasten criminal guilt on Insull, his son, and Harold L. Stuart. The charge was that these three had, in contemplation of bankruptcy proceedings, illegally transferred certain property with intent to prefer selected creditors and defeat the purpose of the National Bankruptcy Act. The court held that the proof offered by the government was not very good and directed the jury to return a verdict of not guilty.

The old man's troubles in the criminal courts were over, though civil litigation continued to harass him until shortly before his death, which came July 16, 1938, in his seventy-ninth year.

In his mellow summing up of Insull's life and times, Francis X. Busch remarks that Insull's codefendants in the government's cases returned to their respective niches in the community life, unharmed either by the prosecutions or the uproar that accompanied them. Memory's view of Sam Insull, says Mr. Busch, "like that of others who have briefly occupied high places," grows dimmer in time's lengthening shadows.

There are some who even now, fifteen years after the old man's death, cannot forget their losses. To them the name of Insull is anathema. Others, even some of the victims of the monstrous mirages of Insull, remember and acknowledge his business genius and "his many contributions to cultural development."

Given another fifteen years, perhaps, and both Insull's cultural efforts and his financial disaster may well be lost to memory. But the record will be there, in the bound records of the courts, and one can picture some Ph.D.-seeking student in American law or finance working up a stout thesis on the proposition *Samuel Insull's Influence in Creation of the Federal Securities and Exchange Act.*

Insull's defenders, of course, can retort that he was found not guilty of all criminal charges brought against him and hence he had nothing to do with the restrictions of the federal securities legislation. Likewise, the defenders of the good name of Miss Lizzie Borden, of Fall River, Massachusetts, could point out that she, too, was found not guilty by a jury of her peers—in spite of which the Yankee spinster is remembered more than sixty years later as an able woman with a single-bitted ax.

PART FIVE

DYNASTIC
SUCCESSION

PHILIP D. ARMOUR

JOHN W. GATES

CHARLES M. SCHWAB

SAMUEL INSULL

Chapter 1 THE DU PONTS

For 150 years the name of Du Pont has been familiar in the United States, and periodically notorious, in relation to explosives. At trading posts and frontier stores for decades a standard item on shopping lists was "Du Pont & Galena," meaning gunpowder and lead. Du Pont Improved Blasting powder ripped the ledges of California's Mother Lode and bored the endless laterals of the Comstock and the Anaconda. Du Pont's Best Stumping removed the debris of logging from uncounted homesteads. Du Pont's Military, either black or smokeless, was fired from American guns at redskins, Britishers, Mexicans, Confederates, Spaniards, Filipinos, Chinese Boxers, Germans, Japanese, and Italians. It's a hundred-to-one chance that Jesse James fell from a bullet propelled by Du Pont powder.

Du Pont is one of the oldest names in American industry. The Du Ponts, who accent the Pont, are perhaps the only group who may be properly described as an industrial dynasty. Yet until comparatively recently, the company that bears the name and the very men who founded and have run the company have been to most Americans little more than vague rumors. That is, outside the state of Delaware and the world of explosives.

One judges that generations of Du Pont liked it that way. Since 1802, when they erected a small powder mill on the Brandywine river, they have operated a closely held industrial barony, built it into a tightly held monopoly, made a good deal of money, lived like squires and, until about 1916, remained aloof from the mainstreams of American capital. In large part, too, the Du Ponts have kept themselves socially isolated from other great industrialists. For well over a century Du Ponts displayed a marked preference for marrying other Du Ponts. Contrary to popular myths about the evils of interbreeding, the family has been standing up remarkably well.

It is characteristic of the clan that no Du Pont ever had a "cottage" at Newport or Bar Harbor. They were never a part of the Gilded Age, though they lived well enough on their estates, which came to number some thirty in Delaware. Their collective and individual fortunes did not become a subject for Congressional investigation until 1934, or 132 years after the founding Du Ponts organized an "Establishment of a Manufacture of Military and Sporting Powder in the United States of America."

A company to make powder was far from the original idea of the head of the family, who was Pierre Samuel du Pont de Nemours, a Huguenot born at Paris in 1739 and sixty years of age when he and a numerous company of relatives arrived in America on the first day of 1800. Included in the group were Pierre's sons, Victor Marie and Eleuthère Irénée, their wives and children.

Pierre himself was already known to and rated by Thomas Jefferson as "the ablest man in France." He had barely escaped the guillotine in 1794. Three years later his house was sacked by a mob and he was arrested and condemned to exile, but the order was countermanded because of Pierre's eminence as a scholar and economist. He had made a fine translation of Ariosto, written much to advocate financial and other reforms and, while in prison, composed his *Philosophy of the Universe*. In 1782, he had been one of the negotiators with England for recognition of the independence of the United States. Such was the founder of the house of Du Pont in America. His elder son, Victor Marie, had served as French consul for Georgia and the Carolinas.

Pierre Du Pont was a moderate, and there was no place in France of the time for a moderate, so Pierre left for America. What he had in mind was to found a colony to which Frenchmen might flee the anarchy of their own country. It was to be no common colony, but a Utopia for a few chosen spirits, the kind of men to whom, before leaving, Pierre had sold shares in his colonization company. These included La Fayette, Beaumarchais, Talleyrand, and Jean Jacques Rousseau. Even so, Pierre meant that his Utopia should not be merely a gathering of intellectuals; the colonists would engage in farming, and also in the manufacture of pottery and glass. It was to be named Pontiana.

Pontiana never came into being. After investigating, and on the advice of Jefferson, Pierre decided that the price of suitable land was too high for his scheme; and he apparently did not think his kind of Frenchmen would be attracted to the wilderness beyond the Appalachians. Meanwhile, he and Son Victor would conduct an importing business.

At about this time, so the family story goes, Pierre's second son, Irénée, thirty, bought some gunpowder for a day's hunting with a Colonel Toussard. He was much impressed with its high price and poor quality. Gunpowder was something this Du Pont happened to know about. For nearly four years he had worked and studied under Lavoisier, the great chemist, who had been appointed chief of the French royal powder works.

Now, with the help of good Colonel Toussard, Irénée surveyed gunpowder conditions in the United States and came readily to the conclusion that a small plant making a good product would return a profit of perhaps ten thousand dollars annually. He returned to France, got machinery, and came back to open a powder factory. Two thirds of the capital required, which totaled $36,000, was subscribed by Pierre Du Pont's colonization company. Irénée was to direct the enterprise for $1,800 a year and one third of the profits.

The new and third President of the United States, Mr. Jefferson, urged the Du Ponts to establish their powder mill somewhere near the infant city of Washington. But no available site there proved satisfactory. In Delaware, Irénée found just what he wanted and for $6,740 got ninety-five acres along Brandywine Creek near Wilmington, plus a dam and a few outbuildings of an abandoned cotton mill. He noted that willow grew in abundance along the stream. This was good. Willow made the kind of charcoal he favored for powder making.

Construction of the works was started on July 19, 1802. The masons and carpenters were mystified that Mr. Du Pont, who designed all the buildings, insisted on walls of triple-thick stone and extremely light roofs which sloped toward the creek. As an experienced powder man, Du Pont knew that explosions were to be expected, in which case the flimsy roofs would blow off into the creek and leave, it was to be hoped, the side walls undamaged.

Early in 1804 the first Du Pont powder went on sale. It was a first-class product. General Henry Dearborn said as much after testing samples at Federal City, as Washington was still called, and he told Irénée Du Pont that he "should do all the government work." He was as good as his word; within the next few months Du Pont's little mill supplied 22,000 pounds for use on the American frigates sent to put down the Barbary corsairs.

Victor Marie did not at first join his brother in the powder venture. His commission business quickly failed, but he still wanted no part of the Brandywine works. Instead, he joined Philip Church, a real estate operator of unbounded imagination who had bought heavily in western New York lands. Church believed devoutly in the power of the printed word. Eastern New York and all of New England was soon plastered with broadsides advertising his wondrous land of milk, cheese, and butter in Genessee County. The excellence of the soil, said Church, coupled with the purity and abundance of water, and the general healthfulness of the region were in themselves sufficient to bring settlers on the run. He spoke confidently of "facility of communication" and of "a Mail Stage," though careful readers of his copy could have discerned that these things were not yet facts. They were "due shortly."

It seems probable that Philip Church's prose and personality hypnotized Victor Marie Du Pont, a gentle, trusting soul, as thoroughly as they had hypnotized thousands of Yankees. After sinking $3,000 of Mrs. Du Pont's little fortune in the Genessee project and seeing it disappear, leaving no trace, Victor found himself bogged down in debt. He assigned his share in the enterprise to creditors and, this time, joined Brother Irénée at the powder works in Delaware.

The brothers worked in harmony. Old Pierre went to France for several years, but returned to live and end his days at the powder mills, the rugged walls and weak roofs of which were subject to periodic if unplanned tests. The first explosion occurred in 1807. Much damage was done though no lives were lost. In 1817 came another when, in the middle of the night, a charcoal house caught fire. Old Pierre, seventy-seven and gouty yet stout of heart, turned out at the first alarm and worked with the crews the rest of the night. Next day the old man fell desperately ill, and died a little later.

In March of 1818 came an explosion beside which all others had been as nothing. The works blew up with a roar that shook windows in Wilmington six miles away, removed five of the six chief mill buildings, and left forty Du Pont employees dead. Irénée's home was partially demolished and his wife severely injured. It is of interest to know that working to aid the wounded and bereaved was a Du Pont guest, who was none other than the Marquis de Grouchy, Napoleon's famous marshal.

It was greatly to the credit of the Du Ponts that the widows and orphans of the disaster were pensioned from company funds, were given houses to live in, and that the Du Ponts also "undertook the education and medical care of the orphans." In that day all accidents and disasters were acts of God, and employees seldom if ever were of the opinion that their employers had any responsibility for the victims of God's acts. The Du Ponts' conscience did not await the prodding of legislation.

The works were rebuilt promptly, larger than before and with a number of "improved arrangements," or new inventions. One of these was a remarkable water-powered sieve for kerneling powder which speeded the process and saved labor costs. The steady progress of the Du Pont business can be seen in their annual production figures. The first year, 1804, Du Pont made nearly 45,000 pounds of powder. By 1808 the annual output was 300,000 pounds. When the War of 1812 broke out, Du Pont was the largest powder maker in America.

Although it seems probable that everyone, including the dimmest witted, is firm in the belief that war increases the profits as well as the production of powder mills, the official spokesmen of Du Pont, and perhaps of all other makers of munitions, are just as firm in *their* belief that the way to treat this subject is by none too subtle evasion, plus the insinuation that war orders are far from profitable, anyway. It is thus that Du Pont's official historians attempt to brush off the War of 1812. They admit that it brought to the firm "Government orders totaling 750,000 pounds of gunpowder," and though this "looked like a profitable assignment," nevertheless the "business realities proved otherwise." They go on to plead that "The company had to risk every dollar and borrow heavily to extend the capacity of the mills"—as if this were a gross imposition from which were derived no profits.

Yet, the official spokesmen say nothing at all about Du Pont profits from the War of 1812. They do say that the profits for 1811 were $45,000. Presumably the war brought them no profits at all, or such at least is the inference to be drawn from the Du Pont party line. From other sources, however, it is made clear that the Du Ponts sold well over a million pounds of powder to the government during the war and were paid for it a price averaging forty cents a pound. Their gross sales for 1812 alone ran to $148,597.

The same war caused the company to purchase adjoining property and to erect the Upper Hagley Mills, which doubled the firm's

252 THE AGE OF THE MOGULS

capacity. To these were later added the Lower Hagley Mills and, in 1838, the Brandywine Mills. (The original plant was named Eleutherian Mills.) By then Du Pont's annual production exceeded a million pounds, in peacetime. By then old Pierre the founder and his two sons, Irénée and Victor, were dead.

The last debts of the company to its French shareholders were paid in 1837, and the Du Pont Company became a partnership of three American-born members of the family. These were Alfred, Henry, and Alexis Du Pont. There were no officers. Alfred, the eldest, was senior partner, a position much like that of the Old Man of tribal societies. All property was communal. The partners drew no salaries. Sums for personal needs were drawn from the cashbox. One clerk kept the books and paid the help.

The next war, which one can hope did not leave the Du Ponts wholly prostrate, broke out with Mexico in 1846. The Du Pont mills, says the official record, took in stride the demands made upon them. And so did a member of the Du Pont clan. Let us leave the powder works briefly to consider this distinguished Du Pont.

He was Samuel Francis Du Pont, born 1803, the son of Victor. At the request of old Pierre, President Madison appointed Samuel a midshipman (there was then no Annapolis) in 1815, and for the next forty years he served in the United States Navy. His record in the Mexican War was cited as distinguished for gallantry, efficiency, and skill. He commanded the flagship of Commodore Stockton, and later the sloop *Cyane,* with which Du Pont moved Frémont's battalion to San Diego, then to San Blas, where a landing party spiked the fort's guns. Du Pont proceeded to seize La Paz. He captured and burned a Mexican fleet at Guaymas. Within a few months he cleared the California and Mexican coast of hostile ships and captured thirty vessels. When occasion required shore action, it was Du Pont's invariable custom to lead his own men in attacking forts and posts.

Captain Du Pont thus came out of the war with a brilliant record. When the Civil War began, Commodore Du Pont was put in charge of all naval operations along the South Atlantic coast. He led the combined army and navy attack against Port Royal and captured it after a five-hour bombardment. It was a notable victory at an opportune time, just when the North had become discouraged.

President Lincoln asked Congress to thank Du Pont and make him a rear admiral, which was done. Admiral Du Pont went on to occupy Beaufort and to capture Tybee Island. A bit later he commanded actions that resulted in the capture of five more southern forts and the occupation of Jacksonville and St. Augustine.

From his first shot up to April 1863, Du Pont went from one victory to another. Defeat, however, attended his attempt to take Charleston, and although competent writers have declared that responsibility for his failure at Charleston should be shared equally by Du Pont and the Navy Department, Du Pont asked to be relieved of his command—but not before he had captured the Confederate ironclad *Atlanta,* one of the chief naval prizes of the entire war. Admiral Du Pont died shortly after Lee's surrender. He was a gallant man, fit for the honor Congress bestowed on his memory by declaring that the intersection of two prominent avenues in the capital should be called Du Pont Circle.

This is the right place to mention that the Du Ponts produced another noted fighting man in Henry Algernon, who, after West Point training and graduation at the head of his class, went headlong into the Civil War to win brevet after brevet for gallantry and finally the Congressional Medal of Honor for extraordinary heroism at the Battle of Cedar Creek. His career with the Du Pont Company will be treated later.

Of the three Du Pont partners of 1837, Alfred retired in 1850. His son Irénée, of the third generation, was taken in as partner to work under Uncle Alexis, while Uncle Henry became boss. Henry the redhead, appears to have been an excellent businessman, obviously a quality shared by most Du Ponts. His first act was to establish an agency in San Francisco to supply the miners. He also had the Du Pont powder works in condition to meet the terrific demands of the Crimean War. These demands were considerable because the chief engagement of the four-year struggle was the Siege of Sevastopol, in which artillery of large caliber was used in unprecedented volume for months on end. How much Du Pont powder was needed by the combined British and French armies seems not to have been published, though the profits coming to the company as a result, says a biographical sketch of Henry Du Pont, were such as to encourage Henry nobly "in his policy of progressive management."

During this period, young Irénée devised and patented a metallic keg which became the company's standard container. It was a good keg, too, but it was no more immune to burning gunpowder than a wooden keg. In May of 1854, 450 of the new kegs went up in a mighty explosion, not at the mills, but in the center of Wilmington. Three drivers, three wagons, and six pairs of horses were blown to bits, along with two innocent bystanders. The villagers of Wilmington, possibly for the first time, were given food for thought on the civic values of powder mills.

The next explosion, which occurred near the mills, took the life of a Du Pont, the first but not the last of the family to die in a plant disaster. He was Alexis, one of the partners, aged forty-one, and had spent all his working life with powder.

Into the partnership now went Lammot Du Pont, recently a graduate in chemistry from the University of Pennsylvania. The first thing he did as a partner was to set up a laboratory in one of the older Du Pont buildings. He had ideas about powder chemistry, and went to work on a substitute for saltpeter, sodium nitrate. Saltpeter comprised from two thirds to three fourths of the content of black gunpowder. Like everybody else the Du Ponts had been getting their saltpeter from India. The product was both costly and unreliable.

Sodium nitrate had been found in large quantities along the west coast of South America. It had been used in powder making long before Lammot Du Pont went to college, but the resulting powder had a grave imperfection—the least dampness made it inert. It wouldn't go off. Young Du Pont devised a method of treating sodium nitrate that not only removed the difficulty but resulted in greatly increased explosive force. On May 19, 1857, the United States granted a patent to Du Pont for "an improved gunpowder."

This product, which the Du Pont Company started to manufacture, was sold as "B" blasting powder. It must have been something of a sensation, for it "swept the coal and iron fields almost overnight." The company claimed that the new explosive was the first important change in the composition of black powder in at least six centuries. Demand for it from the hard-coal country was so great that Du Pont bought a plant in Luzerne County, Pennsylvania, in which to manufacture B blasting near the place where it would be used in large volume.

Lammot Du Pont also produced, at the urging and with the aid of Captain Thomas Rodman, chief of Army Ordnance, an explosive called Mammoth powder, the round grains of which were about the size of a big apple. Mammoth was fired to good effect by the Monitor in its famous battle with the Merrimac.

The Civil War brought the Du Ponts an amount of business incredible until then. They also had a security problem. Delaware was infested with Confederate spies. Two such were captured within half a mile of the works, and in their possession were plans of the mills and grounds. A series of mystifying explosions shook the works periodically and resulted in the deaths of some forty workmen. While no one of these wartime acts of sabotage was a major disaster, both employees and the Du Ponts themselves had reason for saying they worked not far from the front lines.

The war demanded and got some four million pounds of Du Pont explosives. Yet the company lost much of its prewar business with the booming mining industry to quickie outfits that sprang up to capitalize on the opportunity. The United States, moreover, was lax in paying its bills, and the company was often short of operating cash.

At war's end, of course, the Du Ponts, their employees, and their company found themselves attacked as scoundrels who had battened on the blood of Shiloh and Antietam and grown wealthy from four million pounds of a product devoted to murder and destruction. This was as inevitable as it was illogical.

But it should stand to the credit of the Du Ponts, indeed to their lasting honor, that the charge of shoddy was never leveled at them. The powder they made *went off*, and to good effect, even though many of the guns manufactured by the merchants of shoddy stuff were unfit to handle Du Pont powder.

The return of peace could not have slowed the Du Pont mills for very long. Even during the war the United States had been undergoing growth and expansion, and now, with completion of the first transcontinental railroad, the country started to boom as never before. Rails were reaching out everywhere, and every mile of grade called for much explosive. The rails were heading for mines, which required powder in unmeasured quantities. They were passing homesteads, where stumps must be blown and boulders blasted. Meanwhile, powder was being burned to destroy the great buffalo herds, the unbelievably huge flocks of passenger pigeons, and bands of the now desperate Indians.

During this period, the Du Pont Company was run by its senior partner, old Henry, who had taken the reins in 1850 and was to hold them for thirty-nine years. His office staff never exceeded four men and a boy. At a small old-fashioned desk, using a quill, Henry wrote an average of six thousand letters annually. He was a tall man, wore his red fringe beard from ear to ear, and was considered rather gruff; yet he knew the name of every man on the Du Pont pay roll; and was constantly called upon to solve the personal problems of old hands—and to keep peace in a family which generally speaking believed in subordination to the senior partner but whose members had ideas of their own.

Although the company had grown to an immense size for the era, old Henry continued to run things with the primal simplicity that had been common in the United States during the first half of the nineteenth century. As head of the company and head of the house, he considered everything that happened in connection with either was his own responsibility. In his fine study of the Du Ponts, John Winkler told of an incident that showed Henry Du Pont in an emergency. The old man always lived close to the works. Around nine one night his attentive ear picked up a whistling sound somewhere along the powder line. It wasn't right. Lighting his little square lantern, the senior partner of the Du Ponts hastened to the Upper Banks, the workmen's village, and routed out the Upper Yard foreman. The two men traced the noise to the Eagle glazing mill near the milldam. The main shaft had become overheated. It was throwing off sparks like a piece of fireworks. Shouting to the foreman to stop the mill, old Henry tore down to the creek, filled his stovepipe hat with water, and poured it over the hot shaft, averting what surely would have been a fire and explosion.

In the first months of 1880, the Du Ponts broke ground for a new plant to be operated by a new company of which Lammot Du Pont, its organizer, was president. This was the Repauno Chemical Company. It was to manufacture a new product, dynamite, an explosive with a long history which began in 1846 when an Italian chemist, Ascanio Sobrero, obtained a substance he called nitroglycerin. It turned out to be so powerful and so unpredictable that its discoverer was appalled. He warned against its use. A Swede named Alfred Nobel took hold of Sobrero's demoniac material and tamed it somewhat, calling the result dynamite, which he patented in 1867. Here was something that would make Du Pont's B blasting sound like an echo. Dynamite was far and away the most powerful blasting agent known.

The older generation of Du Ponts wanted nothing to do with the new explosive. Old Henry detested it, saying that nothing could take the place of good black powder. He would not even use its right name, but referred to it as "that blasting oil." He took his quill in hand to send warnings to all Du Pont customers of its dangers. And when news came that Nobel's own dynamite plant near Stockholm had blown up, Henry was immensely pleased. He told the Pennsylvania and other railroads they should refuse to carry any compounds of nitroglycerin.

Young Lammot Du Pont, the family's first real chemist, was convinced that dynamite was the coming explosive. He worked hard and long on the old man, and about 1877 Henry grudgingly permitted the California Powder Company, in which Du Pont had a majority interest, to erect a plant to make the new explosive. Then, in 1880, Lammot prevailed on the elder Du Pont to combine with two other firms to start manufacture of dynamite. The Repauno Chemical works at Gibbstown, New Jersey, was ready two years later, and Lammot took charge. Within a few months 2,000 pounds of dynamite were being made every day. Production steadily increased; this was the stuff to move *anything*. Some powder monkey or other called it "rendrock" and the name went across the country.

One morning in 1884 something went wrong in Repauno's nitro department. Lammot Du Pont went to investigate. Just then approximately one ton of the substance exploded, killing Du Pont and five others. There was always a Du Pont to fill any vacancy. Young William now went in as head of Repauno.

In October 1885, Long Island Sound witnessed the greatest submarine blast of the century, when 300,000 pounds of explosives, mostly Du Pont dynamite, shattered Flood Rock, a menace to navigation. It was an outstanding news event, heralded in advance, and Americans were properly impressed with the power of this new agent. So, apparently, were the silver kings of the Comstock Lode in Nevada. With black powder the mines had been producing some fifteen million dollars in bullion a year. With the introduction of dynamite, wrote a Du Pont historian, the "output more than doubled."

Smokeless powder was to be the next improvement in explosives. No writer in a condition of sanity would dream of stating that this or that man invented smokeless. The claimants are beyond number. So far as the Du Ponts are concerned, however, three members of the family perfected the Du Pont smokeless. These were Alfred I., Francis, and Pierre S. After experimenting with guncotton, at the Navy's request, the Du Pont Company added a mill to supply this product for naval mines and torpedoes. Then, urged by General S. V. Benet, Chief of Army Ordnance, the Du Ponts devised a smokeless powder. By 1893 they were making a smokeless that proved fine for small arms; and a bit later hit upon a formula that was accepted by the government for big-gun use.

During the years of old Henry's management, the Du Ponts had been quietly buying up competitors, including many small firms and the big Hazard Powder Company. In 1872 they were active in forming the Gunpowder Trade Association. Like all similar groups, this one described itself with pious words as wishing only to correct practices that were "disrupting the powder industry." Doubtless it accomplished its purpose, for its members came to be collectively known, and cursed, as the "powder trust."

By 1889 the trust controlled ninety-five per cent of the gunpowder and ninety per cent of the blasting powder made in the United States. And there was little doubt as to who controlled the trust. It was Du Pont. One of the last things old Henry did in the way of business was to write letters to critics in which he denied that anybody told Du Pont how much powder to make or how much to charge for it. "We do our own dictating," said he coldly, and figured that that took care of the matter.

Henry Du Pont died in 1889 on his seventy-seventh birthday, the last of the grandsons of old Pierre Samuel, the founder. He had been making powder for fifty-five years. The company was still operating as a simple partnership. Henry's son, Henry Algernon, he of the Medal of Honor, was appalled at the complications incident to settling his father's estate. What was Henry's, and what belonged to the partnership? It was anything but easy. Henry Algernon urged the various Du Ponts to change the business to a corporation. The idea did not meet with immediate favor, but it was discussed for another decade and then, in 1899, the company was chartered as a Delaware corporation.

On Henry's death, Eugene, eldest of the third generation of cousins, became senior partner. Like many of his generation he had married a cousin. So had Eugene's cousin William, who was now in charge of the Repauno works. One of Eugene's first trials, as head of the house, was the first public discord in the family's hundred years in the United States. William divorced his wife.

Eugene Du Pont promptly announced that William had retired from the company and that his duties had been taken over by Hamilton Barksdale, who had married Ethel Du Pont. Later domestic discords of various Du Ponts were not to be settled so easily.

During Eugene's regime, Du Pont brought into the company the brilliant Hudson Maxim, younger brother of Hiram, inventor of the Maxim gun and many other things, including a curling iron, a gas generator, and a locomotive headlight. (Hiram's son Percy invented the Maxim silencer.) Typical of Maine Yankees of the period in restlessness and energy, Hudson Maxim left home early to roam with a schoolmate, Alden Knowles, and peddle a chart of fancy writing styles and colored ink powders. They had a phenomenal success with their own book, a self-instructor in penmanship. Hudson later went to England to work with Brother Hiram in his gun factory. He experimented with various gunpowders, then returned home to take charge of dynamite manufacture for an American firm. He secured a number of patents in relation to smokeless powder, and in 1897 sold these to Du Pont and became consultant to the company, which position he held the rest of his life.

For Du Pont, Hudson Maxim produced a shockproof explosive of enormous power for big guns which he named Maximite. He improved the Du Pont smokeless. He devised various machines, including an apparatus for propelling torpedoes. Du Pont established a laboratory especially for Maxim, at Lake Hopatcong, New Jersey, and there he worked for a quarter of a century, to the great prestige of both himself and the Du Ponts. Maxim was no mealymouthed man, either, and in 1915 he wrote and published a vitriolic attack on pacifism entitled, with characteristic directness, *Defenseless America.*

During Eugene Du Pont's regime, too, the company bought into eleven firms that made powder, dynamite, chemicals, or cartridges; and with Laflin & Rand formed the Eastern Dynamite Company, a merger of three large concerns which, in turn, bought heavily into eight smaller outfits. Du Ponts also were active in forming a cartel agreement with the Nobels and other European explosives makers by which the world markets were apportioned. The last decade of the nineteenth century closed with the incorporation of E. I. du Pont de Nemours & Company. This was not done without opposition of several of the younger Du Ponts, who had logically expected to become partners.

Eugene Du Pont died early in 1902, creating what official historians of the company declare was the greatest crisis in Du Pont history. Just why the death of one Du Pont should have so shaken the company is not at all clear. The vague phraseology of the Du Pont historians only clouds the matter. And the accounts of such honest and objective writers as Marquis James and John K. Winkler still leave one wondering. In any case, there can be no doubt but that the company, after more than ninety-nine years of striking success, had come to an impasse of some sort.

Eugene's brothers, Francis G. and Alexis I., were in poor health, it is said. So, apparently, was the company's treasurer, Charles I. Colonel Henry, the Medal of Honor Du Pont, had never cared much for powder making, and was now obsessed with politics, of which more later. Other Du Ponts had, for various reasons, "disqualified themselves." So now, a few months before the company's centennial, the directors voted to sell to Laflin & Rand, the only other combination in the field large enough to take over Du Pont.

The elder Du Ponts had discussed the matter thoroughly. There was no other way. The great days had passed. The Du Pont energy and enterprise, it seemed, had petered out. Just before the assembled clan were to vote on the doleful resolution to offer Du Pont to Laflin & Rand for twelve million dollars, Alfred I. Du Pont, aged thirty-eight, offered an amendment. "Why not," he asked, "sell to the highest bidder?" This remark, said a company spokesman, "occasioned some surprise."

Alfred I. Du Pont had come to the gloomy meeting direct from the yards, wearing soiled clothes, his face grimy with powder. He was not only young, but several of his cousins had found him erratic. He was a first-class black-powder man, but he had no business experience. Neither did he have twelve million dollars. Did he mean to buy the company? Cousin Francis asked him about that and reminded him that twelve million was a lot of money. But Colonel Henry liked the astonishing idea. He put a hand on Alfred's shoulder. "I'm with you," he said. In reply to Francis's query, Alfred replied yes, he did indeed plan to buy the company. He asked for one week to raise the money.

Alfred Du Pont did not know where the twelve million dollars was to come from, but he believed that he and two of his first cousins, and especially Coleman Du Pont, might be able to figure it out. He left the meeting to get in touch with Cousin Coleman, thirty-eight, and Cousin Pierre, thirty-two, asking them to meet him to discuss an important matter.

The way Alfred figured it was this: he himself was a good powderman. Pierre was a prudent sort, just the man to balance somewhat the high-powered promotion and organizing abilities of Coleman. Alfred thought that the three of them possessed the combination of talents proper for the rehabilitation of a company that seemed to be rotting from the top.

What began to happen at this point will seem less fantastic if one knows a little something of Thomas Coleman Du Pont, who could not have told B blasting from smokeless. He had never worked in powder. He had never been associated with his uncles and cousins of the powder-making Du Ponts. He was physically the biggest of the clan, topping six feet four and weighing 220 pounds, most of it muscle—a Gargantuan character and Rabelaisian, too, with a fund of gamy stories picked up around the coal mines of his native Kentucky.

His father, Antoine Bidermann Du Pont, a great-grandson of old Pierre, at an early age had come to consider the making of powder a monotonous and completely uninteresting business. After a row with his father, Antoine went West to seek his fortune, which he found in Louisville, Kentucky, and environs, in a paper mill, several coal mines, and a thriving street railway. His son Coleman was sent to school at Urbana University in Ohio, where he was an outstanding athlete in every sport. But the massed pedagogues at Urbana could not teach him to spell, or much of anything else. He left Ohio to enter Massachusetts Institute of Technology, where cousin Alfred was also a student. Coleman liked MIT no better than Urbana; they wanted you *to study*. He quit and returned to Kentucky.

In the coal mines of his father and an uncle, Coleman worked with pick and shovel, drove mules, ran an engine, and learned about hard physical labor in every department. He was never looked upon as the typical "boss's son," for he really liked the miners, attended their weddings and other doings, got drunk, was ready to fight anybody, or wrestle for fun, and was even elected by the miners a member of the Knights of Labor, forerunner of the American Federation. When he at last was made mine superintendent, he did much to turn the grubby town of Central City into a spick-and-span community, with decent homes.

The big fellow was a Du Pont still and, as if to prove it, he went up to Delaware and married one of his many Du Pont cousins. But he tired of coal when he discovered that the head of the largest coal company in Kentucky was being paid a salary of only $4,000 a year. Coleman quit and went to Johnstown, Pennsylvania, to manage what became the Lorain Steel Mills. He bought the run-down streetcar line in Johnstown and made it pay him well for the improvements. This was something like it, and Coleman quit the steel business to organize an outfit to build streetcar lines in many states, though not before he had brought in another Du Pont to run the steel company. This was young Cousin Pierre.

Coleman's new firm successfully promoted and built car lines in New Jersey, upstate New York, and Alabama. Pierre became a partner in several of these ventures, all of which paid off handsomely, and Coleman found the younger man most valuable.

It was at this point that Alfred got the ambitious idea of buying the Du Pont powder business and approached Coleman and Pierre. Both men liked the proposition, and so did Pierre's private secretary, a short, stocky young man of twenty-three named John Jacob Raskob, who had a steel-trap mouth and mind. Raskob had been earning forty-five dollars a month with a pump company until Pierre Du Pont came along. Pierre and Raskob were already inseparable.

Coleman Du Pont warmed to Alfred's idea. He told his two cousins that he must have a free hand in the corporate management. He also demanded a larger share than the others of the stock that would be divided among the three purchasers. It was agreed so. It is apparent that Coleman earned the lion's share, too. Here is the deal he promoted and put through so quickly that many Du Ponts wondered how it all happened:

Coleman's inventory of the Du Pont powder business showed the company to be worth about twenty-four million dollars, or twice as much as the family had planned to ask for it. The big-hearted Coleman told Du Pont stockholders that he would pay them $15,360,000 instead of twelve million. But not a dollar was to change hands from buyers to sellers. Everything was to be on the cuff, except for $2,100 which Coleman, Alfred, and Pierre would pay for twenty-one incorporators' shares in a new company formed to acquire the assets of the old one, which was to be dissolved.

Payment was to be made in securities of the new company as follows: twelve million dollars in four per cent purchase-money notes and $3,360,000 in stock. The new company would issue twelve million dollars of 4 per cent notes and 120,000 shares of stock with a total par value of twelve million dollars. All the notes and 33,600 shares of stock, worth $3,360,000, went to the old-company stockholders, leaving 86,400 shares, worth $8,640,-000, which Coleman, Alfred, and Pierre split among themselves under the head of "promoters' profits."

The old-company Du Ponts, possibly a little dazed, accepted Coleman's terms. On an investment of seven hundred dollars, or one third of what the three cousins paid for incorporation of the new concern, Coleman had, in less than a month, emerged as the president and largest stockholder of a big company with shares valued at $4,320,000 in his name. Not even Jay Gould had worked greater magic.

Without a hitch the three cousins took over. It was March 1, 1902. Coleman was president, Pierre, treasurer, with assistant John J. Raskob. Alfred was production boss. It turned out well that he was, not only because he knew every inch of the powder line, but also because it was soon apparent that Coleman had little ambition to learn anything about powder which, after all, was what Du Pont was selling. Coleman wanted to make the company the whale of powder, comparable to Standard Oil and the newly created United States Steel.

Before the end of 1902, Du Pont took over their greatest competitor, Laflin & Rand, for four million dollars, and for another two million got the Moosic Powder Company. Both purchases were made with bonds of Du Pont subsidiaries. In the spring of 1903 the cousins formed a super-holding concern capitalized at fifty million dollars. More firms were bought and put into a ten-million-dollar subsidiary called the Du Pont International Powder Company, into which went International Smokeless, along with its famous president, Colonel Edmund G. Buckner, a noted salesman of explosives who knew all the boys in the ordnance departments of the Army and Navy. Coleman made Buckner sales manager of the bigger Du Pont concern.

Three years after the three cousins took charge, the Du Pont industrial empire had acquired more than one hundred corporations. It was making one hundred per cent of all military powders; and approximately seventy per cent of all other explosives consumed in the United States. The net returns to the company in 1904 were four million dollars. This last item explains why, with all their juggling and exchange of stocks and bonds, the three Du

Pont cousins were not just blue-sky promoters: They were making and selling explosives at a profit sufficient to give their securities value as fast as they came off the printing presses.

The officials of the many powder concerns gathered into Du Pont, no less than many Du Ponts themselves, hardly knew how to take Coleman the dynamo. In his office he was usually coatless, a moose of a man awed by nobody, given to roaring laughter and considerable bragging. He was vain, too, in many ways, yet his sure touch in the matter of promotion and organization could not be denied. His idea of humor was not overly subtle; he liked to hand a caller, preferably a dignified executive, a cigar loaded with a few grains of Du Pont best black powder, and get him to light up while in the office. Other times, he would loose a mechanical frog to hopping about on his desk. He did tricks with cards and handkerchiefs. Men left his office wondering if their own business educations were not lacking and thinking vaguely of buying a lapel rose that would squirt water, or perhaps ink. . . .

The corporate demands of the Du Pont colossus were not sufficient to use up all of president Coleman's immense energy. In 1906 he took charge of the political campaign of his cousin, Colonel Algernon Du Pont who, for more than a decade had been trying to get into the United States Senate but had been blocked every time by John Edward O'Sullivan Addicks, the same fruity character Tom Lawson had first aided, then beaten, in the Bay State Gas war. Addicks was still, in 1906, wearing the great sweeping Cossack mustache he had affected in Siberia; and in a decade of Delaware politics had spent upward of three million dollars in an effort to be elected United States senator. He never had made it. Neither had Henry Algernon Du Pont. Now Cousin Coleman stepped in to aid his kinsman.

Coleman Du Pont went about the campaign the way he did everything else. He set up a whirlwind that blew free cigars and free liquor all over the pretty Delaware countryside, while hired oratory thundered and currency fell gently and as thick as the autumnal leaves of Vallombrosa. In a hard-shell Democratic state, Henry A. Du Pont was elected Republican senator by an almost unanimous vote of its often Democratic legislature. This miracle was greeted by President Theodore Roosevelt with a telegram: "I congratulate the people of Delaware." What he meant, of course, was that Delaware, after ages of darkness, was now on the side of the angels.

The devil himself, however, had been quietly mixing a brew of sore trouble for the Du Ponts. Warning of it might have been seen in the newspapers during May of 1906, though it was clouded in a protective fog. A news item said that Alfred I. Du Pont, vice-president and general manager of the great company, had gone to South Dakota to "inspect sites for a new plant." The real purpose of the trip was to sue for a divorce from Bessie Gardner Du Pont, whom Alfred had married in 1887. South Dakota was then what Nevada became later, namely a place where the bonds of matrimony could be easily and quickly sundered. Alfred's uncontested divorce was granted six months after filing. There had been only two divorces of Du Ponts in 104 years. This was the one that was to split the clan into warring factions as determined as they were bitter.

At the same time Alfred Du Pont left on his South Dakota expedition, Mrs. George A. Maddox, wife of Alfred's secretary, and a cousin to Alfred, left her home on the Brandywine, took up residence in Carlisle, Pennsylvania, and in due time was divorced from her husband. Two weeks later she and Cousin Alfred were married at the Plaza in New York City. The happy couple then returned to Wilmington to settle at Alfred's Rock Manor and await tribal approval. It was not forthcoming. Marquis James says that Coleman Du Pont told Alfred, "The family will never stand for this," and suggested Alfred sell all his Du Pont stock to Coleman and get out of Delaware.

Alfred was never good at taking suggestions, so he and his new wife were given a treatment of social ostracism. They could take it, too, for there was no timid streak in Mr. and Mrs. Alfred I. Du Pont. As the feud grew, says John Winkler, they fought back "viciously and so effectively that they became the 'Terrors of the Clan.'" Gossip of a scandalous nature circulated among the many Du Ponts, although other Delawareans had to read Philadelphia papers to know about it. The Wilmington press printed nothing, not even when Alfred brought suit for slander against his wife's aunt and her friend, Mrs. Mary Thompson, described as "Wilmington's social leader."

Close on these unseemingly doings, the husband of Alfred's eldest daughter brought suit for divorce, alleging adulteries committed while on their honeymoon. The injured husband dropped this charge when Mrs. Alfred Du Pont threatened to "rip the hinges from many Delaware closets, Du Pont cabinets among them," and was content to free himself from the Du Pont daughter on the conventional grounds of desertion.

It is safe to say that never before had the uninhibited newspapers of Philadelphia enjoyed such a gratifying sale in Wilmington and in Delaware generally. The feud was still in its early though far from tentative battles when even the local press was obliged to take notice of a new danger. This was an attack on the whole Du Pont principality by the United States government in the form of a suit for violation of the Sherman Anti-Trust Act. Teddy Roosevelt, who had recently congratulated Delaware for the election of a Republican senator named Du Pont was now in full cry on his trust-busting crusade.

Mr. Roosevelt was perhaps inspired to his attack on the Du Ponts by Robert S. Waddell, a former Du Pont official who had developed ambitions to become an independent manufacturer of explosives. Waddell had been sending congressmen some hot stuff in circulars attacking the powder trust, which he said was one and the same with E. I. du Pont de Nemours & Company. He cited impressive figures, among which was the thirty-one cents he said was the cost to Du Pont of making one pound of smokeless powder, and the seventy-five cents which the government paid for it. This spread was unpatriotic, said Mr. Waddell, who also called attention to a recent statement of the Secretary of War—that the Army alone should have a reserve supply of smokeless of not less than thirty million pounds. Such a supply, if bought from Du Pont, would come to $22,500,000. If made in government factories, the cost would be less than half as much, Waddell alleged, and the saving would approximate twelve million dollars.

Mr. Waddell noted, too, that Colonel Henry Algernon Du Pont had recently been elected United States senator only, said he, after the Du Ponts had contributed $70,000 to the Republican campaign fund; and he, Mr. Waddell, wanted to know if $70,000 was "sufficient to obligate the government" to take twelve million dollars from the poor taxpayers and "give it to the millionaires of this gigantic powder monopoly."

The large black headlines dismayed many of the Du Ponts, though probably less than had been the case with the divorce and slander publicity. In this regard, the Philadelphia *North American* asked editorially why, with the Du Pont Company's very life in jeopardy, the several Du Pont factions should be burning up their energies in a "petticoat row." The family feud did not cease, but the parties to it closed ranks sufficiently to present a magnificent defense of the Du Ponts as a corporate entity.

The government proved that for two generations the Du Ponts had schemed to control explosives in the United States and that under Coleman Du Pont the scheme had been realized. After the trial had droned on for four years, the Circuit Court of Appeals in the District of Delaware found for the government. Du Pont had indeed violated the anti-trust act.[1] Yet the court was faced and baffled with unprecedented circumstances. After remarking that more than sixty corporations had been dissolved after purchase by Du Pont, thus making it impossible to "restore original conditions in the explosive trade," the court said that this "narrows the field of any decree we may make."

So it did. The court solved its predicament by permitting the government and Du Pont, working together, to present a plan for dissolution of the monopoly and a reorganization of the Du Pont Company. This must have seemed mild enough punishment to any Du Pont, after the thunderous condemnation by prosecution, with echoes of horrified astonishment from much of the nation's press. It *was* mild, too. The government and Du Pont discussed matters and decided that a modest portion of the monopoly's assets should be distributed among two new powder concerns.

The happy ending of this story is graphically shown in Du Pont's official history. It is a photograph taken in the big banquet room of the New Willard Hotel, Washington, D.C., one evening in 1912. Men in evening clothes grace the many tables. They appear pleased, and well they should. The caption says this gathering is a "Farewell banquet for those employees who were leaving Du Pont to organize the Hercules and the Atlas Powder Companies." Except for bookkeeping, the four-year battle in the courts had left everything right where it had been in the days before Du Pont had so shockingly shattered the Sherman Act.

Not quite everything: the government gave back to Du Pont more than it had tried so earnestly to take away; the company was expressly instructed to keep for itself *all* of the military smokeless powder business. World War I was less than two years in the future.

[1]Forty-odd years later, or in December 1952, the Du Ponts were again in court charged with conspiring with General Motors and United States Rubber "to monopolize trade and commerce." Old Pierre Du Pont, 82, and Brother Irénée, 76, both wearing hearing aids, were personally in court, prepared to defend what the press was describing as "the $6 billion Du Pont industrial empire."

Neither the anti-trust suit nor its genial settlement appears to have had an ameliorative effect on the inter-clan feud. The New York newspapers were happy to learn about it from their Philadelphia contemporaries, and now the *Sun* and the *World* were particularly spectacular in their handling of this "internecine warfare within the $50,000,000 Du Pont powder company." They also reported a by-product of the strife, which was the new and magnificent estate built for his second wife by Alfred Du Pont. Delaware had not seen the like of Nemours, the white marble palace of seventy-seven rooms set in the midst of three hundred landscaped acres, around which was a rampart of a wall nine feet high. This wall, according to local legend, was, in Alfred Du Pont's own words, "to keep out intruders, mainly of the name of Du Pont." Local legend also has it that the wall was scarcely needed, that only two of the several hundred Du Pont kin ever crossed the threshold of Nemours.

The feud next erupted in the actual command of the company. The executive committee, of which Pierre Du Pont was chairman, announced a plan for "a closer consolidation of authority in the manufacturing department." The plan went into effect immediately. What it did was to relieve Alfred of his duties and install in his place as general manager Coleman's brother-in-law, H. M. Barksdale. Alfred made a protest, which was ignored; Coleman and Pierre were working close together.

The change was made March 1, 1911. It created something of a noise in the press, and even more of a sensation at the Du Pont plants. On February 11, almost three weeks before the announcement was formally made, Ed Bader, an employee at the Hagley Works, heard of it and wrote in his diary: "A. I. Du Pont out!" On that very day, shocked powdermen assembled at Hagley Works and voted to chip in to buy a silver cup for Mr. Alfred. It was later presented to him at a mass meeting of employees.

While the anti-trust proceedings had been moving their sluggish way toward settlement, Coleman Du Pont had been amusing himself with other matters. Apparently he was the first Du Pont to whom New York City presented any attraction, and now he, with Charles P. Taft, a brother to the new President of the United States, formed a partnership to build the McAlpin Hotel. On its twenty-first floor Coleman established his New York residence. He liked it fine. It was a gay place, Marquis James reported, and "Forty people, including half the chorus of a Broadway show, were not unusual at an after-dinner party."

In 1913 Coleman formed a syndicate to erect what he said was to be the largest office building in the world. He was the kind of man who wanted nothing to do with the next to the largest of anything. So, up went a structure forty stories high at a cost of thirty million dollars. It was the Equitable Building.

When the Equitable enterprise was well started, Coleman Du Pont underwent an intestinal operation from which he recovered very slowly. He was in hospital when the bomb went off at Sarajevo. He was still there when Germany invaded France, when Russia mobilized, when British troops crossed the Channel; and still there when all of the great powers, except the United States, and many of the small powers went pell-mell into war.

The first effect of the war on the United States was to scare the daylights out of bankers and investors. The New York money market went into a mild panic. Most businessmen who had "extended" themselves started to trim sail. Among these was Coleman Du Pont, deeply involved in the high finance of his immense Equitable Building. Late in 1914, Coleman, without any previous intimation, wrote Cousin Pierre that he wanted to sell his interest in Du Pont. Coleman was the company's largest stockholder.

Cousins Pierre and Alfred were already uneasy about Coleman's New York venture. Rumors had been going around that Coleman was in so deep as to be "embarrassed." True or not, such talk was bad for the Du Pont Company. And now—it was early in 1915—Pierre got a cable from England asking him to meet the *Lusitania* in New York, to see a Mr. Kraftmeier, a representative of the British Nobel Company, makers of explosives.

Thinking it merely a matter of more orders, Pierre took along Colonel Buckner, the Du Pont sales manager. But Mr. Kraftmeier had nothing to say about more orders. He told Pierre that his firm, as well as the Empire's military leaders, were much worried over a report that "one of Du Pont's large stockholders" had become so financially embarrassed he had sold his holdings to Kuhn, Loeb & Company. It just happened that Kuhn, Loeb were Germany's financial representatives in the United States. This sale of stock "to the enemy," Mr. Kraftmeier went on, had reputedly given Kuhn, Loeb control of Du Pont. Worse, Du Pont was rumored to have already filled powder orders for Germany.

Pierre Du Pont was able to convince the worried man from

England there was no iota of truth in the reports. But Pierre was worried enough too. The time had obviously come to assure the Allies that Du Pont would not sell explosives to Germany. Alfred and William Du Pont agreed. Neither they nor Pierre had any loans against their Du Pont stock. Alfred proposed that any loans against stock owned by the so-called Big Four Du Ponts of the management be taken up by the company.

How much was Du Pont stock worth? Coleman set a price. The cousins thought it too high, even with war orders from Europe piling up in the offices at Wilmington. For the next two months the four cousins haggled—though Pierre, unknown to Alfred and William, did some haggling on his own account. The first that Alfred and William knew of Pierre's secret dealing with Coleman was when they picked up their morning papers one day late in March 1915, to read that "Pierre Du Pont and five associates" had bought all of Coleman's stock in the company, a stroke that gave Pierre complete working control. Coleman's shares had cost the associates fourteen million dollars.

Alfred and William, together with several other Du Ponts not in the deal, were taken by surprise. Their anger mounted as war orders sent Du Pont common from three hundred to seven hundred dollars a share. It mounted again when Pierre changed the corporate setup and came up with a new company capitalized at $240,000,000, which, with the usual exchange of old stock for new, worked out a dividend of eighty-two dollars per old share for the year. The stock which Pierre and his five associates bought for fourteen million dollars had quadrupled in value within a few months. Alfred, William, and other Du Ponts went to see their lawyers.

Alfred Du Pont, it will be recalled, had previously been removed as general manager of the company. In March 1916, he was deposed as vice-president and member of the finance committee. He moved his office out of the Du Pont Building in Wilmington. He was an angry man. He had not been permitted to participate in the lush deal for Coleman's stock. He had been ousted from company management. Yet he was hardly impoverished. His 1915 income from Du Pont had totaled $3,050,089. For the *first half* of 1916 his income from the same source was $3,848,617—a fair indication that despite Du Pont's company historians, war is not wholly a disaster for makers of explosives.

Alfred now read in the papers that Coleman Du Pont had developed gross political aspirations; his name appeared as a presidential possibility. Alfred Du Pont had thoughtfully purchased, a few years before, the Wilmington *Daily News,* which he presently set to ridiculing Cousin Coleman as presidential stock. To the *News* he added a string of smaller Delaware papers, and the entire chain opened up on Coleman and to such effect that Alfred, not Coleman, was elected to sit in the Republican national convention. In the same election, old Henry Algernon Du Pont, United States senator, was defeated.

All of this must have given Alfred, a good hater, some satisfaction, but the suit against the Du Pont Company by Alfred and others of the clan, seeking to prove that Pierre's purchase of Coleman's stock was a breach of trust, was lost in one court after another, and the United States Supreme Court refused even to consider it.

Yet, next to Pierre, Alfred was the heaviest Du Pont stockholder, and the four war years were golden. Du Pont's capacity expanded from 8,000,000 pounds to 500,000,000 pounds annually. Its workers grew from 5,300 to 47,914. They made forty per cent of all explosives used by the Allies. They made, for Du Pont stockholders, a net profit of $237,000,000, or dividends of 458 per cent on the par value of the stock. One short sentence in Du Pont's annual report for 1918 struck Frederick Lewis Allen as worthy of italics. In summation it remarked, "It is difficult to imagine a more satisfactory result . . ." Mr. Allen thought that this was perhaps "the most striking testimony of Du Pont's endurance of the hardships of war."

In what was also an unhappy moment for Du Pont's public relations, Colonel Buckner, the company's demon salesman, figured out that Du Pont business during four years of world war amounted to twenty-six times the business done in any previous year; or if military business only was considered, then the world-war orders amounted to 276 years of Du Pont business.

Colonel Buckner did better when he reported that one day in 1916, J. P. Morgan, Jr., told him that Lord Moulton, head of the British Munitions Board, had said: "The British and French armies wouldn't have held out through 1915 except for the efforts of three American concerns—Morgan & Company in purchasing munitions, Du Pont in supplying powder, and Bethlehem Steel in making guns and shells."

What Lord Moulton said was probably true enough. It was also forgotten a few years later, when Morgan's, and Du Pont's, and Bethlehem's fellow Americans, dismayed and frightened by depression, began looking around for the villains who had brought the country to economic disaster. Du Pont easily topped the list. They manufactured the basic material of war, gunpowder. This automatically made Du Pont more accursed than those who merely made guns and who were bad enough. One wonders what has been the effect on individual Du Ponts and other "merchants of death" of what passes for public opinion. Patriots in wartime. Villains when the enemy has been vanquished. Surely it must make for cynicism.

At war's end, the Du Pont treasury contained a surplus of somewhere around a hundred million dollars. It was up to the company's new treasurer, John J. Raskob, to find a suitable investment. The war that had just ended had been a war, as all good Americans knew, to end wars; and there seemed little future for a manufacturer of military explosives. Mr. Raskob came up with General Motors.

As related earlier in this book, General Motors was the dream of William C. Durant, a superb salesman and promoter but not the kind of financier to inspire complete confidence. He and his company had several banking difficulties before 1915, when the Du Ponts put a token of their war earnings into General Motors. Though at that time they purchased only 3,000 of GM's 160,000 shares outstanding, four Du Pont men were elected directors and Pierre Du Pont was chosen chairman of the board.

A year later the New Jersey GM company was dissolved and the General Motors Corporation of Delaware was formed. Arthur Pound, historian of General Motors, remarked that it was freely prophesied that the Durant-Du Pont alliance would not last. He said that the Du Ponts were alert to technology and finance, but had never taken their projects to the public as promotions; while Durant had promoted General Motors as if it were a four-ring circus.

Yet the Du Ponts seemed to realize there was a place for daring fellows like Durant. Treasurer Raskob probably influenced this opinion. He and Raskob had much in common, and they liked to talk by the hour of electrified farms, a motorized United States, and vast transcontinental highways to take the place of railroads.

During the last war year, when profits were piling up faster than

Du Pont bookkeepers could list them, the Du Pont Company, at the urging of Raskob, really got into General Motors. In 1918, they bought stock to the value of twenty-five million dollars, and inside another year purchased an additional twenty-four million. Mr. Raskob went in as chairman of GM's financial committee.

The Du Pont-General Motors affiliation seemed ordained for great things from the first. Du Pont had already started manufacturing many by-products such as paints, varnishes, cements, and other items that were needed by the motor makers. And instead of demobilizing its huge engineering force, Du Pont had its men do some sixty million dollars' worth of design and construction for GM, including the new Cadillac plant at Detroit. Fisher Body and other concerns were purchased. GM employees jumped to 86,000. GM's capital swelled to more than one billion dollars. On March 1, 1920, Raskob achieved one of those favorite manipulations of talented capitalists: GM's capitalization was increased to 56,100,000 shares. Shareholders got a ten-to-one stock split-up.

This accomplishment was just in time for the short depression of 1920. Dealers refused to accept GM and other cars. Industrial shutdowns swept the country. Raskob and Pierre Du Pont, working with J. P. Morgan & Company, put up a big GM bond issue, retired several bank loans, and took over Durant's stock. Pierre Du Pont went in as GM president. Three years later, with GM back on its wheels and rolling, Pierre turned the presidency over to Alfred P. Sloan, an old GM man, and returned to Wilmington.

The Du Pont control of General Motors has from the beginning exhibited an intelligence none too common in the world of corporate finance. Actual operation of GM was left and has remained in the hands of men who began their careers in automobiles, not in explosives. Fifteen years after Du Pont's original investment in GM, wrote John Winkler, the Du Pont Company had received General Motors dividends of more than two hundred and fifty million dollars. What was more, the motor corporation had become Du Pont's best customer, due wholly to the powder makers' peacetime chemical empire.

This chemical empire had its beginnings back in 1880, when Lammot Du Pont set up a small laboratory at the Repauno works. From that day on, Du Pont men continued to experiment with waste material. As early as 1906 the company was setting aside $300,000 a year for research.

In 1909 Du Pont men were working with synthetic fibers. They had already produced artificial leather, and followed it with various lacquers, plastics, and photographic film. Then, in 1917, the United States confiscated German-owned patents and made them available to American manufacturers at a nominal license fee. (Readers will recall Dr. Koppers in a previous chapter.) Du Pont wanted some of the patents for synthetic dyes. It got them, and its aggressive management, which included not only Pierre but his brothers Irénée and Lammot (the second), all sons of the Lammot killed by explosion in 1884, put twelve and a half million dollars of its war profits into plants and working capital for this new field.

At war's end, too, Du Pont bought several pioneer plastics concerns and combined them into Du Pont Viscoloid, which makes combs, belt and shoe buckles, toilet sets, advertising novelties, and several hundred other items. With Pittsburgh Plate Glass, Du Pont formed the Duplate Company to make shatterproof glass. It organized Du Pont Film Manufacturing Company to supply the movie industry. As early as 1920 it got into the rayon business with Du Pont Fibersilk Company. Before long Du Pont plants were making one sixth of all rayon in the United States and were earning some five million dollars a year.

In 1924 Du Pont bought sole American rights to a new French product called cellophane. It was too expensive until Du Pont chemists cut its cost by almost half and at the same time made the stuff moisture-proof. *This was it.* The whole country seemed to go cellophane mad. Not only foods and cigars and cigarettes came wrapped in it, but almost everything else. This writer vividly recalls seeing in a store window a big refrigerator wrapped in the material, and a desk done up like a cellophane mummy. When repeal at last brought legal liquor, strong and thirsty men cursed as they fumbled and tore at the invisible stuff so ridiculously encasing a sealed glass bottle. . . .

Meanwhile, General Motors, controlled by Du Pont, and Standard Oil of New Jersey combined to form the Ethyl Gasoline Corporation to make and market the new power fuel named in the corporation's title; and the Du Pont Company went into manufacture of the tetraethyl lead used in the process.

During dismal 1934 Du Pont, along with American big business in general, was called before Congress in a frantic effort to place the blame for five years of depression where it belonged—which the elected representatives of the people said was on the shoulders of industrial and banking moguls. Wall Street was the favorite villain, but the victims demanded specific villains, too. No better could be found than the Du Pont family. Either Senator Gerald P. Nye, or some clever press agent, thought up a dandy epithet. It was "merchants of death," and with this on their flag the Nye Congressional committee charged headlong at the Brandywine powder-making family.

"And Du Pont," remarked the company historian with some justification, "praised a few years before as a bulwark of civilization when its munitions were stemming the German tide," was hailed once more before what orators call the bar of public opinion. Irénée Du Pont took the stand with obvious enjoyment. Although the Du Pont historian modestly refrains from giving him any credit and is content to say that the Nye committee hearings were "inconclusive," the record indicates that Irénée Du Pont achieved something of a victory. Blowing reflective smoke rings from his ever present pipe, a medium-long curved briar, he testified that his company had indeed prevented the United States from becoming a province of Germany; and that any agitation for nationalization of munitions making was the work of Bolsheviks. His bland remarks, said Winkler, "robbed the hearings of a great deal of sting, with the result that those who came to hear the cannon roar had, for the most part, to content themselves with a volley of cap pistols."

Yet the hearings, says the Du Pont historian, "left their stamp on public consciousness." Not for long. Within another six years, global war began breaking out and the Du Ponts were again supplying explosives and much else needed by modern armies.

For this second world war, Du Pont built, on United States account, fifty-four plants at a total cost exceeding one billion dollars, for which, says the Du Pont spokesman, the company received a fee, after taxes and other charges, of "$\frac{1}{15}$ of one per cent of the construction cost." At the same time, Du Pont was making smokeless powder at the rate of one ton a minute. It turned out thirty-six million yards of parachute yarn, made from a Du Pont product called nylon and which was to be a postwar sensation in the world of clothing. Du Pont scientists and technicians were also employed on a secret project whose product was dropped on Hiroshima in 1945.

World War II closed with the Du Ponts heroes again, and though their and all other wartime industrial efforts are now largely forgotten, the Du Ponts have not as yet been designated again as merchants of death. (It comes to mind, however, that neither has there appeared, as this is written, any sign of a new depression.)

In 1951, Du Pont's experimental station, ranging along the Brandywine heights within a stone's throw of the original powder mills, represented thirty million dollars. In it and other Du Pont laboratories elsewhere work 5,000 men and women. In Du Pont's Lavoisier Library, named for the distinguished Frenchman who taught the first Irénée Du Pont the secrets of powder making, are framed diplomas representing the 1,680 college degrees held by 850 Du Pont employees. These range "from architecture to zoology," "from Harvard to Heidelberg."

In 1951, the financial statement of E. I. du Pont de Nemours & Company listed an operating investment of $1,553,156,361. That is a pretty big investment even in an era when the tendency of big business is to grow ever bigger. The Du Ponts now consider their very size to be their greatest problem. "The new sin of size," says the Du Pont spokesman, "figures in most indictments of U. S. industry by its detractors . . . Du Pont's position is that in a competitive market size is simply a measure of usefulness; that customer preference will of itself regulate growth or shrinkage." Eighty years before, John D. Rockefeller said something similar.

Though of late years many high company officials, and even one president, have been neither Du Ponts nor in-laws, the family members still connected with the business may be described as legion. The names of eight Du Ponts appeared in Volume 27 (1952–53) of Who's Who in America. Except for one entry, their business affiliations were all given as Du Pont and their homes as Wilmington, Delaware. The exception was Jessie Ball Du Pont, third wife and widow of Alfred, who, after the family and company differences cited earlier, exiled himself to Florida and there created something of an empire of his own before he died in 1935. His estate, probated in the great depression, was $32,736,000.

What the massed members of the Du Pont family are worth would be a task for a dedicated statistician to find out; and to place each member in correct relation to the others would require a genealogical chart of imposing size. Several hundred individuals made up the Du Pont clan in mid-century. There are more than twenty Du Pont estates in the environs of Wilmington, four of them of a magnificence to compare with those of any Astor, Vanderbilt, or Rockefeller.

Beginning with old Pierre Samuel (1739–1817) seven generations of the family have lived in Delaware. Even with Du Pont entry into General Motors, United States Rubber, and other concerns outside Delaware that have nothing to do with explosives, the Du Pont family, by intermarriage and residence, has kept much of its primal feudalism. There has been no other clan in American industry to remind one even remotely of the Du Ponts of Delaware.

Doubtless old Pierre Samuel would be proud of the dynasty he founded in the United States. Just as surely, too, he would be quite appalled at the Du Pont empire. Back in 1812, writing to his good friend Thomas Jefferson, and discussing the division of labor that is the foundation of the modern industrial system, Pierre Samuel said bluntly that he was against it. "One must admit," he wrote, "that this manner to earn and deserve a salary is a very valuable thing, but at the same time one must remember that it is compensated by the misfortune of creating a class of men [employees] weak, unhealthy, condemned to become machines by operating other machines . . . I bewail the fact that Americans are dragged by political circumstances into turning their capital and industries toward enterprises of the sort, which do not create wealth, but permit the acquisition of wealth and make it possible for a few capitalists to get hold of it, with the sad consequence that we have destitute people . . . The class of people who work in factories do not contribute any happiness, or any power, and constitute an evil for a nation . . ."

That, as Gerald Johnson has pointed out, coming from the founder of the Du Pont industrial empire, with its several hundred thousand employees, is one of the choicest bits of irony in American history.

Chapter 2   THE GUGGENHEIMS

THE founder of the Guggenheim line in America arrived almost half a century after the first Du Pont. He was Meyer, fresh from the ghetto of the Swiss town of Langnau, where he was born in 1828.

Meyer Guggenheim came with no capital, nor was he on intimate terms with the President of the United States. His start in the New World was drearily like that of so many Jews before and after him. He filled a pack with shoestrings, laces, ribbons, and other notions and set out on foot to peddle them to miners' wives in the gloom of Pennsylvania's anthracite region.

At twenty, young Guggenheim was already as bewhiskered as a rabbi, yet he made up for his foreignness of speech and appearance with a cheerful and friendly manner. He sold a lot of notions, including a stove polish on which he made a penny on a dime sale. The man who made the polish, he learned, took a profit of seven cents. While on a round of calls in Bethlehem, young Meyer asked a local chemist what the polish was made of, and returned to his home that week end with the formula. It was a turning point in his life. From here on the polish was manufactured in the Guggenheim home in Philadelphia by Meyer's father, stepmother, and stepsisters, one of whom became his wife.

Meyer Guggenheim went out with a pack no more. With a satchel filled with samples of the stove polish and other goods, he rode the steamcars and called on the trade. He now carried spices, a coffee essence, and a household lye for making soap. This last product was so successful that Meyer formed a company to manufacture it in large volume. The Pennsylvania Salt Company promptly sued him for patent infringement. Guggenheim won, and accepted $150,000 to get out of the lye business.

Unlike so many successful Jews, Meyer Guggenheim seems never to have been an outstanding personage in the Philadelphia or New York Jewish communities. He shocked the orthodox because he had no scruples about doing business on the Sabbath. There was nothing impressive about him. He was small in stature. He spoke little. He trusted few men. He believed devoutly that life was a dog-eat-dog proposition. He did not propose to be eaten. He felt no obligations. Business came before everything else. He had done very well at it, too. He meant that his sons should do even better.

Eleven children were born to Meyer and Barbara Guggenheim. Eight were sons. Of these seven grew to manhood, and each was methodically prepared by education and apprenticeship for his role in Guggenheim affairs. The four older sons, for instance, spent their teens learning the lace embroidery business, which their father planned they should follow. Son Daniel was sent to Switzerland to learn German and lace at the same time. Sons Murry and Solomon soon followed, to live in St. Gall, Switzerland's embroidery center. Isaac was sent to New York city to establish "connections" and open an office.

In 1881 all was ready, and the firm of M. Guggenheim's Sons was founded. The four sons were equal partners. Meyer gave them the business but did not become a member, though he kept close watch and was always ready with a loan (five per cent) to tide over any emergency. These could not have been many or serious. M. Guggenheim's Sons were able to undersell all other importers, often by twenty per cent, and the money rolled in.

Eight years later, Meyer rather suddenly urged his sons to get out of the lace business. "We are competing with the Swiss," he told the boys. "When they make $20,000 it means 100,000 francs to them. The cost of living is cheaper in francs in Switzerland than in dollars in America. Get into something that is not in competition with the Swiss."

If the sons wondered what had come over old Meyer, they soon learned what it was—a couple of holes in Colorado called mines. Before the end of 1888, M. Guggenheim's Sons had sold their lace business and they and Meyer took up residence in New York City. By then, the youngest son had turned twenty and the seven Guggenheim brothers were ready to lay the cornerstone of the family's empire, which was to be in metals. But old Meyer had discovered where the cornerstone should lie and he meant to show the boys how to place it.

During the years while the four sons were conducting the profitable lace business, Meyer had not been idle. Among his several ventures was to purchase 2,000 shares in the Hannibal & St. Joseph Railroad of Missouri. He paid forty-two dollars a share at a time when the road was in difficulties and had passed several dividends. He bought in just before Jay Gould decided he ought to have the Hannibal to connect the Wabash and the Union Pacific. In their efforts to get control, Gould's agents ran the stock up to two hundred dollars and more. Meyer Guggenheim was then pleased to sell. On an investment of $84,000 he came out with $400,000, a profit not to be dreamed of in the lace business.

With such a fine killing, most men would have been properly conditioned for further gambling in railroad stocks. Not Meyer Guggenheim. The Hannibal & St. Joe was his first and last. He had other plans for his new capital; some of it would go into a couple of flooded mines in which he had bought half an interest for $5,000. The mines were in the Leadville district of Colorado, recently admitted as the Silver State. They were called the Minnie and the A. Y. Meyer had taken an interest at the urging of Charles H. Graham, a Philadelphia storekeeper who had been a good customer when Meyer was selling lye, stove polish, and coffee essence.

In 1881, Meyer Guggenheim made his first trip into the West. Leadville was in its wild glory. The ex-pedd_r had seen nothing like it anywhere. Twenty thousand people milled up and down its narrow streets, engaged in the usual activities common to mining towns on the boom, such as drinking, gambling, whoring, and selling each other pieces of claims. This was not gold, but silver. The Rockies' first millionaire had just appeared right here in Leadville. He was H. A. W. Tabor and his fortune had come from grubstaking a couple of German prospectors with a jug of whiskey. The Germans proceeded to strike the rich Little Pittsburgh Lode. Other strikes followed to produce millions from New Discovery, Little Chief, Chrysolite, Matchless, and many more.

By then, Leadville was the center of the biggest rush the Rockies ever saw. Row upon row of miners' shacks spread over the hills. Saloons, hotels, sporting houses, and gambling dens went up by the block. The new silver kings built a row of mansions. Five stage lines tried to handle passenger traffic. Two narrow-gauge railroads were approaching. A reporter for the Leadville *Chronicle* told how it was. "Leadville never sleeps," he wrote. "The theaters close at three in the morning. The dance houses and the liquoring shops are never shut. Carbonate Hill with her scores of blazing fires is Argus-eyed. The clock on the Grand Central Hotel points to one. Shots are heard. The roar of revelry is on the increase. The streets are full of drunken carousers taking in the town."

Meyer Guggenheim looked upon the chaotic camp and thought it unfit for savages. The sharp blasts off the fourteen-thousand-foot continental divide chilled his short figure and wafted his dundreary whiskers wildly. He shook his head at the disorder he saw on every hand and spoke to his partner, who had come to Leadville ahead of him. "What a place," he said. "God help you if there is no million dollars in that mine. For no other reason could you ever get me here . . ." And the two partners drove out to look at their A. Y. mine and the adjacent Minnie.

Guggenheim was appalled. The A. Y.-Minnie appeared as a few drab shacks in disrepair, and the shaft looked like any old hole in the ground. A handful of men were working, and Superintendent

Sam Harsh wanted to know if Mr. Guggenheim would like to go
below to see the workings. Mr. Guggenheim looked at the ore
bucket, which was also the mine elevator, and said no. "I know
there is a mine here," he added. "More I cannot know."

Graham tossed a piece of rock down the hole, and the noise of
a splash came up. "That's the trouble with this mine," he said.
"But the new pump will fix that."

Guggenheim knew what *that* meant. It meant that he would have
to buy a pump if he wanted to get his $5,000 back, and maybe a
pump couldn't do that much. He was pretty discouraged as he
and Graham bumped down the mountain to Leadville. There the
two partners, with Superintendent Harsh, discussed the immediate
needs of the mine. Pumps, engines, much other gear, plus cash for
a modest pay roll. It added up to $25,000. Guggenheim grumbled
and swore considerably, calling himself all kinds of fool. "What
a gamble is this!" he cried. Yet without the new equipment, how
could he and Graham know? He put up the money, then got out
of Leadville.

"After that decision," wrote Max Lerner, with complete understanding of the overpowering influence of holes called mines,
"he [Guggenheim] was led by the peculiar logic of one commit-
ment after another to throw his entire fortune into mining ventures."

Back home again, the new mine owner told friends that the only
decent thing he had seen in Leadville was a store well stocked with
M. Guggenheim's Sons lace embroideries. And the demands of the
A. Y.-Minnie seemed voracious. What Meyer called "unwatering"
the mines appeared to be an endless process. To make matters
worse, Leadville had its first miners' strike. The mine operators
called out their private militia companies to protect the properties.
The miners staged a great parade, marching silently with folded
arms. The operators staged another, which included a couple of
hundred girls conscripted from the sporting houses.

Water soon flooded all the mines. When the strike was broken
and men returned to work, Guggenheim had to put up another
$50,000 to get the A. Y.-Minnie unwatered again. But now they
began to pay, and one day, six months later, the Leadville *Herald-
Democrat* wound up to let the camp and the world know about it.
The reporter was no man to fiddle around with short jerky prose.
In one long gorgeous sentence that glittered as it moved up and
down the shafts, then wove from one stope to another, he presented
an imperishable picture of the newest bonanza king's property.

"Of the endurance of the magical foundation which Leadville awoke to find beneath its giant cradle," wrote the *Herald-Democrat* man, "of the fullness of the breast from which she was nourished in infancy and of the permanency of those vaults from which she has derived her parentage amid a wave of tumultuous, if not riotous, approval, she has no better assurances to offer than those which are exposed in the massive blocks of mineral, those pyramids of ore that stand like glistening rows of tenements upon the various levels of the A. Y. and Minnie in California Gulch." When that had sunk in, the *Herald-Democrat's* genius of words told what it meant. "At this day," wrote he, "there is no greater bonanza in the mountains than the A. Y. and Minnie."

He was not far from right. Harvey O'Connor, biographer of the Guggenheims, says that by 1887 some nine million ounces of silver and 86,000 tons of lead had come from the two mines; and that in the next two years "$1,383,000 had been realized clear." He adds that in 1890 the two mines were still valued at almost fifteen million dollars.

Although much of the early production of the two mines was so pure that it went direct to the mint rather than to a smelter, the ore soon changed and smelting became necessary to separate the lead and other base metals from the silver. Meyer Guggenheim looked at the smelter bills. They were big enough, but what troubled him, as it did many another mine operator, was that you had no control of your own metals once the ore had been treated. The smelter took possession, paid you its price, and then marketed the metals. It made two profits—one from smelting, the other from marketing.

Meyer Guggenheim found all this a mystery and an imposition. Possibly he recalled his early experience with stove polish, when he decided to make it himself and discovered the profit multiplied. In any case, it was clear to the new bonanza king that a mine operator ought also to operate a smelter. But first, a Guggenheim should learn something about mines and smelters to make up for Meyer's complete ignorance.

Son Benjamin was sent to the Columbia School of Mines; his vacations were to be spent in Colorado, checking theory with practice. Son William went to the University of Pennsylvania to study metallurgy, plus a course later at the Wharton School of Business and Finance. Son Daniel, who for eleven years had been in charge of lace production in Europe, was brought home, and went at once to Colorado to act as his father's chief lieutenant. Son Murry was soon called to Pueblo, Colorado, where the Guggenheims were erecting a six-stack plant to be known as the Philadelphia smelter. This would take care of what Meyer always referred to as Smelter Extortion, as though it should be capitalized.

The Philadelphia Smelting & Refining Company went into production in 1889. It was capitalized at $1,500,000. No bankers were needed. Every cent that went into the company belonged to Guggenheim. Each of the sons was given an equal share. According to Isaac Marcosson, who wrote the story of Guggenheim's later colossus, American Smelting & Refining Company, the old man provided the funds to build the Philadelphia smelter and charged his sons five per cent interest. He also insisted that the four sons who had made such a success in the lace business get out of it forthwith and go into something big. Who, he wanted to know, would ever hear of the Guggenheim brothers if they remained lace importers? America was developing in the West. Vast fortunes were still to be accumulated there.

The old man had his way. Son Isaac stayed on awhile to wind up the affairs of the lace business, then turned to the financial end of the Guggenheim mines and smelter. Benjamin became general manager of the Pueblo plant. Simon was put in charge of ore buying, along with William as assistant. Solomon was elected to work with Daniel. Murry went in as president of the smelting company. But neither Meyer nor the sons themselves set rigid rules or staked out any borders for the activities within the organization.

The first months of the Philadelphia Smelting & Refining Company were discouraging. It went into the red immediately and for some time showed a loss averaging $50,000 per month. This may have been chiefly because Meyer disliked the idea of paying royalties for use of standard smelting apparatus; he had his men devise a homemade method, which he was at last forced to throw out and to replace with orthodox machinery. Improvement was noted at once. A little more, and the plant was returning a profit of $50,000 a month. This was due in large part to August Raht, a graduate of the Freiberg School of Mines who, says O'Connor, "rescued the Philadelphia . . . and was to remain the keystone in the Guggenheim smelting enterprises . . ."

No little of the ore smelted in the Philadelphia came from Mexico, where Americans had acquired and opened silver mines and built railroads. It was rich ore and it was so cheaply produced that it could be hauled several hundred miles to the Kansas City Company's smelter at El Paso, Texas, and even further to the Guggenheim's at Pueblo, and return a profit. Mexican silver in fact had been underselling the American product. The Colorado mine operators set up a roar that was heard in Congress, where oratory paid for by the operators informed all good Americans that the "flood" of Mexican ore, produced by peon labor, was about "to overwhelm the great industry of the Rockies." In 1890 Congress put an embargo on the silver threat.

The effects of the embargo were immediately noticeable at the Philadelphia smelter. Meyer Guggenheim called Son Daniel. "If we can't bring Mexican ore to Pueblo," he said, "let us take a smelter to Mexico." It sounded reasonable to Dan. He and Murry left Pueblo to spearhead the advance of the Guggenheims. The two young men got along beautifully, for the Mexicans found them astonishingly cultured. They not only spoke a little Spanish, but they were nothing like the brash gringo merchants and crude mining men so numerous and so disliked. The many years Dan and Murry had spent traveling around Europe stood them well here in Mexico.

When the Guggenheims and their local agents had looked at several sites, they concluded that Monterrey in the state of Nuevo León was the place for their first smelter. Dan then went to Mexico City for another round of bowing, handshaking, drinking of toasts, and swapping beautiful compliments; and when these necessary overtures had been completed, the Department of Industrial Encouragement granted to "Sr. Daniel Guggenheim and the company or companies he may organize" a concession bestowing the right to build and operate three smelters. All machinery was to enter the country free of customs duties. Returning to Monterrey, Dan got from the state legislature of Nuevo León another concession, which permitted building and operation of a specific smelter and freed the Guggenheims of taxes for twenty years. It also stipulated that the smelter, or *fundición,* be completed within eighteen months.

Dan and Murry Guggenheim lost no time. They organized the imposingly named Great National Mexican Smelter Company and took off for Pueblo and New York. After a quick conference of Meyer and sons, Solomon and Will, the youngest, left for Monterrey to buy land and start construction of the smelter. The work was fairly well along when what the Guggenheim boys hoped was not a typical Mexican incident occurred; their construction engineer, Van

Yngling, was slashed with knives and killed while asleep in his bunk. Sol called the Monterrey police. Next day General Reyes, governor of the state, appeared to inform Sol that four men had been shot for the murder of the engineer. Sol asked if the men had been found guilty. "Oh," replied General Reyes, "we didn't bother about a trial. They were vagabonds anyway." It was all very simple, the general explained, though he much regretted that the vagabonds had not been shot before they had committed the crime against the American engineer, so much needed now that Mexico was becoming a great hive of industry.

Sol and Will had discovered that if they hoped to keep an American staff to help make Monterrey a hive of industry, they must build decent quarters, recreation halls, and a field for sports. They did these things and, being just as astute as brothers Dan and Murry, they invited good General Reyes and all other state officials to a grand opening. Much food and a plenty of drink were consumed. A band played by day, and an orchestra filled the night with music for a ball. Everything came off fine, and the gringo bowling alley turned out to be an enormous sensation. The like had never been heard of, much less seen. The Mexican officials enjoyed sending the balls thundering down the wooden path to see the pins scatter, while onlookers cheered madly.

The most difficult problem faced by Sol and Will was how to get the Mexican Indians to work. Labor's common wage was twenty-five centavos a day. The brothers stepped up the pay to a peso. It didn't serve the purpose, for the higher the wage, the fewer days the Indian needed to satisfy his simple needs. It merely gave him more time to sit in the sun. A much better plan, which was put into effect, was to offer a rent-free house to those men who would work twenty-five days a month.

At last the smelter was ready, and one day in 1892 the fires were started. The first month's clear profit exceeded sixty thousand dollars. Within a year all expenses incidental to getting the concession and building the plant had been returned.

Dan Guggenheim had been looking into other matters in Mexico. One of these was copper, the metal with which the Guggenheims were to be closely identified. After much exploration, Dan bought a copper mine in the Tepezala district; and at Aguascalientes started construction of a smelter that would handle both copper and lead. The experienced Sol and Will took charge of building and of putting the plant into operation. While this was going on, Benjamin returned East and took up residence in Perth Amboy, New Jersey, where the Guggenheims had decided to build a refinery. It was finished in 1894, ready to refine the ores that had been smelted in Guggenheim plants and dug in Guggenheim mines, along with much ore from other mines.

Meyer Guggenheim, and his seven active sons, now operated an industrial empire in two countries completely integrated from mine head to the finished metal, whether it be silver or copper or lead. The Mexican venture had been entered upon and brought to impressive success in little more than four years. Only a family with energy, resource, and talents could have gone into that country and achieved so much in so little time. By 1895 the family was skimming at least a million dollars a year from its several mines and three smelters. One should bear in mind, too, that the Guggenheims, able as they were, had the best of help. Again and again in his study of the family, biographer O'Connor calls attention to August Raht, the metallurgist "on whom all the growing Guggenheim enterprises depended for profitable operation."

The growing Guggenheim enterprises and all other smelting concerns in the United States were about to take the fancy of Henry H. Rogers, who will need no introduction. He had put together his Copper Trust, which he called the Amalgamated and which Tom Lawson had "floated," in the phraseology of the period, with dazzling effectiveness. The monster had paid off, big. Rogers now wanted to create another monster.

The time was 1896. This was the heyday of the dinosaurian stockjobs, the trusts. The dangerous Bryan had been defeated. McKinley was President, elected on the promise of Mark Hanna that money would be kept sound and dinner pails would be filled to the brim. New Jersey had amended its laws to encourage the floating of any amounts of stock, with no questions concerning its value or lack of value. The federal antitrust laws were museum pieces, antiquities on a par with state laws prohibiting the operation of railroad trains on the Sabbath.

The idea of a smelter trust may have come to Rogers by way of his copper trust, which contained a few smelter properties, or he may have been inspired to it by the Lewisohn brothers, Leonard and Adolph, who had formed the United Metals Selling Company, through which Amalgamated Copper sold its metal in the British market and in which Rogers was a stockholder.

The Lewisohn brothers were ambitious and able, and though

they were not in Rogers' class, they liked corporations that had
size to them, with plenty of stock to float. They joined Rogers to
manage the pool which Rogers said was to be called the American
Smelting & Refining Company. Rogers then called in the principals
of Moore & Schley, the brokerage house favored by Morgan, the
Rockefellers, and lesser masters of capital. Grant Schley was the
intimate and a brother-in-law of George F. Baker, head of the
First National. John Moore was the magnate of both Chase National and Western Union. (Moore, incidently, was soon to cover
himself with a special aura among his clients by getting the federal
income tax law, a weak thing at best yet a "penalty put upon
thrift and enterprise," declared unconstitutional.)

Mr. Rogers told Moore & Schley what was afoot; he and the
Lewisohns were getting together a monopoly of silver and lead
smelters. Would Moore & Schley engage proper agents to go all
over the West and talk to smelter men, tell them of the marvels
brewing to excite cupidity, in the rare case that any sluggishness
in that quarter were encountered, and prepare meanwhile to float
sixty-five million dollars in stock certificates of American Smelting
& Refining, which was to be incorporated in the state of New
Jersey?

The agents of Moore & Schley devoted the next several months
to painting golden-worded pictures of the profits sure to a monopoly. They visited smelters and refineries in Colorado, Kansas,
Montana, Texas, Utah, Illinois, and Pennsylvania, and found the
owners ripe to a man, except the Guggenheims. Even when Moore
& Schley's agent upped the ante, the brothers displayed no enthusiasm.

Rogers could not understand such an attitude. The Lewisohns
were so put out they declared the Guggenheims must have gone
mad. The Lewisohns wanted particularly to get control of the
Guggenheim refinery, the only copper refinery owned by people
in the silver-lead business, because it enabled the Guggenheims to
enter the European copper market independent of the Lewisohns'
United Metals Selling Company.

Rogers wanted the Guggenheims in his trust for more basic
reasons. They were by now the major factor in Mexico, in both
silver and lead, and in copper. Their copper mines and copper
smelter encroached on Rogers' Amalgamated Copper; and their
Mexican silver-lead smelter and mines threatened the whole
smelters' trust.

The pool at last offered the Guggenheims eleven million dollars in stock for their interests, and still was refused. The pool could wait no longer. On March 7, 1899, the American Smelting & Refining stock went on the market. The corporation "combined all the principal smelting concerns in the United States with the exception of the Guggenheims."

Though a veteran of mines and smelters, A. H. Danforth, said publicly that the whole new sixty-five-million-dollar corporation had physical properties worth not more than eleven and a half million, speculators were so keen that American Smelting's entire issue of stock was sold out within two weeks. The happy owners of smelters that went into the trust received approximately nineteen million dollars, and many of them got fine jobs with the new outfit. The promoters were happy, too, to split a few crumbs. These totaled $8,100,000. As for the Guggenheims, old Meyer was immensely tickled. He went around asking acquaintances what good was eleven million dollars in a country like the United States. "For eleven million dollars in their paper we should give away our smelters," he repeated. "What are we without our smelters' mines? Not worth two cents. And anyway, who knows what good their stock is?"

Dan Guggenheim was not pleased. Even though he had stood out against the blandishments of the trust, he knew well enough that he and his brothers had a fight on their hands to survive the attacks of the powerful Rogers combination, with its backing of Rockefeller money. And he, Dan, was now the accepted leader of the Guggenheim brothers. He was forty-three years old. His health was good. His mind was keen as ever, and, aided by the force of circumstances, it conceived something to stand off the smelters' trust. He thought of it as the Guggenheim Exploration Company.

The idea was first to seek out and purchase every good mine in Mexico to hitch to the family smelters; then to follow the same policy in the United States, Alaska, and Canada. The Klondike gold rush was still in full swing. Dan had discussed the Exploration Company with old Meyer as well as the brothers. He called attorney Samuel Untermyer for advice, especially to suggest someone of a speculative bent who could afford to risk a million dollars, possibly more, in Guggenheim Exploration.

Untermyer interested William C. Whitney, a Massachusetts small-town lad who had married a sister of Oliver H. Payne, one of Standard Oil's heaviest stockholders. Whitney had served as Secretary of the Navy in Cleveland's first Administration. He had also participated in the manipulation of New York City's streetcar franchises with Thomas Fortune Ryan and Peter A. B. Widener, through which the trio achieved considerable notoriety and a large though undetermined amount of money running into many millions.

William C. Whitney's fortune was large enough to permit almost any speculation. His temperament was right for it. He was also looking for an opportunity where his son, Harry Payne, might make his mark. Further, anything that would harass the Rogers crowd (though not Standard Oil) appealed to him. He was ready to help finance the Guggenheim Exploration Company. It was understood that his son Harry should have a position in it.

While the Exploration Company was getting started, conditions in the smelting industry, and especially in the smelting trust, were playing into the hands of the Guggenheims. In the trust were many aggressive personalities, men who for years had been dictators in their own domains. Now they were linked in a combine whose orders came from Wall Street. It was irritating.

The miners and the smelter workers were irritated, too. They had tired of the twelve-hour day, and at last the Colorado legislature acted. In June of 1899 a state eight-hour law went into effect. The trust's biggest Colorado smelter at Durango, and smaller plants elsewhere in the state, refused to pay twelve hours' wages for eight hours' work. The workers struck—that is, all except those at Guggenheim's Philadelphia smelter at Pueblo. Simon had agreed to pay the old wage for the new workday.

Many mines were closed immediately because smelters could not accept their ore; there was no place even to pile it. The Guggenheim smelter started operating twenty-four hours a day, seven days a week. The strike continued two months longer, ending with a ten per cent pay increase for key workers but with the twelve-hour shift. The Colorado Supreme Court had held the eight-hour law unconstitutional.

The Guggenheims emerged from the strike as something like heroes. Mine owners, having felt the curse of eastern monopoly, praised them as sturdy men who would not bend the knee to hated Wall Street. The governor of Colorado, Charley Thomas, proposed that the smelter trust be run out of the state. Colorado papers began printing cartoons of trust ogres. The trust had raised smelting charges. The smelters refused to accept small amounts of ore as a nuisance.

The Guggenheim agents were instructed to be liberal with ore shippers. The brothers Ben, Simon, and Will even made small loans to hard-pressed mine operators. Often they bought stock to help develop promising claims. They also posted notice they would pay twenty dollars an ounce for gold, one dollar more than the price set by the trust.

Meanwhile, the Guggenheims were working fast with their Exploration Company. They invested two million dollars in the Missouri soft-lead district and induced producers there to break away from the trust smelters. They leased a lead-silver smelter in Bolivia. In 1899, too, the Guggenheims delivered a smashing blow at the trust by dumping huge supplies of lead on the market, forcing the trust to cut its fixed price below what its metal had cost.

This savage and effective fighting by an outfit with only three smelters and a refinery began to tell on the trust with its twenty plants. It was soon obvious that the Guggenheims had defeated the larger group at half a dozen points, and had thoroughly spiked the hoped-for monopoly. In December, 1900, a little less than two years after its organization, the American Smelting & Refining Company found its capital exhausted. Its worried directors were ready to quit. The white flag went up the pole of the smelters' trust.

American Refining now approached Dan Guggenheim for purchase of his family's small but compact and efficient industrial empire. Dan refused the offer simply because it would not have given control to the Guggenheims. It must be control or nothing, Dan said. That was the way it worked out. For a consideration of $45,200,000 in American Smelting stock the Guggenheims turned over to the trust all of their properties except their mines in Colorado and Mexico and the Exploration Company. Even Henry H. Rogers was to admit that the deal gave undisputed control to the Guggenheims—control of the smelters' trust which he had conceived and so largely created.

For many months Mr. Rogers' attention had been directed elsewhere. Among other things, the billion-dollar steel trust was brewing. Rogers and the other promoters of American Smelting, the Lewisohns, and Moore & Schley, did not fully appreciate what the deal with the Guggenheims meant until it was too late. Or, was it quite too late?

Mr. Rogers had been bruised enough by the Guggenheim defeat of the smelting trust. The sudden realization that control of the trust was now in Guggenheim hands brought him into swift action. Calling in David Lamar, Wall Street's favorite demolition man and one of several characters known at various periods as the Wolf of Wall Street, Rogers told him to wreck the stock of American Smelting.

Lamar began his operations at once. One hundred thousand shares of American Smelting were thrown into the market. The price sagged from sixty-two to fifty-five. But Lamar could drive it no lower. Dan Guggenheim had asked William Whitney for help. Buying started and the bears were routed.

Mr. Rogers took another tack. He got a court injunction to halt the merger of American's and Guggenheim's interests. A legal battle followed, with Sam Untermyer opposing Rogers' noted Vliet Lindabury. The outcome was compromise. The Guggenheims agreed to minor concessions in the corporate setup, but they retained control of American Smelting & Refining, on whose new board sat Isaac, Daniel, Murry, Solomon, and Simon Guggenheim. As if to emphasize matters, the board elected Dan chairman, and Simon treasurer.

It will be noticed that only five sons sat on the board. Ben and Will Guggenheim had broken with their brothers. The reasons for the rift are not clear. Whatever the differences, they came to a head at the time of the merger. Ben went into the mine-machinery business as head of International Steam Pump, with which he continued until April 15, 1912, when he went down on the *Titanic,* along with 1,516 others, when the big new ship struck an iceberg in the North Atlantic. As for Will, he had committed an even greater offense than wanting to leave the family business; he had married a gentile.

The brothers shipped Will to Europe. A doubtful divorce was arranged, and Will returned to the United States. He refused to return to the family business. Instead he would devote his life to philanthropy. The brothers apparently arranged that Will should have a modest income. He soon married again, but for the next dozen years he and the Guggenheim family in general were to be harassed by the ex-Mrs. Will. Attorney Untermyer denounced her motive as "foul and her object blackmail," yet she was a determined woman, and courts in Illinois, where the alleged divorce had been granted, were kept busy with the affair until 1914. Incidentally, Will's was the only divorce in the second generation of the Guggenheim family.

In the last years of his life, old Meyer was sued for breach of promise by a Hanna McNamara, who said she and the head of the house of Guggenheim had been in "constant intimate association" for twenty-five years. Nothing apparently came of the suit, though it made the old man pretty mad and he offered a "$10,000 reward" to anyone who had seen him and Hanna together. In the same period, Meyer submitted to a serious operation. He refused ether, telling the surgeon, "You can't sell a Jew anesthetics or life insurance." He survived the operation, and died in March 1905, aged seventy-eight, happy in the knowledge that at least five of his seven sons were each a multimillionaire. His own personal fortune was more than $2,250,000.

The comparative quiet that followed the end of the smelting trust-Guggenheim war permitted Dan to devote more time to his favorite concern, the Guggenheim Exploration Company. Through one of the company's partners, William C. Whitney, Dan met in 1902 the most celebrated mining engineer of the era. This was John Hays Hammond, forty-seven years old, already a legend in the African gold fields, and reputedly the hero of Richard Harding Davis's popular novel, *Soldiers of Fortune*.

Though born in California and graduated from Yale's Sheffield Scientific School, Hammond had gone to Freiberg, Germany, for a course in mining and had achieved his world-wide reputation as engineer for the great British imperialist, Cecil Rhodes, in Africa. Hammond's status as a mining engineer took on glamour from the fact that the Boers had condemned him to be hanged for his part in Dr. Jameson's Raid, an "incident" leading up to the Boer War. He was saved from the gallows when the United States Senate petitioned the Boer leader, Oom Paul Kruger, for mercy, though Hammond was not released until Rhodes had paid his fine of $125,000.

Here in New York, a guest of the Whitneys, was the brilliant man, returned to his native land as consulting engineer for the Venture Corporation of London, seeking mine properties for exploitation. Whitney had Dan Guggenheim in to meet Hammond, the outcome of which was a contract that dazzled the world. At a salary of $250,000 a year plus a quarter interest in all properties recommended, John Hays Hammond became consulting engineer for the Guggenheim Exploration Company.

No such salary had been paid anyone before. The press reported it with suitable type and the public, including Wall Street, was astonished that the still little known Guggenheims could pay even John Hays Hammond so princely a salary. Somebody figured out Hammond's daily wage and found it to be $277.77. The great man also insisted that Guggenheim Exploration give him Alfred C. Beatty, twenty-nine-year-old graduate of Columbia School of Mines, as chief aide, and pay him $27,000.

Within a month or so, Hammond and his entourage got aboard his private car, named Kya Yami meaning in Zulu "One of My Homes," and rolled down to Mexico City, where an old friend, Don Porfirio Díaz was dictator. Díaz turned out the guard for the engineer, who then and later was treated with more deference than the American ambassador. With courtesies out of the way, Hammond and party proceeded to look into the depths of a mine called Esperanza, then returned to New York. Hammond told Dan Guggenheim that the Esperanza, Mexico's greatest gold mine, could be had for two million dollars. Guggenex, as the Exploration Company was known, took fifty-one per cent, and Hammond sold the remainder to London's Venture Corporation. The mine was to pay for itself and leave six million dollars' profit before being abandoned.

The Esperanza was merely the first of many properties that came into the Guggenheim orbit during the six years of Hammond's contract. These included Federal Mining & Smelting, with most of Idaho's Coeur d'Alene mines, and a smelter on Puget Sound at Everett, Washington. Setting up a new corporation, a grab bag called American Securities Exploration, the Guggenheims put the Idaho-Washington properties into it and added a smelter at Tacoma, others at San Francisco and at Alton, Illinois, and a Baltimore refinery. It proceeded to build a monster copper smelter at Garfield, Utah, said to be the largest on earth. It bought five lead, silver, and copper mines in Mexico.

During the Hammond-Beatty engineering regime, the Guggenheims entered the Yukon under style of Yukon Consolidated Goldfields, with giant dredges and other equipment. At least one hundred million in gold had been panned from Bonanza Creek's gravelly bed during the Klondike rush. The Guggenex engineers estimated there was as much more left. Power machinery would remove it. Stock could be sold, too, and Thomas W. Lawson, Boston's ebullient man of finance and literature, was called in to "make a market" for a subsidiary of Consolidated called Yukon Gold.

The Guggenheims were also ready to enter Africa, a region they had never contemplated until urged to it by Thomas Fortune Ryan, a mogul compared to whom, in 1906, the smelter kings were small change. King Leopold II of Belgium had approached Mr. Ryan, then on a European tour, and asked him to form a company to take over the King's immense personal holdings on the Congo. Leopold knew that the Belgian Parliament was planning to remove the property from the monarch's private purse to the nation's public charge. He wanted Ryan to accept a concession to reorganize, finance, and exploit the Congo rubber plantations.

Ready gambler that he was, Ryan, who had made fortunes from streetcar lines, insurance, and tobacco, told the King of the Belgians he would look into the matter, and cabled Dan Guggenheim. Ryan thought that Dan's Exploration Company ought to look into it. Quickly, too, lest the Belgian Parliament get in its licks first.

Hammond sent his lieutenant Beatty into Africa. When he returned to New York, Ryan and Guggenheim organized the American Congo Company and the Intercontinental Rubber Company. An army of American engineers was sent into Africa, and the wonders of industrial enterprise were displayed to thousands of natives.

Nothing much came of the rubber, but much gold was taken out. The real profits, however, came from diamonds. What the returns have been to Ryan-Guggenheim isn't of public record. One is perhaps safe in saying they have been better than good. In 1926, the Ryan-Guggenheim outfit gained exclusive rights in all diamond deposits it had discovered up to that time, for a period of ninety-nine years. In this respect one may note that Ryan, who died in 1928, after making benefactions to the Roman Catholic Church of some twenty million dollars, left an estate estimated at $200,000,000. Congo diamonds were no small part of it.

The Guggenheims' first venture into Ontario, Canada, did not turn out so happily. Having bought heavily, on Hammond's advice, in stock of the Nipissing Mines Company, another Guggenheim engineer reported that the property's richest vein "pinched out" at a depth of twenty feet. Nipissing stock tumbled. Although the Guggenheims announced they would reimburse the 150 clients who had bought Nip through Guggenheim Exploration, thousands more who had bought Nip on the market, suffered great losses. The Curb was panicked, other mining stocks plummeted, and the Nipissing affair was said to have "nipped the craze" for mining shares.

John Hays Hammond and the Guggenheims parted company in

1908, when his fat contract expired. He had listened to the flattery of men who wanted to make him a candidate for Vice-President to run with William Howard Taft. He spent a great deal of money before the happy picture was seen to be an illusion.

One of the Guggenheims did better in politics. After a bitter campaign, Simon was elected to the United States Senate from Colorado. He did nothing to upset the smooth operation of "America's richest club," which in 1907 was said to contain eighteen multimillionaires, of whom Senator Guggenheim's personal fortune was the largest.

The election of Simon Guggenheim of Colorado echoed loud in Alaska, where the *Daily Dispatch* of Juneau remarked editorially, on February 22, 1907, that the Guggenheims had taken Colorado into camp and were preparing to annex Alaska so far as its mineral output was concerned. "They have begun by buying up most of the land available for gold dredging and are now moving on the immense copper and coal deposits of the Copper River Country."

It was true enough. Though the family's Yukon Gold venture, already described, had been something of a failure, the engineers of Guggenex had continued to explore possibilities in the Yukon, northern British Columbia, and Alaska; and in 1906 Dan Guggenheim went north to see with his own eyes what he could hardly believe from his engineer's reports. But it was true. In the remote and almost inaccessible Wrangel Mountains were copper deposits of incomparable richness and illimitable extent. His new chief engineer, Pope Yeatman, told Dan that this stuff ran as high as seventy per cent pure copper, and that all of it could be delivered to the Guggenheim smelter in Tacoma, Washington, for less than five cents a pound. Copper was selling from twelve to twenty cents.

To get the riches of this godforsaken region, however, would call for a railroad that might cost as much as twenty million dollars. Dan returned to New York and invited J. P. Morgan & Company to join him in a company to exploit what was to become famous as the Kennecott Copper mines. Morgan partner George Perkins approved the idea, which was incorporated as the Alaska Syndicate.

Any railroad to tap the copper region must start inland somewhere along the bleak mountainous coast between Valdez and Katalla. By the time the Alaska Syndicate was ready to begin work, no less than five railroads were being surveyed or were actually under construction, all headed for what Rex Beach, who wrote a novel about it, termed the richest copper district on earth. There was bound to be war, and the shooting started in late September 1907, when a grading gang of the Alaska Home Railway returned to their base at Valdez, bringing one dead man and six wounded. They had, they said, been doing nothing more than minding their own business, which was making a roadbed, when they were ambushed and fired upon by a crew of Guggenheim gunmen.

The Guggenheim crew retorted that they, too, had been minding their own business, which was protecting the right of way of the Alaska Syndicate, when the Home Railway thugs had attacked them with pick handles. Ed Hasey, in charge of the Syndicate "guards," was arrested and put in the Valdez jail, but when mobs formed and shouted something about hanging the tool of the "Morganheims," Hasey was hurriedly removed to Juneau. Here Hasey was acquitted of murder, then found guilty of wounding another man and sent to the federal penitentiary at McNeil's Island, Washington, for eighteen months, where he remained on the Syndicate's pay roll.

The battle between the Syndicate and the Home Railway gangs set off a terrific uproar in the United States which involved chief forester Gifford Pinchot and Richard Achilles Ballinger, Secretary of the Interior, and brought to Alaska such noted journalists as Mark Sullivan and Norman Hapgood. The fight also involved President Taft and ex-President Theodore Roosevelt. It aired in public the information that the Alaska Syndicate had quietly acquired several Alaska steamship companies that would be needed to carry the ore to its Tacoma smelter; that it had bought Alaska salmon canneries and the choicest of Alaska's coal fields.

Two great battle cries sparked the war: one was monopoly; the other, conservation. Was Alaska and its untold riches to be merely another province in the Guggenheim-Morgan empires? Or was Alaska to be locked up in federal cold storage and prevented from developing? There seemed to be no middle ground, no alternative to the desolating effects of either monopolistic control by private interests or the locking up of all of Alaska's natural resources.

While the war roared on in Congress, in the Cabinet, in federal departments, and the courts, the Alaska Syndicate tended to its business, which was getting a railroad to the copper mountains. After spending $1,500,000 in abortive attempts from Valdez and Katalla, the Syndicate hit upon Cordova as a base. Shiploads of working-stiffs were unloaded there, and three gangs worked around the clock during the brief summer that had no night. In winter, the men worked as they could in the bitter twilight. Year after year, gangs drove the rails over mountains, built million-dollar bridges, laid trestles over muskeg and, at last, in 1911, drove the last spike of the Copper River Railroad. It had cost twenty million dollars in money. Nobody ever attempted to assess the cost in misery.

Ore was ready for the first train to the mines. It had to be hauled two hundred miles to port and shipped another 2,500 miles to the smelter on Puget Sound. The first cargo smelted copper to the current value of half a million dollars. The ore had been delivered at a cost of 4½ cents a pound. A year later, the houses of Morgan and Guggenheim divided three million dollars in the first annual dividends from the Kennecott mine. Many more were to follow.

Long before the high-grade Kennecott went into production, the Guggenheim Exploration Company's engineers had interested the family in a lean two per cent copper property in Bingham Canyon, Utah. This belonged to Utah Copper whose Dan Jackling wanted to try the Mesabi iron range technique of steam-shovel mining but needed much more money to put it into effect. Dan Guggenheim bought a quarter interest in Utah Copper, installed a concentrating plant costing $750,000 that would handle the mass excavations planned by Jackling, laid a railroad from Bingham to Great Salt Lake, and began erection of a smelter at Garfield.

Although the Guggenheims, here acting under style of American Smelting & Refining, owned a minority interest in Utah Copper, they really controlled it by reason of a smelting contract for twenty years.

The powerful Anaconda-Amalgamated copper interests did not welcome the lead-and-silver Guggenheims into their world. Almost simultaneously with Utah Copper's rise to threatening stature, the Big Snake of Montana made a bear raid on American Smelting by announcing it planned to invade Utah with a monster smelting works. A second announcement said Anaconda-Amalgamated would build another smelter in Colorado.

Dan Guggenheim fought off the bear raid on American Smelting stocks and also bought control of a new outfit in the middle of eastern Nevada's vast desolation. This was a low-grade copper property put together by Mark Requa and William Boyce Thompson and named Nevada Consolidated. Developing it called for many millions of dollars, and the Guggenheims were happy to let the public in by way of bond issues floated by Charles Hayden, a man who preferred copper to all other metals.

Nevada Consolidated was to be a successful mining operation, but it was not to remain an entity for long. In a dizzying whirlwind of exchanges of stock and of mergers, Guggenheim's Utah Copper swallowed Nevada Consolidated, and also Boston Consolidated, emerging as "a bloated monster," fat with two and a half million shares of ten dollars par value. To the many critics who brought the weary old charge of watered stock, the Guggenheims called attention to Utah Copper's annual report for 1910. It showed earnings of $5,401,000 and dividends of $4,648,000. If that was water, then what *was* cream?

The open-pit mining of porphyry copper had come to stay, and the deep mines of Michigan's Upper Peninsula were to suffer. Dan Jackling had shown Dan Guggenheim the right road and he had taken it. Jackling was already looking around for more porphyry coppers. The tireless Tom Lawson had an option on a long forgotten mine in New Mexico. It had once belonged to Senator George Hearst, father of the publisher, and in 1899 had been bought for $1,400,000 by Amalgamated Copper, which did nothing to exploit its low-grade ore. Ten years later Lawson laid hands on the property, called it the Santa Rita Mining Company, and began spectacular promotion. Though the promotion failed to interest the stock-buying public, it made Santa Rita sound pretty good to Hayden, Stone & Company which bought it on Jackling's recommendation, changed its name to Chino Copper, and, naturally, emitted 850,000 shares of stock and a bond issue of $2,500,000.

The Guggenheims went into Chino, but not in control, and were content with a long-term contract with their American Smelting.

Jackling then looked into another almost abandoned copper property, the English Ray, in Arizona, where a group of young English bloods had played at being copper mine operators until their money gave out. The lads rode about on dock-tailed horses, dressed for dinner in the wastes of Pinal County, and, rather than build a railroad, sought to transport the Ray's ore overland with steam road engines hauling long trains of wagons. All of which helped to put English Ray out of business rather soon. Dan Jackling, with the backing of Hayden, Stone and a group of capitalist speculators known as the Colorado Springs crowd, bought the decrepit property, organized Ray Consolidated Copper Company, refurbishing everything, and went into production. The Guggenheims were glad to sign a contract to do all the smelting.

A revolution and civil wars in Mexico had scared numerous American capitalists, but not the Guggenheims. When things there looked their worst, Dan invested almost three million dollars of

American Smelting money to get some real bargains of mines. (He also advanced cash to the right man, the winner, General Obregón, who came to power in 1920. The new strong man of Mexico made things tough for American oil companies having Mexican investments, but American Smelting & Refining ran on untroubled.)

The next move of the Guggenheims was into Chile, where Albert C. Burrage, a Boston engineer who got around almost everywhere, had come across what he believed was the largest body of low-grade copper ore in the world. He bought up all claims, then went to Dan Guggenheim, whose top field man, Pope Yeatman, was sent down to look it over. Yeatman reported it was all Burrage had said, and more—300,000,000 tons of three per cent copper ore, ready for scooping with steam shovels. The Chile Exploration Company was organized. Nothing the Guggenheims ever did was so perfectly timed, on two counts: Chile Exploration was able to buy cheaply the machinery that U. S. army engineers were beginning to discard on the nearly completed Panama Canal. And the copper that Chile Exploration was to mine would be ready for the demands of a world at war.

The outbreak of war in the summer of 1914 found the Guggenheim brothers and associates ready. With great mines in Alaska, Idaho, Nevada, Utah, Arizona, New Mexico, and Colorado in full swing, to say nothing of the Mexican properties and the immense Chile operation just getting under way, they also had the smelters and the refineries to handle the output. The biggest producers of copper were prepared for the lustiest market man had ever known. There was only one danger. This was in their American Smelting & Refining Company, which many small mine owners and all independent smelting firms resolutely referred to as the smelters' trust.

When all metal markets hit a low point in 1913, the independents began to mutter about the smelters' trust. The trust was an incorporated cheat. It was a penalty on all small operators. Congress was asked to dissolve it just as it was then dissolving the Standard Oil trust. The clamor rose, and finally agents of the Department of Justice were circulating in Colorado. The investigation was warming up when the metals market, including copper, went zooming, and it was permitted to lapse "in the face of this new danger"—meaning war and not the fact that copper had leaped from twelve cents to twenty-five cents a pound. The danger of monopoly, it seemed, was as nothing compared to the danger of not producing copper at the new price. The smelters' trust was not harassed.

The halfhearted attempt to break the smelters' trust may have given Dan Guggenheim an idea: Why not concentrate all of the Guggenheim coppers into one great outfit that would be the U. S. Steel of the yellow metal? Or, it may be that Dan's next step was prompted in part by J. P. Morgan & Company. That house had a heavy stake in Guggenheim's Alaska Kennecott properties. These were rich enough, but Mr. Perkins of the Morgan firm had come to believe the railroad to tap Kennecott had been too expensive; that the mines would not be able to pay for it. The Morgans were so much worried that J. P. Morgan (the younger) himself went to Washington and tried to unload the Copper River Railroad on the government. He failed.

"It became urgent," wrote Harvey O'Connor, "to pass on Kennecott's liability, and what better time than now, when the great investing public was greedy for copper stocks?"

The answer was obvious. Dan, Sol, and Murry Guggenheim acted with alacrity. After conferences with Morgan partners, it was decided to put all the coppers into one big bag called the Kennecott Copper Corporation that would sweat stock and bond certificates until kingdom come, thus doubling the income from mines and at the same time permitting the public to share the expense of the costly Copper River Railroad in Alaska.

Thus in May 1916, while war raged all over Europe and even the United States was talking preparedness, the Kennecott Copper Corporation was formed. Into it went Guggenheim Exploration, along with the many mines. (American Smelting & Refining was not included.) Out of it came a flood of three million shares of no par value which, due to some rather notable churning in the Wall Street machine, quickly rose to fifty dollars. What with bonds, the new Kennecott appeared to have a market value of close to two hundred million dollars.

And how the money rolled in! By war's end, as Mr. O'Connor took the trouble to figure out, "the Guggenheim coppers had paid more than $200,000,000 in dividends and had accumulated lordly surpluses."

Yet, twilight had set in for the Guggenheim brothers. There was no crash, no real disaster. There were even a few more flashes of characteristic Guggenheim enterprise, including heavy investment in Chilean nitrates. There were other flashes when disgruntled stockholders forced American Smelting to seat eighteen "outsiders" to its board of directors; and when Will Guggenheim sued his brothers over dividends from Chile Copper. But twilight had come.

Isaac died in 1922, leaving an estate of ten million dollars after taxes. Daniel died eight years later. The value of his estate was not recorded. Bequests of two million dollars each went to his three children. There were other individual bequests, and more millions went to Guggenheim foundations. Murry, least known of the brothers, died in 1939. He had set up trust funds for his two children but had retained the power of revoking them, possibly in an earnest try to escape federal gift taxes. The government insisted, however, and Murry paid the largest gift tax ever made by an individual. It was for $3,449,000. Both William and Simon died in 1941. It will be recalled that William had long been disassociated with the family enterprises.

It was left to Simon's imagination and money to provide the means by which the family name may endure. This is the John Simon Guggenheim Memorial Foundation, of which more in its place.

Most elegant of the brothers, and the last to die, was Solomon. He educated his daughters in England, where one of them married into the titled gentry. He himself lived to shoot quail and to become a noted patron of non-objective art. He died in 1949, aged eighty-eight.

Two of Meyer Guggenheim's grandsons, Harry F. and Edmond A., have continued their interests in the world of their forebears. In 1951, Harry announced formation of a new Guggenheim brothers partnership, of which he is the head, to "carry on certain of the family's interests" in mining and metallurgical enterprises, and to "engage in research." Harry was Ambassador to Cuba under Hoover, and has justly received many honors for his long efforts in promoting aviation. With his wife he publishes *Newsday,* a Long Island daily. Edmond described himself in 1952 as a business executive with directorships in Kennecott Copper and Guggenheim Nitrate Corporation.

The Guggenheim era of business and finance obviously came to an end with the death of Daniel in 1930. At that time, financial papers generally estimated the wealth of Daniel, Murry, and Simon at $100,000,000, and Dan was listed (1930) as "one of the sixty-four Rulers of America" by James W. Gerard. Four other copperplated moguls appeared on the same list. They were John D. Ryan of Anaconda, Daniel C. Jackling of Utah, Charles Hayden of Hayden, Stone, and William Loeb, Jr., counselor to the Guggenheims in the matters of public relations and politics.

It was significant that of Gerard's sixty-four Rulers, the wealth of the five metal fortunes stemmed chiefly from copper. Fifty years previously, the fortunes of metal millionaires came from gold and silver. In 1930, only one metal fortune was based on gold, even though Americans generally were of the belief that William Randolph Hearst had made his pile from newspapers.

Chapter 3 THE LAST MOGUL

IN the mind of the American public William Randolph Hearst did not appear as one of the lords of capital. He was one of the lords of the press. This was natural enough. For more than half a century he was active as a publisher. For almost as long the Hearst papers had been either a great influence for democracy or a disgrace to the fourth estate. Few of his countrymen thought of Hearst in relation to money. He was never attacked because of his wealth.

Yet when at last he died in 1951, he left an estate estimated at almost four hundred million dollars. Many a man described as a bloated capitalist left much less than Mr. Hearst; and spent much less money during his lifetime. There were silver kings, copper kings, coal barons, railroad princes, and Wall Street tycoons whose fortunes compared to Hearst's were petty change. Most of these lords of creation have been treated as a class or group in books dealing with the great American fortunes. Hearst is not among their number. He remained outside the literary field having to do with masters of capital.

A man who leaves close to four hundred million dollars is a mogul of capital if he is anything. Hearst was that, and more. He was the last to die of his generation of nineteenth-century sluggers who abided by no rules but fashioned their own ethics as they progressed from one killing to another and trampled what reformers said were the grapes of wrath. Hearst merely outlived his era. He belongs in the select company of Commodore Vanderbilt, of Rockefeller, Carnegie, Gould, and Harriman. And of Jim Fisk.

If William Randolph Hearst had never owned a newspaper, he probably would have been grouped with the multimillionaires of mining, for his vast newspaper empire was founded on quartz gold and it was financed periodically for more than half a century by the same substance, most of which was dug from glittering Homestake, the greatest and richest gold mine in North America—which includes Alaska and the Yukon.

Even without Homestake, the young Hearst could have begun his career as a Croesus of mining, for unlike most of our millionaires, his life was not at all in the canon of Horatio Alger, Jr. By his own admission, Hearst spent between ten and twelve million dollars of his family's fortune before he had established himself as a publisher. This money came from Homestake *and* from his father's one-third interest in well-named Anaconda, Homestake's opposite number in the field of copper. Young Hearst could also have drawn on the family's mines in Chile, Peru, and Mexico, in the latter of which was the Hearst San Luis property, good for a monthly profit of $25,000.

Or, Willie Hearst could have set up as a land shark and real estate operator. In 1891, his late father's estate included a one-third interest in the 250,000-acre Victoria cattle ranch in New Mexico. It included 25,000 acres near Phoenix, Arizona; and a little tract of 4,500 acres just south of San Francisco. In Mexico, the Hearst family owned 1,000 square miles of fine land in the states of Vera Cruz, Campeche, and Yucatán; and in the state of Chihuahua was Hearst's Babicora ranch of 900,000 acres, which the elder Hearst had bought during an Indian scare. Lastly, the holdings of the family included some two hundred thousand acres between the California coast and the Santa Lucia Mountains. From this particular property William Randolph Hearst acquired late in life and in the manner of barons of old his title of the Lord of San Simeon.

There is no thought of intimating that Hearst owed his huge fortune and his place in the newspaper world solely to the fact that he was born into a wealthy and indulgent family. Without it, he surely would have worked and won, like the Alger heroes, and gone upward and onward in any business he might have chosen. He had the stuff in him. But his family's fortune was a handy thing. More than once when the young publisher's newspapers seemed about to crumble under the strain of his incredible spending, the sure and abiding golden stream from Homestake saved them. The same stream saved them again when the publisher was old and failing. Seventy-five years after Father George Hearst bought Homestake in 1877, says John Tebbel, it "was still faithfully helping support [his] son in his extreme old age."

George Hearst was a big rugged fellow whose appearance, manners, and success must have gone into the popular conception of the western American miner and mine magnate. Put an indigo-blue shirt on him, place a pan in his hand, stand him in the shallows of California's American River, and you had the model for Portrait of a Forty-niner. Or, put a plug hat on his shaggy head, drape a frock coat on his wide shoulders, comb his long whiskers a bit, string a nugget-laden watch chain across his vest—there you had the veritable western mining man heading for the United States Senate.

He was born in Missouri in 1820. Thirty years later he crossed the Plains to try placer mining at Hangtown and Jackass Gulch, then in the northern diggings around Grass Valley and Nevada City. His luck was only about average, which is to say he did little more than to "make wages." Then, in 1859, he joined the thin trek of prospectors to the Washoe Diggings in what is now Nevada, and for $450 got a half interest in Alvah Gould's gold mine, a hole so lean in gold that Gould figured he had put over a fast deal and went running through the camp yelling, "I've got away with the Californians!" and promptly got most damnably drunk in celebration of his business acumen.

What the California suckers had bought was of course the second-richest silver property on the Comstock Lode, the Gould and Curry. On the same trip, George Hearst also bought for a few hundred dollars a one-sixth interest in the Ophir, the richest of all Comstock mines.

George Hearst was a miner as well as a mining man. He and his partners worked like madmen during that summer of 1859, and just before snow-fly they loaded a long packtrain of mules with forty-five tons of the blue-black ore, and so over the mountains to San Francisco. The ore proved to be worth $2,200 a ton. News of it helped to set off a new rush in 1860. Thousands left the Mother Lode and piled into Nevada. The Comstock Lode went into high gear. Silver was to rule for the next three decades.

George Hearst suddenly found himself almost a millionaire. He went back to Missouri, courted and married Phoebe Apperson, a schoolteacher, went on a wedding trip to New York City, and sailed for San Francisco. There in a house on Nob Hill twins were born on April 29, 1863. One of these was William Randolph. The other infant presumably died soon after birth.

In that same year the Ophir mine alone paid out almost four million dollars in silver. The Gould and Curry was yielding nigh as much. On the advice of a mine foreman named Marcus Daly, Hearst and James Ben Ali Haggin bought the Ontario mine in Utah. Almost at once it began paying dividends of nearly a million dollars a year, and continued so for many years. Next came the Homestake in South Dakota, where Hearst and partners built a town named Lead (pronounced *Leed*) to house the miners. Then, again on Marcus Daly's advice, came the Anaconda property, followed by the ventures in Mexico, Chile, and Peru already mentioned.

George Hearst's acquisitions of land during this and later periods have been cited. His method of getting the thousand square miles in Vera Cruz, Campeche, and Yucatán was interesting. Learning that Mexico did not have a public surveyor, Hearst made a deal with the government by which in return for doing a job of surveying himself, he was given free title to the lands he selected.

He was obliged to put out a little actual cash to get the nine-hundred-thousand acre Babicora tract, though not much. This ranch lay in Chihuahua, a region just then terrorized by the famous Apache, Geronimo. The district had been raided again and again. But in 1887, having received secret information of Geronimo's capture, Hearst hastened to buy the big ranch from its absentee owners before they learned of the event. He got it for about forty cents an acre.

It was quite natural that with his great wealth, George Hearst should aspire to the "millionaires' club," as the United States Senate was often known. The first step in those days was a newspaper. Mr. Hearst bought the San Francisco *Examiner*. The next step was to be governor. The *Examiner* worked hard but its owner failed of nomination. Well, then, the Senate direct. Leland Stanford defeated him in 1885; but the Hearst luck still held, and a year later he was appointed to fill out the term of the other U. S. senator who had died in office. And two years later, Hearst made it again, this time by election.

In the Senate he said or did nothing that is remembered, but his personality made him well known and well liked. He impressed his colleagues, said a biographer, as an unusual man whose life had been a romance in western expansion. He loved whiskey, cards, chewing tobacco, and fast horses. He held that literature, art, and education were all very well, but were toys for the ladies. Coupled with an openhanded generosity, these attributes made George Hearst the American ideal of the western mining magnate.

Phoebe Hearst, however, insisted that her son should have the best education available. Willie was sent to St. Paul's preparatory school at Concord, New Hampshire. Neither Willie nor St. Paul liked the arrangement, and he left, to study at home under tutors. Next came Harvard, which the youth liked no better, though he enjoyed being business manager of the college *Lampoon*. He was asked to leave Harvard after he had sent to each of several members of the august faculty what could be described as a useful domestic utensil, handsomely illuminated with the portrait and name of the recipient. It is worth knowing that at this time the Harvard faculty included William James, Josiah Royce, Barrett Wendell, and Charles Eliot Norton.

Released from the mellow beauty of Harvard Yard, young Willie Hearst went to New York. He already knew what he wanted, and contrary to his father's wishes, he did not want to be a mining man, or a rancher. He wanted a newspaper; especially, because his father owned it, he wanted the San Francisco *Examiner*. He had said as much long before, and his father, to whom newspapers were nothing more than means to an end, had told him no, he should not be a newspaperman.

Young Hearst came to New York from Cambridge with one idea —to learn more about the methods of Joseph Pulitzer, whose *World* Hearst and many others believed to be the greatest newspaper in America. Or, anyway the most sensational. He did not succeed in meeting Pulitzer, but he did just as well; he made the acquaintance of Samuel Selwyn Chamberlain, who had worked on the *World*. Chamberlain had also been James Gordon Bennett's secretary. He had founded *Le Matin* in Paris. He had been editor of the Paris edition of the New York *Herald*. Chamberlain was exactly the man to explain what was needed to make a newspaper successful.

Twelve years older than Hearst, Chamberlain was a brilliant man with the almost standard vice of his kind, which was liquor. He found the young émigré from Harvard good company, as well as a good setter-upper, and the two men discussed the scintillating techniques that had brought the New York *World* from 15,000 to 250,000 circulation within a space of three years. These techniques seemed to comprise a constant appeal to the fundamental emotions of sex, love, hate, and gain, laced with carefully regulated doses of pity running with tears.

The *World's* fine touch included a continuous series of crusades against something, anything. It included a superior vividness in crime stories, with copious use of diagrams showing not only where the body was found, but also the window through which the murderer came, the bed in which the victim was sleeping, and the door through which the criminal escaped. The technique also applied to headlines. The *World* was using bigger and blacker type than any other paper. And its headlines contained verbs. No longer was a *World* headline writer content with "A Vicious Murder"; it shocked the eye and mind with "Fiend Wields Ax in Carnival of Blood."

Chamberlain showed Hearst how Pulitzer had gone beyond James Gordon Bennett in the business of sensational presentation. Hearst decided that *his* newspaper should go beyond Pulitzer. His newspaper was almost ready for him, for he had been working hard on the old man. In March 1887, Willie Hearst was recalled to California and George Hearst told him to go ahead, if he must, and take charge of the San Francisco *Examiner*.

Willie Hearst was twenty-four. He put Sam Chamberlain in as editor. He lopped off the paper's deadwood of retainers. To the staff he added a few of the young men of the Harvard *Lampoon* who had shown unusual ability on the college magazine. He hired Ambrose Bierce, already the arbiter of west-coast letters, to write a caustic column. Bierce left a graphic picture of the young publisher who appeared at his door as a tall and innocent-looking adolescent and muttered bashfully something about the *Examiner*. "You come from Mr. Hearst?" Bierce inquired.

Then, said Bierce, "That unearthly child lifted its blue eyes and cooed, 'I am Mr. Hearst,' in a voice like the fragrance of violets made audible."

The "unearthly child" wrote to his father regarding the *Examiner* that he had all his pipes laid. All that remained was to turn on the gas. He wasn't bragging. The gas went into the pipes and a crazy era began. The *Examiner* office, said George P. West, was a madhouse inhabited by talented and erratic young men led by a mad boss. Hearst only seemed mad. He was really coldly rational, and the ensuing antics of his paper were part of his careful plan to outdo in San Francisco what Pulitzer was doing in New York.

During this period young Hearst virtually lived at the *Examiner*. He never got to bed before two in the morning. He woke at seven and could not regain sleep until he had seen the *Examiner* to compare it with the *Chronicle*. "If we are the best," he said, "I can turn over and go to sleep with quiet satisfaction."

Crusades were begun. They attacked prize fighting, liquor, and prostitution, the *Examiner* meanwhile running columns of classified ads for ladies who described themselves as "masseuses." The two train robbers, Evans and Sontag, were built into epic size as men of refractory genius and virtually cheered for devoting their talents to the sticking up of Southern Pacific trains. Hearst was not a native son for nothing. He knew that a newspaper with the foolhardy courage to attack the SP was sure to be popular.

Sentimentality was not overlooked, and one of the *Examiner* staff, Eddie Morphy, told to fill a Sunday page with sobs, reached into the upper air of his imagination to invent the orphaned McGinty Boys, who brought half of San Francisco to tears and gold pieces rolling into the *Examiner* Fund for the McGintys, the poor lads. The McGintys grew overnight into a sensation, and Morphy was obliged to go forth and scour up a couple of ragged waifs who would look right for McGinty photographs. Meanwhile, Morphy and his comrades made heavy inroads on the McGinty Fund for refreshments to revive their flagging imaginations.

When a train was snowbound in the Sierras and out of food, Hearst chartered a special engine, snowplow, and car to rescue the passengers, resulting in a rousing story of the heroics of the *Examiner* and its men. When it appeared that Golden Gate Park did not have a specimen of the nearly extinct California grizzly bear, the *Examiner* equipped and sent out an expedition to bring one back alive. He was installed in the park while bands played and named "Monarch, the *Examiner's* Grizzly." The incident turned out so happily that a bear was adopted as the *Examiner's* trademark.

In these and all other Hearst enterprises, as biographers Bates and Carlson remark, there was the same curious mixture of reality and unreality, fact and fakery, social service and personal profit. The causes were always good, the means always sensational, and the ends always twofold, one of which was "great improvement in circulation of the *Examiner*."

In 1895 Hearst felt he was ready for New York. The *Examiner's* circulation had more than quadrupled in eight years. Whether or not it was making money is not clear. The great sums its publisher had spent on what looked like causes but were really promotion stunts may well have exceeded the paper's income. If so, there was more money where the other had come from. Senator Hearst had died in 1891. Four years later the Widow Hearst was happy to turn over to her son seven and a half million dollars from her Anaconda interests alone. No publisher, in New York or elsewhere, had started business with such financial foundation.

And Hearst used his copperplated money to some effect. He bought the weak and listless *Morning Journal* for $180,000 from John R. McLean, the Cincinnati publisher who had attempted the Manhattan field and failed. During the first two months Hearst put in another $350,000 remodeling the paper to look and read much like Pulitzer's *World*. The *Journal's* price was also cut in half, or one cent, while the *World* remained at two cents. The ambition of the refurbished *Journal* was apparent: it was going to give its readers more and bigger sensations than the *World* and at half its price. With Hearst running the show, it was a sound proposition.

Although Hearst brought several of his best *Examiner* men to New York, he also wanted the best of the *World's* talent, and began to raid the Pulitzer staff, starting with Morrill Goddard, the Sunday *World's* boss whose specialities were "crime and underwear." Goddard's bloodcurdling horrors, complete with diagrams and sketches of the lace-edged negligee in which he invariably dressed all his female victims, moved over to the *Journal*. So did Outcault, who drew the famous Yellow Kid invented by Goddard. Pulitzer tried to remedy the loss by engaging George B. Luks, later an outstanding painter, to draw more Yellow Kids for the *World*. Both papers had them simultaneously, and from them came the term "yellow journalism."

Pulitzer put Arthur Brisbane in charge of the *World's* features. He was Goddard's equal, and New York was treated to a gorgeous war in which agog was the battle cry and popping eyes the goal. On one and the same Sunday, readers of the two papers were told "why young girls kill themselves" and notified of the "strange things women do for love." These sensations were sanctified, in a way, by the use of Bible texts wherever possible, and good substantial doses of what the editors of the *World* and the *Journal* said was science, including the "jumping Laelaps of 50,000 years ago" and the alleged mysteries of Cleopatra's tomb.

The *World's* circulation went up to 600,000, and still had a comfortable lead, though the gap was fast narrowing. Pouring in another two million dollars from the tireless Homestake out in South Dakota, Hearst established the *Evening Journal* to compete with the *Evening World,* and bought a special color press that could turn out sixteen pages of comics or of colored supplements about the leaping Laelaps and the harems of East Indian potentates. The Sunday *Journal* now rocked the eye with what it liked to call "iridescent, polychromous effulgence." It was soon followed with an addition which became the *American Weekly,* the typical story of which, said one of its editors, was one that could support its classic headline: Nailed Her Father's Head to the Wall.

Two years after the Pulitzer-Hearst war started, Brisbane came over to Hearst, not only because Hearst agreed to pay him two hundred dollars a week plus one dollar for every thousand readers he should add to circulation; but also, said Brisbane, because Pulitzer had refused to let him run "headlines a foot deep." Two years later Brisbane's salary went to $50,000, and eventually topped $250,000.

Hearst was ready to spend more than half a million dollars in coverage of the brief Spanish-American War, which many historians think might never have taken place without the inflammations set going by the *Journal's* enterprising crew of agents provocateurs. Although Joe Pulitzer hated war, his *World* got into the excitement and fought Hearst with special correspondents and special dispatch boats. The *World* and the *Journal* combined in vilification of General William Rufus Shafter, a brave and competent soldier who was not to be hurried by headlines into needless slaughter of his soldiers.

With the war, the *Journal* began to pay. On its staff was a group of highly talented men and women who were getting the fattest salaries in the trade. To put the paper into this flourishing condition, Hearst had dipped into the Hearst mining properties for more than seven million dollars. He dipped again and started to buy and to found newspapers. In 1900 it was the Chicago *American.* Four years later "at request of leading trade unionists in Los Angeles who wanted a paper friendly to labor," he set up an *Examiner* in that city. In 1904 he appeared in Boston with his *American.* After a lull, he bought the *Georgian* at Atlanta. Shooting the decrepit paper full of comic strips, leaping Laelaps, and big headlines, says Herbert Asbury, he soon had Atlanta by the tail and was swinging her high, wide, and handsome.

ANDREW MELLON

DANIEL GUGGENHEIM

HETTY GREEN

During World War I Hearst bought the *Advertiser* of Boston, then got the Chicago *Herald*. In 1919 he added to his chain the Wisconsin *News* of Milwaukee and the *Times* of Washington, D.C. Two years later he purchased the weak Detroit *Times* and made it into the likeness of his other papers. What made the likeness of his papers, according to the Hearst editorial writer, Arthur McEwen, was the "gee-whiz" treatment. The gee whiz, said he, was a reader's emotion when he saw the front page of a Hearst paper, any Hearst paper. Page two fetched a "Holy Moses!" Page three brought a climactic "God Almighty!" The formula worked very well with one generation after another of Hearst readers.

The year of Hearst's greatest acquisition was 1922, when he added the Syracuse *Evening Telegram,* the Rochester *Evening Journal,* the Washington *Herald,* the Seattle *Post-Intelligencer,* the San Francisco *Call,* the Oakland *Post-Enquirer,* and the Los Angeles *Herald*. A year more and he got two dailies in Baltimore, the *American* and the *News*. In 1924 he bought the *Times-Union* of Albany and "started his first tabloid, the New York *Mirror."*

In the decade after 1924, the Hearst empire grew with the Milwaukee *Sentinel;* the *Sun-Telegraph* and the *Post-Gazette* of Pittsburgh; the Omaha *Bee-News;* the San Francisco *Bulletin,* which was merged with the *Call;* and the Los Angeles *Express*.

As early as 1903 Hearst had bought *Motor* magazine, and followed it with *World Today,* which became *Hearst's International* and was later merged with *Cosmopolitan*. Then came *Harper's Bazaar, Good Housekeeping, Pictorial Review, Town and Country, House Beautiful,* and several trade magazines.

The Hearst newspapers were served by the Hearst-founded International News Service (1906) and several Hearst-owned syndicates, of which King Features (1914) became the colossus. King Features, said *Fortune* in a survey of the Hearst properties in 1935, served more than two thousand newspapers in the United States, and other papers in ninety countries, where "In thirty-two languages . . . Jiggs and Popeye are homely U. S. Ambassadors."

How was Homestake standing up during the years of Hearst's continuous if erratic expansion? It was standing up well. By 1912 more than a hundred million dollars had come up from its deep and long corridors, and the bonanza was far from played out. It went on to pay $5.86 a share in 1928, $8.00 in 1930, $10.60 in 1932, and $30 in 1934. These rich dividends were revealed in the latter year, when a suit by an investment trust, which owned a mere one hundred shares of Homestake, drew back the veil of secrecy that had always enveloped Hearst-controlled enterprises. The plaintiffs claimed that Homestake officially valued its property and equipment at less than five million dollars when in reality the figure should have been at least eighty-six million. A year later, Homestake dividends jumped from thirty to forty-four dollars a share, and a financial magazine said that for ten years past Homestake dividends had exceeded Homestake earnings.

At this period, too, other properties in which Hearst was a large owner were flourishing. The American Metals Company, for instance, had assets of more than seventy-seven million dollars and presumably paid dividends. A director of this company was Edward H. Clark, financial manager for W. R. Hearst, a position he held for decades. Mr. Clark was also president of the Cerro de Pasco Copper Company, which, said *Moody's Manual,* was "one of the oldest and richest in the world," with assets of forty million dollars.

Hearst's principality of land was not shrinking. His agricultural and timber holdings approximated almost two million acres. On his Babicora ranch, which he visited infrequently, "Mr. Hearst must travel seventy-three miles to reach his own house, and beyond it he can still travel sixty miles without leaving his own land." His hardwood forests in Vera Cruz grew on 260,000 acres. Near the forests was his Campeche ranch of 350,000 acres. From Campeche came about five per cent of all the chicle imported into the United States, a fact of interest to Hearst critics who liked to remark that the Hearst newspapers were favorites of gumchewers. There were 70,000 acres of oil lands, too, in the Hearst Mexican properties. As time passed, it became increasingly apparent that old George Hearst had accumulated and bequeathed to his widow and son a more solidly grounded estate than many better known fortunes.

Son William did not add to the fortune by his excursion into the movies. This experience, it has been variously estimated, cost him between two and seven million dollars' dead loss. Yet from the unreal world of the films he got the idea of how a moneyed lord ought to live and, as we shall see a bit later, he translated the idea into the movie-like grandeurs of San Simeon.

His motion picture experience began with the making of newsreels in 1913 in conjunction with Pathe. With Pathe, too, Hearst won his sole claim to movie immortality with the concocting of

The Perils of Pauline, the first of the cliffhangers. It amounted to being a sort of animated Hearst Sunday supplement and it was an enormous sensation to people able to read subtitles. (Pathe-Hearst tried to capitalize on *Pauline* with *The Exploits of Elaine* and *The Mysteries of Myra,* neither of which seems to be remembered.)

Mrs. W. R. Hearst took a great interest in the new art form. She had been Millicent Willson, of the dancing Willson sisters when Hearst met and married her in 1903. She retained her liking for things of the theater, and among her philanthropies was the helping of young women get a start on the stage. In 1918 one of these deserving females was Marion Davies, then appearing in the Ziegfeld Follies. Mrs. Hearst brought her home and introduced her to her husband, who was planning to produce several film epics.

Miss Davies, born either in 1897 or in 1900, had been christened Cecilia Douras. From the chorus line at Ziegfeld's Mr. Hearst moved her directly to the starring role of a couple of Hearst-produced films. Simultaneously she was "discovered" by the Hearst chain of papers from Boston to the west coast. Hearst soon moved his picture outfit to Hollywood, and there Miss Davies starred in other films. By then it was no secret that a triangle had formed, and for the next thirty years it was the most talked-about liaison in the United States. How many thousands of movie-struck girls dreamed of emulating Miss Davies is not to be known. But the number must have been staggering. Though it was far from typical, the Hearst-Davies romance was the Hollywood idyl without compare.

Biographer Tebbel handled the affair with considerable grace and with as much dignity as possible. He remarks that the fiction of the Hearst marriage was maintained, and Mrs. Hearst assumed her position whenever it was advisable on occasions of state. The Hearst sons were able to spend some time every year with both parents. Mrs. Hearst continued to make her home in New York, while Hearst had already started building the old San Simeon ranch of his father into a place that defied belief in the people who saw it. Here he was the Lord of San Simeon, a title he enjoyed as much as he did that of Imperial Hearst, used by one of his less favored biographers, Ferdinand Lundberg.

Hearst the motion picture producer soon petered out, though not before his ocean-going yacht was the scene of the death of a well-known movie director, Thomas H. Ince, whose passing was officially ascribed to "heart disease, superinduced by an attack of indigestion." Due possibly to the fact that the yachting party included a crowd of popular movie stars, both male and female, the death of Ince created more public curiosity than usually accompanies heart failure.

When Hearst ceased actual participation in the making of movies, Miss Davies retired, if that is the word, to San Simeon and her Santa Monica house, which was "slightly larger than the historic Vanderbilt residence on Fifth Avenue." He had failed as a movie magnate, as the phrase had it. He had failed, too, as a politician. New York City's Tammany Hall machine had been glad to send him to Congress, where he seldom responded to roll call. Then, turning against his Tammany pals, Hearst cooked up the Municipal Ownership League and ran for mayor. He was defeated in a close contest. He next turned his cold blue eyes on the governor's chair, but he was no match for Charles E. Hughes. Again he ran for mayor, being terribly beaten by William J. Gaynor.

Meanwhile, Hearst's name was put forth in a Democratic National Convention considering candidates for the presidency. He was not nominated. Well, perhaps he could be a president maker. In 1908 he spent $300,000 promoting an Independent Party candidate named Hisgen. William H. Taft was elected. The Hearst candidate ran fifth in a field of five.

There were smaller defeats, too. In 1913 he locked horns with the heirs of old Commodore Vanderbilt by suing the New York Central Railroad to enjoin it from switching freight cars at night on the West Side of Manhattan, where Hearst lived on Riverside Drive. He testified that even though he had put double windows on the Clarendon, his slumbers were broken by the noise. He won, only to have the decision reversed by a higher court.

Then, out in San Francisco, where his *Examiner* seemed to him to be slipping in journalistic fervor, Hearst ordered one of the old-time crusades that had been so successful as circulation getters in the past. He would clean up the notorious Barbary Coast. To be a hero of the campaign (along with the *Examiner,* of course) he chose the Rev. Paul Smith, whose church was located close to the red-light district that was to be scourged.

But Fremont Older, the energetic editor of the *Bulletin,* took a hand, and also the headlines. On the evening when the Rev. Mr. Smith was to open the crusade from his pulpit, into his church trouped hundreds of prostitutes, brought there by *Bulletin* reporters and primed with suggestions for embarrassing questions, with which they bombarded poor Mr. Smith. He could not answer the racy queries, and was soon in such complete confusion that the only mass meeting of San Francisco harlots of record had to be called off, and it was not mentioned in the *Examiner,* though the *Bulletin* made much of it. The *Examiner's* crusade died before it got under way.

The next Hearstian crusade was on a national scale. The time was 1914. War broke out in Europe. The Hearst papers had had no hand in starting *this* war, and Mr. Hearst would have none of it. He turned pacifist. That is, so far as the European war was concerned; but he warned his readers that Japan planned to invade the United States.

As 1915 came in, Hearst's opposition to the war in Europe became bolder. His attack was chiefly on England, a country he had never liked. His papers stressed British interference with American commerce on the seas. They also supported a propaganda outfit called the American Truth Society, which was composed about equally of English-hating Irish Americans and German Americans. The Hearst reporting of the fighting, moreover, was obviously loaded to favor Germany. Little wonder. The (Hearst) INS correspondent at the front, William B. Hale, was a former employee of the German Embassy in Washington.

In 1916, England and France denied further use of the mails and cables to INS. Canada barred all Hearst papers from the Dominion. Then, in April 1917, when the United States declared war, the Hearst papers from coast to coast gave a mighty heave and broke out with their front pages carrying brave American flags in color. In spite of which, later that year anti-Hearst demonstrations took place in many cities. Hearst was denounced as pro-German. The New York *Tribune* cartoonist showed him in a German army uniform holding a copy of the New York *American* with defeatist headlines. Hearst was burned in effigy in several cities, including four towns in his native California.

So far as Boston was concerned, however, the Hearst *American* was one hundred per cent patriotic—and often one hundred per cent inaccurate. Here is what happened, according to one who was there: For Wednesday, October 24, 1917, the troops at Camp Devens, Massachusetts, planned a monster field day for the whole division. Secretary of War Newton Baker was to review the soldiers.

There were also to be regimental, brigade, and divisional field and track meets. Several football games were scheduled between companies and batteries. For a week or more, all efforts at Devens were directed to making the huge camp presentable for the thousands of wives, relatives, and friends of the soldiers who were expected.

Dawn on Wednesday was cloudy. By eight o'clock rain was falling. It increased to what some said was a downpour and others called a cloudburst. In any case, there was no review, there were no sports, and almost no visitors. Secretary of War Baker did not come. The whole affair was called off long before noon.

Late in the afternoon from Boston came great bundles of the Boston *American,* favorite newspaper of the cantonment. Its front page was devoted wholly to an alleged account of the 76th Division's monster field day and review. There were many photographs, all of which merely showed barracks, and troops marching, and had obviously been taken days or even weeks before. The text of the *American's* newsbeat was pretty vague. You could just imagine some poor guy sitting there at his typewriter, composing a scene of forty, perhaps fifty thousand soldiers and visitors; telling of the march-by, the sports, the games, and all else, yet not once citing a specific fact, and not once mentioning a name, save for that of Secretary Baker, who was declared, though not within quotes, to be mighty pleased at the division's showing.

This monstrous piece of fakery had of course been cooked up during the previous night. "Whether its effect on other soldiers was as lasting as it was on myself," remarks the man who was there, "I don't know. So far as I was concerned, it left me with a permanent skepticism of anything that has since appeared in a Hearst paper. I'm certain that such blanket skepticism is not warranted, yet the shock of reading a long account of something I knew never happened proved too much to overcome."

There were to be a few more Hearstian sensations, including a bitter and unsuccessful attempt to prevent Al Smith's nomination for the presidency; the printing of Mexican "documents" which turned out to be forgeries and which almost involved the United States in war; Hearst's summary expulsion from France as an enemy of that country; his pleasure at the rise of Hitler; his attacks on Communists and "communists"; and his later attacks on, after first supporting, Franklin D. Roosevelt.

Less known was Hearst's vast accumulations of new properties. Back in the nineties he began buying around New York's Columbus Circle, with the idea of making a magnificent Hearst Plaza; and for another thirty years added properties for this project. He bought three Manhattan hotels, the Ritz Tower, Warwick, and Lombardy. He bought the Ziegfeld Theatre and the Clarendon apartments. He was quick to get into the radio field and established broadcasting stations in New York, Baltimore, Pittsburgh, and four more in California.

At the same time, Hearst was buying thirty-five million dollars' worth of art and antiques. These included pretty nearly everything from whole castles and monasteries to paintings and other small works of art.

"Money," said one who knew him well, "meant absolutely nothing to Hearst except that he could spend it for what he wanted."

The whole wild and indiscriminate accumulation at last began to tell on the man's finances, and in 1925 the first Hearst bond flotation was made, a fifteen-million-dollar loan being secured. The crash of 1929 found him "extended," to use the bankers' favored term for such things; and in 1930 he staged another flotation, this time with a gigantic holding company along Insull lines called Hearst Consolidated Publications, a Delaware corporation. For the next seven years the stockholders of this corporation were in clover; they received an average of seven per cent dividends at a time when any dividend from any source was something of a rarity.

Yet, the gigantic mass of scattered properties was shaking. In another effort to bolster credit and to escape income taxes, a new corporation was formed. It was called American Newspapers. Into it went Hearst Consolidated and no less than eighty-nine more Hearst concerns. Over it went a cloak or, as some worried stockholders began to think, a shroud. Hearst biographer Lundberg called American Newspapers, Inc., "a secret chamber." It was not a public corporation. It published no reports. Yet it controlled everything else.

No matter these various efforts, or dodges, the structure was still tottering. Something other than new incorporation papers was needed. Hearst at last sliced off 165,000 acres from his San Simeon ranch and sold them to the government for two million dollars. He still had 75,000 acres left.

Hearst's good friend, Miss Davies, now stepped forward—of her volition, says Tebbel—to lend the publisher one million dollars.

If it disappeared never to return, well, what of it, what did it matter? "I didn't have anything when I first met him," she told a friend, "—what's the difference?"

Even more heroic measures were called for. The New York *American* was folded up and put away, though the official announcement termed it a "merger" with the *Journal*. The Rochester *Journal* went next, followed by lease to Cissy Patterson of the Washington *Times* and Washington *Herald*. The Omaha *Bee* was sold. Then came another "merger": Hearst's Universal Service disappeared into International News.

Worse was coming. In 1937 it was announced that Hearst had turned over all of his finances to Clarence Shearn, one of his top lawyers for more than three decades. Hearst himself became an employee of his own pyramid of corporations. His salary was cut from $500,000 to $100,000 a year. Mr. Shearn went bravely ahead to straighten out what must have been as complicated a mess as any American capitalist ever got into. He sold the Ritz Tower; and soon uncounted tons of Hearst antiques and objects of art went on sale, many of them over the counter in New York department stores. There were suits by disgruntled stockholders, one of which took two years to settle.

While Shearn and his comrades in salvage operations, such as John Francis Neylan, continued their great labors, war broke out. War in 1898 had played no little part in making the New York *Journal* a sensationally successful newspaper. War from 1941 to 1945 did much to lift the Hearst papers and magazines out of their financial bog. All newspapers, Hearst's and others, made money. The lush period continued. Hearst even expanded again, this time to buy several paper mills in Canada. Hearst's personal salary went up to $300,000, which was pretty fair for a man in his eighties who had no real duties and had long since concentrated on creating the character of the Lord of San Simeon.

The lord died, aged eighty-eight, on August 14, 1951, though not at San Simeon. He lay on a bed in a typically ornate, typically overdone rambling stucco house in Beverly Hills that belonged to Miss Davies. Outside was the characteristic swimming pool, Southern California's contribution to the symbols of affluence and success.

In the New York *Post* Max Lerner wrote that "here surely was one of the most loveless and unloved figures in our history." The

New York *Herald Tribune* and the New York *Times* were more sympathetic, the former believing "that it will be long before his mark fades from our times"; the latter remarking that Hearst brought "the printed word to many who had previously come close to ignoring it." There were many, many other comments, but *Life's* obituary may have summed up the reason why there was almost no agreement as to the departed's good points and faults. *Life* remarked of Hearst that his newspapers had managed "to antagonize just about every existing segment of informed opinion."

One fact that few if any of the obituaries failed to point out was that Hearst was the very last of the nineteenth-century style of monolithic individualists. Personal journalism passed with Hearst as personal railroading passed with the deaths of Hill and Harriman.

Unlike so many of his peers of late last century and early this, Hearst, as we have seen, was not a self-made millionaire. Homestake alone prevented that. But he was like those peers in his ruthlessness and in his often arrogant individualism. Long before he died, almost anonymous managements were directing the affairs of big business. Income and inheritance taxes, along with government restrictions without number, had come to prevent the rise of any figures to compare with Commodore Vanderbilt in his prime, or William Randolph Hearst in his. The three quarters of a century that elapsed between the passing of these two men saw the attrition, almost imperceptible yet continuous, of the opportunities for the conception and nourishment of moguls of the very top class.

What their kind contributed to making the United States the materially powerful nation it is today must be immeasurable, though our professional economists are in no manner of agreement about it. And our professional historians, until recently, have ignored their lives and works. Yet one may be excused for believing that they had as much and possibly more influence on our country than a like number of generals and statesmen—who almost automatically get into the history books. Whether this influence was "bad" or "good" also has been debated by moral philosophers, or at least critics, many of whom are of the opinion that, no matter the quality of the influence, it cost the nation far too much. Hence the restrictions already mentioned.

That these restrictions on what one school terms ability, energy, and foresight, and another school calls by the name of piracy, have become increasingly effective is perhaps most obviously seen in regard to the homes and the playgrounds of the rich. By the time Hearst died in 1951, most of the imperial or merely gaudy of their mansions had been torn down or turned to other uses; Jay Gould's palace was an antique shop, Carnegie's is a schoolroom serving students of social work. At Bar Harbor and Newport still stand a number of the ostentations in marble or granite of the great days. Like so many of England's palaces they are mostly boarded up. If not, then they have been turned into religious retreats or community enterprises; or are open only as museums, where for a small fee the public may see something of how the enormously wealthy lived.

When the homes of a class of people cease to house them and become museum pieces, it means the class is extinct or nearly so. That is what happened to the class which Americans came to know as the idle rich. It would seem that their very manner of living, by calling attention to their incredible millions, contributed something to their virtual extinction. If this is so, it adds strength to the theories of Darwin as interpreted by Herbert Spencer, who seemed to say that the mogul species, like the brontosaurus and the saber-toothed tiger, became dominant by the laws of the jungle. They became extinct because they were too stupid to comprehend the danger from the changes of jungle environment which their business methods and their ways of living had helped to bring about. It was full circle. Darwin had explained their origin and prophesied their end. . . . Let us see how they lived in their most favored times, which spanned ninety-eight years, from the day Commodore Vanderbilt put to sea in a "yacht" costing half a million dollars, to the day William Randolph Hearst ceased to be the Lord of San Simeon.

PART SIX

WHAT THEY DID WITH IT

Chapter 1 ELEGANCES AND BEQUESTS

W E come now to the elegances of the new rich which Thorstein Veblen called conspicuous consumption of valuable goods as a means of reputability. To cite these extravagances without mention of other uses to which accumulations of money have been put would be unfair, and this chapter will have something to say about the benefactions from the same sources. It is not proposed to be definitive in either category, but rather to sample the ostentations and eccentricities, as well as the bequests, of the immensely wealthy.

Veblen believed that conspicuous consumption antedated even the beginnings of what he chose to call predatory culture. Stuart Chase put stress on the fact that the practice was double-barreled. "Superior people," he said, "lord it over their pecuniary inferiors by wasteful expenditures, whereupon the inferiors move heaven and earth to improve their status by spending to the limit themselves." This is so true that we have imbodied it in an expression— keeping up with the Joneses. The expression is not quite exact; it really means getting ahead of the Joneses.

One of the earliest notable efforts to step to the head of his class was the great and gaudy private steamer *North Star* of Commodore Vanderbilt, already mentioned, in which he and his numerous family, with a large company of retainers including a personal clergyman, toured the world in 1853. Both the ship and the cruise were so fantastically extravagant as to call wide attention to this new multimillionaire, and no other of the day attempted to outclass him on the high seas.

But A. T. Stewart, New York City's merchant prince, who often vied with Vanderbilt in matters of ostentatiousness, including charity-giving, erected on Fifth Avenue a mansion of a size and quality that made all other residences in the United States seem to shrink and fade into mediocrity. The Stewart mansion was pictured in all illustrated magazines, on calendars, and in popular colored prints. Neither the Commodore nor any other rich man of the time made any effort to match it. Nor did they match Stewart in death, for the merchant prince's remains were dug from their resting place in St. Mark's churchyard by body snatchers and held for ransom.

It was left to the Commodore's son William H. and grandsons Cornelius and William K. to show what could be done for conspicuous waste in the form of residences. Like Stewart, the Vanderbilts favored Fifth Avenue, but north of Forty-second Street. William H. had lived for some years on Fifth at Fortieth. It was something of a mansion, but hardly in keeping with the fast multiplying fortune of the head of the New York Central Railroad.

So, in 1879, he purchased the entire block facing Fifth from the west between Fifty-first and Fifty-second. On it, he told his architects, decorators, and contractors, to erect a block-long residence. His home was to be in the southern half; the north side was for his two daughters, Mrs. Shepard and Mrs. Sloane. Vanderbilt said what he wanted could be built for about three million, give or take a hundred thousand dollars or so.

His first plan was to use red and black marble, which he favored above all other building materials. But perhaps he was superstitious. In any case, he recalled what had happened to both A. T. Stewart and William B. Astor so soon after *their* marble mansions had been completed: they had died. Make it brownstone, Vanderbilt told his men. Brownstone would go up much more quickly. So, sixty imported sculptors and seven hundred laborers went to work. The house was ready late in 1881.

This was the same superb mausoleum that caught the eyes of young Mr. Frick and young Mr. Mellon, both of Pittsburgh, on a visit to the metropolis. They stopped their cab to consider what the Vanderbilt homes had cost and how much might be their upkeep. Frick figured the upkeep would run to $300,000 a year, then calculated: "That would be six per cent on five millions . . . say a thousand dollars a day; that is all I shall ever want."

Mr. Vanderbilt was so pleased with his new home and its contents that he authorized publication of a preposterous "art album" entitled *Mr. Vanderbilt's House and Collection,* which was "purchased with solemnity," says Wayne Andrews, by Vanderbilt's friends and business associates, including J. P. Morgan. The album remarked that the new Vanderbilt home stood as "a representative of the new impulse now felt in the national life."

The new impulse turned out to be a glorious hash of styles and periods from much of the known world—French tapestries, Florentine doors, African marbles, English china, Dutch old masters. These were mingled happily with Oriental magnificence which included a Japanese parlor lined with bamboo and fairly a-crawl with jeweled crickets and dragonflies. The album was more assured than modest, remarking how "completely elegant, refined and artistic" everything was.

In the art gallery of his new home Mr. Vanderbilt hung his collection, heavy with Meissoniers. None was of "an indelicate or questionable nature." Only one could have been termed a nude, and she was patently no hussy. Vanderbilt held strong opinions on Art, and what he liked best was a picture that told a story. Being a horsey man, too, he stocked up with several Rosa Bonheurs.

The great house was completed in time to permit its owner almost four years of residence; and there he died in 1885. He died in harness, too, for at the moment of death he was discussing with Robert Garrett the possibility of a Baltimore & Ohio terminal on Staten Island. He was laid away in a cozy three-hundred-thousand-dollar job of marble, which Richard Morris Hunt had designed for him, at New Dorp. The family did not propose that body snatchers should profit from a Vanderbilt, so "they required the lonely watchmen of the tomb to punch a time-clock at fifteen-minute intervals."

Mr. Vanderbilt's estate, as reported earlier, exceeded two hundred million dollars, the largest fortune to date. It was sufficient, says his biographer, to provide, "amply, for his widow and eight children." The "amply" apparently described the difference between two hundred million dollars and the $1,050,000 which was bequeathed in varying amounts to hospitals, churches, a home for drunks, and Vanderbilt University. This school was originally Central University of the Methodist Episcopal Church of the South, at Nashville, and had taken the name of Vanderbilt in 1873, when the Commodore made it a gift of half a million dollars. His son and grandsons continued the tradition of giving to Vanderbilt.

No matter the elegance of his new home, it remained to the wife of one of William H. Vanderbilt's sons, Willie K., to breach the social barrier that neither William H. nor his wife were able to surmount. This fort was operated by Mrs. William Backhouse Astor, belle dame of Manhattan society, whose chamberlain was a curious dude named Ward McAllister. This fop had set up the premise that there were no more than four hundred socially possible persons in the city. These did not include the Vanderbilts, who, for no very clear reason so far as Astors were concerned, McAllister said were invaders of a barbaric sort.

Young Mrs. Vanderbilt's crashing of the four-hundred barrier is generally credited to her taste in architecture. She did not like the brownstone piles in which her mother-in-law lived. Even Mrs. Astor was sheltered in brownstone. So, on Fifth Avenue young Mrs. Willie K. had Richard Morris Hunt build her his great chef-d'oeuvre. It was more than reminiscent of the Château de Blois in France; and it cost three million dollars. What is more, it unnerved Mrs. Astor, still lodged in her chocolate horror of cheap brownstone. It did not matter that Louis Sullivan, America's revolutionary architect of the period, remarked that a gentleman in a silk hat and frock coat coming out of this new Château de Blois was a pathetically absurd sight; because of it, Mrs. Astor felt she could no longer hold the invaders at bay. Thereafter, the blue-liveried servants of Astor and the maroon lackeys of Vanderbilt became acquainted if not actually chummy.

Mrs. Willie K. proceeded to throw a ball which, so the *Sun* reported, "In lavishness of expenditure and brilliancy of dress . . . far outdid any ball ever given before in this city." The boys of the *World* scurried around to consult dressmakers, florists, and such, and came up with the estimate that the Vanderbilt doings had involved expenditures of approximately $250,000.

Acting apparently on the proposition that New York had been properly stunned by the Vanderbilts' local elegances, Willie K. thought up a nice birthday gift for his wife. At Newport, Rhode Island, he built a seashore cottage, Marble House, for two million dollars, then spent nine million more on its interior. It quite paralyzed the dude resort.

Marble House did not, however, quite paralyze Mr. and Mrs. Cornelius Vanderbilt. (Cornelius and Willie were brothers.) They erected close by a true monster of a Newport cottage and named it The Breakers. Yet Marble House retained first place simply because Mrs. Willie K. was a born leader of the idle rich and there were no limits to her energy or ambition. She soon married

Daughter Consuelo off to His Grace the Ninth Duke of Marlborough. It was perhaps from the standpoint of "prestige" the most
notable marriage of an American heiress, though regrettably, as it
turned out, it did nothing to promote Anglo-American unity and
ended in divorce.

The marriage also came pretty high, even by Vanderbilt standards of pecuniary values. To achieve it, Willie K. transferred to
the house of Marlborough 50,000 shares of the Beech Creek Railway Company, an incredibly rich subsidiary of the New York
Central. The shares had a current value of two and a half million
dollars. In addition, Vanderbilt agreed to pay each of the presumably happy couple the sum of $100,000 annually. An interest-
ing item in connection with the Marlborough-Vanderbilt nuptials
was Mrs. Willie K.'s gift to her daughter—the pearls of the late
Catherine, Empress of All the Russias.

A sort of footnote to the union of the noble English and the
wealthy American houses was another divorce: Mrs. Vanderbilt
charged in court that Willie K. had been intimate with one Nellie
Neustretter of Eureka, Nevada, far beyond the western limits of
New York Central territory. Mr. Vanderbilt, always the gentleman, did not question his wife's allegations.

The several sons and daughters of Mr. and Mrs. Cornelius
Vanderbilt had so far been content to marry Americans; but it
would not do to permit the Willie K.s to have the only title, so
Gladys, youngest of the Cornelius clan, was married off to Count
Lâzló Széchényi of Hungary. It was generally regarded as nowhere
near so brilliant a match as that of Consuelo with a Marlborough.
Nor could it have cost so much, or at least nothing was made
public as to the contractual charges of the groom.

Incidentally, it is somehow satisfying to report that though the
family of Jay Gould was never invited to Vanderbilt social affairs,
Daughter Anna was a countess before either of the Vanderbilt
girls had titles. A few months previous to Consuelo's marriage,
Anna Gould was joined in holy matrimony to Count Boni de Castellane. The count was a jolly sort. In some ten years or so he went
through almost six million dollars of Anna's money that had been
sweated out of the stocks and bonds of the Erie, the Missouri
Pacific, and half a dozen other railroads. Whereupon she divorced
him and promptly married his cousin, who was not only a count but
also a duke.

It is not to be thought that the Astors were not gunning for a title

—and at last they got one, not through marriage but from a king of England. The Astor so honored was William Waldorf, who inherited about a hundred million dollars in 1890 from his father, the third John Jacob Astor. His name was fairly well immortalized by the building of the Waldorf-Astoria Hotel. But he was defeated on a try for Congress, which embittered him. He tired, too, of the con-- tinuous social warfare carried on by his wife and his aunt for supremacy of the idle rich four hundred; and in 1890 he moved with his family to England.

In England the Astors had to start at the bottom of the social scale. The rise proved hard going. But the Astors had a lot of money, which, it became apparent in time, could perform as great marvels in England as it could in America. Astor became a British subject in 1899, and his "life in England was characterized by vast expenditures, a somewhat obtrusive effort to win social recogni- tion." These efforts included purchase of several estates, plus the castle that had belonged to Anne Boleyn; the buying of newspapers and magazines; and fat contributions of cash to the right people. They paid off when he was made Baron Astor, and a year later was promoted to viscount. (It was one of his many cousins, John Jacob IV, who went down on the ship that removed so many rich men, the *Titanic,* and "the testimony of many survivors bears wit- ness that Mr. Astor showed great disregard of self and displayed great courage and coolness.")

In the matter of bequests, the Astors were known neither for outstanding generosity nor niggardliness. John Jacob, first of the name, left $400,000 to found a library bearing his name, and suc- cessive generations added to its size and excellence until it was un- questionably the finest in the city. The Astor Library was merged with two other great collections when the present New York Public Library was built on Forty-second Street.

The four hundred of dude-chamberlain McAllister had failed to keep Mrs. Willie K. Vanderbilt in the outer darkness. She swept into the fancied realm of high society and on her gilded heels came a host of still newer rich. The society gold rush had begun in the seventies. It was to reach its height late in the century. As early as 1890, *Life* magazine (not the present periodical) remarked that the four hundred had risen to the fifteen hundred because Wall Street got control and watered the stock.

Many of the theoretical eleven hundred new members of the big

show-off had come to New York from all over. These were what
Charles Beard referred to as the bravest of the socially venturesome.
They came to the place where they could best display their money to
the gaping multitude, and advertised their arrival in the most obvious manner by erecting palaces, buying Art, and all the exhibi-
tionism they could invent.

They gathered here from the blast furnaces of Pittsburgh, from
oily Pennsylvania creeks, from Michigan forests, from the copper
mountains of Montana and the deep silvered stopes of the Comstock, from the murk of Chicago, and from quiet New England
villages. With them they brought the wealth of Midas and the
dreams of potentates. There were no classical traditions to inhibit
their appetites for display; and because few of them had acquired
canons of propriety and aesthetics, they put on a show as staggering
as anything Phineas Taylor Barnum could have conceived. It was
the era of the porte-cochere, and a popular anecdote concerned
the brand-new millionaire whose architect asked him if he wanted
a porte-cochere on his new chateau. "Hell, yes!" replied Midas.
"Better put in five of them—and make sure the flush don't sound
loud."

Calla lilies became the favored flower; they had size to them.
Heraldry bloomed. So did Art, and old masters were manufactured
in gross lots. Portrait painters flourished. One of the new millionaires, having somehow heard of John Singleton Copley, told his
secretary to get in touch with that artist. "I want for him to paint
the kids," he said.

The most amusing critic of the times was another artist, Charles
Dana Gibson of *Life,* whose jibes must have penetrated the whale-
bone and thickest weskit of even the brassiest climbers. Because
there are no snobs so insufferable as the new rich who think they
have arrived socially, Gibson pictured the climber's progress as
pitilessly as Hogarth did the rake's. Gibson's overblown dowagers
were obnoxious. They led their consorts, the captains of industry, by
the nose. These commonly domineering characters followed their
women meekly if wearily up mountains of moneybags and skulls
of the proletariat and lent a hand as the girls tried to pickax their
way into the homes of slightly less new "aristocrats."

One of Gibson's best pictures was Mrs. Steele Pool's House-
warming. It showed a vast ballroom, elegant beyond measure, empty
of people except for Mrs. Pool herself, who appears as an obese,
overdressed old bag, waiting for guests who would never come.

Gibson also hammered away at the Anglomania of the new rich who sought "to deck their family trees with a British or Continental title."

It went without saying that before any of the climbers could be considered, they must have a magnificent house in New York, and so the region of Fifth Avenue became a continuous construction job. The ambitious must also have a summer retreat, and Newport and Bar Harbor, the Berkshires and Long Island witnessed the rise of "cottages" and "country seats" that were designed as evidence of the great wealth and barbaric taste of their owners.

These homes were virtual billboards advertising the pecuniary condition of stocks and bonds representing steel tonnage, barreled pork, mile-deep copper, and rivers of petroleum. They were an indication of the great thaumaturgic powers of whole oceans of patent medicines guaranteed to cure all human ills, put babies to sleep, and restore what the labels said was lost manhood. They were proof that sewing machines, telegraph wires, tin plates, and wooden matches contained more magic than the technology that went into their invention and manufacture. Castles of solid marble arose on understructures of juicy black chewing tobacco.

Erecting a palace in the city and a cottage by the sea or in the mountains did not by any means assure their owners that their families would be admitted to this or that one of the many social groups that came into being as the four hundred changed to fifteen hundred, and then grew into a horde. You couldn't build a big mansion and sit there and wait. You had to compete for notice in the new society pages of the metropolitan press.

The competition took many forms. One banquet was given for the pet dogs of the rich. A hundred canines participated, says Cleveland Amory in his *The Last Resorts,* "most of them in fancy dress; the menu was stewed liver and rice, fricassee of bones and shredded dog biscuit." One dude gave a dinner on horseback. A dowager thrilled her guests by seating a chimpanzee at her dinner table. One of the Pittsburgh millionaires sat guests down at a table in the center of which was a large glass tank. In it disported a shapely houri clad lightly in golden scales. A competitor for attention put *his* houri in a huge pie out of which she bounded, along with a flock of brilliantly plumed birds.

The wife of a new and minor capitalist let it be known that she had a bedstead for which she had paid $200,000. Another regaled friends about her $55,000 piano, which was little enough when an acquaintance bought a pair of opera glasses for $75,000 and a small dressing table for $65,000.

All of this and a great deal more was exactly the right climate of research for Veblen, who was then composing his extended remarks on the leisure class. "The canon of reputability," he wrote, "must adapt itself to . . . the degree of spiritual maturity of the particular class whose scheme of life it is to regulate."

The spiritual maturity of the particular class Veblen was writing about reached high noon on February 6, 1897. This was the day of the Bradley Martin ball, and the Bradley Martin ball is almost the only social affair of the Gilded Age to get into the history books. For more than half a century it has been turning up in critical writing where, without competition, it occupies the position of horrible example of capitalism at its worst.

The time was one of country-wide industrial depression, and bread lines were the only form of alleviation for the worthy if improvident poor. Bread lines were overly long that winter. It seemed like a good time to Mr. and Mrs. Bradley Martin to "put money in circulation" on the theory it would thus help to feed the hungry, of which New York alone had at least two hundred thousand.

Now, the Bradley Martins were petty-cash minors in the big-money circles. But they were consummate exhibitionists. Engaging the Waldorf-Astoria Hotel, these "rich ninnies" as Thomas Beer characterized them, announced they would give therein a "Fancy Dress Fete." The hotel's interior, the Bradley Martins told reporters, was to be transformed into a replica of Versailles, with rare tapestries, exotic flowers, and myriad lights to do justice to the costumes of the several hundreds of guests who would come attired as court characters of the times of the great kings and queens of France and England. For the sake of publicity, too, the Bradley Martins were pleased to estimate that the cost of the fete itself, coupled with the expense of costumes of the guests, might run as high as $370,000. A gay time would be had by all, they promised, and just think of all that money put into circulation to improve the condition of the needy.

Good Dr. Rainsford, rector of St. George's, a church to which excessive wealth was no bar, was alarmed when he read of the Bradley Martins' plans. He called in reporters to warn that the affair would "draw attention to the growing gulf which separates the rich and

the poor, and serve to increase the discontent of the latter needlessly." He could see no point in the chatter about setting money
into circulation.

Dr. Rainsford's warning was ignored. The Fancy Dress Fete
came off on schedule and it was a real dinger. One of the rich
ninnies told how it was. "I do not think there was ever so great a
display of jewels before," she said, nigh swooning at the memory.
"My sister-in-law personated Mary Stuart and her gold embroidered
gown was trimmed with pearls and precious stones. Bradley, as
Louis XV, wore a court suit of brocade. The suit of gold inlaid
armor worn by Mr. Belmont was valued at ten thousand dollars.
The value of the historic gems worn by the ladies simply baffles
description."

So did the fete's aftermath baffle the Bradley Martins. The press
gave the affair more than generous space, immortalizing it in many
columns of gush and pictures, while the editorials almost without
exception snarled and bellowed at such display in the midst of unemployment, misery, and starvation. Not only the left-wing populist
sheets, but sound Republican papers denounced people who seemed
to wonder why the breadless did not change to a cake diet.

Mark Hanna, something of a capitalist himself, was greatly
annoyed. The whole thing struck him as cruelly reckless. He thought
it would serve the witless Bradley Martins right if some terrorist
had heaved a bomb and blown "the dancing fops and their ladies
to spangles and red paste." A little later, when Hanna saw a copy
of *The Theory of the Leisure Class* on a friend's table, he picked
it up and snorted. "What's their theory?" he wanted to know. "More
fancy-dress balls?"

Another wealthy and reflective man, Frederick Townsend Martin, had watched the aberrations of the newly rich with increasing
loathing touched with fear. He believed devoutly in capitalism and
just as devoutly that decay follows idleness and extravagance. He
wanted his class to correct its abuses. Finally, he could stand their
doings no longer and he wrote a book which, like Tom Lawson's,
was first serialized in *Everybody's Magazine*. He called it *The Passing of the Idle Rich*. In it he cited affairs like the Bradley Martin
ball and other idiocies, though never by name; and he cried that
"only the morally and intellectually deaf" could not hear the sound
of the rising storm of the common people. "It sweeps from the
plains of Kansas in the breath of the rustling corn," he wrote. "It
moans from the sweat shops of New York, and the charnels of the

packinghouses in Chicago." He called for a Marius, a strong man of the people.

No Marius arose, however—or none strong enough to overthrow the plutocracy, though Eugene Debs made an effort so frightening that eventually it was thought best to restrain him in prison. Yet the Bradley Martin ball was not wholly without effect. The alert tax gatherers of New York City had taken notice of it, and the empty champagne bottles had little more than been collected by Waldorf-Astoria flunkies when the tax men visited not only the home of the Bradley Martins but the homes of many of their guests of the ball as well, to reappraise them for the rolls. The sudden boost in valuation of the Bradley Martin residence was such that, coupled with the blizzard of criticism and abuse, Mr. and Mrs. Bradley Martin took off for England, to live abroad ever after.

In addition to residences and fine entertainments, certain appurtenances were almost obligatory. One of these was a yacht, even though such a capitalist as William H. Vanderbilt refused to have one. He preferred the rails. But his son Willie K. went to sea in the *Alva,* named for his wife, which cost more than half a million dollars and was 285 feet long, the longest afloat when she was launched in 1886. Jay Gould's *Atalanta* ran 250 feet, William Astor's *Nourmahal* 233 feet.

J. P. Morgan's *Corsair* was a pretty nice ship but she was a mere 165 feet. *Corsair II* was forty feet longer. And the third of the line, launched in 1898, was a regal 302 feet. Morgan told his boatman that except for size, *Corsair III* must be identical with *Corsair II*. This raised a problem. It was discovered that the kind of carpets bought for the earlier boat were no longer made. "What of it?" Mr. Morgan asked. Then he ordered the old patterns set up anew on the looms and the old design woven.

Then there was the matter of private railroad cars. The elder Morgan seems not to have owned one. When he had a rail trip of any consequence it was his custom to engage an entire train, say four or six luxurious cars. On one of these occasions he commissioned a special train to take him and his guests to a convention of Episcopal bishops in San Francisco. That his guests might not suffer unduly while crossing the Great Plains, Morgan—says Lucius Beebe —had a part of the diner torn out and special wine racks built in to accommodate Morgan's favorite vintages with a minimum of jarring. "The wines were mostly champagnes," Mr. Beebe reports, "but

one bin was allotted to the financier's favorite Rhine, a Johannis-
berger, which had been bought at auction by his Berlin agent for
thirty-five dollars a bottle." The San Francisco *Examiner,* after a
brief skirmish with wine measures, and sums, informed its readers
that every glass of this number consumed by Morgan and his
ecclesiastical guests, set the old man back four dollars. Incidentally,
the man in charge of Mr. Morgan's diner on this trip was Louis
Sherry, the lad from St. Albans, Vermont, who had gone to the city
and made good as a Manhattan restaurateur.

It was probably natural that the Vanderbilt and Gould families
should go in for private railroad cars. Jay Gould owned several,
the finest of which was the Atalanta, costing $50,000 and which
ended its days as the yardmaster's shanty at Overton, Texas, a town
on the Missouri Pacific. Gould's son George, who inherited the
Gould lines and attempted to run them, was not content with a
private car; he owned a private train, and his brother-in-law, the
aforementioned Count Boni de Castellane, recalled that on the
Gould train all hands scrupulously dressed in formal style for
dinner.

At the time it was built, in 1882, William H. Vanderbilt's Vanderbilt was the finest on wheels. It cost $50,000, or more than the
car of Leland Stanford, head of the Central Pacific. The Vanderbilt
was a sight for the astigmatic. It was painted a circus-wagon yellow
with red trim. Its exterior was decorated with monstrous oil paintings of Niagara Falls and other scenic assets along the New York
Central. Since that day, no Vanderbilt generation has been without
its private car or cars, down to Harold V.'s comparatively recent
Idle Hour.

Even Henry Ford, for all the fact that he did much to ruin railroad passenger traffic, liked a nice train ride on occasion, and to
take it he had the Fair Lane, a massive job of eighty feet, longer
than the Moultrie, the redwood and satin-upholstered rolling palace
of Henry Flagler, the Standard Oil man. Perhaps the longest private
car ever built was the eighty-three-foot Errant, built in 1927 for
the son of Nevada's Silver Senator William A. Clark. It was later
bought by William Randolph Hearst.

Mr. Beebe himself often takes to the rails in one of the largest
and most gorgeous private cars of record. This is the Gold Coast,
an eighty-two-foot rosewood and mahogany job, owned by Beebe
and his associate Charles Clegg. It is almost the last privately owned
car on American railroads. These symbols of wealth began to fade

at almost the same rate as the mortality of first- and second-generation moguls. Their last stand was in the twenties when, as Mr. Beebe noted, he saw the cars of Goulds, Vanderbilts, Armours, and others "drawn up twenty deep in the private railroad yard of the since vanished Royal Poinciana Hotel in Palm Beach."

The fast horses of the wealthy began to disappear even before the private cars were parked in forlorn places to perform duties as shelter for yard hands, though here and there a scion of one of the moneyed houses keeps up the tradition. Many of the racing stakes still carry the names of long-dead capitalist sports. Race horses are expensive, wasteful, and useless, hence are suitable "to the canon of pecuniary good repute of the leisure class." In some respects, however, dogs are even more suited to the canon, and dogs and dog shows have remained favorites with leisure-class people and their imitators, both of whom are gluttons for "the fawning admiration characteristic of the dog to his master." Though the dog is, in Veblen opinion, as well as in the opinion of a few others, "the filthiest of the domestic animals in his person and the nastiest in his habits," yet he makes up for these shortcomings with "a servile, fawning attitude toward his master, and a readiness to inflict damage and discomfort on all else." Taken all around, he holds "a well-assured place in man's regard as a thing of good repute." We should never be astonished that the wills of many wealthy persons have bequeathed vastly larger sums for the care of an aged canine than was left for charitable purposes. Over the years such bequests have become commonplace.

Even J. P. Morgan the elder recognized the dog as a thing of good repute. Dixon Wecter tells that when Morgan found some bright and personable young man who might make a good Morgan partner, he sent him a collie from his own kennels.

Neither Morgan, father or son, had any social ambitions. They did not need to rise; they were *there*. Yet the elder liked to get around to the several resorts maintained by and for the wealthy, and seemed to favor Bar Harbor. Because he was a strong traditionalist, his visits, says Cleveland Amory, varied little in routine. When the great *Corsair* entered the harbor and dropped anchor, all manner of sailboats, motorboats, rowboats, and canoes put out from shore to form "an impressively fawning flotilla." Then, headed by Bishop Doane or some other Episcopalian eminence, a small group of Mount Desert's solid people went aboard to deliver the resort's official welcome.

Later in the evening, the great man was most circumspectly put ashore, where he called on one or both of two ladies, neither of whom was young, giving rise to one of Bar Harbor's favorite bon mots—that Mr. Morgan "not only collected Old Masters, he also collected old mistresses."

Morgan's old masters, his rare books and objects of art were his greatest extravagances. Not even his biographer Allen attempted to estimate their cost beyond saying that they must have amounted to "millions a year." They were bought in some part through Henry Duveen, of whom Morgan was very fond; and once he saved Duveen from considerable trouble by advancing him almost one and a half million dollars. But Morgan did not like Joe Duveen, the better known member of the art firm.

As early as 1871 Morgan bought a country place on the Hudson just below West Point, and here the family spent a good part of each year. His town house from 1880 to his death in 1913 was the massive brownstone at 219 Madison Avenue. It did not matter that the fashionable rich were building on Fifth Avenue and continually moving farther north; where J. P. Morgan had his home was exactly where he wanted it. As if to emphasize as much, he later built a marble library next door to his house, fronting on Thirty-sixth Street. This is the structure famed in business circles as the place to which old Morgan summoned bankers and capitalists to instruct them how to stem the wave of disaster that seemed about to engulf the country in 1907.

Once a year Morgan went to London, where he maintained a town house, and usually visited the Continent. His trips abroad gradually lengthened, and much of his time was devoted to searching for books and pictures to add to his collections. He ignored all contemporary art and literature. What he wanted must be heaped with venerable tradition. Roger Fry, adviser on paintings to the Metropolitan Museum, remarked of Morgan that "a crude historical imagination was the only flaw in his otherwise perfect insensibility" toward art. But Fry had had several run-ins with the financier and resented what he said was Morgan's "domineering" attitude.

During the last fifteen years of his life, the elder Morgan was the greatest collector in practice, which may have been one reason why at death his estate was estimated to be worth no more than sixty-eight million dollars. He had expected that the Metropolitan would erect a wing to hold the paintings he planned to give to it, but this was not done and his collection was left to his son. Somewhat later a good part of the fifty-million-dollar collection did go to the Metropolitan, but many things were sold and went to other institutions.

Not all his money could rectify what affliction did to Morgan's fiery nose. The condition is called rhinophyma. Though he consulted specialists the world over, the nose tended to get worse rather than better. It was the subject of one of the favorite pieces of Morgan folklore.

When Dwight Morrow was about to become a Morgan partner, his able wife thought it would be nice to have the eminent man for tea. Morgan graciously accepted the invitation. Mrs. Morrow was quite competent to tender a tea party to the old man's liking. What worried her was her precocious young daughter Anne, who, childlike, might innocently pass some remark about the astonishing nose. So, Mrs. Morrow drilled Anne. When introduced to Mr. Morgan she was to let her gaze wander no higher than the guest's collar, make no remark other than "Good afternoon, Mr. Morgan," then to bow prettily and go upstairs.

Little Anne did perfectly, and as the child left the room good Mrs. Morrow was wildly relieved. She turned to the great man. "Mr. Morgan," she asked, "do you take nose in your tea?"

Morgan the elder, the great, the magnificent, died on a Monday, March 31, 1913, in Rome, aged not quite seventy-six years. Funeral services were held two weeks later in St. George's, New York, and burial was at Hartford, Connecticut, where he was born. He left, as related, a fortune of about sixty-eight million dollars, aside from his collections of pictures and books. Half a million went to St. George's, $100,000 to the local Episcopal diocese, and another $100,000 to the House of Rest for Consumptives.

To all hands in the employ of J. P. Morgan & Company went the equivalent of a year's salary. There were legacies to his daughters and sons-in-law. All the rest went to his only son, J. P. the younger.

Morgan biographer Allen points out that Morgan made many large gifts in his lifetime and says they mostly were secret. He wanted no mention of them. One was for more than a million dollars to the Wadsworth Athenaeum in Hartford. Another went toward construction of the Cathedral of St. John the Divine. Then there was Harvard, a typical instance.

Harvard University was planning a new group of buildings for its medical school, and its fund raisers cruised the country to tap wealthy graduates and wealthy nongraduates. Morgan the younger had gone to Harvard. So, when the elder was approached for some money, he said he should be pleased to see the plans for the new medical school. In the meantime, John D. Rockefeller had made a contribution, but not before he had taken six months to have the project thoroughly investigated. When the Harvard men came to see Morgan at his office and were shown into an inner room, in walked the old gentleman himself, watch in hand.

"Gentlemen," he said brusquely, "I am pressed for time and can give you but a moment. Have you any plans to show me?" As soon as the drawings were unrolled on the table, Morgan swept them with a glance and began jabbing with his finger. "I will build *that*," he said, "and *that* and *that*. Good morning, gentlemen." He left the room abruptly, having in three minutes committed himself to financing three buildings at a cost of a million dollars.

There were many who believed it was the Pujo committee's investigation of Morgan affairs that hastened Morgan's death. The old man was on the stand for many hours (it was 1912) and withstood the relentless questioning of the government's lawyers with characteristic firmness. If the ordeal did have any effect on his health, it was only one more sad item in a world that had begun to doubt its great men of finance. The muckrakers had had their day lambasting Standard Oil, and even Morgan's own child, United States Steel. Theodore Roosevelt had made a lot of noise about malefactors of great wealth; and under his successor, the serene Taft, the United States had conducted even more prosecutions against big business.

All of these things must have seemed like a world upside down to America's foremost financier. "Well," he exclaimed sadly to a son-in-law, "it has come to this!" He was speaking of the anti-trust suit against U. S. Steel, and he brooded long over what he considered a public affront. Then, not long before his death, he was called to Washington again, this time to explain his campaign contributions of earlier years. Harassment was on every hand. It was all pretty terrible.

Morgan had always done what he thought was right. He was too sure of his rightness to change his thinking about it. He *couldn't* change his thinking—about anything. Almost sixty years before, when he entered the business world, he wore an enormous blood-stone attached to a cable-like watch chain. When he died he was wearing the same chain and the same bloodstone. For almost sixty

years, too, he had distributed to friends annually exactly six tons
of especially fine tea. It was distributed every year, on the same date,
from the era of Buchanan to the era of Woodrow Wilson.

He *couldn't* change his thinking. He believed in Holy Writ, but
he believed no less in Holy Writ than he did in the proposition expounded so effectively by William Graham Sumner—that all yearning after equality by one's inferiors is the offspring of envy and
covetousness. He invariably dressed in dark clothes, whose style
never changed, wore a wing collar and an ascot tie, and an old-
fashioned square-topped derby. He was completely insulated against
the mass of his countrymen. The idea of democracy evaded him
wholly.

Thus he lived and thus he died. Forty years later, his name is still
redolent with the idea of the power of money; and his personality
can be sensed in the masterful portrait Edward Steichen took of
him. Of his meeting with Morgan, the photographer recalled best his
subject's eyes. Meeting his gaze, said Steichen, was like confront-
ing the headlight of an express train bearing down upon you. As an
abstract force, Morgan was unequaled in his element, one composed
solely of money. One would hesitate to say what his contribution to
making America had been.

His son, Morgan the younger, lived for forty-six years in the
shadow of the old man alive; and lived another thirty years in
shadow of the old man dead. Allen described him as a quiet and
courteous gentleman, content to listen to the counsels of partners
more brilliant than himself. He was stiff and remote, contemptuous
of democratic blunderings, yet far more conscious than most financiers "of the imperial obligations which accompanied imperial
power."

At Glen Cove, on Long Island, Morgan the younger built in 1910
a fifty-six-room mansion of stone, considerably larger than any
home of his father. He built another *Corsair,* too. It was the largest
private yacht afloat when finished in 1929, being 343 at the water
line, forty-one feet longer than the elder's *Corsair III.* The old man's
shadow might be longer, but the son could have a bigger house
and a longer ship.

At the time of his death in 1943, most Americans recalled
Morgan the younger as the elderly man of a photograph which
showed him holding a female midget on his knee, the result of a
press agent's efforts to advertise a show. The public had by that
time forgotten the incident that made the younger something of a

hero. On July 3, 1915, while having breakfast with his guest, Sir Cecil Spring-Rice, the British Ambassador, Morgan was attacked in his Glen Cove home by an assassin with a revolver in each hand. Morgan grappled instantly with the intruder and overpowered him, though not before being shot twice. The attempted assassination was inspired in the gunman, Dr. Erich Muenter, a German national, by the fact that Morgan & Company were purchasing agents for munitions in the United States of the British Government, then at war with Germany. The press hailed Morgan for his courage and ability to handle a madman with two guns.

By a piece of the irony that seems often to dog the efforts of the great, the Morgan mansion at Glen Cove came, in 1949, to house the Soviet delegation to the United Nations. The Russians installed seventy-one beds, an "apparent violation," so the New York *Herald Tribune* remarked with a straight face, of the one-family restriction of the community of Glen Cove. The Russians moved out in 1951, leaving "the once-beautiful gardens a mass of weeds," while inside, plaster and paint were peeling from the ceilings and torn drapes hung at the windows. Taxes on the property had gone unpaid, and in 1952 the place was sold for back taxes in the amount of $29,506.

The white marble library still stands at Madison and Thirty-sixth Street, Manhattan, however, and it serves adequately to indicate the magnificence of the imperial Morgans at its best.

The answer as to what they did with their money is quite simple in regard to only one of America's wealthy persons—the she-mogul Hetty Green. Hetty kept hers. At her death in 1916 her fortune was much larger than that of the elder Morgan's, even if his collections of art and books were included. Hetty left no art, no books, not even a mansion. She left one hundred million dollars of what are called liquid assets.

She was born Henrietta Howland Robinson at New Bedford, Massachusetts, in 1834, and from her father and an aunt inherited a total of approximately six million dollars. In 1867 she married Edward Green, a well-to-do Vermonter who had made his pile in tea and silk. On their wedding day, Hetty and Edward signed an agreement that each should remain independent in all financial affairs, which is why Edward is forgotten while the memory of Hetty lives on not only because of her ability to match wits with the bulls and bears of Wall Street and the wolves of business anywhere, but because of her way of living.

When she moved upon the New York Stock Exchange, Hetty Green became the first and only female operator in a place considered for males only. She quickly demonstrated what a fatuous notion *that* was. She engineered several astounding coups in railroad stocks and took part in the manhandling of many other properties, all of which increased her fortune.

Meanwhile, she lived in obscure and shabby boarding houses, sometimes in unfurnished rooms, where she installed a single gasplate and did her own cooking. She invariably wore what had once been a black dress, which must have been of practically indestructible material. It turned brown, then green, and still she wore it; and carried an umbrella and handbag of about the same era as her dress. In the handbag she carried graham crackers—bought in bulk—on which she munched from time to time, remarking she was thus saved from paying the "prohibitive prices" of New York's restaurants.

It is remembered that when Edward Hatch, Jr., was active in the management of the Manhattan store, Lord & Taylor, he once commented to Hetty that her veil was torn, and told her that if she'd come to the store, he would give her one of the best veils in stock. "Will you?" she said, as pleased as a child. "That is nice of you." Hatch had forgotten about the incident when one morning an agitated floorwalker in Lord & Taylor came to him, saying that Hetty Green was downstairs at the veil counter demanding a veil for nothing. Hatch went down and had a salesgirl drape the best veil in stock over Hetty's battered straw. She liked it fine. "I wonder," she asked Hatch, "if you have any skirts you could let me have at a reduced price?" Hatch let her have a dandy for fifty cents. She paid for it, and ever after told her friends that Lord & Taylor was the best store in town to buy things at reasonable prices.

Another time, in Bellows Falls, Vermont, Hetty wanted a horse and rig, but discovered that the owner wanted two hundred dollars. Hetty thereupon went to another man who had once owned the horse and also had a grudge against its current owner. From him Hetty learned all the faults of the horse in question. She went back to the first man, listed all of the alleged faults of the horse, beat him down to sixty dollars, and bought.

In April 1916, the old lady suffered a stroke brought on by a fierce argument with the cook in the home of a friend with whom Hetty was living. The cook and Hetty both swore at each other like a couple of troopers. The stroke followed, and Hetty was taken to the modest brownstone house of her son, at 5 West 90th Street, New York. Here, while bedridden for weeks, she was cared for by nurses engaged and paid by the son. The nurses were instructed never to appear in their white uniforms, but to dress as servants, which were relatively inexpensive compared to trained nurses. The young Mr. Green remarked that the appearance at her bedside of a white-uniformed nurse would have been sufficient to kill his mother at sight.

Doubtless Hetty Green was partly the victim of a newspaper tradition, yet there was more than a little substance to the stories of her parsimoniousness. The same may have been true in regard to John Warne Gates, the Bet-a-Million man. He is best remembered for immense betting at horse races, roulette, whist, faro, and any and all other games of chance. Even at such a big-money place as Saratoga, Gates managed to leave a permanent mark for stakes.

In one day at the Saratoga track, he lost $400,000, and that night appeared at Canfield's clubhouse with the intention of winning back his losses at faro. The play went on, and by ten o'clock Gates was out another $150,000, making more than half a million loss for the day. He then rose from the table and went to see Canfield himself, to ask belligerently that the limit of the game be raised. Canfield asked him what limit he wanted. "Five and ten," he replied. "You may have it," said the professional. Gates resumed play. By midnight his luck began to turn, and when the game ended at dawn, he had recovered his loss of $150,000, and also another $150,000.

Gates dressed like a gambler. He liked to have three diamonds in his shirt front, three more on each gallus buckle. Portly and florid, he chewed or smoked a cigar during his waking hours, had a whole suite at the Waldorf by the year, bought Corots and Meissoniers by the square foot, and maintained a hunting lodge in France and a town house in Chicago. His weakling son Charlie, however, probably cost Gates more than all of his elegances together. Charlie got into one scrape after another, and they turned out to be inordinately expensive. And after his father's death in 1911, Charlie married again and erected in the Lake of Isles district in Minneapolis, a monstrous home costing four million dollars. It was characteristic of Charlie, as a symbol of the playboy sons of moneyed men, that he died at a party, in Cody, Wyoming, where he had gone for a hunting trip with another able drinking man, who was William Frederick Cody, better known as Buffalo Bill.

Charlie Gates died in his private railroad car, Bright Eyes, and was taken to New York, for burial beside Bet-a-Million, in a "huge

HENRY FORD

WILLIAM RANDOLPH HEARST

mausoleum in New York's Woodlawn Cemetery." He will do as the perfect example of the wastrel, the shirt sleeves to shirt sleeves in one generation tradition which, however, is more myth than fact.

A great contrast to the extravagances of John Gates and his son was the parsimony of a much wealthier man. This was Russell Sage, one of the most durable capitalists of all time. We have seen him working with Jay Gould and others in the acquisition and manipulation of railroad stocks, from which he usually came off richer than before. He built a home on Fifth Avenue that was rated "remarkably unpretentious," and a modest place on Long Island. Neither was for show. They were for comfort only. Sage was no epicure; plain food suited him best. His clothes came right off the rack of whatever store was having the hottest "fire sale." He was known to haggle over the price of an apple, or a pound of butter. At the age of seventy-five, in 1891, a bomb tossed into his office blew his clerk into bits and also killed the assassin, one Henry Norcross, but Sage quickly recovered from his wounds. He died at ninety, leaving a fortune of seventy million dollars, at least one quarter of which went into the Russell Sage Foundation, established in 1907.

The other durable capitalist, of course, was John D. Rockefeller, who had no more social aspirations than Sage. Rockefeller came in time to live on a colossal scale, but he cared nothing for pomp and elegance. He merely wanted to live a prudently well-ordered life unmolested by the many dangerous enemies incident to the forming and operation of Standard Oil; no man with a bomb or a gun was to get into the old man's presence without effort.

At his chief residence in the Pocantico Hills, near Tarrytown, New York, he gradually built up a large estate, though the house he lived in, which was one of seventy-five structures on the place, was far from elegant. There were nearly a hundred miles of private roads on the estate. The guards and other employees numbered more than a thousand. The guards were probably needed in the earlier years of the Pocantico place, but the old man's longevity came to be his greatest protection. He outlived all of his greatest enemies, outlived even many of their sons and some of their grandsons.

We have seen how the coming of the gasoline age increased the Rockefeller fortune many times over. John D.'s first attempt to reduce it somewhat was a $600,000 gift to re-establish the University of Chicago. This was brought about in part by the efforts of the Rev. Frederick T. Gates, a Baptist minister and no relation to

John W. (Bet-a-Million) Gates. The elder Rockefeller was impressed with the extraordinary ability of the forty-year-old preacher, and in 1893 invited him to become associated with the Rockefeller interests. Gates, says one of his biographers, was primarily instrumental in acquiring for Rockefeller the iron mines of the Mesabi, in their development, and also in establishing the ore railroad and ore-carrying fleet.

To such business ability, Gates added the imagination of a poet and the mind of a scientist. He was also outspoken, and now that he had Rockefeller's ear, he talked turkey. "Your fortune," he told Rockefeller, "is rolling up . . . like an avalanche! You must keep up with it! You must distribute it faster than it grows! If you do not, it will crush you, and your children, and your children's children!"

Rockefeller was willing to listen and ready to believe. He gave royally when Gates convinced him of the worth of what became the first of the Rockefeller foundations, the General Education Board. Gates then conceived the Rockefeller Institute for Medical Research, and finally the Rockefeller Foundation, chartered in 1913 to "advance the well-being of mankind throughout the world." Gates, wrote Henry Steele Commager, was curiously more concerned with the cure of bodies than the cure of souls. He remained opposed to almost anything except the improvement and spread of medicine; but in 1928, when the foundation was reorganized, there was a marked shift to the social sciences. Since then, 10,000 fellowships in seventy-five countries "have trained the best brains for leadership." Flynn estimated that at least $575,000,000 of Rockefeller money had gone into gifts, yet the "fortune has grown through mere increment faster than he could give it away." By 1950, the several Rockefeller foundations had made grants of more than $821,000,000.

There is no way of estimating what the impact of eight hundred million dollars may have done to "advance the well-being of mankind throughout the world." In an excellent book, published in 1952, Raymond B. Fosdick told the story of the Rockefeller gifts and what had been done with them. It is a heart-warming story of the impetus given to education, medicine, science, and religion by the money that flowed into the greatest industrial monopolist of modern times. But it is the story of a mass of money and a horde of people, and because it is, it lacks the appeal of individual philanthropy.

Henry H. Rogers, one of Rockefeller's ablest associates in Standard Oil, and one of the most ruthless in business, was never known to contribute any money to mass charities. Good works with him were pretty much a matter of individuals. How many unfortunate people he supported in whole or in part was never known, save that they were apparently a great many. But at least two of his philanthropies became known. "It was he," cried Elbert Hubbard, who for once got his facts straight, "it was Rogers who gave Helen Keller to the world. Without his help that wonderful woman would still be like unto the eyeless fish in the Mammoth Cave." In her *Midstream,* Miss Keller speaks of Rogers as having financed much of her education, which came through the devoted Annie Mansfield Sullivan.

Rogers' other private philanthropy that became public knowledge was in connection with Mark Twain. When Rogers and Mark met in the Murray Hill Hotel in New York one evening, the famous writer had got to the bottom of his barrel. He had invested and lost a fortune in a typesetting machine; and his own publishing venture had failed and gone into bankruptcy. Forty-eight hours after the meeting, Twain's tangled and nigh hopeless financial affairs were in Rogers' able hands. With charm and unparalleled delicacy, and possibly with cash that the writer never suspected, Rogers put Mark Twain's financial world right side up again, and saved his copyrights, which were worth "more than the gift of half a million dollars in cash." Until his death, Rogers continued to act as Twain's business manager and general counselor. . . . The great Negro leader, Booker T. Washington, remarked of Rogers that "He never failed me" when it came to cash donations.

It was characteristic of Rogers that when he got around to having a summer home, he did not build a cottage at Newport or Bar Harbor. His summer place was in his native Fairhaven, a small Massachusetts village where his old friends continued to call him "Hen" and where he established the Atlas Tack Company, "the largest concern of its kind in America." Rogers also paved all the Fairhaven streets. He gave it grammar and high school buildings, a Masonic hall, and a fine Unitarian church and parsonage.

Although Veblen was of the opinion that it would be misleading to ascribe to Divinity a jealous regard for His pecuniary standing, this was not true of a majority of capitalists who favored religious denominations above all else for their gifts and bequests. Possibly they shared the belief which one of their number, George F. Baer, expounded in a statement that is as fresh and resonant now as when it was made half a century ago. "The rights and interests of the laboring man," wrote Mr. Baer in a famous letter during a strike, "will be protected and cared for . . . by the Christian men to whom God . . . has given the control of the property interests of the country." This might seem to exclude the Guggenheim brothers, but one feels sure Mr. Baer did not mean it that way; he thought he was speaking for all men of big business—Christian, Jews, and Andrew Carnegie.

It is probable that the twenty-odd millions of dollars which Thomas Fortune Ryan gave or bequeathed to the Roman Catholic Church was the greatest gift of an American capitalist to a religious group. Though James J. Hill was a Protestant, he gave a million dollars to establish a Roman Catholic seminary in St. Paul, saying he did not care what denomination it was so long as a true religious spirit governed it. Remarked Mr. Hill: "Look at the millions of foreigners who are pouring into this country and to whom the Roman Catholic Church represents the only authority that they either fear or respect. What will be their social view, their political action, their moral status if that single controlling force should be removed?" Mr. Hill himself was a foreigner, a native of Canada, and doubtless felt he knew what was best for foreigners.

"The mighty churches of New York and Chicago," observed Matthew Josephson, "were filled to bursting with the Astors, the (younger) Vanderbilts, the Rockefellers, the Wanamakers, the Morgans, the Armours, the Pullmans, and all their kin, who paid for these churches."

There was at least one notable exception to the rule that the Christian men to whom God had given control of the property interests of America were ready to support the church. Andrew Carnegie did not even consider himself a Christian. When one of his early partners, E. M. Ferguson, a most religious man who never missed a Sunday service, came into the office one Monday morning, Carnegie greeted him brightly, then said: "Well, Fergy, how was your friend Jesus Christ yesterday?" The dignified Ferguson blew up and quit the firm.

Carnegie's mentor in philosophy and economics was his great good friend Herbert Spencer. His own creed, he said, was that of the great Englishman, which was a devout belief that man "is ever in the presence of an Infinite and Eternal Energy." And when he came to start distribution of his immense fortune, no church entered his plans, though he was seemingly inconsistent and bought many fine organs which he gave to churches. Yet these gifts he considered in the category of music, not religion. "A taste for good music," he said, "is as necessary as a taste for good reading."

Though he lived well enough, Carnegie was not of the ornate rich. His block-long home at 2 East Ninety-first Street was sumptuous though not "elegant." His own bedroom there was extremely simple. Almost its only wall decoration was a portrait in oil of Captain Bill Jones, the incomparable maker of steel who did so much to make little Andy the prince of steel, before he died, with his boots on, in a slag pit at the Edgar Thomson works on the Monongahela.

Early or late, Carnegie never had anything of the playboy about him. His one great elegance was to buy 40,000 acres in Sutherland, Scotland, and there build Skibo Castle, where pipers played reveille and heather covered the moors and the vales.

The benefaction with which he is popularly associated, that of the gift of library buildings, began as early as 1881, with a Carnegie-built library at his birthplace, Dunfermline. He built in all 2,811 Carnegie libraries, of which 1,946 were in the United States. The total amount spent on them was sixty million dollars. Of all his benefactions, which amounted to $350,000,000, libraries were closest to his heart.

Unlike John D. Rockefeller, Carnegie did not need a Gates to tell him how to spend his pile. Once he had sold his steel empire, he went with all his energy into giving away his money. He even used the process of making steel as an analogy for his spending. Steel is made, as most everyone knows, by the removal of certain substances inherent in iron. One of these is phosphorus. Well, said Carnegie, human nature needed dephosphorization if mankind was to be improved.

The best way to improve mankind was to improve the understanding. The removal of ignorance could best be accomplished by exposure to books. Carnegie did not believe there was any sudden magic in books, but he did believe in the eventual triumph of intelligence. Give 'em books.

Hendrick says that Carnegie's first offer of a library to Pittsburgh was ignored, and local newspapers denounced it as a scheme to immortalize the benefactor. Yet, says Hendrick, not one third of the libraries for which Carnegie furnished the money bear the

donor's name. In Indiana alone are 155 Carnegie libraries, not one
of which carries the giver's name. He did insist, at first, that the
phrase "Let There Be Light," preferably with an open book in
bronze or stone, appear somewhere on or in the building. He later
dropped the specification.

He did not fill the buildings with books. That was up to the
village or city, and so was the library's upkeep. Carnegie often referred to these gifts as bribes. By dangling before the popular eye
"a neat and commodious building," he tempted the city fathers to
do their duty.

It was in January 1901, when Carnegie really started to give
away his fortune. He had just then sold his business to United States
Steel. His first act was to set up a five-million-dollar pension fund
for Carnegie employees. For the next eighteen years his chief interest was to deplete his fortune. He seemed to enjoy doing so as
much as he had the making of it; and he was just as successful at
giving as he had been in accumulating. At his death, in 1919, only
ten per cent of his $350,000,000 remained.

The originality of the man is to be seen in the diversity of his
gifts. There was the Peace Palace at The Hague; a ten-thousand-
dollar annuity to President William Howard Taft; $5,000 a year for
the widows of Grover Cleveland and Theodore Roosevelt; the sixty
million dollars for library buildings; $10,000 a year to Lloyd
George of England; the sum of $50,000 to prevent foreclosure on
Lord Acton's personal library; ten million dollars to Scottish uni-
versities; twenty million to American colleges; twenty-two million
dollars each to the Carnegie Institutes of Pittsburgh and of Washington; ten million to Hero Funds; and other bequests, including
$125,000,000 to the Carnegie Corporation of New York, described
in legal argot as the residuary legatee, established to carry on after
his death the various good works.

The formal biographies of Andrew Carnegie ignore the Cassie
Chadwick incident. This is a mistake, for he came out of the affair
with reputation unsmirched, and even something of a hero. Mrs.
Chadwick, an adventuress of Cleveland, Ohio, confided to a banker
that she was an illegitimate daughter of Carnegie; and through a
series of diabolically clever moves with forged documents prevailed on the banker, and other bankers as well, to loan her almost
one million dollars. She lived high for a time, buying a thousand
dollars' worth of imported handkerchiefs at a lick, hiring a special
train to take Cleveland friends to the New York opera, buying

houses and farms, and taking twelve local high school girls on a cultural tour of the Continent. It was these didos that interested a couple of reporters of the Cleveland *Press*. They did some investigating and came up with the most sensational news story of 1904.

Cassie Chadwick was shown to be a complete hoax. She was the daughter of Canadian parents, honest folk whom Cassie had bilked before she went to the United States to become a palmist, a psychic reader, and a convict before ever she thought up the illegitimate daughter business. Andrew Carnegie, when the hoax blew up, testified that he had no illegitimate children. He had never so much as heard of Cassie Chadwick. The public believed him. Mrs. Chadwick was sent to prison, where she died.

It was in little Oberlin, Ohio, where Cassie's touch hit hardest; a small conservative bank there closed its doors, and officials admitted they were holding the woman's notes for half a million dollars. One of them went to prison. Another died of what was thought to be shame and grief.

When he heard about the bank failure, Carnegie paid all the claims against it by Oberlin College students whose meager savings had been swept away. Almost fifty years later, one of them recalled with gratitude that a man who gave away his money in units of millions should have troubled to make good the sum of $130, for which he had not the slightest obligation. One feels sure that little Andy would have liked that. He was as filled with sentiment as he was with ruthlessness.

It was a woman, and quite remarkable, too, who did noble work in dispersing the great fortunes accumulated by the two Huntingtons, uncle and nephew, respectively Collis P. and Henry E. Her complete name was Arabella Duval Yarrington Worsham Huntington-Huntington. Biographers agree that her early life was, at best, obscure. Mr. Worsham, also obscure, was her first husband. Then, in 1884, she married Collis P. Huntington, the greatest of California's Big Four, the west-coast railroad kings. Until then, and in spite of his great wealth, Huntington had been content to spend no more than two hundred dollars a year on himself.

Two hundred dollars a year was not Arabella Huntington's idea of living. She quickly induced her husband, as Oscar Lewis tells it, to build a two-million-dollar home in New York City. It arose at Fifth Avenue and Fifty-seventh Street, and looked a good deal like a fancy warehouse. Into it Arabella stowed another two million dollars' worth of tapestries, paintings, and assorted elegances, including fragile gilt chairs, which her two-hundred-and-fifty-pound husband tried only once.

When all was ready, Mrs. Huntington threw a party to which virtually all of New York's fifteen hundred were invited. Few came. Whereupon, she reconsidered matters and returned to San Francisco to build another big house and give another big party. Few came this time, though the snub was due less to snobbery than to the implacable hate which her husband had earned by his "scrupulous dishonesty" and domineering business methods.

In 1900 Collis died, leaving a lot of money to Arabella and a lot more to his beloved nephew, Henry E. Huntington. Henry accepted the bequest with pleasure, even though he really didn't need it, being in his own right the sole proprietor of the Los Angeles city transportation system and of much valuable property. Henry was also fond of his widowed aunt, in fact found her so charming as to ask her hand in marriage, thus concentrating in one happy couple the greatest fortune west of Chicago. The wedding took place, and possibly was also consummated, in 1913, when the bride was an unblushing sixty and the groom sixty-three.

By this time Arabella had become something of a patron of the arts under the tutelage of Joseph Duveen, the sycophant salesman of old masters to America's new rich. Through him she had bought paintings of Rembrandt, Velásquez, Hals, and other ranking artists of the long ago. Duveen had also assisted her in tossing out much of the expensive stuff in her New York mansion, replacing it with even more expensive stuff recommended and sold by Duveen. She even turned to Duveen to make all the wedding arrangements. Thus were Arabella and Henry E. Huntington taken in tow by the great peddler of Art.

Before his marriage to Arabella, Henry had built up a fine estate at San Marino in Southern California. On it he erected the marble library and museum gallery in which it was his ambition to display the rarest books and finest paintings obtainable. The library portion was already filling with rarities. The gallery contained some nice paintings, but not rich enough for the taste Arabella had acquired. She was a most astute woman, however, and did not seek to turn Henry's taste away from paintings by the English masters. He doted on these and his wife meant he should have them.

So, loading herself and Henry aboard the *Aquitania,* and with her mentor, Duveen, in an adjoining suite, away they went to England. The outcome of this trip was the art sensation of the decade: for $620,000 the Huntingtons bought Gainsborough's The Blue Boy. (Duveen's biographer, S. N. Behrman, remarks that the twenty-thousand-dollar portion of the purchase price was doubtless tacked on by Duveen to cover the cost of a telephone call.) The painting was bought from the Duke of Westminster.

Duveen staged The Blue Boy's departure from England as Barnum might have handled it. The public was permitted a last look at a public showing, while hundreds and thousands of Britons wept or cursed because a national heirloom was going to the Americans. When The Blue Boy arrived in New York, Duveen refused to permit its exhibition at the Metropolitan, though he showed it at his own gallery, then had it packed while the newsreels recorded the event. He personally escorted the picture to San Marino.

The affair received as much attention in the press as a World's Series. The Blue Boy also got into a Broadway musical, into vaudeville, and into what must have been millions of cheap colored prints. Both The Horse Fair of Rosa Bonheur and the September Morn of Paul Chabas went into oblivion. The rumpus must have captivated Arabella, and probably pleased Henry also, for they went on to hang the San Marino gallery with more Gainsboroughs and paintings by Reynolds, Turner, Lawrence, Constable, and other English masters; and to fill the library with letters, documents, manuscripts, and books, until the building and contents reached a value of more than thirty million dollars, with an endowment of eight million for their care. In a day when few railroad stocks or bonds are considered gilt-edged investments, the San Marino monument to Henry and Arabella Huntington is evidence that there *was* a time when at least one railroad paid off big.

Henry Clay Frick, the king of coke, also built up something of a library museum for posterity. Moving like Carnegie to New York, he put up a mansion on Fifth at Seventieth, a good twenty blocks from his former partner, with whom he was no longer on speaking terms, and started to fill it with paintings, various objects of art, and art reference books. He had made his pile in the murk of Connellsville and the soot of Pittsburgh, but now he was going to live like a Medici. One judges that he did; the most revealing picture of Frick at home is that left by Anna Burr, one of his biographers, who has him "seated on a Renaissance throne under a baldachino, holding in his little hand a copy of the *Saturday Evening*

Post." He loved music of a sort, too, at least on Saturday afternoons when an organist came to fill the mansion with the melancholy "Silver Threads Among the Gold," and the inspiring "The Rosary," his favorites. Frick hung his house with a catholic assortment that included Turners, Van Dycks, Rembrandts, Fragonards, and Bouchers. He left it all to the public, along with an endowment of fifteen million dollars. To Pittsburgh, Frick gave a public park, plus a two-million-dollar endowment.

It was Andrew Mellon, of course, who bought old masters in wholesale lots. In 1931 he paid seven million dollars for twenty-one paintings which the Soviet government had confiscated from the collections of the Czar and various grand dukes. A few years later, from Duveen, Mellon purchased forty-two paintings for twenty-one million. To house them, and many more from his own and other collections, Mellon built in Washington and presented to the United States the magnificent National Gallery, five and a half acres enclosed in marble. He refused to have his own name on the structure. Not one man in a million, he said, could tell you who Smithson was, though millions knew and used the Smithsonian Institution.

Joe Duveen and a few other American art dealers were among the foremost aids in helping wealthy men to dispose of their fortunes. Their one monumental failure was to accomplish anything with Henry Ford. It seems rather strange, in view of Ford's well-known tastes, that the art dealers even made an attempt on him, yet they did. The time was 1920, a terribly bad year in the art world, according to Behrman, who tells how it happened in his amusing book on Duveen. So, in desperation five of Manhattan's leading dealers ganged up to make an assault in force on the squire of Dearborn.

First, they prepared a come-on in the form of three magnificent volumes in which, reproduced in full color, were what the gang said were the hundred greatest paintings in the world. It was odd that the hundred greatest were for sale, but they were and the five dealers meant that Henry Ford should buy them all in what would be the biggest art sale of all time. When the gorgeous volumes were ready, five representatives of the dealers went by appointment to Dearborn, there to meet Mr. Ford.

The New York slickers were astonished at the simplicity of the Ford residence, and took heart in the belief that a man who liked a Stag At Bay etching and a Currier & Ives print, along with a couple of Ford calendars for décor, would be bowled over by the hundred greatest paintings in the world. And they were heartened again when Mr. Ford looked at the books with the utmost delight. "Mother," he called, "come in and see the lovely pictures these gentlemen have brought." Mrs. Ford admired the books as much as her husband had.

Then, Duveen, spokesman for the dealers, thought the time ripe to start the con. "Yes, Mr. Ford," he said, "we thought you would like them. These are the pictures we thought you should have." Ford, the rustic, still did not quite perceive the reason for his callers, the gentlemen from the big city. "Gentlemen," he said, "beautiful books like these, with beautiful colored pictures like these, must cost an awful lot!" Duveen tried again, telling Ford that he was not expected to *buy* the books; that they had been gotten up especially for the automobile magnate; that they were a gift to him from his bighearted visitors. Ford was still foggy. He replied that though it was extremely nice of the gentlemen, he really could not accept so expensive a gift from strangers.

Duveen and the four other worldlings were confounded. The complete innocence of the great mechanic was too much for their oversophistication. It was an American morality play in real life; the Honest Farmer too much for the villains of Metropolis.

When at last the ineffable Duveen found speech, he was obliged to humiliate himself by admitting that he and his comrades were really nothing more than so many peddlers. "Mr. Ford," he explained, "these books were gotten up to interest you in buying the pictures represented in them."

This was clear enough. Mr. Ford's simple amazement vanished instantly. "But, gentlemen," he asked, "what would I want with the original pictures when the ones right here in these books are so beautiful?"

There was no answer to that remark. Uncle Si had refused to accept the green goods. The dejected dealers went away from Dearborn, Michigan, forever. One hopes that they left the come-on volumes on Henry Ford's fumed oak parlor table. . . .

On his death in 1947, Ford left, besides the Ford empire intact, the largest trust fund in the world. This became the Ford Foundation, to be used for the welfare of mankind, in ways some of which, remarked Garet Garrett, Ford would have withered with comment while he lived.

During his life, Ford's chief interest outside his business was to restore as much as possible, and in one place, something of the America he had done more than any other man to destroy. This took form as Greenfield Village, a monster museum based on pre-twentieth century (or pre-Ford) artifacts erected at Dearborn. Into it went everything that Ford and his many agents could discover and move. When he came across something he wanted that could not for one reason or another be moved, Ford bought it, repaired or restored it on the spot, and endowed its continuance. Such was the case with the Wayside Inn in Sudbury, Massachusetts, where because the roar and smell of passing automobiles impinged on the idyllic scene, he moved the highway out of sight and sound by leave of the state, and paid for it himself. His fine work collecting Americana was in contrast to his notorious effort in international relations. This was the so-called Ford peace ship, which, loaded with well-meaning but difficult idealists, set out for Europe to halt World War I by pleading and argument. Nobody would listen, and the idealists bickered among themselves on one of the strangest voyages in history.

The Du Ponts, who through ownership in General Motors became Ford's big competitor, have set up a Du Pont Foundation but it is chiefly to advance chemistry. Foundations, indeed, have for many years been the style for the distribution of wealth by individuals and families. How many foundations there are is probably not answerable; new ones, mostly of modest size, appear almost continuously, and a large book has been written about them.

A foundation takes the place of a new church, or merely a bell for a new church, which once upon a time was the fancy of more or less generous capitalists. Foundations or funds were the method chosen by the several Guggenheims to disperse their millions—or a part of their millions. First was the Daniel Guggenheim Fund for the Promotion of Aeronautics, which was not meant as a permanent endowment, but was to be spent to rouse America to keep up with world aviation. Harvey O'Connor reported that two and a half million dollars was spent to this end and that it had a great deal to do with speeding up aviation in this country. Another Guggenheim foundation of some four million dollars was started to provide summer concerts in New York City's Central Park. But far and away the best known of the family's bequests is the John Simon Guggenheim Memorial Foundation, established in 1925 by Simon and his wife in memory of a son.

This foundation is in the form of fellowships "to assist research and artistic creation." It is open to citizens of the United States, of all other American republics, the Republic of the Philippines, of Canada, and of the British Caribbean. The fellowships granted for 1953 numbered 184. The average grant was $3,000 for a year of twelve months. The 1953 fellows were to engage in all manner of things—from "a study of some aspects of cultural pluralism in the United States" to "studies of the apochryphal stories of the Flood." The foundation is currently endowed with twenty-five million dollars.

How objective can these Guggenheim fellows be? O'Connor pointed out that a critical book about "American captains of industry written by an author subsidized by the Foundation failed to mention the Guggenheims." Yet Carleton Beals, who wrote *The Crime of Cuba* on a foundation grant, "minced no words about the responsibility of a Guggenheim for Cuban affairs under the dictator, Machado."

Murry Guggenheim came to the conclusion that Brother Simon's aid to scholars was too limited, so he and his wife founded the Murry and Leonie Guggenheim Dental Clinic in New York City. Thousands of school children are treated there every year, and the only condition is that their parents are unable to pay. Murry and wife paid for the million-dollar building and added two million more for endowment.

The benefactions of the Guggenheim brothers, says O'Connor, won them such praise as to drown most of the queries as to where and how had come their wealth. He figured that the brothers had "made a remarkable bargain in public esteem." Yet he wondered if the surviving brothers did not find it melancholy that the Guggenheim corporations, because none of their sons thought it worth while to continue in their fathers' footsteps, were heading toward anonymity; and that the once sturdy name of Guggenheim appeared in the papers more often in connection with third-generation divorces than for any other reason. There were eight of these within a comparatively brief period.

If the Guggenheims failed of a dynasty because of a disinterest in the family business by the younger generation, this is not true of the Hearsts. Five sons survived William Randolph, and they are all working on newspapers of the Hearst chain. Technically they are third-generation newspapermen, for it was their grandfather George who bought the first Hearst paper.

Neither the younger Hearsts, nor anybody else for that matter, is likely even to attempt to make a career like that of William Randolph, Sr. It isn't that the race of giants has expired. It is rather that the land of Gath, together with its unique climate has undergone a change. It is not probable today that a William Randolph Hearst, with a Homestake mine, gold all the way down, and bottomless, could accomplish what he did in the fifty years after 1890.

Nor are we likely to know another mogul who lived like Hearst. That he left an estate estimated in 1951 at around four hundred million dollars must have struck those who knew something of how he lived as fantastic. Here was a man who *spent money*. His personal expenses probably ran to fifteen million a year for at least thirty years on end. If the elder Morgan was "magnificent," as he has been termed, then Hearst surely earned the "imperial" that was attached to his name. Though their tastes had little in common, Morgan as a spendthrift was not in the other's class. Nobody else was, unless it was some one of those Indian princes whose extravagances are popular in the Sunday supplements.

It seems a pity that Thorstein Veblen was never a guest at San Simeon, one of Hearst's six homes and where his expensive ostentatiousness reached its height. San Simeon documented everything Veblen wrote in his famous book, and added examples of which the author never dreamed.

Hearst's other homes, owned simultaneously with San Simeon, were a whole apartment house in New York City, a latter-day castle on Long Island, a genuine castle in Wales, a beach house at Santa Monica, and an imposing "ranch" called Wyntoon. The latter two, like San Simeon, were in California.

After their marriage in 1903, the Hearsts lived for a time in a four-story brownstone at 123 Lexington Avenue in New York, where Chester Alan Arthur had died. The house was already piled deep with the art and antiques Hearst had bought before marriage; a child was born in 1904, another was on the way. So, Hearst leased the three top floors of the new Clarendon on Riverside Drive. All thirty rooms were soon not enough, and the master asked permission to rip out a few partitions and make other alterations. When the owner seemed hesitant, Hearst was annoyed, a condition he assuaged by buying the entire building, for which he paid $950,000. Now he might do as he pleased. He straightway took over five floors and a penthouse. He altered things to make a sort of Gothic hall in order to hang his immense tapestries and to display his collection of armor. Somehow the Hearsts and their five children managed to get along, and for twenty-five years the Clarendon was their headquarters.

As part-time affairs, Hearst later had apartments in the Beaux Arts Building and in the Warwick Hotel, both in New York, and an entire floor in the Ambassador at Los Angeles. In 1929 he bought for Mrs. Hearst the château and estate of August Belmont on Long Island, which had the Gothic towers he so much admired, plus a big lighthouse. At about the same time he purchased, without seeing it and on the strength of a photograph, the nine-hundred-year-old St. Donat's Castle in Wales.

By cable Hearst set a corps of restorers and decorators to work, quickly added a crew of servants, another of gardeners, and three years later went to see the place for the first time. It pleased him a great deal, but it still had no plumbing to speak of. An army of plumbers were set busy in the 135-room house until they had installed as many bathrooms as the master thought right for a castle.

What was more, he had the boys dig a large swimming pool. During Hearst's infrequent visits to St. Donat's, John Tebbel remarks, he and his guests often dined on mutton, yet the table service, which included a pair of Cellini cups flanking the centerpiece, had cost a quarter of a million dollars. For a while he wondered what to do with the dry moat, but inspiration happily came and he made it into a nice lawn for croquet.

Yet all of these manifestations of grandeur were not enough. They paled in contrast to the triumphs Hearst achieved on his California estates. (In both cases the land was inherited from his father.) Then there was the stucco palace built for his good friend Miss Davies.

The lesser of Hearst's two ranches was mile-high Wyntoon, on the wild McCloud River in northern California. Originally it had been a rustic retreat for his mother. He built it into a Bavarian village. It was considered to be "remote," and even though Eleanor (Cissy) Patterson managed to arrive there in her private railroad car, Wyntoon *was* remote from the usual haunts of Hearst's friends and sycophants, who were often one and the same. It consisted of three main buildings called Fairy House, Cinderella House, and

Bear House. There were numerous outbuildings and quarters for the varlets.

Bear House alone, a rambling Alpine château, bedded sixty people, even if they all slept alone. When the master really wanted company Wyntoon entertained around two hundred. Cuckoo clocks that performed on the hour, on the half, and even on the quarter, with supplementary music boxes, kept them well posted as to time. But time meant less here than at the other Hearstian caravansaries. It was harder to get to. Guests commonly stayed longer.

There were only two troubles with Wyntoon. Miss Davies did not enjoy it, and is said to have indelicately referred to it more than once as "Spittoon." And physicians of the aging master told him the place was too high for his health.

So, he who was to be the very last of the downright imperial moguls of America turned to the vast San Simeon property which George Hearst had acquired more than half a century before. It covered 275,000 acres, with the Santa Lucia Mountains running diagonally across it. On it, before Hearst started his transformation, were his mother's hacienda and the barns and corrals common to a ranch. For years it had been a favorite outing place in the summer for Mr. and Mrs. William Randolph Hearst and their sons.

In 1919 Hearst got the notion of converting honest San Simeon into something else. Bates and Carlson traced his ambition to his interest in Hollywood, which naturally "led him to recognize in the meretricious charms of the cinema the perfect realization of his own pseudo-aesthetic ideals." No more damning sentence was ever written about Hearst. Or truer. Out of those "pseudo-aesthetic ideals" arose a bastard "Venusberg" that would have blinded the most rococo architects of the Gilded Age together with all their clients. Perhaps Jim Fisk alone could have appreciated its cinematic elegance. Here, by the grace of God and the Homestake mine, lived the mogul of moguls, the Lord of San Simeon.

Just what part did he think he was playing at San Simeon? Was he a Spanish grandee? All the many buildings were given Spanish names. Was he an Italian gentleman of the Renaissance, a Roman senator, a French knight of the Crusades, an English lord of the manor, or a German baron? All of these parts and ages were represented by artifacts and portions of architecture at hybrid San Simeon. Set cheek by jowl with these medievalisms, within shouting distance of Cardinal Richelieu's bed, was a ping-pong table, a genuine Hollywood swimming pool, the flying field, and the tennis and croquet courts.

So far as possible, everything was made to look like something other than it was. Next to a monkish refectory was the cinema theater, at which all San Simeon guests were expected to attend every evening of their stay. For their entertainment also was the San Simeon zoo, where roared four lions, along with two pumas, and a leopard; elephants trumpeted, hordes of monkeys chattered, and assorted zebras, llamas, cassowaries, emus, yaks, gazelles, antelopes, giraffes, eagles, and cockatoos provided the sounds common to their species.

Guests were brought to San Simeon and taken away by a fleet of Hearst limousines and a plane. In the closets of their suites they found complete outfits, male and female, for all occasions—riding habits, sport suits, lounging robes, even dinner clothes, though formal doings were rare. This was the "ranch" and though the table services were collectors' items, no cloth was on the table and the napkins were paper. As in a restaurant, a menu card was at every place.

There were no uninvited guests at San Simeon. The estate was fenced to stop everything short of an army with tanks and artillery. The gates were strong. At each gate was a guardhouse and guards. No gate could be swung until the lord had given permission by telephone. Not even Miss Davies could have a gate opened without personal endorsement of the lord.

Miss Davies, the chatelaine, or at least the mistress of San Simeon, had the Celestial Suite, in the bedroom of which hung an old-master Madonna. In all the suites were a list of house rules. Tebbel says these did *not* include prohibiting use of the word "death" in conversation. They did include a ban on drinking in the suites. You might have all you wanted to drink but you were to get and drink it at one of the several bars maintained especially for guests.

The most authoritarian house rule was that all guests must come at precisely 7:30 P.M. to the great hall of the chief of the four main castles, called La Casa Grande. Here, while cocktails were served, the lord made his entrance, accompanied by Miss Davies. And presently she and Hearst led the grand march, somewhat similar to that in *Aïda,* into the Gothic refectory, followed forty, even sixty, strong by the Hollywood, newspaper, and assorted but indescribable characters Hearst liked to have around. The guests were seated in the order of their wealth or importance, with Hearst in the center and Miss Davies opposite.

Behind Miss Davies a special servant stood throughout the meal for the purpose of holding her powder compact. Next to Miss Davies sat her dog, named Gandhi, and behind the animal stood its special flunky, who gravely brought him his favorite provender, which Bates and Carlson reported to be sliced ham and turkey, on a silver platter. It is just possible that here was the height of pecuniary show, for it is of record that although showy Jim Fisk and *his* chatelaine, who was Josie Mansfield, were fond of dogs as animals of good repute, they did not entertain them at table with their guests. The San Simeon example seems to prove beyond cavil that the manner of living of the last of the moguls was considerably gaudier than anything achieved by Fisk. Nor did Fisk leave an estate of four hundred million dollars. One should not, however, be too hard on the Prince of Erie, but bear in mind that Fisk had no Hollywood to inspire him. Nor did he inherit a Homestake mine . . .

It is improbable in this era of high taxation that San Simeon will be maintained by an individual no matter how wealthy and no matter his tastes. The best one can hope, if the place is obliterated, is that some agency in go-getting Southern California will see fit to erect on the estate a historical marker, preferably of colossal size, calling the tourists' attention to the fact that here lived the man who was apostrophized by Mr. Nick Kenny, the Hearst papers' poet laureate, as The Chief is gone, the man we all called Boss/ Colossus of an age that changed the world/ The galleons of his genius knew their course/ His finger tips around the cosmos curled. . . . If that seems too rich, even for Southern California, then a simple line would do: Site of Home of William Randolph Hearst, The Last Mogul.

Hearst will do to close the story, not because he was the greatest, which he wasn't, but simply because he was the last.

Thus the moguls died, one and all. Likely no one will ever be able to draw up a satisfactory balance sheet of their age. They plundered and wasted, and for half a century it has been a popular literary exercise to attack their reputations as great enterprisers and to deny that their labors were other than futile, or even harmful to our country.

Yet the moguls were also builders. Reflect upon Commodore

Vanderbilt, tossing off half a dozen eggs at seven of a morning, tamping down his breakfast with a cheekful of Lorillard's plug, then going forth in his fur-lined overcoat to wreck or blackmail weak railroads in order to form the first great consolidation, unmatched in its day both as a transportation system and a gilt-edged investment. When he was born, Americans faced a vast continent that was largely empty; the very land was unmapped beyond Ohio. When he died a railroad spanned the United States, and the East, South, and Midwest were networks of rails. Then came Hill and Harriman to fight wasteful wars yet manage, too, to reach and dissolve the last vestiges of the frontier.

Or, Carnegie in his number-five shoes, a mite of a man but all dynamo, moving swiftly about in the pall of smoke and cinders, grabbing a furnace here, a rolling mill there, welcoming money panics that dropped frail companies into his hands; seeking the best brains to make the best and the cheapest steel, bluffing down or massacring competitors, all to the end that he should be the greatest steel man on earth. He *was,* too, and with him he took the United States, lifting it from fifth to first place as a producer of steel. It was accomplished in less than thirty years.

There was the shy pious Rockefeller, aghast at the chaos of wildly spouting petroleum, bringing it to order by control of storage, then building a monster from the bodies of his corporate victims so quickly and quietly that almost before his name was known to fellow Americans, all were using his kerosene, and camel trains were toting Standard Oil products over the Sahara and Standard Oil tins were cherished domestic utensils in Hankow and Reykjavík. But his immense contribution was to the philosophy of American enterprise: he invented big business. Big business has been operating American industry ever since.

Ford, the lone wolf, accepted big business and also added something to it. While he tinkered, without realizing what he was doing, to bring a whole new era into being, he came to believe that one's employees were consumers and should be paid accordingly. Other manufacturers thought him mad. He was not mad. His theory of wages is now as much a part of American philosophy as big business.

Those Chicago butchers to the world were well named. They brought about a revolution in food that was felt from the Argentine to Siberia; and their contemporary, McCormick, made possible an almost incredible increase in wheat production the world over.

McCormick's contemporary, Montgomery Ward, did not invent anything but he brought about a revolution in marketing whose influence is felt more than eighty years after Ward's first catalogue.

Many of the men of this narrative lived to see the United States lead the world in railroad mileage and tonnage, in the manufacture of steel, aluminum, explosives, processed foods, electric light and power, oil, motorcars, and all manner of things, including magazines and newspapers. The moguls alone did not do all this, but they were chiefly responsible for the miraculous speed with which it was done. They were in a hurry, those men, and they set our national style.

They were not the idle rich. They were rich enough but never idle. The idle rich were their widows and descendants. The very nature of moguls would not let them be idle, even when they had made their millions. Consider Jim Hill coming out of his private car to wield a shovel in a blizzard, a Swift rising at dawn to check the waste grease at his abattoirs, or a beaver-hatted Du Pont walking his powder lines by starlight.

Most of them were well paid for their fearsome energy, but I cannot bring myself to believe they were moved solely by the profit motive. They wanted profits, of course, and got them, but there was something else. I am naïve enough to think their tremendous drive came from the same source that drove Genghis Khan and Napoleon Bonaparte.

It has been noted that as the moguls died, there were no replacements. This was true less because of a lack of ability in later generations than because of a change in public temper. Americans had been educating themselves in patterns of government which left less elbow room for acquisitive individuals. Business and industry were taken over in the managerial revolution, to be run almost anonymously.

One can believe that the moguls earned every dollar they got, and that they earned, too, the restrictions that brought an end to their kind and to their age. Without realizing it, they committed class suicide—an ironic and rather pleasing circumstance.

Irony also attends their efforts to make their names secure in history. The stone and marble palaces which they called homes and which were built for the centuries have already been leveled or turned to other uses. Given another hundred years or so and the actual accomplishments of the mogul class may well be forgotten save by historians; and if their names survive otherwise, it will be through their bequests in the fields of art, literature, science, and education, matters they largely scorned in their heyday.

Though Drew could barely read, and Vanderbilt and Stanford wouldn't read, and Armour read little enough, their names even now would have dimmed or faded except for the institutions of learning which they had a hand in founding. Though neither Frick nor Mellon really cared for art except as an expensive hobby, their fine galleries are a superb heritage to come from coke and aluminum. And there are the Morgan and the Huntington libraries, left by men who didn't read books and bought them only when they were rare and costly. (Of all the moguls, only the highly literate Carnegie escapes the irony.)

Then, there are the several foundations. Russell Sage is already forgotten except for his name on such a bequest, and the same will soon be true of the Guggenheim clan. Perhaps in another century or two, the memory of Ford and Rockefeller will also rest chiefly on the enormous bequests those men left "for the welfare of mankind."

It is amusing to contemplate the possibility, years hence, that the very names of these semi-literate or at best unlearned moguls will survive and somehow carry the authentic flavor of art, letters, and scientific inquiry; and Americans of that day will be proud to look back on the New World Renaissance which came so astonishingly into being in so young a country as the United States. It *could* happen, for history is filled with paradox.

ACKNOWLEDGMENTS AND BIBLIOGRAPHY

MOST of the research for this book was done in two fine libraries, the New York Public, and the Portland Public in Oregon, in both of which I was accorded the wholehearted help of the staffs, and had special aid from Ivor Avolino and Sylvester Vigilante in the one, and from Katherine Anderson, Louise Prichard, and Elizabeth Johnson in the other. No writer, I feel certain, ever received better assistance or any more generously bestowed.

Then there were others, nonlibrarians, who made the way easier, and I must mention Sarah Truax Albert, Lucius Beebe, R. C. Brummer, Howard Cady, R. G. Callvert, M. T. Dunten, Lewis Gannett, Roderick Lull, Dr. Miriam Luten, M. M. Marberry, Dorothy Lawson McCall, Philip H. Parrish, Robert W. Sawyer, Sylvia Stallings, and James Stevens.

To all of these go my best thanks, with more left over for Sibyl, my wife, who helped to prepare the manuscript.

In the matter of books, along with articles in newspapers and magazines, the following list includes the writers to whom I am most indebted.

BOOKS AND ARTICLES IN NEWSPAPERS AND MAGAZINES

Adams, Henry. *The Education of Henry Adams.* 1918.
Allen, Frederick Lewis. *Lords of Creation.* 1935.
———. *The Great Pierpont Morgan.* 1949.
———. *The Big Change.* 1952.
Amory, Cleveland. *The Last Resorts.* 1952.
Andrews, Wayne. *The Vanderbilt Legend.* 1941.

Baker, Ray Stannard. *American Chronicle*. 1945.

Barron, Clarence W. *They Told Barron*. 1930.

————. *More They Told Barron*. 1931.

Bates, Ernest S., and Carlson, Oliver. *Hearst*. 1936.

Beard, Charles A., and Mary R. *The Rise of American Civilization*. 1947.

Beer, Thomas. *The Mauve Decade*. 1926.

————. *Hanna*. 1929.

Behrman, S. N. *Duveen*. 1952.

Bennett, Harry. *We Never Called Him Henry*. 1951.

Breasted, Charles. *Pioneer to the Past*. 1943.

Bridge, J. H. *The Inside Story of the Carnegie Steel Company*. 1903.

Busch, Francis X. *Guilty or Not Guilty?* 1952.

Carlson, Oliver, and Bates, E. S. *Hearst*. 1936.

Clews, Henry. *Fifty Years in Wall Street*. 1908.

Commager, Henry S., and Morison, Samuel E. *The Growth of the American Republic*. 1938.

Cotter, Arundel. *The Story of Bethlehem Steel*. 1916.

Crofutt, W. A. *The Vanderbilts and The Story of Their Fortune*. 1886.

Deardorff, Neva R., and Rich, Wilmer S. *American Foundations and Their Fields*. 1948.

Denton, Frank R. "The Mellons of Pittsburgh," *The Newcomen Society*. 1948.

Dictionary of American Biography. 1936.

Downey, Fairfax. *Portrait of an Era*. 1936.

Du Pont, The Autobiography of an American Enterprise. 1952.

Flynn, John T. *God's Gold*. 1936.

Garrett, Garet. *The Wild Wheel*. 1952.

Glasscock, C. B. *The War of the Copper Kings*. 1935.

Grace, E. G. *Charles M. Schwab*. 1947.

Gregory, John S. "Henry H. Rogers," *World's Work*. May 1905.

Hendrick, Burton J. *The Life of Andrew Carnegie*. 1932.

————. *The Age of Big Business*. 1921.

Holbrook, Stewart H. "Ex-Bodyguard of Insull Talks," *The Oregonian*, Portland, July 1. 1934.

————. *Iron Brew*. 1939.

————. *The Story of American Railroads*. 1947.

Howard, Joseph Kinsey. *Montana: High, Wide, and Handsome*. 1943.

Hubbard, Elbert. "Philip D. Armour," *Little Journeys*. 1914.

Hunkins, R. V. "America's Greatest Gold Mine," *The Black Hills*, edited by Roderick Peattie. 1949.

James, Marquis. *Alfred I. Du Pont*. 1941.

Josephson, Matthew. *The Robber Barons*. 1934.

Kennan, George. *E. H. Harriman*. 1922.

Kogan, Herman, and Wendt, Lloyd. *Bet a Million! The Story of John W. Gates*. 1948.

Lawson, Thomas W. *Frenzied Finance*. 1906.

Lewis, Lloyd, and Smith, Henry, J. *Chicago; The History of Its Reputation*. 1929.

Lewis, Oscar. *The Big Four*. 1938.

Lundberg, Ferdinand. *Imperial Hearst*. 1936.

Marcosson, Isaac F. *Metal Magic, The Story of the American Smelting and Refining Company*. 1949.

Martin, Frederick T. *The Passing of the Idle Rich*. 1911.

McCarthy, James R. *Peacock Alley*. 1931.

Moody, John. *The Masters of Capital*. 1919.

Morison, Samuel Eliot, and Commager, H. S. *The Growth of the American Republic*. 1938.

Myers, Gustavus. *History of the Great American Fortunes*. 1936.

Nevins, Allan. *Grover Cleveland*. 1932.

————. *John D. Rockefeller*. 1940.

O'Connor, Harvey. *Mellon's Millions*. 1933.

————. *The Guggenheims*. 1937.

Owen, Russell. "Samuel Insull," *The New York Times*. April 8, 1934.

Parrington, Vernon L. *Main Currents in American Thought*. 1930.

Rich, Wilmer S., and Deardorff, Neva R. *American Foundations and Their Fields*. 1948.

Schriftgiesser, Karl. *Families*. 1940.

The Searchlight. San Francisco. July–August 1952.

Seitz, Don. *The Dreadful Decade*. 1926.

Spearman, Frank H. *The Strategy of Great Railroads*. 1904.

Sullivan, Mark. *Our Times*. 1926–1935.

Sumner, William Graham. *Folkways*. 1940.

Tarbell, Ida M. *The History of the Standard Oil Company*. 1904.

Tebbel, John. *An American Dynasty*. 1947.

————. *The Life and Good Times of William R. Hearst*. 1952.

Veblen, Thorstein. *The Theory of Business Enterprise*. 1904.

————. *The Theory of the Leisure Class*. 1934.

Warshow, Robert I. *Jay Gould*. 1928.

————. *The Story of Wall Street*. 1929.

Wecter, Dixon. *The Saga of American Society*. 1937.

Wendt, Lloyd, and Kogan, Herman. *Bet a Million! The Story of John W. Gates*. 1948.

West, George P. "Hearst, A Psychological Note," *The American Mercury*. November 1930.

Winkler, John K. *Incredible Carnegie*. 1931.

————. *The First Billion*. 1934.

————. *The Du Pont Dynasty*. 1935.

INDEX

Accessory Transit Company, 14, 15, 17

Addicks, John Edward O'Sullivan, 170, 264

Alexis, Grand Duke, 43

Alger, Horatio, Jr., 89

Alton Railroad, 116

Aluminum Company of America, 217, 222

Amalgamated Association of Iron and Steel Workers, 83

Amalgamated Copper Company, 137, 163–68, 169–73, 179, 286, 287, 297, 298

American Bridge Company, 152

American Smelting & Refining Company, 287, 288, 290, 291, 297, 299, 300

American Steel Hoop Company, 152

American Steel & Wire Company, 145, 152

Ames, Oakes, 49–51; Oliver, 49

Amory, Cleveland, 330, 335

Anaconda Copper Mining Company, 157–68, 170, 297, 298, 303

Andrews, Samuel, 65; Wayne, 325

Apperson, Edgar, 202; Elmer, 202; Phoebe, 305

Archbold, John Dustin, 67–68, 71, 135, 136, 138–39

Armour, J. Ogden, 111; Ossian, 108; Philip Danforth, 107–10, 236, 363

Arnold, Thurman, 236

Astor, Henry, 21; John Jacob, 9–10; John Jacob III, 328; John Jacob IV, 328; Mrs. William B., 325; Viscount, of Hever Castle, 9; William B., 3, 7, 9, 324, 333; William Waldorf, 328

Atchison, Topeka & Santa Fe Railroad, 97, 194

Atlas Powder Company, 267

Averell, Mary, 100

Bacon, Robert, 151

Baer, George F., 346

Baker, George F., 287; Newton, 315–16

Ballinger, Richard Achilles, 296

Baltimore & Ohio Railroad, 91, 148

Barksdale, Hamilton M., 259, 268

Barnard, George C., 30

Barnum, Phineas Taylor, 10, 329

Bay State Gas Company, 170

Beatty, Alfred C., 293, 294

Beaumarchais, Pierre de, 248

Beebe, Lucius, 227–29, 333, 334–35

Beecher, the Rev. Henry Ward, 5, 46

Beer, Thomas, 331

Bellamy, Edward, 133

Belmont, August, 357

Benet, General S. V., 258

Bennett, Harry, 208, 209; James Gordon, 306–7; William, 5

Bent, Silas, 219, 226

Berkman, Alexander, 86

Bessemer, Henry, 78

Bethlehem Steel Corporation, 183, 85, 187–90, 224, 271

Bielaski, John, 153

Bierce, Ambrose, 307

Big Four Lines, 94

Bismarck, Otto Eduard Leopold von, 187

Bissell, George Henry, 63–64

"Black Friday," 39–41

Blaine, James G., 50, 54

MAINSTREAM of AMERICA